EXISTENCE

AND

THERAPY

EXISTENCE
AND
THERAPY

An Introduction to Phenomenological Psychology and Existential Analysis

Ulrich Sonnemann, Ph.D.

Formerly Associate Professor, New School for Social Research, and Clinical Psychologist in Federal Service

GRUNE & STRATTON   New York   1954

By the same author:

HANDWRITING ANALYSIS
As a Psychodiagnostic Tool

TABLE OF CONTENTS

▼

INTRODUCTION

Nowhere less, perhaps, than in the sciences of man, but in psychology least of all, has the universality of knowledge remained a living truth. In an age in which advances in the physical, technological, and medical fields are internationally communicable without any barriers at least in the scientists' own minds, *psychology* in America and Europe now seems to share hardly more than the name. Since much unification, if also technicalization, of research and theory has been characteristic of the thinking of psychologists in the United States, how understandable is their inclination to despair of their skeptical European confreres who, stubbornly, seem forever bent on examining "fundamentals"! Nevertheless, this strange insistence has recently led to tangible enough gains, chiefly in such an eminently practical domain as psychotherapy, and the vigor with which the new ideas in psychotherapy abroad assert themselves cannot help but bring the whole divergence in thinking more sharply into focus. If this divergence, however vast, would take the more articulate and fruitful form of a debate on just as vast a scale (and just as fundamental a level) its implications would be less disquieting, but there is at present no such debate.

This state of affairs is the more deplorable as American psychological research still owes some rather recent debts to theoretical impulses, such as psychoanalysis and Gestalt psychology, that came to it from abroad. However, very little actual communication with the newer work in Europe has been in progress, and such communication becomes ever more difficult in view of the growing depth of the split; the split by no means merely divides—as it does in fields not involving human existence—theories about commonly accepted subject matter and their problems, but involves such most elementary points as the definition of subject matter, the conceptualization of problems, the aim of knowledge itself, and scientific method. If certainly this creates obstacles to our attempt to present the dominant trend of western European psychology, psychopathology, and psycho-

vii

therapy in an outline, the difficulties are of lesser magnitude for at least one of the principal phases of this task. Of the two whole contexts of ideas now in the foreground of psychological theorizing in Europe, *phenomenology* has been introduced to American psychologists in the past at least in its most restricted form as a method in the exploration of such basic processes as perception; on the other hand, conveying anything like a full understanding of the new thinking in differential and abnormal psychology, which in recent years has sprung up under the influence of the (phenomenologically oriented and derived) *philosophy of existence* appears to be incomparably more trying.

Of *Existential Analysis*, a personality theory as well as a treatment method that since the last war has replaced older approaches in the focal attention of psychotherapists in western Europe, hardly more than whisperings have reached these shores. On the whole, the belief seems widespread that this movement is a kind of outgrowth, a possibly interesting application-to-psychiatry, of Jean Paul Sartre's *existentialism*, that is, of "metaphysics" and perhaps of a particularly unacceptable metaphysics at that. It is evident that scientists who, according to their own honest belief, have severed their relations with metaphysics long ago will be frightened by such speculative associations of a theory purporting to be science; on the other hand, it is also evident that no fright should be so great as to prevent the scientific mind from checking its justification.

The relations between *Daseinsanalyse* and the philosophy of existence —which is not really a system of metaphysics but the first radically *empirical* way of philosophizing since pre-Platonic days—will be clarified as we unfold the heavy implications of Kierkegaard's, Husserl's, Jaspers', and, most of all, of Heidegger's thought for the anthropological sciences generally, and psychology in particular. No direct connection, on the other hand, links the scientific work of Ludwig Binswanger, Eugene Minkowski, Jacob Wyrsch, and Medard Boss (who are thoroughly indebted to Heidegger) with Sartre and the branch of existential philosophizing that happened to catch the attention of a wider American audience in the years following the second World War. This is not to deny some common ground—recognizable, however, only at the starting point of the thought of each—in which these two ramifications of "existentialism"[1] share and which they have in common with virtually every articulate intellectual force now at work in western Europe. Attempting a rough and preliminary characterization of this dominant and common trend, we may say that it decidedly steers away from positivism, functionalism, instrumentalism, pragmatism, and operationalism, and toward a rediscovery of *spontaneous man in his world*; in this process, such older metaphysical beliefs as "rationalism" and "empiricism", "complementary errors" to the phenomenological glance, are analyzed and rejected. Also rejected are the newer *metaphysics in disguise* which, ever since the middle of the nineteenth century, have prevented man's understanding of himself in his world from keeping pace with his growing power of and interest in, *object-manipulation*, impeding the inner growth of what, somewhat inadequately, is called the "social" sciences. Existentialism which has been called a philosophy of crisis, of the crisis of modern man caught in the cogwheels of his ever more dehumanized civilization, is rapidly turning the designation into a title of honor by its achievements in diagnosing the nature and depth of the debacle, and by discovering, at the bottom of the twentieth century whirlpool of evanescent realities, despairing man's forgotten power to *be*. The insight that man, as the encompassing experiencer of everything that can become the "material" of science, as the indispensable *referent* of objects insofar as they are objects, can in principle not be conceptualized as an "object" himself—that the very idea of a science of man, in order for such a science to be true, must be rethought rather than thoughtlessly patterned along preconceived naturalistic lines—brings this new thinking into a necessary and increasingly radical conflict with any doctrine, philosophic or scientific, that attempts (nowhere successfully) just such "objectification". Existentialism, to sum up, uncovers and questions exactly those constant and implicit assumptions of the functionalistic theories of man which to the functionalists themselves have become so completely self-evident that they are hardly aware of them, let alone of their aprioristic nature. Such premises and foundations of one's whole thinking tend to be protected by the most militant defenses, and much of what, a long time ago, the *Wiener Medizinische Gesellschaft* said about Freud will conceivably be said about *Daseinsanalyse* by today's Freudians; yet it is obvious, lest of the "free intercourse of ideas" little more should remain than the slogan, that the existentialist argument in psychology and psychotherapy should be stated in America.

The task of familiarizing the American reader, particularly an expert in some field, with *existentialism* at work is difficult on two counts: it is a philosophy of crisis of man, and it has the crisis of philosophy already behind it. The crisis of man is, or until recently has been, less far advanced in this country than in Europe. The crisis of philosophy has not yet passed the dead point. It has, in fact, stayed there so long that the scientist, accustomed by now to obey the instrumentalist's decree to turn his eyes from all philosophy, except that of the instrumentalist, needs courage to break that spell. The scientist's problem, at any rate, parallels this writer's: to explore independently the vast number of theoretical implications of *Daseinsanalyse*, not all of them yet enucleated by those Swiss and German scholars who have been its foremost promoters. This study, because the peculiarity of linguistic differences blocks literalness, does not come close to unfolding the total expanse of daseinsanalytic thought; on the other hand, no mere digest and rendering-in-English of the sizable and largely untranslated literature that phenomenological psychology and existential analysis proper have accumulated could even suffice.

Like any other elementary movement in the history of thought, the one that led to Binswanger's theorizing has many different sources and currents. It is natural, then, that discrepancies in the specific direction of theorizing exist in great numbers, but there also exist, binding them organically together, a core of common perceptions and a common way of posing problems. A detailed historical analysis of the movement would be too indirect an introduction to it; to restrict this presentation to rendering the specific views of Binswanger only, would, on the other hand, leave their entire ideational background unexplained, and the gulf that separates them from objectivism unbridged in the American reader's understanding. The only key that promises to open up this so different world of thought has been supplied by the subject matter of psychology and psychotherapeutic theory itself: existentialism in this orbit can be explained only through a fresh formulation and systematization of its common perceptions. An approach of this kind, one venturing into untrodden paths of inquiry, not only is made imperative by the existent cleavage in psychological thinking, but the fruitfulness of the existentialist conception of a science of man may be shown by nothing quite so much as the apparent im-

possibility even to state it without partaking in some measure in the
development of its underlying tenets.

NOTES

1. Heidegger's decisive repudiation of his disciple and admirer, Sartre, contained
in his *Letter Concerning Humanism* (1947) abrogates his share in any "existentialism" constructed along Sartrean lines. Since Heidegger continues as both the
most penetrating and most influential philosopher of existence, the use, in this
study, of the term *existentialism* refers primarily to the thought of Heidegger,
secondarily to that of his followers in the sciences; references to the thought of
Marcel, Jaspers, and Sartre, where they occur, are made explicit.

PART ONE

The Crisis of Knowledge and the Rise of Phenomenology

CHAPTER 1

Behavior and the Psyche—The Psyche as "Object" and as Referent of All Objects—Causal Analysis and the Nature of Understanding—First Determination of the Phenomenological Quest.

I SEEK REFUGE UNDER A TREE FROM THE GLARE OF the July sun. This tree protects me, and everything about it reveals itself as true to the idea of this service: by no means only its shadow, of which the bulldozer next to it would provide a far more "perfect" specimen, unpatterned by the interspersing light falling through the branches. These light spots only accentuate the protectingness of the tree's shadow by being slight, domesticated reminders of what glares beyond: could it be, then, that quantitative perfection should be different from *true?* The bulldozer, after all, is just a "thing" that people have put there. It can be made to come and go; it can be shipped to Jubbulpore, India, and on arriving in Jubbulpore be just the same bulldozer. It is made to serve certain purposes, the same, astonishingly, in Jubbulpore. Its whole existence is this serving purpose: a *being* of its own the bulldozer has not. It does not belong, has no roots, here, and its function, everywhere, is to level, to obliterate; can it be expected, then, to protect anything or anyone? How different is the tree! The shape of its crown, its soothing green, the stable power of its trunk against my back, all accentuate the idea of protection. This idea is not a thought of mine, even though it has meanwhile become one.

The idea is immanent to the situation in which I discover myself under a tree. It was immanent already in my selection of the tree, not

1

the bulldozer, a choice I know I arrived at neither by "contacting" other trees in my memory (however, there was a moment of recalling the shape and function of bulldozers), nor by studying my own "motives", nor by reasoning about the shadow, the crown, the trunk; any psychology that would *explain* my choice by referring to these phases, be it as "valences" or as "sign-like qualities" or as "discriminating features", would be reversing the true order of events, known only to myself. Yet, at the moment when the idea of the situation becomes a thought in my head, it demands to be accounted for, and for just another moment I cannot help isolating each of the phases I have named. Man, on a certain medium level of reflection, inclines to understand his world in this way, and in many of his dealings with it derives great benefit from this spontaneous propensity of his reason toward a conceptual isolation of abstractible phases as *factors*. Does it follow that it would also be reasonable to assume, against the only available evidence, that my original experience of the tree, from which the analysis only took off, had already occurred in its pattern? If it had not, on the other hand, how could psychology—as any other science, supposed to be true to nothing but the observation of its subject matter (in this case, my choice)—account for it? Psychology has a choice at this point, not wholly unlike the choice between the tree and the bulldozer, and just as restricted to two positions only.

*   *   *   *

Since the choice I described was a decision of my own, the locus of the subject matter is the locus of decisions, the psyche. But although we know that our choices are decisions, a scientist may decide to ignore that knowledge. The choice, then, becomes a behavioral event observable in physical space. Behavior itself, of course, is to a large extent always "understandable"; but the understandability of it is no longer of interest once the decision to explore behavior radically from without is taken. For any admission of the relevance of either the subject's own phenomenal data of experience or of their occurrence on a level of *lesser immediacy*, of their understanding by others, has in fact to be eliminated: to be explored as nothing but a series of coordinated physical events, behavior must first be "freed" from even the slightest trace of its own spontaneous intelligibility.

Except for the mysteriousness surrounding the continued use of the name psychology, there is nothing in such a decision for the principle of *behaviorism* that in any way is unclear, illogical, or illegitimate; we do well, however, to realize in advance the methodological consequence that the decision must entail to be meaningful. If understanding is to be eliminated radically, "explanatory" descriptions of "processes" not only must be free from *any* terms that we ordinarily apply to observed behavior because we are able to follow it with our own comprehension as human beings; they must also be free from any terms that, according to an analysis of our way of understanding them, refer to a within, to "subjectivity", as their cognitive prerequisite. It is important to visualize the extent of this requirement. Such terms, the comprehension of which will rely on our inner experience, rather than on our perception of measurable magnitudes in space, would have to be absent from the ultimate explanatory account; for example, we could never, in such an account speak of the protectingness of a tree, nor of our memory of other trees, nor of the purpose of the bulldozer, nor even of "seeing" either of the two, nor of "selecting" one of them; and any attempt to replace these concepts by more "objective" ones, such as "response signals", turns out to be ultimately inadmissible. Both *response* and *signal,* so indispensable in behavioristic literature, would remain incomprehensible unless we already comprehended them in analogy with such understandable entities of human phenomenal reference as responses to questions or signals to a railroad engineer; with these provisions, however, no argument against the logic of the behavioristic *quest* remains.

We may ignore "molar" behaviorism, a rather unprincipled compromise, since it constantly violates these conceptual restrictions, between "objective" and "understanding" psychology,[1] and confine our attention to the true objectivistic concern. To be consequent as physics has been consequent, behaviorism must first refer its phenomenal observations to the level of neurophysiological processes; ultimately, it must strive to speak the very language of that most dephenomenalized, most (in one sense of science) *radical* science, physics itself, a language consisting as much as possible of mathematical formulae. Could it, speaking in this language, be expected ever to account for such complex human actions as the evolution of quanta theory or the creation of a great poem? Could it ever help our understanding of ourselves and others, even if it should finally be able to accomplish, in its "different" language, such theoretical accounting? Would the retranslation into an understandable idiom not lead back simply to the original behavioral observations that behaviorism started out with? Certainly no other test can be conceived for the truth of its theorizing about man than the attainment of *predictability* of behavior, not in experimental situations already altering the object by narrowing the scope of behavior to isolated reactions or predefined tasks, but of spontaneous behavior in its full observable breadth. The repulsiveness of this idea, which in principle turns man into an automaton, is not an argument in science, not even in the science of man; it is very much, however, a problem for such a science, since the idea seems to clash with a timeless knowledge in us that such predictability, by interfering with freedom as a fact of our experience, would *destroy* the very order that science originally had set out to *explore.* Inasmuch as science can be conceptualized as one of the many processes partaking in this order of man's existence, it is this very order that would turn out to be self-destructive in a far more radical sense than any advances in atomic knowledge now threaten—provided *objectivistic psychology ever passes that test.* There are, in any case, strong reasons to doubt this. The quest of the radical objectivistic school calls for the progressive analysis of processes, into their single given cause-effect connections; modern biology, which preceded psychology in this, found out, however, that with increasingly successful isolations of such single connections their concomitance in the organismic total process has been becoming more incomprehensible rather than less, and that no introduction of quasi-physicalist field concepts has helped this matter.

Why, then, this reforming of the known *inside* of behavior to still rather unknown neurological *outsides,* which generically are so different from the former that nowhere does there exist even the faintest trace of a bridge? We shall return to this observation and to the whole question of objectivism; however, the perhaps most decisive point can be made now that no necessity for the behavioristic quest can be discerned, since to the comprehension of human behavior, unlike that of events in physics, we fortunately have *constant free access* provided by the immediate data of experience. That other choice which psychology can make must be subject, of course, to the same principle of as much epistemological purity as possible, which before was required of objectivism. This principle has nothing to do with terminological quibbling; what it concretely means in behaviorism as behavior-

ism *should* be, on the contrary, is something self-evident for any kind
or form of explanatory science (such as behavioristic psychology),
since explanation is a referring of phenomena to different levels of
description: for example, the explanation of lightning nowhere presupposes the phenomenality of lightning, but "dissolves" this phenomenon by accounting for it in terms of such objectified concepts
as electric discharges. What, now, does the principle entail in an
analysis of the immediate data of experience? These data, claiming
the most direct access to their understandability conceivable, must
again, as radically as possible, disclaim as misleading any attempt at
"explanatorily" referring them to different levels. Evidently, the
principle turns out to mean the opposite of what it means in behaviorism; the theoretical account must be free from any term the referential
implications of which should fail to be justified by the structure of the
phenomena *as they are given*.

This requirement is emphasized by the fact that in returning to
phenomenal experience we face two well-known and often repeated
objections. One is that phenomenal experience is by definition "subjective", meaning unreliable; the other is that it is unobservable, since
any observation of ourselves in experiencing not only must disturb
but in fact *split* the psyche into an observing subject- and an observed
object-pole, so that the observed state of the psyche can in principle
never be the state-to-be-observed. To the first of these arguments we
shall return later; the second could not be more true. Besides throwing
out some already historical methods from the early, introspectionistic
psychology of basic processes, it has great bearing on the current understanding both of many abnormal states of personality and of certain
currently prominent methods of their observation, explanation, and
treatment.

But how much has the argument to do with the immediate data of
experience? This consciousness, with which our first attempt at theorization meets—what general properties does it show in the first place?
If it were itself an *object* to be observed, as the introspectionists
believed, "subjective" psychology indeed could never get out of the
dilemma in which it found itself or was found, but was this belief
empirical? Is it not already a dictate *to* experience? It appears at a
glance that our first attempt at theorization already has by-passed the
immediate data of experience *qua data*, for nowhere do these data

resemble any such thing as an "objectified psyche" or "experience as
a process". The data, on the contrary, if I may refer back to the particular experience with which I began, are whatever constitutes the
situation in which I discover myself under a tree. Consciousness, being
centered—as I can abstract from the fact of this discovery only upon
reflection—on what gives the situation its togetherness, the idea of the
tree as protector, is present only as consciousness *of* that idea; the
idea itself, if I describe its appearance more fully, is in a state of
"spatial unfolding": it first occurs to me as the order of that whole
protective tree situation, which, unlike consciousness, I originally perceive. Consciousness, on the other hand, even in its nearest possible
observability, is by no means that conceptual entity into which it only
subsequently may turn itself through self-objectifying reflection; moreover, in its actual first appearance, it is not even a state of myself but
the diffuse horizon of the *what* of my experience, of "world"; characteristically, in some languages still directly connected with their
origin, being conscious to this day retains its primal meaning as a
state, not of the subject, but of the things experienced. But even in
objectifying one's consciousness, or trying to, all one can cognitively
catch is an abstraction from oneself as the experiencer; in any true
sense, *experiencing* never occurs as its own datum, consciousness never
as object, all objects occurring to it.

Phenomenological psychology, then, has nothing in the least to do
with introspection in the sense of self-observation; the phenomena, no
matter whether of inner or outer experience, objects of thought or
imagery, or percepts in environmental space, are invariably *beyond the
self* as the experiencing agent, and self-observation makes no exception
from this law since "the eye cannot see itself"; it needs a mirror to
approximate this feat. This beyond the self, this self-transcendence of
all psychic events is itself empirical in the strictest sense conceivable;
for example, the irreducibility of the objects of cognition to cognition
as a psychical process is demonstrable already on the basis of such most
simple data as the observation that even though I have different whole
"contents of consciousness" each time I fixate an everyday object from
a different angle, each time I see the same whole object. It becomes
clear that I cannot have this perception according to any comparative
study subsequently undertaken among the random selection from the
infinite number of possible patterns of geometric retinal distributions

either by my intellect or by any discoverable process mechanism; the *whole* object is seen according to the immediate conviction (*intentio*) of each "partial" perception. In other words, experiencing, if we try to conceptualize it from the side of the subject, inevitably has what early phenomenology called *Aktcharakter*, the character of *action*; it has this character inasmuch as action, to be just that, must go beyond itself, "transcend itself towards its task", be more than aimless motion. The concept, historically understandable from Brentano's need for a term that would articulate, against the associationistic psychology of his time, the irreducibility of experience in any terms of mere processes, is nevertheless not too fortunate since it somehow seems to suggest a conception of experiencing as either an action in any literal sense, or at least something deliberate, or else a *production* of phenomenal objects by the organism. This is about the opposite of what it does imply: the fundamental structural characteristic, in all experiencing, of a *directedness-toward*.

In the actuality of experience, to which non-behavioristic psychology is referred as its only legitimate subject matter, this directedness-toward is never a "function" of subjective needs and drives. Even in the case of needs and drives *emphatically conative* what occurs to the subject is the relevance of the object itself. Functionalistic psychology may speak of an organism's striving for food as the function of a drive, but in doing so has already "forgotten" that this entity *drive* is nothing but an abstraction from what, in the organism's concrete experience, is the direction-setting relevance of food. Object-relevance remains in principle prior to any "strivings", conceptualized in isolation from their objects; the concept, for example, of a libido only *seeking* cathexis reveals itself at once as senseless from the viewpoint of both observation and logic[2] but becomes understandable as a concept once we realize that the reification of "striving to unite with the loved one" into "libido" made this, if only terminologically, possible. Nowhere more clearly, however, than in such experiential acts as thinking does the object of experience transcend experience itself: an *idea* which appears in the medium of the psyche like everything else that may occur to a subject, is itself nothing psychical: a mathematical proposition has a structure that thinking reveals as independent of the psychical act of thinking it. Such phenomenal orders as mathematics are more evidently compelling because they lend a direct, short-cut access to the certitude that inheres in all possible orders which can occur phenomenally; yet, in principle the structure this discloses applies to the acts of experiencing throughout, and the "drives", the "emotions", are not exempt from this principle of experiential self-transcendence: the reified feeling is in actuality a conceptual inference from a *what* that is felt. The psyche is in principle never an object but is "given" (*datum*) always and only insofar as "world" is *given to it*.

Without this referential quality of experiencing throughout, living would not exceed the definitive criteria of objective processes. Living would be worldless, and worldless is what it tends to become in the focus of any *immanentistic* doctrine[3] that insufficiently realizes the incisiveness with which this referential quality of experiencing distinguishes the psyche from any object-processes conceivable or met with. This most fundamental observation, that a psychical event always refers to a phenomenal content, or, more strictly speaking, is a becoming manifest of that content, characterizes as unempirical from the start all objectifying functionalistic psychologies, regardless of how introspective their method. Conceptualizing their observations *as though* they were cognizing object processes in physical time-space, they fail to notice that this analogousness is wholly unjustified since not a single object process in physical time-space is constituted as a *reference beyond itself*.

The subject matter of differential psychology, from the vantage-point of phenomenology, is not the psyche in isolation, but the observable whole expanse of man's possible ways of man's being-in-the-world: of his *existing*. Any explanatory analysis of nature (as context of physical objects observable from without) necessarily understands what it observes by referring it to ever more isolated component processes in their past-to-future successivity. Understanding, as the Gestalt school's experiments in perception, thinking, and learning have demonstrated, is not subject to this principle; understanding, on the contrary, refers all single "sensory" elements as much as possible to the meaning contexts in which they are embedded. These contexts stubbornly defy causal reduction, for example, to past experience, *if* such experience is understood as more than the executive agent of the axiomatic knowledge in us, an agent required only for *actualizing* the understandability (never explicable in terms of this agent) of our environments; for every recurrent experience, insofar as it holds meaning, is a *presence*. Its meaning does not emerge from the past; it is the past that is allowed to emerge here (if and when it does) because what the experience means *re-calls* it. But from where does the meaning of the thing experienced itself emerge? It does not. We already prejudice the structure of the event, we become untrue to the first duty of the scientist to be wholly observing and unreservedly descriptive if we pose the question that way. It is *we* who emerge, and what we emerge into in experiencing the meaning of something is the *truth* about that thing, which truth thus reveals itself to experience as an opening, a clearing, a phenomenological rediscovery of the greatest import and the starting point for Heidegger's fundamental-ontological re-interpretation of truth itself.

This is confirmed by nothing so much as that the experience of sudden insight, the "Aha" moment of which Wertheimer spoke in his early investigations of this experience of cognitive emergence (which he conceptualized as one on the part of the meaning or truth) involves an experienced widening of the very limits of our existence. The linguistic structure of the "Aha" itself confirms this: analysis of the genesis of all language (early historical language and the first formation of language in infants) shows that the phonetic *a* is the most immediate expression of a combined experience of *upward* and of *sideward in all directions,* that is of height and breadth (the *h* the most immediate expression of an innermost experience of *revelation* and of the implied need for *spreading* it, of communication from the heart). The spontaneity and universal consistency in the linguistic emergence of such space-analogous apperceptions *of direction,* both in infantile speech and in figurative conceptual usages of language, utterly defy their causal attribution to any *a posteriori,* any empirically derived analogisms with spatial-environmental experience: the (conceptual) analogism itself, if used or understood by a subject, already presupposes that the analogy must at one point have *occurred* to him. But, in an instance of this kind, on what "empirical" basis can it occur? Of the two analogates, only one refers to the environment, the other forever to an event within.

As is easily seen, empiricism, as it ordinarily does in such cases, solves a problem by burying it quite naively in a term. If this term is analogism, structural "likeness", or simply "similarity", the similar, for example, between the low of the ground beneath our feet, and the low of "feeling low", a "lowly character", an act of self-*abasement*, is tacitly implied as self-evident by the empiricistic explanation; yet what the empiricist overlooks is that this self-evidence, which directs his own thinking so imperatively that his thinking does not even seem to "know" it, *constitutes the whole problem*, which no causalistic going back in time can solve.[4] The empiricist explanation therefore moves in a circle; and at any point of the circle it has already by-passed the problem. With a preconception about genetic *tracing* as the key to all problems that data may raise, the empiricist's observation never gets a chance to perceive structural orders that intersect at any point the path of causal time, because they themselves are timeless. Are they, thereby, unununderstandable? In the case we last presented these orders refer us to a simple enough fact: they remind us that at any point of our life course we *exist already into space*.

This insight dispenses with problems that are typical artifacts: not only orientation *in analogy with* three-dimensional space, but also orientation *in* three-dimensional space, the learning of which still awaits "explanation", it reveals as far more fundamental than the empiricist or nativist psychologies have traditionally surmised. For evidently, what we are dealing with is not anything that can meaningfully be conceptualized as inborn faculty, let alone a learned function, nor indeed as anything that would be subject to any kind or form of evolution, but a constituent attribute of the very mode of our being, as angularity is of the triangle, a relationship never comprehensible in any terms of time as the dimension of changes. Regarding space-analogous experiences, what we are forced to conclude from this constituentness of the spatial for our very form of existence is an original presence in us of axioms of directional meaning (*allgemeine Bedeutungsrichtungen*), which with equal priority distribute their rule to the spheres of inner (symbolic) and outer (visual motor) experience, a clarification of the problem first offered by Löwith.[5]

It is evident that an unlimited number of similar observations could be added to this first presentation from a small sector of the phenomenological theory and critique. The comprehensive discovery that links all of them together is the constituent presence in experiencing of a system of *a prioris* that unlike the *a prioris* of the idealistic metaphysics of the past are themselves empirical; they are *evident to experience* and, indeed, to experience down to its most sensory levels.

Nowhere reducible to any explanatory causative laws, these a prioris (*isomorphically,* as Gestalt psychology understands it) determine the structure both of the world as phenomenon and of its basic comprehension by the mind of man; or, to eliminate the still substantial trace of un-phenomenal Cartesian dualism in this Gestaltist conception, they determine the structure of our being-in-the-world. Empirically, then, the subject matter of psychology, nowhere needing physiological or physicalistic justifications, but only to be explored, as Freud quite justly saw, on its own, refers the inquirer to an outward-from-within-the-subject, rather than to objectification in either its behavioristic or introspectionist form; to meaning constancies, *essences*—rather than to causal components of processes; to comprising contexts standing ready for analysis because they articulate their own part-systems, rather than to field *constructs;* and to understanding rather than explanatoriness, since explanatoriness, which cannot but objectify whatever it lays its hands on, which must by-pass in principle any immediacy of phenomenal meanings, ignores the true data of psychology, pointing in the direction of physics. Psychology, therefore, to comprehend any single experience-fact (or set of such data) must strive for an essential account of the most comprising contexts of experience in their most axiomatic constancies discoverable. This means that, to be radically empirical, it must first explore experience worlds of individuals as they actually are.

NOTES

1. Since much of behaviorism has more recently become molar, the arbitrariness of its conceptual compromises, such as manipulanda, discriminanda, etc., can now be studied on a basis of extensive materials.

2. No experiential states to which the term *libido* can conceivably refer are ever found *objectless,* even though—in states actually meant where psychoanalytic theory speaks of an *unattached libido*—the phenomenal object may be in a state of extreme diffusion and little power, for this reason, to "polarize", that is, direct, the subject's strivings. Since language itself—a fundamental tenet of phenomenologists and existentialists alike—tends to be spontaneously true to any meaning which can appear in its medium, this merely confirms the logical self-contradictoriness that we notice: in terms of concrete linguistic experience rather than of any semantic theory, it remains unclear what "objectlessness" can possibly be supposed to mean.

3. Andras Angyal, *Foundations for a Science of Personality,* 1941.

4. Neither do such detours, denied by observation and ultimately leading back into the same dilemma, as an attribution of such phenomena to "cultural factors" or "conventions": the axioms of experience transcend cultural boundaries (let

alone "conventions") throughout. What the relativist forgets is that "cultures" themselves were born from human experience and survived only so long as they stayed reasonably true to it. In a manner peculiar to the *specialism* of all process psychology, functionalism here simply ascribes an understood phenomena within its own field to *deus ex machina*-like factors of the same generic order as these phenomena but happening to lie within another "field", so that they can more fully be reified as "factors", that is, excluded from analysis without the gap becoming apparent.

5. There is, in other words, neither Kant's and Lotze's "primary perception of space", not the building up of space from "optic and kinesthetic impressions" (for example, P. Schilder, in *The Image and Appearance of the Human Body*, p. 21, who overlooks that "impressions" already presuppose "space") but a pre-given spatiality of experiencing. The abstraction of a space *concept* that is evolved from it at a certain point in the life course is only contingent, then, on this *existential a priori* of the spatial.

CHAPTER 2

The Charge of Subjectivism—A Logical Confusion and Its Consequences—Husserlian Phenomenology and Radical Transcendental Idealism—Why Had the Immediate Data of Experience Been Overlooked by Science? —Objectivism as Metaphysics—Second Determination of the Phenomenological Quest: the Essences and Their Position in the Structure of Knowledge—Jaspers' Schizophrenics and the Limitations of Husserl's Method —The Foundational Position of Being—Heidegger's Existential Analytic and the Thematic Gap in Psychology.

BUT HOW CAN WE KNOW INDIVIDUAL WORLDS OF experience other than our own? We cannot: inasmuch as such knowledge must be *our* knowledge, such experience *our* experience, it is exactly that *other than our own* that already ceases to hold true the instant the knowledge here meant becomes an event of our understanding. Evidently, then, the question has not been posed right. Its tacit premise, the way we first posed it, is a *duality* between two different experience worlds that mysteriously can be in contact with each other. But this premise—taken for granted by all objectivistic attempts to answer the question—is a fixation of thought, if certainly a powerful one; it has no foothold in the data of experience. The image it suggests is comparable to the contacts made between two radio stations; it is untrue to what the phenomenon of understanding (as well as the eidetic origin of *understanding* as a word in the English language) shows, and which is not a duality between the separable positions, not a standing opposite one another, but an identity, a standing under. Identity here connotes not an identity of any two objects (the understander and the understood); we may remember at this point that the understander is, as such, no object in the first place. But is the understood, as such, his object? We shall later meet

13

with reasons to extend our doubts to this still widely unquestioned assumption as well. At any rate, analogies with relations from the world of physical facts seem of little help in furthering our understanding of *understanding*.

The customary accounts of the phenomenon of spontaneous interpersonal understanding, which center on the utterly unclarified concept of empathy, take recourse, peculiarly, to what is least likely to provide clarification: emotion and feeling. Though it is evident that any kind of understanding, and intersubjective understanding most of all, naturally involves our emotions inasmuch as it engages us as whole beings, it remains illogical to select a reified stratum of experience that is itself insufficiently understood to explain so articulately cognitive a category of events as understanding. The historical "explanation" of understanding, which was founded upon this error of Lipps and some others, has contributed to the general tendency of the behavioristic school to discredit the validity of immediate qualitative cognizing, of "intuition", even in instances in which, according to behavioristic criteria, such "intuition" proved to be objectively valid, that is, capable of such objectifiable accomplishments as successful matchings of personal identities on the basis of expressive movement patterns offering no clues but their physiognomic characteristics. How, with his insistence on scientific rigor, was it possible for the behaviorist not to notice this inconsistency? A first brief clarification of the whole current usage in science, and in psychology specifically, of the terms *objective* and *subjective* seems in order. Without such clarification, it would be impossible to answer the behaviorist's second argument, cited earlier, that direct qualitative experience is subjective in the sense of being arbitrary, cognitively unreliable.

Refuting this argument offers little difficulty once we recall the true situation to which the behaviorist's argument originally referred, the situation of psychology at the Wundt-Titchener stage of its history. Since we can never say of a "thing", but only of a statement or a judgment *about* it, that it is objective or subjective, it is evident that the reproach of subjectivism is meaningless if it refers not to a method of inquiry, but to a subject matter itself as data context, or to any of its given attributes. The reproach remains valid for introspectionism. The very fact of self-observation here introduces to the cognitive situation a clear-cut dichotomy between a subject and an object pole, and subjectivism can be charged to the operations of the subject pole since no objective verification of the cognitive accomplishments of these operations can even be conceived—an observation that is simply in accordance with the basic arbitrariness, already shown, of turning the psyche into an object in the first place. It is clear, on the other hand, that the reproach of subjectivism is quite thoughtless if it pertains instead to the inalterable experiential mode in which, prior to any inquiry, a context of data *occurs*. The subjectivity of the legitimate data of psychology is not a feature of scientific method but the constituent mode in which these data are presented to the inquirer from the start; any attempt to eliminate this element, regardless of how empiricist the doctrine on which it bases itself, is therefore bound to be a violation of true *empiricalness*, a dictation *to* the data at the very start of inquiry.

There are a number of reasons why the methodological confusion which this reflection exposes and which underlies the charge of subjectivism, is not easily seen by the functionalist. Most of these reasons we cannot expect to understand more fully before making an analysis of that major underpinning of modern science, the Cartesian subject-object split. This task still awaits us, but we can at least attempt to account for the fact that the issue has proved most explosive in psychology. Unlike the physicist, the psychologist, if he is a functionalist, investigates processes that belong to the same general order—perception, learning, thinking—as those by which he conducts his investigation. As a result of this cognitive nearness to his subject matter, he confounds the two types of processes and forbids those considered as object from leading to conceptual forms to which he would not allow the process of investigation to lead. Empiricism, therefore, when applied to psychology, tends to turn into its own opposite: historically beginning with a justified abjuration of transcendentalism as a premise of scientific method, in attempting to be true to nothing but observable data, it falls into the trap of dogmatism once the data themselves (as they do in psychology) show transcendence, reference to phenomenal contents, as their central constituent. At this point, empiricism no longer is "true to data" but quite unsuspectingly postulates in advance what the data should be to be scientific.

The form this postulation takes protects it from discovery chiefly by using circular methods of inquiry that yield the desired types of data by inconspicuously altering the object under attack: suggestive questions geared to preconceived theorems; whole "inventories" of trait-dimensions, the intrinsic relevance of which has never been demonstrated by the subject matter, personality. This simple discovery has far-reaching implications: it explains at once why in psychology radical empiricalness and empiricism-as-an-ideology are now at opposite ends, and it sheds light on the trend toward manipulatory routines in present-day applications of functionalist theorizing. From this insight into the nature of reductionism, the *naiveté* of rationalist speculation becomes only too understandable: for example, the debunking as irrational of a subject's beliefs (or other experiences) in which the inquirer does not share. This reduction to "misunderstood", "projected", or "sublimated" "subjective needs" of that subject, is not an attack on them by frontal argument; it does not ask, not seriously, at least, "is this true"? but "why does he say so"? and it thus misses out from the very start of the inquiry on the nature of conviction *qua conviction*. Yet, if human conviction would legitimately allow of such debunking, why should the convictions just of the debunker himself (his theorizing, for example) escape his own reductionism? Why, to put it more briefly, should the reductionism escape itself? An outstanding and instructive example of the ideological character of this error is the superficiality and enlightened narrow-mindedness with which Jungian theory, which has been concentrating on religious experience with less epistemological prejudice than other doctrines, has for a long time been tabooed by various "objectivisms"; the sterility of this opposition blocked the *actual* errors of Jungian theorizing from the objectivist's sight.

This arbitrariness is very human; it is implicit in the very act of psychological objectification; the psychologist who thus objectifies his subject forgets that his own world access remains bound up forever with his own subjectivity. He may, of course, strive to eliminate such subjectivity; but however strong the striving is he can succeed in eliminating only what he is aware of. His awareness, *qua* awareness, being subjective, it is not to be seen how he ever could get out of it. It becomes evident that another misleading *object image*, as though subjectivity and objectivity were quasi-substances of which world apperceptions are somehow mixed together (so that the mixture allows of something like quantitative changes in proportion) is getting into our way here. The subjectivity and objectivity of an experiential event cannot be understood in this manner. They are not even among the qualities of such an event; they are its definitive constituents in the same manner in which such concepts as matter and form are the definitive constituents of physical objects. This means that their polarity is itself an abstract one; it is not a polarity between two actually existing poles. It is an abstraction from a unity which itself knows of no such poles as subjectivity and objectivity as *components*; but in the manner of many abstractions it misleadingly suggests such a composite relationship as something (so to speak) concrete. Underlying this deep-rooted misunderstanding in its effect on psychology, a dissection, itself strictly metaphysical, of personality into blind (conative) and orientative (cognitive) "functions" will be found later, and the inevitability with which this dissection had to lead to a *thematic gap* in psychology will then readily become transparent.

From the very start, therefore, the orientation of phenomenological inquiry is objective in the only legitimate sense of focussing outward with the subject's own focus of experiencing; if this is done, "reductionism" not only becomes impossible but becomes understandable, wherever it occurs, as a direct consequence of an inquirer's lack of understanding, that is, of his own phenomenal improverishment, so frequently accompanying professional specialization in our age. Wertheimer's statement that a "thing which is black and uncanny is just as uncanny as it is black, yea, if it is both at the same time, it is uncanny in the first place", not only is representative of the consistency with which phenomenology focusses outward from within, but it becomes even more instructive once we visualize the unempiricalness as well as lack of logical principle with which any immanentistic doctrine in psychology would at once set out to "psychologize away" the perception of uncanniness, while arbitrarily allowing for the objectivity of so irreducibly phenomenal a percept as *black*.[1]

It is in opposition to this very kind of confusion, then called "psychologism", that, early in this century, the phenomenological method was first formulated and proposed. Brentano first argued the objectivity of knowledge in the sense of an irreducibility of the phenomenal contents of consciousness to an objectified psyche. The immediate origin of the method lay in Edmund Husserl's rediscovery of what transcends experiencing as an objective process throughout: the essences or noetic constituents of all the "things" that can *appear in*, rather than be produced by, consciousness—consciousness being understood here as their condition of actualization in the temporal individual psyche. Husserl, in his careful analyses of the structure of knowledge, rediscovered those stable and comprehensive conditions of all thing-awareness which are axioms because they are irreducible; any genetic accounting of them which seeks their causes in past states of the organism turns out to be a mere description of their past occurrences, and in the same manner, environmentalism has no answer here, since such phenomena of consciousness as insight cannot by any conceivable process be derived from the mere facticity of sensory materials. The most intrinsic stabilizers of knowledge, identity, form or essence, definitive compellingness, anything that constitutes meanings, are never contained in "reality" (which Husserl therefore parenthetically excludes), but, vice versa, are constitutive to the very *possibility* of reality as a continuous one in which appearances are what they are and can be recalled in their meanings in subsequent environmental encounter. Consciousness therefore has its origin (which evidently is not meant to connote any point or points in its temporal lineage but connotes essential constitution) *beyond* reality, if reality is understood as the time-stream of ever-changing facts going on without; working from the most timeless (perennially self-evident) elements of consciousness toward the actuality of existence, Husserl described the succession of intuitive acts whereby the transcendental ego, "making room" for itself in the physical universe, turns into the physical ego only through the encountered pre-constituted presence of its own body, the encountered co-presence of other bodies presumed to refer to other selves, and the "public sphere" of intersubjectivity thus established which allows all these selves to share in a common universe of communicable experience.

Naturalistic criticisms of the account are pointless, inasmuch as the genesis Husserl describes is explicitly *not* the temporal-causal genesis of a process of consciousness. Instead this genesis *intersects* with time; it is the ever-present hierarchy of the ego's intuitive awarenesses according to their levels of comprehensiveness for all *possible* knowledge. Likewise, Husserl's use of the term *intuitive* has nothing to do either with the loose use now colloquial or with its traditional use in metaphysics: the *noemata* do not exist in a separate world of ideas, as in Platonism, but *apply* themselves to the physical fact world in a manner of interpenetration much closer to Aristotelian thought. Intuition, accordingly, in the sense in which the phenomenologists use that term, is, in Collins' definition,[2] "not some sybilline, mystic utterance but only our direct acquaintance with our situation in existence. . . . (It) does not take the place of careful analysis but is its grounding in reality and its priming point." Correspondingly, Husserl's transcendental ego, unlike Kant's, is linked with the empirical ego through a successive continuum, reaching far beyond the Kantian *categories*, the Kantian *Anschauungsformen*, of degrees of certitude in immediate experience; it is not a postulate of reasoning, but an empiric discovery, resulting from a systematic reduction of the contents of consciousness to only such constancies as are contained in their own direct descriptions. Unlike Cartesianism, furthermore, this "empiric transcendentalism" does not "suspend the belief" in a contingent physical reality to ascertain first the reality of the ego as subject but suspends the ordinary notion of the ego as subject along with the notion of the sense world; in this suspension, neither of the two is ever fundamentally held in doubt as in the Cartesian method, but each is "put in brackets". Husserl's transcendental ego, as an inference from the *a priori* givenness of knowledge his inquiry encounters, is not a subject opposing the essences as objects, but itself *constitutes* or "intends" the essences. Since the essences are the true contents of consciousness constitutive to all temporal applied knowledge, *being* and *being known* become one: the order of knowing coincides with the order of foundation of being, "things" are radically understood as being *what they appear to be*,[3] and the Husserlian ego, cutting straight through the subject-object cleavage of both metaphysics and science, no longer stands in apposition to "world" but squarely *in* it as its "founder" and "knower" in one, a version of transcendental idealism that despite (if not perhaps because of) its derivation, is indeed more extreme than any of the past.

It is the epistemological neutrality of Husserl's thought, its attempt to unite the sources of logic and of ontology, its attempt at radical empiricalness, that accounts for its influence on the subsequent rise of the existentialist movement; even at that point where the existentialists, under the impact of the thought of Nietzsche and Kierkegaard, break away from Husserl's version of phenomenology, in their reversal of the predicative order of knowledge and being, the very

fruitfulness of the challenge proves their indebtedness to his purification of philosophic method. The mere rediscovery of the immediate
data of consciousness had been Bergson's merit, but Bergson (as
shown by his time theory) had not succeeded in working out a system that, without involving concepts extraneous to these data, allowed
their theoretical enucleation.[4] Why had the immediate contents of
consciousness, of experience altogether, been overlooked by science?
According to the very idea of science, no self-articulated context of
data is of any less cognitive dignity, that is, merits inquiry less, than
any other; yet, what the phenomenologists discover is that the one
data context basic to all others, basic to our very apperception of
reality and thereby to everything science *does* deal with, had been
completely overlooked by even that science upon which the exploration would most naturally fall: psychology. Psychology, the phenomenologist finds, has *by-passed* its subject matter; by-passing it, it
has replaced that subject matter by abstractions that are analogisms.
These analogisms, as shown by the terminology of all objectivistic
schools, are borrowed from the physical fact world, which argues
against their meaningfulness, since no analysis of the physical fact
world can find the psyche anywhere among its data.

This analysis would remain incomprehensible without an actual
detection of positive preconceptions about the whole order of the subject matter of psychology on the functionalist's part. Preconceptions
about the whole order of the subject matter of a science are by definition metaphysical premises. In principle, this is acknowledged by all
schools of thought. No reason thus is visible that the definition should
fail to apply in the case of scientists not only unaware of the aprioristic
character of their presuppositions, not only claiming empiricism with
perfect good faith, but being enabled by their very unsuspectingness
of their own operations to be militantly "against" metaphysical
premises.

Opposition to metaphysical premises, of course, is an indispensable and meritorious characteristic of science. In the fields where the
principle was appied correctly, as in physics, none of the stupendous
gains of recent times would have been possible without it. The entire
emancipation of the scientific mind from the bonds of dogma depended
on this opposition, and it is important to remember what it meant
concretely in physics: a complete *openness* toward whatever the sub-

ject matter should reveal; no pretense to know anything before having observed; a readiness to revise even such most fundamental categorical schemes as one's conception of space, once observation came to demand it. Contrariwise, what we find at the root of, for example, Thorndike's objectivism in psychology is a metaphysical assumption not any less dogmatic for this scientist's anti-metaphysical beliefs; these beliefs succeed only in completing its blindness because, very much in distinction from metaphysical assumptions directly posited or otherwise explicit, nothing that lies beyond the horizon of the premise is any longer conceivable to the scientist. Thorndike's psychological method begins with a postulation (believed to rest on empiric grounds) according to which the subject matter of psychology is conceived of in analogy with physical things. Physical things, in Thorndike's implicit interpretation of the term, are pure *objects* and nothing besides. They are objects insofar as[5] they are occupants of space already isolated from their phenomenal contexts, purged of their meanings, with which man finds them in his world. Thorndike's postulation is based on the "observation" that *everything that exists exists in a certain quantity.* According to observation, this is untrue, and we need not even go into the subject matter of psychology to show it.

Since Thorndike's statement refers to *everything, anything* must bear the statement out. How about an elephant? The elephant exists in a certain quantity—of what? Of elephant? This would be true only in the world and language of a butcher of elephants, but in any non-butchering, any intrinsic account it would be true only if the big beast were a homogeneous mass or multitude instead of a structure, a unified manifold in which no part is either equal to any other or already fulfilling the definition of elephant as a part. Far from applying to everything, Thorndike's statement holds true for masses and multitudes only. But the proposition has blocked the accesses to the true horizon of phenomena-centered problems for a whole generation of behavioristically trained psychologists. The subject matter of psychology was prejudiced: objective, in the sense of scientifically valid, and quantitative, were uncritically synonymized. The idea of measurement (as though one were dealing with masses or multitudes of homogeneous materials, of "traits" that can meaningfully be subjected to the counting operations of statistics) protected whole sectors of

psychological subject matter from ever being discovered in their own
unmitigated order. It is easy to recognize quite similar prejudicing
of the subject matter in the way in which the early empiricists of
perception, under the influence of the metaphysics of the sensory
datum of J. S. Mill and others, preached the nothing-but-observation
to themselves and the world, but had in fact already decided that,
for example, our visual perceptions ought to be due to a merely additive agglomeration of many single stimulations of retinal neural fibres.
They did not derive this doctrine, so completely shattered since, from
observation; the experiments they conducted to prove their point were
constructed to create the very special conditions under which the
doctrine attains a semblance of truth. The doctrine derived from the
a priori of their own existence; a pre-given fact, the historical situation of their thinking, made them unable to conceive of it in any
other way.

What accounts for this dogmatism with anti-dogmatic gesturing?
Before we can reach an answer, the whole epistemological background
of modern positivistic science quite evidently needs clarification; the
clarification, however, calls for a definite vantage point, which must
lie wholly outside the boundaries of positivistic science, since it demands a more detailed and concrete account of the phenomenological
position. How can the immediate data of experience be ascertained
reliably? To account for knowledge, any "knowledge" not deriving
from the immediate data of experience, must be "put in brackets".
For example, in understanding our concept of *spring*, it does not help
to dissect spring into multiple single sensations; their ordering in the
concept of spring cannot be derived from an addition of them in our
minds: we see that the "single percept" already refers to a conceptual order that it implements. Nor does it help to trace the concept
bio-historically, culture-historically, or along any other genetic lines,
since at any point along such lines the experienced emergence of
the concept, or *ours into it*, presupposes understanding, the potential
presence of the concept in our consciousness. Is spring, then, primarily an abstract idea in our heads, a Platonic shadow that we
somehow bring along? This would contradict the fact that we encounter it without; the experienced direction of its apperception is
from its *occurrence* to us inward, not from our *abstraction* of it outward; the abstraction only encloses and conceals the idea, reducing

a concrete mental presence to a "spaceless" position within the purely concept-relational context of our applied logical operations. The idea, which thus is isolated and reduced, originally is not immanent to any operational context of thought but is immanent to an encountered order that takes part in our world. The true sources of knowledge, then, the essences or *noemata*, as discreet order-makers which they are, are neither "single perceptions of fact things" nor ideas *qua* abstractions. They occupy a zone between these, in which we discern them as ideas in the original sense of that term, as pure *Anschauungen*, images of *a priori* valid meanings. The term ideas with this connotation is used by Plato himself, and only in consequence of his way of philosophizing about ideas did our present use of the term emerge: to connote abstractions constituting a merely subjective (subject-immanent) inner sphere of thought. This has occurred through the long history of western metaphysics that begins, not with authentic Platonism, but with the traditional "Platonic" misunderstandings of that doctrine that date back to Speusippos. This loss of the original concept of ideas as subject-transcendent, world-constituent, inter-individually shared *Anschauungen*, has had consequences in modern psychology which we shall meet when we turn to such acute and important propositions as the so-called loss of abstract behavior in some categories of mental patients, especially those with organic brain disease.

At least an inkling of what such loss really consists of is already forthcoming once we concentrate descriptively, with phenomenology, on the whole sphere of ideas as *Anschauungen* (eidetics)[6] which perpetually surrounds normal man as experiencer, and reaches to the very core of his *existing*, the active self. Both facts, that the objectivists overlook it and that its theorization presents general difficulty, are understandable from its own mode of *givenness* alone; since the axiomatic constancies underlying any act of *noesis* are continually distributed to our perceptual and logical operations at once, the direction of conscious attention[7] thereby established points away from them: consciousness, which these constancies *constitute*, therefore *by-passes* them, more properly, has already by-passed them at any point. This requires a special effort at detached, nothing-but-observing, contemplative attention, at eidetic intuition, to use Husserl's term, to bring their fixation about. This discovery, that consciousness tends to by-pass its own immediate data *in their immediacy* (in Heidegger's language, that "logic" tends to by-pass its own foundation in pre-ordered *being*) is the perhaps most revolutionizing element of phenomenological inspection in existentialist thought and the empiric basis for the existentialist break with idealism (including Husserl's) and empiricism at once. The significance of its psychological and clinical truth for the entire concern of abnormal psychology is neatly demonstrable by an analysis of the states of consciousness of schizophrenic subjects, not according to induced introspection, but according to their own spontaneous complaints. In its most cogent form, this demonstration was undertaken by Jaspers in his *General Psychopathology*[8]; the experiential order it reveals is basic to all "psychic events", and consequently to any theorizing about experiential orders.

In many instances of acute schizophrenic psychosis, the patients complain of qualitative changes in their perceptual world; the voices of others seem to come "from very far" or as though the patients are hearing them "through a wall"; or it seems as though they are seeing everything "through a veil"; or they complain that all things have "flattened out", turned into almost two-dimensional reliefs. All these expressions are meant pictorially; since language is grounded in normal experience, no directly descriptive words are available to these subjects, who are well aware of this inadequacy and of the fundamental alienation of their worlds, and are groping for the nearest possible expressions to convey its character. Testing their perceptual faculties invariably shows that their vision, hearing, and touch are sharp and distinct; for example, even in instances in which the complaint directly suggests changes in the inner geometric proportions of the field of vision—"everything looks so far away" or is "so terribly near"—in its tested objectivity the field of perception shows no changes. Jaspers concludes that there are disturbances in perceptual experience that effect neither the sensory data, nor the apperception of meaning, nor the perceptual judgment. "There must, in normal perception, still exist something else which we would not notice if these patients would not produce their peculiar complaints." We notice this something only when it is missing in some subjects; otherwise it is far too fundamental to experience to be an object of experiential awareness. Jaspers goes on to show how the phenomenal descriptions become ever stranger with higher degrees of the disturbance. They increasingly affect those axiomatic constants of all perceptual experience—identity, togetherness, meaning—which are so constitutive to reality itself that loss of reality, in cases such as he describes, occurs on a far more fundamental level than in the delusional systems of *thought* usually referred to by clinicians using the term. These constants are so basic to reality that the objectivist cannot be aware of them as axioms of experience, precisely because they determine his own reality apperception, including his theorizing; he can therefore believe he knows what he is talking about when he speaks of reality or the loss of it, as in schizophrenics. Invariably, his conception of reality *per se* is grounded in his own personal world experience, but just because it is grounded there it focuses away from the ground. Thus he isolates elements that the phenomena of Jaspers' patients reveal as entirely extrinsic to the constituent sources of reality, the axioms of consciousness, and concludes that loss of reality must involve (as it precisely does not) a severing of orientative connections between the objectifiable ego and the total gamut of environmental objects, the sensory world. The objectivist may affirm either, with Freud, the indissolubility of the psyche into its physiological substrate, or, with Gestalt psychology, the correlative structuredness of this substrate and the sensory environment. But no matter how emphatic he is about either, reality to him is, explicitly or implicitly, the sum total of the contents of perceptual judgments made from sensory experiences through apperceptions of meaning; these apperceptions themselves, as we will show in our analysis of Gestalt psychology and of psychoanalysis, invariably remain mysterious. The objectivist's notion of reality, then, is invalid; the reality of his theorizing is precisely that which in concrete losses of reality remains wholly unaffected.

Is there a phenomenal common denominator from which we can understand both this so-called loss of *abstract behavior* which deteriorated schizophrenics share with brain organics, but which is experienced as *catastrophic* only by brain organics, and the *acute* schizophrenic's own *catastrophic* "losses of reality"? Any such denominator could not be sought successfully with Husserl's method, because Husserl's version of phenomenology has no room for the pre-logical, for experience in its groundedness, for the phenomenal primate of existence in human experiencing; its tacit presupposition, from which

the empiric ego is only derived, and existence only predicated, is the
encountered fact of knowledge already given as conceptual knowledge,
the *logos*.[9] But from where does the logos arise—from objectifying
"from without" constructions that by-pass its actuality or from experience itself? Jaspers, psychopathologist and existential philosopher in
one, and of all existentialists the one least influenced by Husserl, was
in a particularly good position to make observations that at once
defy transcendental idealism and the notions of the objectivist. But
although his *General Psychopathology* remains a source book of the
first order for phenomenologists, Jaspers' unwillingness to admit in
principle the explorability of the "ground of existence", *being* itself,
forbade him to go further.

It is this going further, which Jaspers rejects and which Sartre
does not conceive of, that evidently is preliminary to any true attempt
at enucleating the pure data of experience; without these data, existences as individual modes of *being-in-the-world* can never be cognized.
The decisive discovery of Heidegger, the groundedness, ontic as well
as experiential, of existence in the all-constituentness of *being* as the
phenomenal *wherefrom* of all language, all logic, all objectifications,
even of the "superficially perceived self", the *I*, therefore becomes
basic to Binswanger's and all other attempts at an applied existential
analytic. Heidegger's philosophy, his reversal of the phenomenological formula (which we will develop in detail) leads to an existential
analytic that for good reasons has a fundamental ontology (exploration of being) rather than any anthropological applications as its
goal; but just because of this fundamentalness of the level on which
his phenomenological inquiries are conducted they become incisive
for psychology. As has been noted increasingly by psychologists in
Europe, both the material and the methodological implications of
Heidegger's thought finally permit a closing of the traditional thematic gap between the psychology of cognitive and of conative "functions", of perception (in addition to some other basic processes) and
personality, a gap of exceeding endurance and exceedingly sterile
effect, to which we shall turn next.

NOTES

1. The irreducibility of phenomenal color to its neural "correlates", regardless
on what level of physiological complexity, will be taken up later. For a fuller
discussion of phenomenal impoverishment as typical of specialization processes,

cf., the author's "The Specialist as a Psychological Problem", *Social Research*, 1951, *18*, 9–31, esp. pp. 20–23.

2. J. Collins, *The Existentialists*, 1952, p. 122.

3. It goes without saying that appearance in this sense has little to do with the "appearances" naive realism focuses upon. The phenemenological contention is exactly that ordinary weak observation by-passes the full richness (and onto-logical revealingness) of phenomena as beings, retaining, at the phenomenal level, "appearances" that suggest a search for the "real nature" of something "behind" its appearance, that is, refer the inquirer to objectifying analysis. The character-istic consequence not only is an explicit abandonment of "naive realism" but also an implicit completion of the original (naively realistic) concealment of phenomenal truth.

4. For example, Bergson's denial, in itself perfectly true, of the experiential authenticity of mathematical time, must first demonstrate the "unreality" of the *past*; the demonstration then comes to depend on an analysis of the experience of the past as *no longer real*, which still presupposes an original apperception of mathematical time in the subject. Concerning Heidegger's phenomenological clarification of original time, cf. p. 114.

5. The fundamental significance of this "insofar as" for the entire quest of quantitative explanatory science is discussed on p. 61.

6. From the Greek *eidos*, idea, arch-image, linguistically relating to *idea*. In phenomenological usage, the term has a wider connotation than in Jänschian psychology; eidetic images as in the now ordinary sense can be understood as instances of a particularly free and active, unblocked, world-participation as a pregiven characterological fact in some subjects.

7. Both in academic psychology and in psychoanalysis, *attention*, especially in its more autonomous manifestations, has remained practically unexplored to this day. In the view of phenomenologists the general tendency of the objectivisms in psychology to construct theories of consciousness (as well as of the unconscious) without first investigating the foundational phenomena of attention, is a character-istic example of their own inattentiveness, their inveterate *by-passing* of authentic experience.

8. 1946, pp. 53–54.

9. The paradoxical use that some versions of logical positivism have been able to make of Husserl's method is explicable wholly from this unempiric limitation of experience to consciousness, more precisely, of consciousness to its own oper-ational aspect in which logic, the systematic context of intra-subjectively operant categories, is encountered as an already finished entity. While Husserl only in his late period develops his "absolutism of mind" and even then still sees and empha-sizes his original discovery, the eidetic constituents behind all logical operations, the new positivists no longer do. The operational aspect of knowledge being absolutized, reality can be subjected to objectification even more limitlessly than either Descartes, Kant, or, for that matter, any of the older positivists envisaged. Concerning the existentialist interpretation of logic, see p. 117.

CHAPTER 3

The Gap in Psychology: the Missing Link between Personality and Cognition—The Subject-Object Problem and the Contingency of Being Object *on* Being—*The World as Phenomenon and as Process—The Diltheyan Gap and* Explanatoriness—*Gestalt Psychology and Phenomenology—Parallelism and Interactionism—The Isomorphic Circle—*Values *and* Requiredness—*The Gestaltist Movement as a* Time Gestalt *of Weak Closure.*

BOTH THE NATURE AND IMPORTANCE OF THE GAP ARE evident at a glance. Its obstinacy plagues the functionalist, and the literature on its problems is swelling. Without being able to unite in one conceptual scheme the structural and dynamic (motivational) laws of the subjective *in* the person with the structural and dynamic (cognitive) laws governing objective reality as it occurs *to* the person, no one can claim to have built a science that does justice to the given unity of the context of experience (or of behavior). For the gap, of course, is not in the "object" of that science. The gap is in the functionalist's mental presentation of this object which keeps eluding his grasp with a kind of mocking trickery. It is torn there by the diametric opposition between his two foci which must be directed at once toward outsides and insides: toward the constant and variable elements of objective fields of perception, learning, and thinking as they present themselves from the vantage point of the subject on the one hand and the objectified inner conative processes of that subject on the other. Why, in all the desk and laboratory research on the problem of the relations between personality and cognition, has only the production of brain models, expected to further its solution, made progress, the solution none? Because the diametric opposition is not even one of two conflicting directions in a single field of observation with one identical observer. Whereas data from two conflicting directions of observation can be related systematically, those from two fundamentally *disparate*

28

fields cannot, because no conceivable common denominator exists in which the two sets of data could find one ultimate referent; the observer of phenomenal reality, focussing outward with the subject, and this same observer studying the latter's "processes", are quite literally two different observers because the fields of observation are untranslatably heterogeneous in their entirety. The two referents, therefore, from the very start of the cognitive operation, are mutually exclusive. The directional conflict is not located in any one field but in the theoretician himself. In the theoretician's very subjectivity we find two incompatible attitudes, one accepting—in fact if not in principle—subjectivity as the given existential premise of objective reality, the other insisting, against this inexorable constitution of the cognitive situation, on turning subjectivity as such into an object. It appears, then, that the relations between motivation (attitudinal facts) and cognition observable in the operations of inquirers *into* these relations present clues *for that inquiry*.

But before examining this possibility we are faced with demands for implementation as well as with objections. One of the objections concerns the question whether an acknowledgment of the stated disparateness would not destroy the unity of knowledge by destroying ultimately the unity of all-things-that-are. In facing this issue, one cannot help noticing two important clues: one, that it is the very *being* of a process that would correspond to the functionalistic constructs of processes in psychology—not of correlated neurological ones, which no one questions—that remains wholly unproven, since processes, in any strict sense of science, are observable (or deducible from observation) changes of *things in space*; second, that the notion of the all-things-that-are still refers to a subject holding that notion. The holding of a notion, if we describe it in its givenness, means that the thinking subject has the content of that notion in front of him; he himself, inasmuch as he *has* a notion, is inevitably excluded from its content. This is not changed by any decision of his to extend the reach of the notion to himself as object of thought (one-who-is); to alter the constellation described, this extension would have to dissolve the given premise of subject-object confrontation between the thinker and the thought-of. Since this result is not forthcoming, the thinking agent as such remains excluded from the contents of his thought. What can be inferred from this? Certainly not that the all-things-that-are fails to include him (the one who thinks it) but only that the subject as one-who-is (object) is *not* the subject who conceives of this (and any other) object: the very *is* or *are* of the notion presupposes a position of the subject outside of the context of things-that-are, since, except from such a position, the *is* or *are* could never be "seen". The *is*, in one sense, implies the *naught* as its alternative becoming perceivable at the point of thinking the *is*; in another sense, it refers to the possibility of thinking *any* "is", that is, to *being* as the tacitly presupposed constituent of all-things-that-are. This constituent, therefore, is the subject himself, not in his "subjectivity", in which he has "severed" his existential links with the object in order to subject it to his cognition as to a *power*, but the subject in his original situation of openness-toward (being-in) the encompassing, the *world*. Foundational to all existents and to his own existence, this pre-given status of being-in-the-world thus remains as the only possible cognitive source of the notion of being that self-evidently enters the *is*. The presupposition is tacit and consciously unelaborated wherever we use the "is . . ." in judgments about objects because *being* and the subject are in a state of identity in cognizing, whereas the object (literally, that which is "thrown against") is *encountered*. This establishes an irreducible duality between subject and object once objectification (logical subjection) is achieved. The world as object which presupposes such subjection, is then misunderstood to be the source and testing criterion of reality, an assumption that clinical cases such as those cited by Jaspers refute as unempirical.[1]

Although this assumption continues to be held the only one objectively possible, it merely clouds the issue. For is reality, which evidently shares in being, our object? This Cartesian notion can be challenged on many grounds. One is that the more any object is *made* object (the less, to use Heidegger's term, it is allowed to remain *open* to our spontaneous participation in the given contexts of its meaning) the more it is inevitably excluded from our understanding (original cognizing) also, since understanding is the immediate manifestation in us of being in its authenticity, in which we *share* with the world. The subject's own being, therefore, is thoughtlessly by-passed in the explanatory operations of objectivism, buried in the inconspicuous *is* of our cognitive judgments; these judgments first isolate things from their contexts, then, isolating molecular and atomic elements within the context of the things, lose reality (in its authentic mode of occurrence) while becoming increasingly useful only for its manipulation. The result is the fundamental world- and self-alienation (nihilism) that has become the common lot of man and the hidden suffering at the existence-basis of the typical neuroses of our time. The essence of this double alienation is loss of *being*. This has come about with the rise of modern object-manipulatory science and technology, although its roots dig into a common historical ground with the roots of these phenomena themselves. The implication of this insight is not irrationalism. It is not a denunciation of objectivity, but an acknowledgment of the necessity for *both* thinking and living to put objectification back in its place, to "remember being", "recall man to being", in Collins' formulation of Heidegger's fundamental concern.

The polarity of being and the naught in which man's—and only *man's*—existence is caught will be exposed more fully in our subsequent presentation of Heidegger's doctrine. Returning to our present problem, we face another objection to our contention of an unbridgeable gap between objectified subjectivity and the phenomenal: if only physiological processes "correlated" with phenomenal experience can be objectified in principle (their objectification in fact continuing to lag conspicuously), do these processes or their hypothetical models not legitimately, inasmuch as science is *supposed* to deal with objects, replace the data of psychology? The phenomenologist's answer to this argument of behaviorism is twofold. One, the perennial idea of science, which not having been born with Cartesian dualism is likely to survive its present self-reduction *ad absurdum* in the anthropological sciences, has never been restricted to the objectivistic quest; second, a simple requirement of scientific logic, the replacement would ultimately have to account for the phenomenal data in their phenomenality, just as the most boldly observable hypothetical constructs of physics must finally be tested on their ability to account for the physical facts. Whitehead's thesis about the universe as process, on which (phenomenal) reality is only contingent, seems to overlook that we have no possible conception of such a process, except as one "in reality"; ultimately, then, the very conception of a world process hinges on its phenomenality as an at least conceivable one.[2] The attempt to found reality on process, rather than vice versa, as the direction of analysis would indicate, is contingent on the successfulness of a prior attempt to sever the experiential "bridge behind" that still links to our

existence even the remotest objective conception, such as that of the
universe as a process both blind and invisible. It is evident that such a
feat neither could nor would have to be completed: it might be held
accomplished in principle once we can account for any phenomenal
data of experience strictly in terms of physicalistic laws.

According to the very careful analyses of Goldstein and most other
holistic biologists, this is impossible, by no means only in fact, but in
principle: no *not yet* is involved; "organic nature cannot be *understood*
with the tools of mathematical, natural science."[3] Does it follow from
this that experience, as a peculiar characteristic of organic nature,
cannot be explained? The statement quoted says nothing about explanations; the question of the possible physicalistic explanation of life
processes remains completely open. But the more molecular, sub-
microscopic the research becomes, the less the explanation accounts
for what it has deliberately excluded from the start, the unity of the
organism as an encountered one in our immediate experience, even
should physics ultimately find an explanatory principle for the given
coordination of single molecular processes. For the phenomenality of
the organism, the encompassing unity of expression (character) pervading its static physiognomic aspects as much as its behavioral forms,
refers to principles of reduction that *a priori* have to do not with atoms
but with essences: the unity encountered is prior to any explanatory
principles that may account for it from the vantage point of physics.

This by no means holds true only for organisms but extends to the
entire world as *our* world, that is, to anything having a being of its
own and thereby sharing in being: a landscape—more distinctly if
interpenetrations with the existences of generations who lived there
have shaped its spirit; a historic situation or scenery; an idea in its
authenticity; a snowfall; an autograph; the atmosphere of a city; a
piece of music, a story, a poem, or a painting.[4] It is quite possible,
of course, to conduct a physicalistic analysis of the colors in the painting as well as of their point-to-point distribution, and conceivably,
by including the artist's brain processes, the analysis could extend also
to the production of the painting. But the analysis would be futile, for
it is bound to lose the painting *qua* painting at the start[5]: the analysis
as an act is a cognitive exclusion of the being (intention, character,
style) of the painting, which refers to disciplines more essential to
paintings than is physics. What does this situation imply? Evidently,

that explanation is a cognitive account that takes place only in one specific predetermined direction. This observation was made when deterministic explanatory theories of everything were first beginning to bloom, in the late nineteenth century, and it led Dilthey to his unsatisfactory dichotomization of science into *Naturwissenschaften* and *Geisteswissenschaften,* the former explanatory, the latter understanding, with the line of division, significantly, running straight through *psychology.* Explanation, then, by deliberately excluding the phenomenality of the things it sets out to reduce to what it believes to be ultimate laws (but where has there been less ultimateness than just in physicalistic explanations?), not only fails to account for the *being* of that which it reduces but in the end stands itself in need of a psychological account.

A full insight into this situation is preliminary to any understanding of the major attempt that has been made in psychology to close both the gap between perception and personality and the Diltheyan gap and to account for phenomenal experience by ultimately referring its data to the laws of physics. This does not mean, strictly speaking, a causal reduction of experience to preceding physical events—which Gestalt psychology rightly rejects—but a strict structural correlativeness between the two "parallel" sides of the organismic total process as an explanatory principle supposed to account for experience. The necessity for refuting, not the valuable experimental work of Gestalt psychology, but its *a prioris,* the presuppositional and purposive (theoretical) frames within which this work was interpreted by the Gestaltists themselves may seem surprising if it follows almost immediately affirmative references to Gestalt psychology's friend and neighbor, holistic biology. The apparent closeness of the phenomenological and Gestalt views, the almost indistinguishable presence of both viewpoints at once in the thinking of the late Wertheimer, and the extensive use that the phenomenological method has found in the experimental work of that school, may make such a refutal seem even stranger. That closeness, however, has more and more become one of two adjoining realms, each drawn inexorably into different whole orbits, with the effect that they contest each other more vehemently than the hinterlands within each orbit, knowing little about one another, may incline to. As Gestalt psychologists will confirm most readily, Gestalt psychology has questioned the objectifications of psychical processes

undertaken by older schools but never has questioned the epistemological validity of the very aim of objectification.

The concrete accomplishments of Gestalt psychology have without
exception been phenomenological. Experimentally securing given
constancies, for example in visual perception, as both independent
of the geometric retinal distribution of environmental objects and
irreducible to past experience; demonstrating the peculiar translation
(made evident as well as understandable but strictly speaking never
explained[6]) of minute time distances in bilateral auditory perception
into differences in the experienced direction of sound; demonstrating
an encompassing predominance, in memory, thinking, and learning,
of stable and transferable structures (configurations, *Gestalten*) over
fleeting sensory media, essences over elements—all these are confirmations of the phenomenological contention of an objective irreducibility
of immediate experience as the very constituent of objects. Peculiarly,
the purpose of all this experimentation at the margins of the field
was not, as it could have been, an autonomization of psychology as a
science in its own right (from then on dealing with its data with just
as little concern for physics as the physicist shows for psychology in
dealing with his), but a justification of psychology before the tribunal
of physical science. In acceding to the claim of physical science to
embody all ultimate truth, Gestalt psychology bowed to the fundamental idea of the nineteenth century at the very point where it seemed
to rebel against it.

The magic key was the theory of psychophysical parellelism, according to which pervadingly identical structures (isomorphisms) determine the events of the psyche (of phenomenal experience) and the
correlated events on the physiological (neurological, muscular, motor
behavior) side of the organismic total process. This theory is, in one
respect, of great plausibility: although it does not *explain* anything, it
enables us to understand—for example, an infant's understanding of the
smile of his mother as manifested by his own first smile, which we
can never attribute to past renumerative experience with his own
smiling, for there has been none, nor to imitativeness, for nothing else
of the mother's behavior is imitated by the infant. The fundamental
contention of Gestalt psychology, a lawful and encompassing relation
between any insides and outsides of experiential-behavioral events, is
evidenced by an infinite number of possible observations, many of

which have been cited often and need not be repeated. The peculiar characteristic of all these observations is just that they are immediately plausible: they themselves presuppose what they are supposed to explain, understanding, and the range of such observations consequently varies with the individual. When this range of primary understanding has been narrowed by phenomenal impoverishment, as in many specialists, the inevitable consequence is that any *understanding* achievements by others, regardless how analytic and how verifiable experimentally, that lie beyond the horizon of those understandings that one is used to and therefore need not find problematic, will automatically be attributed to an uncanny and disorderly something.

This something, the given order of which cannot be re-experienced by the critic and consequently cannot be seen, is called intuition in a derogatory sense by all those who thoughtlessly identify the fundamental direction of human cognitive behavior with the direction of explanatoriness. The derogation does not remove intuition, primary understanding, from its position at the basis of explanatoriness as of all cognition: just as the order of a work of music must be intuited before it can be subjected to *any* theorizing, so must every single deductive step in the solution of a mathematical problem. This pre-given order contains important clues. For one, it allows us to account for the fact that there continue to engage the experiential "processes" of human beings uncounted phenomena of their being-in-the-world which the objectivist, not sharing in the experience of these in the first place, unempirically excludes as unreal, an attitude which he now extends to the debunking of the reality of any ultimate essences but which he could extend to the debunking of such undoubted realities as a Beethoven symphony also, if his phenomenal impoverishment would attain to complete unmusicality and if even in that case his life in society had not led him nevertheless to "believe in" the reality of music. Since Gestalt psychology, in its search for phenomenal constancies which it believed would allow to *explain understanding* (that is, reduce a more authentic to a less authentic mode of cognition that itself wholly depends on the former as its presupposition) never concentrated on what only seemed capable of muddying its findings, personality psychology, it never did investigate modes and degrees of *phenomenal receptiveness* in the person, thus missing one of the two sliding scales (the range of *Prägnanz* constituting the other) along which—if one attempts a merely circumscriptive objectification of phenomenal experience—the two margins of immediate reality, the "subjective" and the "objective" ones, are seen to shift.

Second, we are enabled to account for the misunderstanding behind the theory of psychophysical parallelism. Our first observation will be that the theory itself is evidently in need of clarification since it cannot possibly cover the ground of experientially encountered body-mind relations, which show the enormity of the dynamic (phenomenally causal) impact of bodily states on psychic conditions as well as, with probably just as much generality, of the latter on the former, even though only since Charcot, Janet, Freud, Bleuler, and A. Meyer, more attention has been paid to the latter direction of psychosomatic interactiveness. The reservation is not made in order to side with interactionism against parallelism but just in order to expose the confusion behind this already historical dispute. For "psyche" and "soma", in either one of the two doctrines, have connotations wholly heterogeneous from the ones they find in the other. In the field of observation theorized by interactionism, "mind" and "body" are entities which refer to a "my"—*my* stomach, *my* fears—and therefore themselves to unreflected phenomenal experience. This discovery implies, (1) that "body" as the "my body" (*Leib*) of a subject is a different concept from what the same "body" (*Körper*) is under the focus of strict explanatory science; the latter at least can continue to postulate, with parallelism, a pervading correlativity of two processes in the organism. This heterogeneity, in turn, explains at once (a) the legitimate importance of the whole sphere of *Leib* experiences for the understanding of the "my body" (and altogether of phenomenal causality), not as methodological tools but as *data* for an existential psychology, (b) the confronting, by the psychoanalytic schools, of phenomenal causality with strict explanatory causality, and (c) the seemingly insuperable difficulties which biology has found in trying to "nail down" phenomenal causality, always involving the organism more or less as a unit, in terms of any strict explanatory analysis of single causal processes which it was able to isolate. (2) Since, what is left of "body-mind relations" once we deduct the phenomenal of their immediate (subjective) experience, becomes hypothetical on the side of either (mind as well as body), the question arises whether Gestalt psychology offers anything that could turn the parallelistic hypothesis into a verified theoretical picture.

In order to assess even the nature of the problem correctly, the experiential origin of the parallelism theory must be remembered first. "I move my hand", and "my hand moves in space" are not "causally connected". In order to be causally connected, one would have to precede the other, a fundamental line of criticism which cancels out many other "causal" functionalisms likewise, such as the James-Lange theory of emotions, as well as the older theory which it reversed. The naive causalistic misunderstanding of many instances of "because of" relations, the implicit identification of the very concept of explanatory *reason* with the very concept of genetic *cause*, should, of course, never have gotten into nineteenth century psychology in the first place. Schopenhauer had clarified the heterogeneity of the various *why* relations[7] at the beginning of that saeculum, and the breakdown of his philosophy has in substance been survived by that feat. But if "I move my hand" and "my hand moves in space" are not *causally* connected, what connects them? Evidently, identity: they are not even just simultaneous, they are the same event. But how do I know this? This knowledge, with which—rather than with the *ego cogito* of Descartes—all knowledge begins, can for this very reason of its fundamental (existential) givenness never be successfully made an object of explanatory knowledge, for explanatory knowledge, itself grounded in that givenness as its inevitable premise, deals with processes taking place in an external field of observation, whereas the peculiar characteristic of the stated identity as a given *a priori* of our knowledge is that it lies forever in two "fields" at once: inner experience of *my* hand as mine—but not even as anything I "have" but as sharing in what I *am*—and perceptual experience of this same hand as an object in space. Since any attempt to theorize this most fundamental (epistemological) mind-body relation must be true to its data—the phenomenal self-identity of "hand" and the "my"[8]—it must account for them, and this only a double aspect theory can: while a double aspect theory explicitly acknowledges both its own eternally postulatory nature and the unbridgeable gap between the two "fields" (which yet are bridged at any point by the foundational fact of the full experience of "my hand"), it does not fall into the error of stipulating one field with two "parallel" chains of events where emphatically there are given two fields with only one chain of events that appears in both at once. For what does "parallelity"—which Gestalt psychology here claims—imply? For one thing, separation

between two processes, for which, in *experience,* there exists not a
trace of a basis; secondly, their directional homogeneity within one
field. For what can be the meaning of *parallels* not accounted for in
their parallelity by the axiomatics of a single multidimensional domain?
The phenomenal peculiarity of the one-in-two which Gestalt psychology
consistently turns into a two-in-one, is exactly that no such domain is
given to begin with.

In consequence of this error Gestalt psychology has to construct the
one domain hypothetically. In turn it has to postulate, to make this
one domain plausible, the "two-ness" of all given *ones* that pervade
the two domains. A smile is one event but it pervades the domains of
inner experiential and outer expressive appearance and thus phenomenally occurs to the smiler and the smiled-at at once, uniting them,
with Binswanger's term, in one—more or less close-knit, more or less
stable—dual mode of existence. Gestalt psychology turns this into two
and possibly several *processes* ("process levels"⁹) by confounding the
static plurality of the given appearance-domains with a dynamic
plurality of separable occurrences. The basic misunderstanding involved is visibly the conversion by Gestalt theory of the isomorphism
concept from a regulative principle of reason in the Kantian sense,
necessitated by the phenomenal evidence and its explanatory irreducibility, into a factorial entity supposed, as such, to partake in "processes"
themselves hiding *behind* the phenomenal: the isomorphism concept,
in this manner, comes to assume at once the position of a pervading
characteristic (datum) to be explained and of its principle of explanation.

Once the illogical in this procedure, its circularity, is understood,
the inevitability of failure in the ensuing search of Gestalt psychology
offers no difficulties to our comprehension. Since Gestalt psychology,
while rejecting positivism in "principle", yet prides itself on its
adherence to explanatory principles of positivistic science, ultimately
it must prove the existence of these processes or process levels, prove
their "correlativity" independent of any argument of our immediate
understanding—since our immediate understanding itself is to be
explained in this enterprise—but how can it conceivably do this?
How can structural relationships that must not be "understood" *be*
understood or vice versa? In order to raise its argument to explanatory dignity of the exact, that is, unphenomenal, variety, Gestalt psy-

chology must refer its data to a *different*, a *more abstract* level, where they can be stated in acceptable physicalistic terms rather than in terms merely circumventive of the original dilemma such as "field organization", "dynamic self-distribution", and so forth. Its data are the given "isomorphisms", for example, of the phenomenal experience state of a subject, his facial expression, and the understanding of his mien by another. Since, according to principles of explanatory science, the "understanding" of all this (*qua* immediate understanding) is admissible only as *datum*, never as methodological point of argument, it must be referred to generically different laws; consequently, the neurological process itself must be explored in the end.

Since this is difficult, Gestalt psychology—before its recent recourse to the investigation of the electric discharges of the brain became available—for a long time contented itself with anti-atomistic postulations of a field-functioning of the brain. These not only were supported by much partial experimental evidence arguing at least against any mechanistic localization of the more complex accomplishments of the psyche, but received added support from the general insights of the holistic biology of recent years and from the conspicuous absence, which only an atomistic metaphysics had cast into oblivion, of any good primary reasons for the space-localization of so manifestly trans-spatial an entity as the psyche. Since all these arguments, however, remained unsatisfactory to the physicalistically-minded psychologist, Köhler took recourse to observations in physics itself. Gestalt-like phenomena were found in dead nature, wherever a process-field was relatively independent of its topographic surroundings; for example, the distribution of the electric charge on the surface of a conductor was found to fulfill the *Ehrenfels criteria* for the phenomenal *Gestalten* of psychology. The physicists were not stirred by this, and their imperturbability was founded on good reason, for whereas the Gestalt principle (although misunderstood by the Gestaltists as an ultimate, an immanent law of organization upon which *meaning* was held contingent) had been demonstrated as indispensable for a theoretical account of the phenomenal data of psychology, the *Gestalten* encountered among the data material of physics did at any rate not require it in order to be fully—or as near to fully as possible—explained. What Gestalt psychology had tried here was a short-circuiting of the (necessarily ever more radical) tension between the whole

explanatory and the whole phenomenological quests; yet the introduction of lyricisms into physics not only remains unjustified in
cognitive principle but in the last analysis is not poetical either, since,
in that discipline, it is hopelessly out of style. The consistent phenomenologist leaves physics alone, trusting that the claim to all ultimate
knowledge inhering in that science may eventually be shattered but that
it will never be shattered unless the claim is allowed to pursue without
the slightest extraneous disturbance its *dissolution of reality* to the
point where the introduction of holistic concepts into physics
becomes imperative from the vantage point of the situation in physics
itself. This criticism may appear "formal"; however, if considera-
tions of its kind argued in principle against the Gestaltist venture into
physics, observations of a more material nature invalidated it beyond
hope.

At a close glance, Driesch found incompatibilities between the two
orbits of observations. The experiments with physical *Gestalten* all
had to guarantee a stability of their topography as a limiting condition (and a *condition of limit* in the over-all range of observable
physical events); the organism and its process did not require such
guarantees. It was molding its own topography, the *stabilizer* here was
not topography but still the "psyche", "life", or whatever one desired
to call it. Köhler subsequently dissected the arguments of his critics.[10]
The resulting topographic theory, as shown by Goldstein,[11] linked
Köhler's hypothetical conception of the substrate of the *Gestalten* of
psychology with topography-involving processes in physics in an
already far more satisfactory way, but all the more now failed to
link it with the actuality of the *biological Gestalten;* the "essential
nature"[12] of the organism was truly irreducible to physics.

This allows additional inferences concerning the possible scope of
the new electroencephalographic enterprise of Gestalt psychology,
whereby structures correlative to those of the phenomenal experience
of a subject shall be shown in the pattern of his simultaneously
recorded brain electric events. Tragically—since a "debunking of
the debunkers" is its declared ultimate aim—this enterprise, which
fights its opponent's shadow much rather than his reality, *atomism*
rather than *objectivism,* has much of a Don Quichotery, for either it
must—as according to the record of the previously presented efforts
it may—end up with a renewed postulation, for lack of evidence, of

strict correlativity as something still to be demonstrated later; or it
must cancel itself out, still ending up with a renewal of the same
postulation *as a postulation,* precisely *if* the desired evidence is attained; for what, if not again its understandability (which is to be
explained) would make such evidence evident? The logical difficulty
in which Gestalt psychology is caught is truly insoluble. This theory
must, as we saw, refer its isomorphisms to generically different laws,
yet, since these isomorphisms are the only lawful pervaders of
generically heterogeneous media in which the events investigated take
place no such laws are even conceivable *formaliter*; consequently,
none can be found. This dilemma is the source of unending con-
fusions among Gestaltists and non-Gestaltists alike, for example, when
it comes to any such attempts as an "explanation" of synesthetic
experience spontaneously linking together in a subject's phenomenal
experience a certain color with a certain sound. Since the only link
here always turns out to be the phenomenon of synesthetic experience
itself (or of its possible re-experience by others), which is *datum*,
consequently cannot be its own explanatory referent, the datum, in
the end, is invariably either debunked—synesthetic experience being
declared just the fantasy of the subject who has it, without, in most
cases, any explanation of such fantasying following the debunking—
or it is hypothetically accounted for by "isomorphic" formulas that
bury the dilemma in a term. What, then, can the optimal outcome of
the new enterprise of Gestalt theory be? Modern chemistry once sprang
as an unintended by-product from the manipulations of alchemists,
and great gains for neurophysiology may result from the Gestaltist venture; but what has psychology to expect from it? Any structural analogy
—as is most likely to exist—of cerebral wave patterns to patterns of
phenomenal experience must be recognized by some observer in order
to be stated. To recognize it, the observer must understand the analogy
already. How is this generically different from his understanding of
the inner meaning of a facial expression, likewise "physical" and likewise understandably expressive of the observed subject's experience?
The *physiognomic* evidence for the unity of psyche and organism,
which as understandable unity of appearance and behavior needs
no intrasomatic augmentation because it is constantly exposed to the
full light of the day, is traced to its hideouts; but, if found there,
what is found is the same kind of understandable "isomorphic" evi-

dence as before, not any explanatory principle that would account for
it as a datum.

Clearly meaning is not a factor. It is nothing that can be arrayed
with other factors on one plane of analytic presentation. As the "being
of being" (Heidegger), it escapes any analyses that try to reduce it
to anything seemingly beyond itself, such as "structure", as though
any structure not already depending on its meaning for *being* one
can even be conceived. Since meaning is the encompassing constituent
of the very possibility of knowledge, how could knowledge, that
depends on it, hope to explain it? This pregiven fact of our existences,
the unbreakable supremacy of meaning over structure, inheres in the
very self-transcendence of experience, which we discussed before, and
it illuminates two further aspects of Gestalt psychology: its claim
to have bridged the Diltheyan gap between explanatoriness and understanding, and its traditional withholding of commitment from the
field of personality. The latter point has been touched upon before,
if only in its relation to the one-sidedness of the Gestaltist explorations
of phenomenal experience in the sphere of basic processes; its fuller
exploration still awaits us.

Dilthey's splitting of the sciences into explanatory and understanding ones has never been satisfactory. Its comprehension is helped
by a comparison between whole domains of human knowledge. Let
us consider astronomy and the history of literature. What is the primary difference in the occurrence of their data to us? The movements and magnitudes of celestial bodies are given the observer in
such a way that a context of quantitative laws governing the four-
dimensional domain wherein the observations are made can be
abstracted from, as well as re-applied to them, making verifiable pre-
dictions possible; in the history of literature, a theorization of this
kind would at once be sensed as ridiculous—but why would it?
The difference, of course, will most readily be explained as arising
from an absence of strict *lawfulness* in the history of literature; but
this tends to obscure the problem rather than to solve it, for it fails
completely to account for either the immediate effect on our experience
as stated or for the true literary scholar's typical experience of insight
into the necessity with which a single line of a single poem "could
not have been written by anyone else, at any other time, in any
other country"—an experience of certitude not any less illuminating

than that of a mathematical solution. As is readily seen, the explanation itself just referred to stands or falls with a rather superficial
generalization *a priori* of what is specifically applicable to such fields
as astronomy only; a confounding of lawfulness with mathematical
lawfulness and of strictness with exactitude. This confusion is favored
by the general present trend of our civilization. Phenomenal impoverishment, directly fostered by the gearing of education to technological
object-manipulatory ends and a corresponding reversal of the natural
hierarchy of human values, may account for the readiness with which
the physicalist debunks experiences of immediate understanding.
Preliminary to this trend but dating back farther, a preconception
alleging the cognitive validity of quantification *only* has been exposed
before in this text but still demands more radical analysis. For the
present, the *Diltheyan* complex of problems may be summed up as
follows: in our example, the direction of the cognitive quest of
astronomy is set by the relative "immediate meaninglessness" of the
facts observed on the one hand, their submission to predictive calculation on the other; contrariwise, the direction of the cognitive quest
of the history of literature is set, on the one hand, by the immediate
meaningfulness of the phenomena *encountered,* on the other by their
refusal to survive any dissections into "facts".

The situation surrounding the cognitive quest in the latter case
can be qualified further. The stated immediate *meaningfulness* a) is
individually accessible in varying degrees; b) yields the perception
of true structural (morphological) laws—such as recurrent cycles in
the historic phaseology of styles—*only* where individual accesses to
it (phenomenal understanding) are fully and freely possible, the
whole person, not just the intellect in its isolation, having to partake
in the experience; c) only where phenomenal perceptions are not
interfered with by explanatory speculations, are theoretical coercions
avoided—such as improper re-applications of abstractly homogenized
type concepts to phenomenal materials; d) the question of predictive
verification does not pose itself because no static laws requiring such
verification are hypothecated in the first place and because, e) phenomena that are *historical,* that is, arise from constellations of inner
and outer circumstances which by definition are unrepeatable can in
principle not be reproduced experimentally, nor can the recognition
of this impossibility be construed with any legitimacy as a conten-

tion that such phenomena are in any sense *unlawful*. While Dilthey recognized the latter point clearly, he failed to discern that the "structural" (analogistic) laws governing *historicity* hinge on their verification, not by their "superficial" appearance to us (since our perception of them is itself predetermined by *our* historical situation) but by their appearance to us after the achievement of a break-through to their phenomenal authenticity, which takes the question form (Binswanger): how has it really been? rather than: what went on?[13]

The implications of this phenomenological criticism of much of historiography in general for the specific *life historical* interest which ever since Freud has been mounting in personality and abnormal psychology, are evident: in order to gain an understanding, for example, of the childhood experiences of a subject, it is already inadmissible to leave unexamined any applications to them of concepts the implicit understanding of which derives from their applications to *adult* experience. Thus, if a psychoanalyst, supported by passages in Freud's writings, concludes from Freud's discovery of infantile sexuality that infantile innocence has been a pious myth, he not only overlooks that the acknowledged lack of functional differentiation in infantile sexuality forbids *any* unexamined conclusion drawn in analogy with the situation of adults; more fundamentally he also overlooks that the very *concept* of infantile innocence presupposes both the adult's *experience* of adult guilt and adult phenomenal perceptions of the minds of children. In order for the contents of these perceptions (and of whatever other perceptions may conflict with them) to be clarified, that is, for the very idea of *childlike innocence* to be understood intrinsically, the child's world has first to be examined *as it appears* to the child. If this is done, it becomes evident not only that what Freud exploded is a superficial adult notion of children's innocence, but that this notion already is worlds apart from the original (the real as well as, of course, the mythical) mode-of-being of childlike innocence of which that notion just catches a last dim shadow.

With such dissipation of conventional semantic shadows, in order to see again the phenomena that cast them, neither Dilthey nor the early phenomenologists (as absolutizers of logic) were properly concerned. The break-through to existence on the part of phenomenology itself is historically later than the phenomenological inculcation of psychology from which Gestalt theory sprang. In consequence of this birth situation of their doctrine, the scientists of that school brought along a notion of phenomenology which Köhler quite properly sums up in his verdict against Husserl but which suggests, much rather than Köhler's conclusions,[14] that extension of phenomenology to the very existential prerequisites of the appearance of essences in the mind which, outside of Gestalt psychology, had meanwhile gotten under way. Instead, Köhler mistook a mainstay of early phenomenology, the concept of essence-*appearances* (*Gestalten*; emphatically a notion of aesthetics) as connoting both the ultimate of human phenomenal experience and the neglected feature of physical organization itself that would finally allow an explanatory linkage of experience with the "paralleling processes" of events in the brain. The fundamental belief behind this "unification" of the field of knowledge was dualistic only in appearance. Köhler's transphenomenal, which according to all signs we have is accepted as the truer[15] version of reality by the Gestaltists, is not transcendent phenomenality but the physicist's world-as-process. The fundamental belief of Gestalt psychology turns out to be a monistic metaphysics and a monistic metaphysics, inevitably, becomes a unification par force.

The over-all line of argument along which the closure of the Diltheyan gap is attempted in Gestaltist literature takes the form: we have to understand explanations to call them such, and whatever we understand we experience as explained. The first half of the argument evidently is true, demonstrating, as it does, the fundamentalness—not yet the nature—of understanding; the second becomes a striking untruth once we reflect upon the restrictive connotation of "explanation" as a reduction of phenomena to laws themselves attained through an analysis of physical magnitudes abstracted from the phenomena (away from their *immediate* understandability) through a selective isolation and comparative measurement of certain of their properties and phases. We do not, for example, need to be able to explain why a train presently rushing by at the speed of eighty miles an hour will not be standing still the next moment in order to understand that it will not, but neither is this, that it will not, explained already by our understanding in its instantaneousness. Explanatoriness and understanding, themselves fundamental facts *of* the psyche as much as existential fundaments of scientific theorizing *about* it, are not inter-

exchangeable modes of cognition, as Koffka believed.[16] But neither
was Dilthey justified in seeing them as separate ones of equal noetic
"dignity". Understanding is basic and all-comprehensive, explanatoriness a specific form of the cognitive quest that completely depends
on the former for every single operation; characteristically, man's
experienced need for explanations which grows with the relative
alienation of phenomena in his world while shrinking with their relative familiarity, is reduced to nothing whenever he immediately and
fully understands. Whether explanations in the latter case can improve
his world-orientation at all, is questionable on this account alone. The
vogue of explanatoriness in recent centuries has not accidentally
coincided with the alienation from *being* that has led to man's crisis;
what that crisis demands is not a renunciation of explanatoriness (as
irrationalists teach) but a remembrance of its own basis in understanding.

Returning to Gestalt psychology, we may understand why this
doctrine so emphatically focussed away from personality, not in the
sense of persistently focussing outward *with* the person but of ignoring
the personal: once explanatoriness and understanding were "unified",
any behavior not already submitting to generalized laws of a common
field of behavior, threatened to explode that seeming unity. Even within
the limits of the world of sensory perception that Gestalt psychology
so concentrated upon we find uncounted Gestalt ambiguities neither
reducible, like those of certain visual patterns, to generally accessible
properties admitting of alternate "organizations", nor to lacking opti-
mality of understanding on the perceiver's part. To cite an example
by Katz[17] the arrangement of books on a scholar's desk, which to the
chamber maid may be plain chaos, is a *Gestalt*, but only to him, whom
we have to know first in order not to share in the chamber maid's
perception. What else does this mean but that, in order for a sensory
function spontaneously to operate "thus" or "thus" *as* a function,
entirely non-perceptual entities turn out to be not just influential, but
field-constituent? Since in the chamber maid's perception the scholar's
desk-*Gestalt* is a mere agglomeration, Gestalt psychology here can
answer, without, however, solving the stated difficulty too truly, that
the chamber maid is operating on a lower level of understanding,
but the difficulty becomes insuperable once another and more obvious
Gestalter, with Stern's term, for example, a painter of still lives steps

in, to whom the books on the desk also form a *Gestalt*, but a weak one which he undertakes to make more perfect in a manner wholly ruinous to the scholar's. Whose *Gestalt*, now, is the "objective" one? It is evident that the relative functional independence of the perceptual sub-systems only accounts for those aspects even of sensory perception in which the *worlds* of human beings happen to coincide, or rather, toward which they converge. The more complex the meaning of any one perceptual constant, such as in the case just cited, the more is its interpersonal realm restricted; the more simple, that is, exposable in terms of such pervasive laws as phenomenal size constancy, the wider (and tending to extend beyond the human species) that realm. Without reference to the inter-subjective, interorganizational convergences and divergences of the being-in-the-world, the constancies of cognition cannot be determined; correspondingly, the "subjectivities" their referents imply cannot be determined without reference to the phenomenal constancies. What resulted from this situation for research and theory has been a fruitless swinging of the pendulum back and forth between alternate accentuations of the "subjective" and "objective" "factors", with cognition continuing to be misapprehended as a kind of quantitative admixture, interpenetration, or compromise between these. What that situation actually implies, is, contrariwise, something simple, namely the complete spuriousness of the subject-object polarity as a real (factorial) one. The roots of this misconception, the historic power of which may account for its stubbornness in modern psychology, will be examined. Already it is clear that the premature Gestaltist unification of the field of knowledge has only concealed the true unity of the events of cognition which is given indissectibly in the origin of all reality experience, man's *being-in-the-world*.

Since Gestalt psychology, with this insistence on unification, cannot tolerate theoretical implications of phenomenal structure unless they readily enter a hypothetical world model, the non-factual among them —the constituents of *world*, the values, with the positivistic term for them—are themselves interpreted as phenomenalizations of objective requiredness by the Gestaltists—a semi-physicalistic notion which the physicists refute and which conceals, as Gestalt psychology does altogether, an onlooking, fundamentally tired, aestheticism. The paradox of all aestheticism is that it combines a world-observing disengagement *from* the world with the inability, for this very reason of its disengagement, its resulting want of primary existential participation, to observe the action-sources from which the world is continuously created anew; in Spinoza's terminology, it is sold to *natura naturata*, seeing *natura naturans* objectively and therefore more clearly, but always as what it *has become* at any moment, never as what it *is*. For what kind of objectivity, of clarity, is this? Its intrinsic validity can at best—in the case of a world view of the Hegelian type—be compared to that of the clear objectivity of a perception of the sun at the moment of setting: the power of the sun at noon, which defies the power of the observing eye, defies clear objectivity, not because it eludes human experience, but because it *engages it so much*, can never be deduced from such sunsets, and the deductions of aestheticistic objectivism are, in this sense, in the end the least objective of all— the least objective even when it comes to such tasks as the understanding of phenomena within its own apparently closer domain, such as a work of art not itself born from aestheticism. What this Gestaltist aestheticism entailed in its encounter with the personal, with human motivation, now, was not, certainly, any naive reduction of it to environmental "facts", but the hypothecation of an objective principle which it supposed to organize the fact world for us, so that an immanence in the structure of reality was claimed for what in its authenticity both *constitutes* reality and *transcends* all objective structures towards the encounter of absolutes: *human values*. How could human values receive a half-way plausible position in the Gestaltist unification system? It is obvious that the theoretical demand of Gestalt psychology to explain values from structure-immanent principles of requiredness could never be implemented in concrete research without a prior substitution of artifacts for true data; Lewin, therefore, believing to have found the Gestaltist key to *personality*, resorted to a bracketing-in of the individually different as a separate objective factor (the ego and its tension systems) in a quasi-physicalistically unified field.

The self-contradictions in this are striking: the field, by definition the behavioral environment of a subject, intersecting with other behavioral environments but referring to *his* experiential vantage point, is unified with the behavioral environments of other subjects; but to whose vantage point, then, does this common field refer? How is it to be constructed? On what primary data are its mathematics to be

based, and where does there exist a valid criterion for the quantitative
translation of qualitative phenomenal contents of experience? Except,
nevertheless, for this continued dubiousness, both of the ultimate possibility (as well as the relevance) of mathematics for such ends and of
the specific method of mathematization the Lewinian group applied to
its experimental designs, little difficulty appears inherent in the proposition wherever the field is phenomenally given as a readily perceived
natural unit, as in the case of a group of small children (or kittens)
at play, but what when the ego systems start playing their incalculable
roles? It is evident that, in group situations, common denominators
for these systems, if they could be found, offered the only basis for
experimentation conceivable but that, if they could not, constructs
had to replace them in such a way that the method of inquiry—for
example, of subject interrogation—which one employed would itself
safeguard the unmendable artifact-nature of these constructs against
any threat of a ready detection.[18]

For our present purpose, the most important observation that can
be made in connection with the Lewinian turn of Gestalt psychology
in its later years is its increasing lack of consistency in employing the
phenomenological method. What is "bracketed in" in the ego and its
tension systems phenomenally refers no less, of course, to a beyond-
the-subject, to *world*, than any of the subject's perceptions refer to the
facts of the immediate situation; consequently, a subject's in the
Lewinian field preoccupation with a matter exclusively of his personal
concern, located on another continent and perhaps not even in the
present, would have to be introduced into this field on equal terms with
the comparable distal tensions of the other subjects in the field as well
as with the immediately effective proximal valences of the situation,
yet still in complete fidelity to the whole qualitative differentness of
its phenomenal content. Within the frames of quasi-physicalistic field
theories, this is no more possible than it is beyond them, and since
quasi-physicalistic field theories were what Gestalt psychology resorted
to in encountering personality as a topic, it failed in the very domain
wherein lie all the tasks that *ultimately test psychological doctrines.*
The fate which unavoidably overtook Gestalt psychology beyond that
point of decision, was the common technicalism[19] of hypothetical constructs which dismisses the very *land of man*, the phenomenal sources
of all knowledge, including any knowledge of its cherished "measurable

variables in the environment", as a *no-man's land*,[20] on its part insists on the existence of an undiscovered mid-land of functional processes[21] neither clearly neurological nor deducible from phenomenal experience not already altered by the inquiry,[22] and is shared by most of objectifying psychology in its present efforts to find the bridge between what it believes cognition and what it believes personality to be like.

NOTES

1. Hornbostel, a psychologist from the fringes of the Gestalt school whose insights failed to influence the main trends of this movement, recognized this existentialist truth, and Goldstein follows him: ". . . a thing is not real because of its stability, rather it is stable because of its 'reality'" (*The Organism*, p. 376). While the Gestalt school as a whole has not been articulate on this view, doubts that it shares it are justified by its pertinacious attempt—also criticized by such Gestaltists as M. Scheerer—to reduce the meaning of Gestalten to their *Prägnanz* rather than vice versa, and related tendencies.

2. For example, the Einsteinian cosmos cannot be visualized (what cosmos ever could?) but the failure inevitably refers the failing subject to the spontaneous conception of a being from the vantage point of whom it can. In terms of original phenomenal experience, the compellingness of this reference is not any less axiomatic than that of any of the steps of thought themselves which lead to the conceptual construction of the Einsteinian cosmos, but a realization of this experience may be dulled by certain metaphysical preconceptions while the compellingness of the physico-mathematical steps themselves, since these particular preconceptions favor rather than forbid them, will be encountered in its full authentic impact.

3. *Ibid.*, p. 409; whole sentence italicized in Goldstein's text; present italics supplied.

4. Evidently, since the cognitive quest in any of its versions cannot recognize topical reservations as legitimate limits, it would be arbitrary and even illogical to let objectification stop just short of man. With the discovery that the explanatoriness of objectivating thing-isolation (the starting point for both causal atomization and its possible corrections by holism) by-passes the being of whatever it lays its hands on, this Sartrean error is avoided. The line of division which ensues does not run between man as a topic of science and all other topics of science, but between the whole gamuts of beings and of objects. Man (as in principle everything else also) is both at once, but as an object remains a topic of biology (and of its possible physicalistic fundaments) only.

5. This, of course, implies also the complete irrelevance of the often cited antagonism between Aristotelian and Galilean principles of inquiry for the problem of the lawfulness of the *unique as phenomenon*.

6. While the Gestaltist explanation has closed in on the problem as much as explanations can close in on it, it still has to rely on the "immediate understandability" of the "translation", that is, it still fails completely to account for

the decisive fact of the primary possibility of a conversion of time into direction, of unexperienced time differences into experienced spatial ones; any explanatory solution presupposes a valid theory of the fundamental static relations between time and space which are locked in the pre-givenness of our spatio-temporal existence. Such a theory, therefore, appears possible only from an Archimedian point outside of time and space at once, but the existential impossibility for us to solve this central problem, which physicalism, limiting itself as always to a descriptive account of their given *functional* relations, by-passes, does not remove it as a problem from a strict explanatory point of view.

7. Arthur Schopenhauer, *Über die vierfache Wurzel des Satzes vom zureichenden Grunde*, Berlin, 1891.

8. This "my", while being formally identical with the one of phenomenally encountered psychosomatic interaction, is materially quite different. The experiential prerequisite, for example, of any bodily complaints is the self in its *otherness*, with Hegel's term, that is, a manifest being-different of "my body" in apposition to the experiencing subject, implying a primal temporary suspension of their absolute identity. In the situation presently discussed, this identity, in turn, is the *primal* fact of experience which only radical epistemological reflection itself—never phenomenal experience—can "suspend".

9. Rudolf Arnheim, "The Gestalt Theory of Expression", *Psychological Review*, 1949, 51, 358–74.

10. W. Köhler. *Gestalt Psychology*. New York, 1929.

11. K. Goldstein. *The Organism*, pp. 383–390.

12. *Ibid.*, p. 387.

13. The preoccupation of historiographers with the what-went-on (regardless of its sociological breadth) leads inevitably to the perception of comparable *time-Gestalten,* that is, to an esthetic of history in either its better (Hegelian) or worse (Spenglerian) forms, rather than to a perception of historic existences in their authentic modes of being. Dilthey's self-misunderstanding, his own failure to see the necessity for the "break-through" spoken of, accounts for much of the misunderstanding, during the first half of our century, of the—allegedly unscientific—nature of the *historical* on the part of systematizers of knowledge. In substance the phenomenological argument is already contained in Count Paul York von Wartenburg's correspondence with Dilthey (cf. Bibliography).

14. W. Köhler, *The Place of Value in a World of Fact*, 1938, p. 409.

15. This is evidenced already by the otherwise hardly intelligible direction of the entire Gestaltist quest which tacitly acknowledges a requirement for "justifications" of phenomenal experience.

16. K. Koffka, *Principles of Gestalt Psychology*, 1935, pp. 20–21.

17. D. Katz, *Gestaltpsychologie*, 1948, p. 86.

18. Previously demonstrated (in the development of the Lewinian theory on the *Level of Aspiration*) in the author's "The Specialist as a Psychological Problem", *op. cit.,* pp. 21–22.

19. More specific implications of this *technicalism* will be expounded in the following chapter. In its present form, it appears as the result of a gradual, if

still incomplete, unification process between the (molar) behavioristic and Gestalt movements, a convergence which is itself the result of their correlative inconsistencies: both fail to follow through their original quests, the radical objectivistic and the phenomenological ones, to the last consequences of either.

20. Cf. Egon Brunswik, "Remarks on Functionalism in Perception", *Journal of Personality*, 1949, 18, 56–65, esp. p. 59.

21. It has become increasingly more evident that this preoccupation interferes with both at once: consistent conceptualization, as in the instance of such a term—suggesting a concept where there *can* be none—as *memory trace*, which links a notion of purely subjective inner reference (memory) with an entirely heterogeneous objective notion (trace) neither true to the phenomenality of memory nor itself allowing to be joined to any other but concepts of movements in space or their justified analogates; and with phenomenal perception itself, as when a specialist of perception theory speaks of his having the impression that he perceives meanings in objects even though realizing that they do not come to him through his eyes at the moment of perceiving them—as, such remarkable impressionism notwithstanding, they obviously do according to the *perceptions*. The true extent of the inroads which functionalism already has made on the fundamental human faculties of observation and description only awaits its explorer.

22. For example, denaturized by dissections of cognition into "purely perceptual" and "purely intellectual" phases. As is readily seen, this entire dichotomy, which is strictly unempirical on the side of either "percept" or "idea", depends on a continuation of the already characterized metaphysical fixation traceable to the traditional misunderstandings of Platonism (cf. p. 23).

CHAPTER 4

Gestalt Psychology and Psychoanalysis—Functionalism as a Blind Alley—Further Inquiry into the Cartesian Subject-Object Split—Max Weber and the Place of Values in Sociology—Scheler's Contributions to Phenomenology—The "Double Nature" of Man and Its Implications for Science—The Jeopardy to Being-in-the-World in Schizophrenics and in Brain-Organics—The Existentialist Attack Upon "Most Evident" Notions, and an Inquiry into the Nature of the Why—The Dimensions and Limits of Explanatoriness—Cognition, the Will, and the Virgin Territory of Existence: Third Determination of the Phenomenological Quest.

In the history of modern psychology, the Gestalt school appears as one of two simultaneous movements. The other is psychoanalysis. The directions of attention of the two movements diverge. Together, in the total dependence of each of them on only one of the two sides between which the gap in psychology runs, they characterize the loveless and dissonant thinking-about-man of an already bygone period of recent European history, the 1910's and 1920's, the age both of radical disillusionment and horizonless self-preoccupation, and of a radical aesthetic formalism cultivating the deliberate.

Since the power of the Cartesian split to prejudice the very subject of science not only does not allow the psychologist who thinks in its terms to recognize existence, the being-in-the-world, as the given topic of his quest, but fails to offer him any workable substitute; since he is dependent on his own experience-world as his unquestioned frame of reference, he cannot at once direct his glance toward a postulated object, the inner workings of another psyche, and that other psyche's experience-world, which lies beyond his frame of reference, with no possible unbiased vantage point even remaining. Instead of the truth which is missed, two half-truths—an error split into two complementary

53

ones—make their appearance. The tacit presupposition of Gestalt psychology is that experience, rather than being the *Gestalter* (and as such, prior to either "subject" or "object") is contingent upon an objectively existent physical reality of the *Gestalten,* which are viewed as determining characteristics of the world and its process. Vice versa, the tacit presupposition of psychoanalysis is that this objective world is given the "Gestalter" as a factually determinable topography of incentives for, and obstacles to, *wish fulfillment,* and that any *Gestalten* into which it is turned subjectively are products (sublimations, substitutions, etc.) of instinctual needs and drives. Both viewpoints lead to absurdities, the first to an aestheticized pseudo-physics which ignores the whole depth and authenticity (the inner wherefrom) of human experience; the other to a biologistic prejudicing of precisely that *wherefrom* and a worldless immanentism in the wake of which the very criteria of cognitive truth are gone, while the psychoanalyst continues to act as though they were not. The criteria of truth are gone in psychoanalysis because the psychoanalytic conception, for example, of someone's world as his *projection* (and of similar mechanisms supposed to account for man's cognitive and valuative behavior) implies that the projection *qua* projection, that is, its distorting effect upon the reality picture, can be shown, which in turn presupposes that a projection-independent reality picture remains *available.* But why should such an independent world picture—for example, of the world as a topography of drive-incentives and obstacles—not be just another projection, this time of the analyst? Within the frame of this doctrine (Freud's later general-psychological extension[1] of his original clinical theory of projection[2]) nothing indeed is left which could still provide even an access in principle to anything like a true world. In turn, it is evident that if no possible implementation of the whole proposition of a true world is left—a consequence Freud himself, personally holding on to the notions of a true world and indeed of an independent truth, never noticed—the whole proposition of an untrue world (projection in the Freudian sense) is voided likewise; what remains, in the way Freudian theory then naturally tends to apply itself in practice, is a primal suspicion of projective world distortions as an attitudinal characteristic of some analysts, that is, as an ideology rather than an idea.

Since the inconsistency is not noticed, both psychoanalysts and Gestaltists hold on to the notion of one objective reality. The relativistic implications of the theorizing of either are therefore bound to affect, not that reality, but *truth*. In its phenomenal actuality, as shown by Heidegger,[3] truth is encountered as the open and encompassing medium the pre-givenness of which alone allows of a convergence of realities (subjective experience worlds) and indeed of communication, of the very possibility of language, a situation which the traditional metaphysical dispute concerning the "absoluteness" or "relativity" of truth has been instrumental in obscuring. For the very form of our judgments, *that is true*, defies any attempt at defining the true in terms of a *that* itself defined in terms of the true; the judgment evidently presupposes a notion of truth which is prior to the notion of this *that* or any other *thats*. Truth, therefore, is never the material content of a judgment—an observation which explodes the dispute referred to as meaningless—but the *wherefrom* of the experience of its convincingness, its certitude, a phenomenal constellation that restricts the absoluteness of truth to its source. Truth, then, as the tacit orientative premise of all thinking and theorizing, is a manifestation of existence; it is the pre-given horizon within which any communicative event, dissension no less than consensus, may occur. Lawfully, it escapes definition: there is no definition that, as a definition, would not already presuppose truth. How, with such horizonlikeness inhering in its constitution, can truth be made dependent on an unaccounted for reality, as in the *reality principle* of psychoanalysis? How, on the other hand, could it ever be understood *truthfully* as a physicalistically conceived reality function with which the organization of the brain field is endowed, as in Gestalt psychology?

Both movements still accept as an absolute measure *for* their subject matter what, empirically, is made a data context only *by* that subject matter: reality. Both absolutize—even though historically, interindividually, even intraindividually, just reality has been subject to the greatest conceivable fluctuations—*one* image of that-which-is, fleeting with uncounted other such images across the place (clearing, opening) of Truth (Heidegger) which alone remains stable as the common and distinctive, in itself never changing, home of man as the knower. What are the consequences of this absolutism? Since both movements run their courses in the shadow of positivistic thought, even though in imperfect agreement with it, it is to positivism itself that we shall first turn.

In the literature, the most telling example of the way in which the

absolutization of physicalistic world conceptions fails to work out is
furnished by Reichenbach's *Rise of Scientific Philosophy*.[4] According
to Reichenbach, if we have the picture of a tree in our minds and
say so, the words "picture" and "tree" lend themselves "only to an
indirect expression of what we mean". What we really *mean* is that
our body is in "a certain state", the state that would be effected by the
falling into our eyes of light rays emitted from a tree. It is only
because our language is so poor that it has no terms directly referring
to bodily states that we express ourselves so indirectly. "I see a tree"
and "my body is in a certain state" are therefore *logical* equivalents.

The example is important because it shows the extreme lack of
observation, the factual disregard for experience, to which a philosophy
allegedly relying on experience only can attain, the unfathomed depths
of dogmatism which can be reached once sober rational analysis,
always faced with the alternative to be either an operant procedure
or the idol of an ideology, has emphatically become the latter. For
every single statement in this—according to Reichenbach—psychological account is untrue either to experience or to thought. Working
backwards and, by way of giving the thesis the benefit of the doubt,
assuming that the two judgments are equivalents in some yet undefined
sense, it becomes evident, first of all, that they are in no conceivable
way *logical* equivalents since their contents, being heterogeneous in
their forms as much as in their subjects, are not even related, let alone
identical. If logic has nothing to do with their *intrinsic* relationship,
however, what kind of logical relationship can still be said to obtain?
It is evident that they are supposed to "refer to the same state", not as
judgments, for "I see a tree", according to its content, refers to a tree
and not to that "state", but as *events*. With this clarification, which
for the time being disposes of "modern" functionalistic logic, we may
turn to the relationship retained—which no logical identity of the two
judgments resulting from their analysis, is evidently a contended factual
identity of the "states they refer to" (namely as *events*).

But just this factual identity, as has been shown, remains necessarily
a postulate. Nowhere even from that part of the "I see a tree"—the *I*—
which implies the subject, is there any bridge to the subject's body,
not as a phenomenon of his self-experience, which of course is always
implied in the *I*, but as a physical object with such characteristics of
perceptual behavior *qua* physiological functioning as retinal cones;

nowhere, in turn, is the tree or any of its characteristics discoverable in the neural process, and no success of the Gestaltist venture discussed in the preceding chapter could change this, even if we disregard the logical difficulties there exposed, for the hypothecated and conceivably discoverable isomorphisms of the brain are themselves restricted to event patterns articulated along the dimension of time; they can therefore never cover pure *qualities* of experience, themselves independent of any time *Gestalten*, such as phenomenal *green*. The Newtonian ring, as we see, fails to close, and Goethe's side on the old issue of the *Farbenlehrestreit* emerges unvanquished in the twentieth century: those most understandable experiences which are characterized by absolute immediacy *phenomenally* remain just as absolutely unreachable *physicalistically*, even if we make allowances for looseness of logical principle at the basis of the explanatory enterprise itself.

Returning to Reichenbach's equation, we are struck, first by the contention that our language, which abounds in terms so far more directly referring to bodily states than the pale abstraction "in a certain state", should be so handicapped as to warrant the services of functionalistic logic; next by the characteristic unempiricalness in the contention that the state of the body in which we *see* a tree is one with the state of the body in which we have a tree only *in our mind*; and finally by the statement that we mean a bodily state of ours when what we have in mind (and say so) is a *tree*. According to the meaning of *to mean*, how can anyone know better what we mean then we ourselves? At this point, the core of functionalistic logic is unveiled: in order to construct a world picture true, allegedly, to nothing-but-experience, experience, in functionalistic world accounts, is to be decreed away first.

But we may go still further, grant further benefits of doubt, for the *reductio ad adsurdum* of a doctrine implies a demand to follow it through to its conceivable consequences. What the functionalist wishes to do, is a complete translation of the being-in-the-world of our phenomenal experience into the language of the world-as-process.[5] In this world-as-process, since otherwise it would not be all-inclusive, consequently would not be a world, no observer in his phenomenality, nothing that says *I* can be left; consequently there is no observation, no statement about it, no understanding of the statement if there were one. There is nothing, but far from noticing the radicality of this principle which he has imposed on himself, the functionalist allows his logic to break down already in the formulation of a single state-ment of a single finite event: in the "my body is in a certain state", what does the *my*, which so unobjectively implies the *I*, signify? Is it not perhaps "an indirect description in terms of internal objects"? And if we eliminate it, and all other such internal objects along with it, who remains as maker of the statement?

An oversight. But if we correct it, nothing indeed is retained in the end, not even, then, the image of the world-as-process, and so it indeed becomes questionable whether want of circumspection alone can be made responsible for it. If we look closely, we detect a neces-sity for oversights of this kind in the troublesomeness of the task which the functionalist has set for himself—a cybernetic theory of man—and which calls for oversights as well as artifacts, if on the whole more visibly for the latter. Since, as we have seen, precision of thought is what is most dangerous to the functionalist's quest, it must be rendered harmless; the procedure chosen for this end then comes to follow the maxim *divide et impera*. How is the maxim applied? Precision of thought, first, is divided into *precision* and *thought*. Of these two, thought—thought in its authenticity—is debunked, to be replaced by utopian vagaries set forth in the known and already some-what tiresome vocabulary of the ever greater progress and enlighten-ment. Whatever precision, on the other hand, the *theoretical* operation still can muster, is understood already as the precision of the opera-tions of a machine. Functionalistic thinking, therefore, tacitly recog-nizing the robot as its own model, can combine conspicuous clumsiness in its logic with the ideal of mathematical precision, that is, exactitude. The specific precision of mathematical thought—just exactitude—never extends, of course, to any check on the truth of the data which it is made to analyse; "precision" here always operates only within data-set boundaries that are *a priori* fixed. The data themselves may be arbitrary and even completely spurious: the precision of the mathe-matical operation is not diminished thereby. But neither can anything lying beyond these boundaries ever become visible through the opera-tions of mathematical thinking, and just this closedness of its topogra-phy, then, finds its counterpart in that of the robot: the robot carries out mathematical operations the entire scope of which has been fixated in him in advance. Yet, since the robot's exactitude, in itself only the consequence of a special application of the precision of thought to the conditions of physical processes steered by man himself along the finite predetermined pathways of a closed topographical system, always will outmatch the functionalist's own exactitude by mere operational (quantitative) standards of achievement, the functionalist indeed will be enabled to make plausible at least the possibility of an attainment of a cybernetic man model.

At this point, it is to be remembered that the functionalist nevertheless remains human as a *being*. His roots in authentic existence can be severed only in theory. The absence of intrinsic precision from his thinking therefore is felt by him. It calls for compensations, which an attitude stands ready to grant. In accordance with his valuative orientation toward images of mechanisms, this attitude will articulate itself in assertions of cold toughness: exactitude alone would not do, not only because his attainment of it is imperfect; it would also not do because "there must be something more". This *more*, of course, is not acknowledged in principle; it is acknowledged by the functionalist's attitude which remains human in the sense of being emotional. In what way, now, is it emotional? An analysis of the cherished cold toughness yields the answer. Where the functionalist believes that he is engaged in precise thinking, he is emoting about the unemotional, the make-believe life and make-believe spirit of an arrangement of fast-turning cog wheels senselessly dissecting the path of mathematical time with their motions, in brief, about the qualities of his guiding ideal.

There are uncounted observations today which corroborate this analysis. The analysis makes them more understandable but does not provide already their historic account. If we investigate what now calls itself general semantics, an attempt at dealing with words as though, contrary to phenomenal evidence as much as historic facts, language consisted of "symbols" voted into existence by some theretofore non-verbal convention of methodologists, rather than being the irreplacable mode-of-being, constitutive to all true conceptual symbols and even to all untrue accounts of its own constitution, of thought itself; if we read in Reichenbach's comments to his already presented equation that "modern logic has means of dealing with equivalences of this type", as though this "equivalence" were a fugitive (which it is) and modern logic a steely police outfit determined to put an end to such disorderly elusiveness; if we read that "act psychology has dealt with the tender in a tender way, whereas we methodological positivists try to deal with the tender in a tough way",[6] we can assess the magnitude of the change-over from the transcendent nothing-but-the-truth to such self-preoccupied and frankly voluntaristic consider-ations of a scientist's "feel" of his own operations. But we cannot yet understand why, in the twentieth century, a theoretician of man should believe that he has taken even a step nearer to the solution of a problem in his field once he has succeeded in couching it in "tough", that is, technical-sounding, language. The answer that the example which the successfulness of technological science has set should be of hypnotic strength in suggesting imitations of its "style", if not of its successfulness, is a circumscription of the difficulty rather than its removal, even *as* a circumscription, however, it is markedly unobserv-ing, for such unfree emotionality toward their subject matter is hardly typical of the physicists of today. Where does the circle moving in which these frustrated theoreticians of man can be seen originate? It is time for us to analyze the often referred to Cartesian world-split more painstakingly. Regardless of the functionalist's denuncia-tions of rationalism, regardless of the Gestaltist's denunciations of the split itself (as a tenet in the theory of personality-as-an-object) the split continues to determine their own whole scope of thought.

In the world picture of Descartes, two substances, "meeting in man", thought (*cogitatio*) and the spatially extended (*extensio*), themselves contingent only upon an ultimate third (God), are placed in an appo-sition of far greater radicality than their prereflective unity in us stands ready to affirm. The starting step is a heuristic suspension of belief in the reality of *anything*. Since thought itself is the agent of the doubt, the doubt cannot extend to it, and what thus stands up under this doubting test, the undoubted *I think*, even though the *I* of *I think* is evidently contingent on its *being*, becomes foundational to the *I am*. The "subject" in the subject, therefore, is conceptualized as his *thought*, which as the only participant in the whole of the cognitive situation is not extended spatially, existing instead purely in time. Anything that lies beyond thought, then, a) is found standing in appo-sition to it, b) is real inasmuch as this standing in apposition implies it, c) is extended in space as the locus of *objects*. The apposition, in turn, through the thinking activity of the mind (*cogitatio*), becomes a *subjection* of the *extensio* under the domination of the mind; since

the body itself is found to partake in the *extensio,* it, too, thus becomes man's object, that is, that part of the extended world which the
mind has appropriated (subjected) only in a more definite manner.

This account, of course, is strikingly belied by experience. The
existentialist critique of Cartesianism centers on this misinterpretation of the phenomenal givenness of the body as *my object.* Any
reduction of the self to a spaceless pure mind is artificial, if no more
artificial, of course, than the heuristic doubt it serves to dissipate.
Man *is* (in one sense of his being) his body, rather than has it. The
body, in turn, must be thought of as being more than a *thing.* Man
does not "have" it in this Cartesian sense of a mere (and no matter how
unconditional) ego-separable possession, as a claim to an object in
space, extended "beyond him"; or rather, before, in his self-experience,
any such reflection, according to which the contention *could* be affirmed,
even becomes possible for the doubter, the *I* has already encountered
itself: the *being-one's-body* as a pre-given fact of existence, as the
horizon-like constituent of the *I-am-in-the-world,* has already been met
with across any such rationalist cleavages. Exposures of the fallacies
Cartesian thought so manifestly feeds on have been frequent, of course,
ever since its revision by Kant. The existentialist critique is only the
one most radically empirical. The earlier ones do not push their
analyses far enough to contribute to either an understanding or
remedying of the deep-reaching and obdurate effect which Cartesianism
has had on the history of western man and his science, from those
fields of knowledge which understandably benefited from the split
to those which can benefit only from its closing.

In order to understand this strange and powerful fixation, the
dynamics of Cartesian dualism bound to unfold from its—just introduced—position of start rather than its scholastic inception must be seen.
Once thought is assured of its absolute sovereignty over its materials,
it no longer partakes of being any more but instead subdues the
counter-substance, that is, objects found in space. The things thus
objectified are alienated through this neutralization, which recognizes,
not their self-articulated mode-of-being any more in an encompassing
existential context with the cognizer as a person, but only their occupancy of a dead stereometric domain. Since space itself is nothing
except for the fact that it stretches, thought itself, no longer sharing
with what it encounters in an all-pervading primal truth, must "stretch"

from here on out, that is, replace by more and more quantified determinations, measurements superimposed on phenomena and cutting them
up into facts, more and more extensive new intakes and dispositions
of such fact-materials, what it has lost in doubtlessness, that is,
immediacy, of grasp. Accordingly, this manipulatory imperialism of
the new rationality must become all-inclusive of whatever *can* be
"spatialized". Before its cognitive absolutism, everything indeed must
turn into an object, and less and less, then, can it *penetrate*, but less
and less also can it *tolerate*, anything in its authenticity, its spontaneously occurring doubt-preceding import.

Almost imperceptibly, with the establishment of this situation in
the beginning Baroque age, the whirl of atomism is unleashed, but its
movements first are slow. The whirl reaches full speed only during
the first half of our century. Where it hits upon man as an object, a
peculiar cognitive vertigo ensues, a collision of the Cartesian subjectivity with its own basis. What happens in this collision is that the
absolute claim of the *cogitatio* is extended to "itself", that is, the
objectification comes to hit its own substrate. This substrate now partakes in the *extensio*, as just another subject matter in the quasi-space
of an objectifying psychology, and, nowhere escaping the *cogitatio's*
demand to submit, it is, as everything else within the reaches of the
extensio, dissolved as much as possible into functional determinations.
The claim of the *cogitatio*, therefore, becomes ever more absolute:
no longer, to be sure, in the form of an explicit assertion of the
claim, of rationalism as a philosophy, but of an implicit assertion of
it by way of the growing *factual* unlimitedness of the "empiric"
operation itself. At the same time, however, the logical implications
of that very same imperialistic procedure negate its own basis, just
that sovereignty of the *cogitatio*: once the subject himself is radically
"extensified", no independent mind can remain to justify the claim.

Since the claim itself is no longer explicit at that stage, rationalism
having been discarded, no articulate self-conflict can ensue—which
explains why there is none. The process of functionalization thus can
go on in an ever more schizophrenic manner, being absolutistic on the
operant subject side, and dissolving the subject as object in the operational accounts. The functionalist, *qua* specialist, not only does not
recognize what he is doing but protects himself from any awareness by
erecting walls round his thinking in the form of operational definitions

of truth itself. Yet just the truthlessness of an enterprise which is
based on false presuppositions, its intrinsic lack of success, for example,
in trying to bridge *that gap*, cannot escape his feelings, and the result
is frustration; the frustration, in turn, taking such forms as have been
shown.

The untenability of the cognitive claims of an unlimited rationality-
in-operation, the peculiar atomism and nihilism inherent in it, was
first recognized in sociology by Max Weber in his observations of
values. The demand for a value-free sociology dealing with nothing
but fact data and understanding the demand for analyticalness about
them as a demand for their dissection into ever more elementary
causal factors had been general and strong, in the assumption not
only that values were "subjective" but that such itemization itself was
analytical. What Weber discovered was by no means that values were
not subjective but that they were just as objective in the sense of partaking in the fact material as irreducible constituents of the observed
phenomena themselves: whole historic societies and their developments
became understandable only in their terms. This established sociology
as a field inseparable from human existence: for any sociological interpretation of history, the existents' authentic experiences were found
to be what mattered most, and whatever accounts were to be given of
social attitudes and their changes, had in substance to be true, therefore,
to what the generations, groups, and individuals had *lived*. Weber's
methodological position is important also because, in his search for
transparent contexts of lawfulness articulated by the fact-materials
themselves in their immediate givenness to the observer, he first recognized in social history, as later Jaspers and other existentialist
scientists do in biology and psychopathology, the cognitive legitimacy
of *phenomenally evident* causal relations, which Weber defends at
once against the claims of a radical quasi-physicalistic causalism and
against the Diltheyan determination of scientific method applicable to
such "understandable" subjects as those of sociology. Weber's thought
nevertheless only grew upon ground which Dilthey's *Aufbau der
geschichtlichen Welt in den Geisteswissenschaften* had fertilized for
a whole generation of re-thinkers of man as a subject matter of science
and which proved equally propitious for the more radical revision that
Husserl and his disciples meanwhile had proposed.

The beginnings of an exploration of whole spheres of *validities*, independently persisting essence-structures in religion, ethics, and art, in all realms of the mind endowed with a mind-transcendent order of their own, as a foundation for any true science or sciences of man, were the accomplishment of Scheler, the most empirically-minded phenomenologist among the earlier generation. In its inception, an important fundament of social science, the sociology of ideas, traces back to Scheler's propositions; in psychology, paralleling the comparable if more descriptively analytic work of Pfänder, an empiric study of *Grundeinstellungen,* axiomatic valuative attitudes, was proposed and largely carried through. The whole problem of the relations between life and the mind, man as organism and man as a person, was first expounded by Scheler, who, not unlike Freud, claimed a deep-seated, indeed irreconcilable, antagonism between the two. Since Nietzsche's teachings at the latest, this conception was in the air: for example, Bergson's vitalism and the more emphatic irrationalism of Klages, who is concerned with the same duality but, unlike Scheler and Freud, sides with the *chthonic,* the Dionysian forces of life, differ from the basic psychoanalytic account in their value premises only; if we look closely it is this difference and nothing more that keeps these hostile brothers, modern objectifying rationalism-in-operation and its perverted form, irrationalism, divided. In the extent to which it is bound up with these common preoccupations of his whole generation in Europe, Scheler's doctrine, only more articulate in this respect than Freud's, is beset with metaphysical tenets which are now as thoroughly antiquated as any and which the later phenomenologists discard; as Freud's thought has to be cleansed of metaphysics to make its core of concrete empiric observations visible and lasting, a similar purification of Scheler's yields the valid and important insights which he contributed to the whole problem of the psyche-organism relation in man.

His most far-reaching discovery—translating it into more objectified structural terms as biological subjects require—is the presence, in man as an organism, of a hierarchy, consisting of mutually discontinuous levels of determinacy, each becoming operant and inoperant with shifting centerings of motivation. From Darwin to Freud, the nineteenth century had stressed man's animal nature, assigning him but the highest rung on a ladder of biological organization thought to be comprehensible throughout in terms of such narrowly deterministic concepts of motivation as drives for organismic need satisfaction, an entity hypothecated in essential analogy with animal instincts. Between this biological causalism and the physicist's "strict" causality a line of distinction has been drawn before. Strict physicalistic causality, first of all, lies beyond the immediately (phenomenally) given; those observations which serve to enucleate it *behind* the phenomenal, discard morphology not only procedurally, but physicalistic thought has no room for any *Gestalten*. Since the concept of cause-effect relations in the human mind is itself realized first by immediate observations in the person's actual life space—since *original causality* is itself a phenomenon among others—it is only consistent with this policy of discarding the phenomenal that precisely a radical causative search dissolves causality itself in the end; the probabilistic statistical norms which it retains at that stage replace explanatory concepts by calculative ones that by-pass the original *why* already more visibly. This dilemma of radical causalism, in turn, as shown by the reflections of such physicists as Niels Bohr, Schrödinger, and Dessauer, does by no means call for an abrogation of the why. It means no abandonment of the principle of strict determinacy in objective nature but only requires some fundamental revision of past conceptions of it; in the measure, in which, for example, the classic conceptions of time and space underlying classic causalism are relativized, causality itself has to be re-thought, and thus through the very efforts of physics, swinging back in a wide circle to an almost forgotten historic point of their origins, the timeless question of the *ultimate determinant* is posed afresh.[7]

But causality not only assumes a new aspect as an ultimate result of the explanatory quest; a doubtfulness of a quite different kind surrounds those of its immediate appearances in the phenomenal world of man which precede and induce *some* explanatory operations. Its superficial appearance, for example in the understandable connection between a childhood trauma and an adult neurotic symptom, claims a dependence of the latter on the former, but the silent premise of this claim is the scientist's knowledge of the symptom as that which became of the trauma. The causative connection, as psychological causalism understands it, hinges on the meaning of the trauma for the traumatized. But just this meaning of the trauma, far from being contained in the mere facticity of the trauma as an outer event, rather

is determined, in the concrete understanding for example of the
psychoanalyst, by what he supposes to be determined by it—the
adult neurotic symptom. The direction of determinacy, therefore, as
in all biologic causalism, turns out to be the opposite of the one
which causalism claims; with this modification (which psychoanalysis,
as Jaspers first pointed out, since it turns understandable into strictly
causal connections, disregards) no argument against the relevance of
phenomenal causality for the understanding of life histories remains,
but precisely in a strict sense of determinacy what does such
"causality" imply? Evidently its own opposite, teleology, and it makes
no difference at this point whether the scientist likes it or not: phenomenal causality in psychology implies finalism as its logical consequence. No teleological order of the object world is claimed thereby,
of course, but only the empirical validity of teleological concepts—
such as any notion of drives—within that central zone between radical
objectivism and the phenomenally understandable to which holistic
observations—observations of whole organisms as such—necessarily
are geared. The realization that drive theories—since without understandable implications of *goals* no plausible one can be constructed—
are inevitably, whether the holistic causalist is aware of it or not,
teleological ones, will interest us later; in introducing Scheler's thought
on the motivational nature of man, the all-important point is not this
but rather the impossibility which he demonstrates to account for
human experience and behavior on the basis of any such theory of the
mainsprings of motivation in man as mere biological drives: the distinction between man and animal consists precisely in man's ability
to act in freedom from any such limitations of the scope of behavior
as *could* in principle be predicted on the basis of pre-formulated
animal-analogous drive concepts.

While psychoanalysis contests this, claiming, in the nineteenth
century spirit, a quasi-mechanically conceived process, for example,
of sublimation, that it supposes to transfer impulse energy from the
drives into moral, spiritual, and aesthetic strivings in man, it fails
to implement this explanatory postulate by means of successful predic-
tions of behavior, the only admissible evidence for explanatory postulates in this realm; the argument, instead, is invariably an interpretation of experience and behavior which traces their data backward
to their assumed instinctual moorings. The inference which this situa-

tion imposes is not an abandonment of depth psychology but only of the preconceived zoologism which depth psychology in its psychoanalytic form took over from nineteenth century thought: in order theoretically to account for existence in its self-determining freedom, for the entire spiritual aspect of the phenomenon man, this aspect must first be seen in its given experiential actuality. If this is done, it turns out to be no less *elementary* than any of the instincts observable in animals, consequently no good empiric reason to reduce the former to the latter is recognizable to start with.

While the argument will be expounded in greater detail once we turn to the existentialist critique of psychoanalysis, a simple example may be in order to illustrate Scheler's insight. If we speak of self-preservation, of the drive for survival, we are used to understand its connotation as requiring an avoidance of biological death by the subject, yet we know of countless instances of human biological self-sacrifice motivated by the resolution to preserve oneself in the totally different and even opposite connotation in which the *self* is not the carrier of the subject's life as a biological state but of his self-determining spiritual and moral identity—which, in an instance of this kind, is experienced by him as mortal *only* if he should shun biological death. How can any biologistic drive theory account for any case of man's dying to survive as a super-biological entity as which he represents, not his own organism, but an idea in its timelessness? Any explanations that derive his motivation, wherever it shows determination as well as clarity of purpose, from internalized societal morals operating through a coercive superego are belied by the inspiredness of his spontaneous motivational experience and the corresponding elementary unity of action which becomes phenomenal even to his closest observers. This leaves biologism still with several alternatives; a) the subject *qua* subject may be acutely swallowed up motivationally by the collective psyche of a group striving to survive as a superindividual entity, b) his death in his own account ("conscious" or "subconscious") may serve the survival interests of a more distal collective entity in which he biologically partakes, such as a race, c) it may be motivated by the death instinct of Freudian theory. Of these, a) and b) fail to account for all instances in which—as in the historic case of the death of Giordano Bruno—the identity to be preserved is undefinable in terms of any specific biological collective, representing instead the subject's

personal cause or idea as the quintessence of his existence, while c)
is phenomenologically incompatible with the life-affirmative purposivity
of this entire mode-of-action which withstands death precisely by
recognizing death's ultimate identity with the condition of a *mere*
(truthless or non-transcendent) living, a living as though life was not
more in man than what it is in any other creature. Scheler's conclusion
from observations of this kind is not a denial of man's share in animal
nature, which in fact determines much of everybody's observable
living, but an empiric securing of the *other* sphere of existence in which
man, as the only existent among organisms, shares *also*, and in just
as elementary ways. Transcendence toward *world* which before was
recognized as a tendency inherent in any psychic event thus not only
receives its full actualization only in man,[8] but man only thereby is
enabled to recognize his own *genetic* transcendence from the closed
instinctual topography of the bonds of animal life. We can, of course,
readily think of many comparable media of man's world in which,
as in a piece of music, an emergent phenomenal order comes to
determine the structure of what otherwise would forever have to
remain referred—without even substantial hope for any plausible
account in the end—to a postulated, never quite implemented explanatory exploration of unending webs of single cause-effect connections,
as in the cited "sequence of sound waves" following each other without
an explicable order. Transcendence, then, in the sense of a relatively
discontinuous emergence breaking through abruptly into a higher and
freer order of determinacy, reveals itself as an elementary and
immanent principle of phenomenal reality itself.

Of the host of biological implications which unfolds from this discovery, the most important one is this evident discontinuity between
the levels of motivational determinacy operant in man: inasmuch as
man shares in phenomenal freedom, he "abruptly" becomes subject
to a new context of determinant laws while nevertheless remaining
subject to the postulate—so far unimplemented by either biology or
physics but remaining a necessity of reason—to be strictly accountable-
for in terms of physicalistically understood objective causes. What
fails to apply to him at this level is not this unimplemented radical
physicalistic *causalism* which just for the reason of its infinite remoteness need hardly concern us, but the phenomenal causalism of the
drive theories. The latter misunderstands itself in two ways: it mis-

takes understandable connections between the meanings of successive events for determinations of the latter event by the earlier, and it illogically conceptualizes what it understands by way of analogy with what it understands, not more, but *less*—animal behavior.

But how can Scheler's picture of the special position of man be related to our whole conception of organic evolution? As far as phylogenesis is concerned, not a single one of the substantial elements of Darwinian theorizing is even touched: what takes place is a shift not in evolutional tracing but in emphasis and in our perspective for the way in which one significant genetic step is realized in the actuality of the existences concerned. As, with man, evolution abruptly emerges into the wholly different order of conscious existence, like a movement slowly climbing up through the depths of the ocean and yet at only one point breaking through its surface into the horizoned openness of an entirely new element, thus a second, only far more sudden and incisive, conquest, comparable to the earlier overcoming of aquatic existence in the development of the species, must be assumed. No "amphibious" transitory forms at least have survived to mark this second change-over, yet, just as new elemental laws begin to govern the organism of the new land' animal, no reference to animal instincts can any longer account for human existence and conduct precisely in their authentically experienced depths. It is clear that by biogenetic standards only a short period has elapsed since this enormous leap into a new elemental order occurred; man's "new lungs", his capacity of transcendent purposes, is still far too precarious a possession to forestall alternations, just as abrupt and unbridgeable, between the two whole levels of determinacy "available" to him.[9] Existence, in Heidegger's word, is equi-originally in untruth as it is in truth: it *can* "determine itself" by referring itself motivationally to what man still inclines to believe are the elements in him (as though he would need this self-reminder if they were) and he can be in *his* element by being radically articulate and spontaneous—true to truth itself.[10] While we are touching here on the central problem of neurosis, which existence-analytically can be defined as a state of truthless living induced by a self-misunderstanding of the very quest for truth, some more general implications of Scheler's theory demand our attention first.

It is evident that the very conception of the biological life space

is altered with his discovery. Man's environment does not even come
only to include the geographically distal but comes to include such
generically "different", non-factual, entities as images, ideas, and
ideals. How can even the most holistic objectivism incorporate them
as they are in the framework of its theory? At a closer glance, we
recognize in images, ideas, and ideals the very powers which, in man,
"organize" the world of his experience throughout, ultimately determining its whole perceptual aspect also; but this truth is concealed
by the fact that in the structure of perceptual worlds, as we follow
them from their encompassing valuative axioms which are different
ones in each subject, toward the objective axioms of the ordinary
perceptual *Gestalten*, a convergence is seen to take place without which
perception itself could never be studied "objectively". Yet in principle
the determinant power of the "subjective" world axioms, as has been
shown before, is stronger *even* than that of the common *Gestalten* of
a sensory world mistakenly conceptualized as an independently existent
objective reality, and the problem of the biological incorporation of
the cognitive and the valuative—images, ideas, and ideals—thus widens
into the problem of the bridge between biology and psychology *per se*.

Several attempts to solve it have been made by biologists. Üxküll,
in his descriptive applications of his conception of *Umwelten* ("worlds
around") by which he tried with altogether too little caution to reconstruct the orientative experience-spheres (*Merksysteme*) not only of
human beings but of animals as well, contributed greatly to our
insight into the very problem of phenomenological method in all its
thorniness, as much as to that into different subjectivities. The quasi-
physicalistic attempts of Lewin have been characterized before. Within
the frame of a biological field theory, the only logical (if hard to
implement) solution appears to have been found by Angyal (*Foundations for a Science of Personality*): only the most cautious objectifications of the psychophysically neutral organism in its unity
("system"), of its "principle", and of its "functional ramifications",
are formulated, phenomenal experience and the correlated specific
behavior being parenthetically excluded throughout.

The only alternative to a formalism of this type that remains is a
frank acknowledgment of the methodological difficulties surrounding
the leap from the determinate objectivity of the organism to the
transcendent subjectivity of that organism's "psyche"—without which

the objective organism must ultimately remain ununderstood. Many quotations which have been brought before testify to this frankness in the biological theorizing of Goldstein; the particular research central to his whole work, his concrete exploration of the changes that experience-behavior contexts undergo in brain organics, indeed forbade any "bracketing in" of subject matter in itself psychological.

As shown by Goldstein,[11] the brain organic, 1) is unable freely to refer the immediate and momentary of his sensory experience to what is required to make it meaningful, a constant background of images and ideas; 2) reacts to this failure with panicky anxiety; 3) reacts not to the experience of specific failure in a task but to the encounter of a void where meanings used to be, that is, of nothingness.[12] What collapses catastrophically in such cases, because it no longer can realize itself *into* the world, is the patient's existence itself. As Jaspers' cases of schizophrenics showed the irreducibility of reality to sensory data, its contingence upon an unbroken existence, Goldstein's of brain organics, vice versa, demonstrate the irreducibility of existence *qua being* to any merely intra-organismic principle: being "is" *into the world,* or else collapses. "The source of anxiety", to quote Goldstein, "is the inner experience of not being confronted with anything or being confronted with nothingness". The common phenomenal denominator for the anxiety in either case, then, is the destruction or profound disturbance either of self-realization in the world (schizophrenics) or of world realization in the self (organics), but in either case of what never is being considered by the objectivisms in psychology precisely because it is so self-evident to the normal human being, including the objectivist: the being-in-the-world as the pre-given constituent of all data, whether environmental or organismic. The existentialist revision of psychopathology, therefore, not only recognizes in the being-in-the-world the foundation of all states of the psyche, both normal and abnormal, but recognizes the inevitability with which this fundamental truth was bound to be concealed at the pre-existentialist stage of the social and anthropological sciences by the unreflectedly existence-bound thinking of the scientists themselves.

The problem which remains is whether the organic's incapacity of world realization within the self is fully understood if conceptualized as a loss of *abstract* behavior. Goldstein's own description of the actual losses which this concept is meant to comprise reach far beyond its true scope—this true scope, if we take the term abstraction as literally as possible, being far narrower and more specific than the scope of psychological symptoms which it is supposed to cover. Attempting a more encompassing definition, we may say that the organic fails in the ability to relate the fleetingly sensory of his immediate situations to a stable background of axiomatic meanings which can make these "concretenesses" understandable in their depth and thereby accessible, not only to thought (both analytic and creative) but to its (normally) constant and silent underpinnings, feeling and volition in their time-transcendent roles as well. While abstraction will naturally be affected most conspicuously by this for the simple reason that achievements in it far better than in any other "functions" lend themselves to testing according to definable standards, it does not follow from the presence of this greater technical facility that what the facility lends access to must necessarily also be the essence of the brain-organic psychological change. In specific circumstances, where abstraction as a routine activity has become part and parcel of an organic patient's habitual dealings with his situation, of his "concrete" relations to the immediate daily environment, it may, in fact, remain relatively unaffected at a time when any independent ideation of his already is blocked by a total inaccessibility of the original eidetic background of his world. In the case of one brain organic, an insurance mathematician whom the author had occasion to observe over a period of several months, the ability to follow fixed sequences of formulas in the solution of routine algebraic problems survived longer than did almost any other of this subject's intellectual abilities.

Since, in their most recent versions, Goldstein's own observations and actual theoretical accounts of the psychological changes in brain organics exceed in essence the limits of the concept here criticized the question must arise why the concept has not long been revised by holistic biology. The most likely explanation lies not in any intrinsic inconsistency on the part of the biologists but in the historic necessity for them, once problems involving phenomenal experience became relevant for their research, to make contact with the most holistic psychology in the neighborhood of their own field that could be found at the time of their theorizing. Precisely, indeed, this misunderstanding of abstraction, itself wholly contingent upon the *concrete* presence of fact-transcendent meaning constancies in the mind, as the source of meaning experience, no longer offers difficulties to our comprehension, since we now discern it only too readily as the consequence of the Platonistic tradition discussed before and as the central error, likewise expounded earlier, of Gestalt psychology in its contention of a structure-immanence of meaning: the Gestaltist derivation of meaning from a physicalistically conceived, if never actually explained, "self-distribution" of sensory data in the brain field evidently underlies this actual, if never express, identification of the essential with the abstract. Yet, if meaning were itself abstract, rather than eidetic, why should experiences of meaningfulness presuppose an implementation of concepts by *Anschaulichkeit* (readiness to be visualized)? Why, on the other hand, should concatenations of abstract terms in a text reduce its phenomenal meaningfulness rather than enhance it, if this belief were true? The necessity, suggested before in our first presentation of the existentialist revision of phenomenology, for thought to first go back behind its own operational system—inasmuch as logic bypasses also the actuality of that experience wherein its own compellingness is rooted, the phenomenal *unfolding* of thought—once more becomes imperative.

Evidently, this undoing of conceptual surfaces by radical phenomenology is the first step any true analysis of existence must take. The step, in turn, cannot be taken without violating basic tenets in the social and anthropological science of our day, so that the revision takes the form, in part of a total exploding, for another part of a reversing of *everybody's* most unquestioned (and most unproved) notions. To show this, we may turn to issues which have been introduced already, as the problem of the predicative order of truth and reality, where we recognize this constellation easily once we realize the enormity of the hold which the unempirical conviction about the one ("absolute") reality and the many ("relative") truths has come to exercise upon the average intellectual of our day. While a further development of this particular issue has to await a more systematic introduction to existentialist philosophy, already we discern the depth of the problem which is posed for psychology by the peculiar nearness, characterized before, between the subject matter of this science and the available conceptual tools for its grasp: no longer, like the student of the physical sciences, is the psychologist faced merely with the issue of correct versus incorrect solutions of problems, but primarily he is

faced with the issue whether these problems themselves are posed
meaningfully, whether his very posing of problems, owing to his own
existential involvement in the topics of his theorizing, does not already
articulate itself in concepts and tenets that obscure the subject matter
in its actuality and hence themselves must first—with the existentialist
expression—be "thought back to their sources".

This thinking of concepts back to their sources, to human conceptual
experience *in statu nascendi*, reveals itself as the only solution to the
problem of language as a tool in the sciences of man: its current
alternative, the so-called general semantics, is founded upon the conspicuously mistaken belief that an Archimedian point for the
definitive analysis of the axioms of conceptual language—a point
beyond the reach of these axioms—is accessible to man. As though
definitions not themselves consisting of words to be defined existed,
as though a single "symbolic" term-representative could be discovered
the meaning of which would not already have to be intuited, and as
though any compelling criteria for the truth of the representation
were even conceivable, the semanticist and the symbolic logician
establish their headquarters in the still constantly spreading *naught*
which intrudes on human existence from wherever operationalism is
adhered to. Their claim concerning the misleadingness of language
makes language itself responsible for both its misuses and their own
failures in understanding language of a wider phenomenal scope: *as
though* the physical frailty, the mechanical destructibility, of a great
work of art would argue against the eternity of its message, they conclude from their ability to intersperse any text not of their liking with
demands for definition that the text lacks that significance which it has
when understood.

Since no analysis of human cognition anywhere breaks through the
barrier of the irreducibility of understanding to anything not already
pre-requiring it, the phenomenological reversal of the cognition problem comes to question precisely the other side of the *Diltheyan gap*:
if, despite all the efforts of psychologists during the last seventy years,
understanding cannot be explained, can, perhaps, explanatoriness be
understood? The dependence of explanatoriness on understanding has
been touched upon. In the strict (causal-genetic) sense of the term,
explanations, as likewise pointed out before, are referrals of events to
different descriptive levels, therefore, to advance on the problem, these

levels must be investigated, their recognizable order be explored. Even before this is done, the very *why* with which the causative question opens must be subjected to phenomenological reflection.

As an example for our study we may attempt to understand the meaning of this *why* in the mind of a child asking his father, *Why is there a moon?* According to an unbiased perception of the child's thought experience in asking this (readily verifiable by a radically unsuggestive method of interviewing but transparent in the question), such a *why* could just as well have involved the *purpose* of the paperweight on our desk or nature's *aim* in equipping a desert plant with fleshy leaves. In other words, behind the question there stands no conception as yet of the relevancy for it of a dead causal tracing of the moon's genesis but rather the spontaneous trust in an intrinsic order of the universe that assigns a task, mission or purpose to everything in it, so that it turns out to be this "What's the idea?" that the child's *why* implies. Yet, if the father, as in many instances today he will, happens to reply with one of the many existent hypotheses of astronomers concerning the physical origin of the moon, the inevitable effect on the impressionable mind of the child of so imposing a knowledge must be a concealment of the original meaning of his own question and of perhaps innumerable such questions later in his life: increasingly, from here on out, their very first appearance in his mind will attach itself to the image of the world-as-process by the limiting availability of genetic answers only—as the *only* acceptable "serious" ones in an enlightened society—a condition which, in by-passing the original *why*, yet succeeds in projecting a shadow of it, easily mistaken then for the *why* itself, upon the endlessly stretching plane of causal time. This quality of endless stretching is itself a guarantee that the substitution will not easily be noticed; since it always refers to a *farther-on*, a *not-yet*, a *keep-going-as-long-as-you-can*, no alternative sets or directions of the total cognitive quest can finally even come into focus any more once, historically or individually, this hypnotism of explanatoriness has started on its path. What originally is but a position of limits to which the *why*, actually here turning into a *how*, may apply itself, the "*how* has it come to be this way"? as the specific quest for past states of a thing in their succession *becomes the standard for the why itself*.

The first conclusion which this observation suggests recognizes the capacity of answers to questions to alter the questions by tending to block from sight—once the answers have been given—the authentic meaning of the questions *as they were asked*. The peculiar self-by-passingness of consciousness which our discussion has exposed before and which calls for the many reversals and revisions of "self-evident" objectifying notions at the hands of existentialism, shows up in this as in many of the categorical instrumentalities of explanatory objectivism. For example, in our illustration of Thorndike's fundamental contention the existence in a certain quantity of an elephant was found to be spurious, shattering the claim of objectivism to a quantitative reducibility of qualities, but this insight initiates rather than completes an analysis of the error. As always where objectivism, in going off on a tangent, follows that tangent into the naught of its ever more thoughtless, imageless abstractions, it is the reverse relationship that is readily seen to obtain: bigness, a concept referring to quantity, is unquestionably encountered as one among the many phenomenal *qualities* of this "object", and the basis of quantitativism, the isolation of a thing-property from its authentic context, thus becomes transparent at a glance. Here and always, restoration of the original experiential order first has to remove the block on everyone's mind which the successfulness of the by-passing phenomenon has obscuringly put in front of that order; while this attempt is difficult, it can be said to receive increasing *moral* support from the unsuccessfulness of mere quantitative explanatoriness in making understandable even such a legitimately objectifiable sphere of events as that of biologic processes with their peculiar interpenetration between strict causality and irreducible holistic parameters in the phenomena observed. The insight of holistic biology[13] that systems previously assumed to be merely more complex concatenations of single two-factor relations, can in principle not be derived from them—that vice versa, the two-factor relations will have to be regarded as the *borderline cases*, as most radically simplified systems—is a characteristic feat of true twentieth century thought: the building stones of explanatory analysis finally being discerned as mere positions of limit at the fringes of the range of the phenomena to be explained, the forgotten experiential order is ultimately verified by the revised objective conception, and explanatoriness itself undergoes a relativization in the end.

So far, its relation to mathematical time as only one of the endlessly stretching dimensions along which it operates and which make
its hypnotic power over the modern mind understandable has been
exposed. Two more such infinities can be discerned in its make-up,
the dimension of the *ever-smaller* into which its analyses are drilled,
and of the *ever more abstract* by which it replaces, first the visible,
then anything ready to be visualized or visually analogized (*veran-
schaulicht*). Granted now that explanatory analysis, with these dimensions as its tacit premises, succeeds in finding ever more Archimedean
points for object manipulation in technology and applied science, this
rather specific line of successfulness cannot obscure 1) that its concentration on only one of the two comprehensive orders penetrating
each other in reality, its total replacement of the world-as-essence by
the world-as-process, is itself *not* compelled by scientific inquiry but
as a valuative (existential) decision *precedes* a specific line of scientific
inquiry, setting its direction from the start; 2) that, accordingly, along
this line of inquiry, the world-as-essence remains unaccounted for
throughout; 3) that the increase in manipulatory power over nature
which the inquiry gains is not necessarily even an increase in power
per se. The average person in our age is on the contrary becoming
constantly more powerless, for at the rate at which he comes to depend
in every action and thought on anonymous forces of his own "mechanisms" within and of the technological collective without, his life-
course is pre-set along ever more narrowly-determined and machine-
like topographic lines. We may add, 4) that this increase in
manipulatory power is only a substitute for essential knowledge; the
substitution, in turn, for a long time, but hardly forever, being able
to cheat the original *why* which comes to the fore again once, 5) the
discovery is made by man that the perpetual widening of the limits
of his knowledge about nature is, by definition, also a perpetual
running-away from him of these limits; as he never catches up with
them, he fails to progress a single step towards the dissolution of the
boundary between the known and the unknown, which thus merely
shifts. For a psychological account of explanatoriness, the latter
observation corroborates other implications contained in the dependence of this mode-of-cognition on the three infinities named: the
explanatory quest takes over from the original *why* not only the
a priori demand for certitude but also an *a priori* sensing of the infinite

as the given source of all possible certitude attainable. The infinite, no longer understood in its authentic givenness-to-experience as that ultimate which experience can never hope to implement "objectively", comes to exercise—if we may say so—a function of background.

This may seem paradoxical since the infinite by definition would seem to defy such conversions into "ground." However, it is not any stranger than the fact, for example, that the infinite of the sky is perceptually converted into a ground on which airplanes can write figures, such as the names of cola drinks. The question, which touches on the fundamentals of our culture, whether this is a proper use to be made of the infinite of the sky, is, of course, a different matter, and in the same way we may question the appropriateness of the use which positivistic science makes of the three infinities (explanatory levels) to which, in accounting for man in his world, it refers its observations. For the present, it may suffice to verify the background functions of the past (mathematical time), of the ever smaller ("analyticalness"), and of the ever less *anschaulich* (abstraction) by reflecting upon the experience of cognitive satisfaction which they ordinarily seem to impart but immediately stop even to *seem* imparting once this satisfaction itself is made the object of our quest: evidently, what accounts for it is not any going-to-the-end (for there is no end to infinities and consequently never even the slightest progress in moving closer to one) in any of these dimensions, but the opportunities which they grant *as backgrounds* to refer to them. What does this mean? The explanatory relation, by projecting singled-out features of phenomena against the background spoken of, only succeeds in replacing by conceptual shadows what it claims to explain, but in ordinary human experience the replacement assumes the status of a theoretical account, for any experience of *distance* promotes orientation: the very act of referring things to their conceptual shadows turns these shadows into distal formulas that the dimension of reference, the "sky" itself of the explanatory projection, legibly and authoritatively spells out for our reading.

But once this is seen, the *original why* no longer can be cheated: at the moment, for example, when a glance at the evolution of species in its combined Darwinian and Mendelian account comes to notice that nowhere along its path in mathematical time this cavalcade of forms, moving according to the laws of heredity and natural selection, anywhere supplies intrinsic reasons, either for the forms in their specificity or for their unfolding in its directedness as a phenomenon of time itself, the combined accounts turn out to be no more than a description of the recordable "mechanism" (the *how*) of a change, the essential cause of which has still entirely escaped us. Time itself, then, is, as mathematical time, only descriptively explored in such an enterprise, explored in a manner which, in principle, is in no way different from that of descriptive explorations of orders-of-things in space; and just as descriptive explorations of orders-of-things in space cannot claim to be already their theoretical accounts, descriptive enucleations of the mere *how* of orders in time (morphological changes) cannot claim to be already an inspection of their true causes. Not any less than this phenomenological reflection, the relativization of time at the hands of physics, reducing it from an *Anschauungsform* (Kant) to a quasi-spatial objective dimension, destroys the claim to special causal-explanatory privileges traditionally accorded to time by the philosophical apologists of explanatory objectivism, but this is still rarely noticed, for in what if not phenomenal time does the physicist himself observe as well as think? If the *a priori* of time is not a transcendental absolute, if time is an objective dimension according to the ultimate implications of phenomenal experience, it all the more emphatically remains one of the absolute (existential) constituents of experience *as such*; the physicist's cognition may dissolve the phenomenal as radically as it can, it continues with every step to hinge on his existence. Only time means something different in its *original* connotation[14] than it means once the very concept of it has become founded on a mathematization of observed successions of events, and thus the crisis of knowledge which must arise once mathematical time has been discerned in its intrinsic emptiness offers two clues to its solution: man can come to perceive in his own existence along the dimension of time the source of his inclination to locate causes in the phenomenal past and thus to obscure his own insight, for a certain stretch of his history, into the essential equivalence between orders of things in mathematical space and orders of events in mathematical time;[15] and man, once this discovery is made by him, no longer can legitimately take recourse to mathematical time as the locus of what—originally and now again—he means by *cause*.

Since the second dimensional infinity of explanatoriness, the *ever smaller,* has already been shown in its irrelevance for an analysis of phenomena insofar as they are meaning-determined, only the misleadingness of the third of these infinities, the dimension of abstraction, remains to be shown in a representative example. Contemporary psychiatry—in its breadth as a social phenomenon, not, certainly, in its *avant-garde* positions as an orbit of thought—offers such examples plentifully, most tellingly, perhaps, in the peculiar uses it makes of its nosological concepts. We may, for example, read in a psychiatric diagnostic study that "we understand now that this anxiety formed part of a hysteria", and ask ourselves what it is that is truly understood here, or read in another that certain ideas of a patient in which the examiner fails to follow him may be "attributable to a schizophrenia", and ask ourselves about the logical essence of such an act of attribution. The peculiar power of conceptual reification over objectifying psychology has been explored before, and it is not difficult to see how the results apply here: as though nosological concepts such as hysteria or schizophrenia in their definitive constitutions anywhere exceeded the descriptive classification of symptom patterns; as though they were comparable with such nosological concepts of somatic medicine which refer symptoms and their patterns to actually demonstrable processes *beyond* the symptomatic, psychiatry, in such cases, "understands" symptoms in terms of their own classifiability, that is, it attributes them to themselves by attributing them to terminological entities standing for nothing but again the same categories of symptoms; yet the impression as though an explanatory reduction to a process beyond the symptomatic were made cannot fail to be received both by the psychiatrist himself and his audience. Dynamic psychiatry not only has not changed this essentially, since all disclaiming of the importance of classificatory nosology cannot do away with the ultimate necessity of diagnosing according to *some* categories, but in many respects has made it worse by 1) replacing symptom-classificatory reifications by unverifiable speculative ones, 2) failing to recognize or remember the logical nature of the difficulty surrounding psychiatric nosology as shown, so that the very dependence of descriptive classifications on descriptive vantage points is allowed gradually to sink into oblivion. The consequences are diagnostic disputes, for example, on whether a patient is a schizophrenic or not,

which would be exploded at once by examining the definitive constitution of the concept of schizophrenia *as understood* by the disputants,
and not stopping at the terminological level: while the definitions may
still seem compatible with one another, they require a consistent interpretation of symptom concepts as they apply to individual cases. The
reality of psychiatric training and practice largely fails to fulfill this
condition, but the reason for this—for the often completely different
concrete understanding of such a symptom concept as emotional shallowness, as revealed by inter-judge discrepancies in its diagnostic
application—is not any phenomenal ambiguity on the part of the
concept of shallowness. Rather is there insufficient differentiation by
the original nosologists among the many posible forms and degrees
of this quality; the insufficient training in phenomenal observation
and phenomenological thought characteristic at least of the more
typical examiner then adds to the defect.

Since strict empiricalness of his science seldom is doubted by the
average psychologist, this is most strange: the picture we receive of the
stated situation in psychodiagnostic work is one of a reign of
"realism" in the medieval sense of the word but hidden behind a
"nominalistic", that is, empiricistic, ideology, so that this actual
absolutism of terms is hardly ever discovered by the average clinician;
what keeps changing is not the absolutism, but the terms that wield it.
Its worst consequence, and with this we may return to the general
misleadingness of the dimensional infinity of abstraction, is the concealment, by the very availability of abstract terms *qua* abstract ones,
of the authenticity of human experience and human existence which
these reifications come to enclose like coffins: problems which individual cases present and for which an as nearly as possible full understanding of the patient's world *first* offers the only hope of solution,
will be referred away from the authentic to an abstractness incapable
of theoretical achievement precisely for the reason of its own merely
classificatory constitution, no longer realized as a rule by the practicing
diagnostician. It is manifest that the misleadingness of abstraction here
analyzed is a specific yet representative instance of it, since it is
typical at once of early twentieth century modes of thinking-about-man
in general and of the hypnotic role which the three infinities of explanatoriness can be seen playing. What remains, once this essential
futility has finally been registered on the mind? The forgotten *world*

as essence is rediscovered by the scientist, and beginning with man as the subject matter most imperatively calling for this *phenomenological revision,* the direction of the cognitive quest of science itself must change.

Science being one according to the very idea of it in its timeless and compelling universalism, a reintegration, not now predictable in its concrete forms, of the phenomenological and objectifying world accounts must be expected. It is evident that this hope stands or falls with the one for a recognition, by science at large, of two necessities: abandonment of the figment of an objectifying psychology even as a link between phenomenology and the physical sciences, and a re-examination of the teleology problem. Within the orbit of objective science, holistic biology, as shown before, has re-posed this problem compellingly by demonstrating the interpenetration in the organism of a causal order of lawfulness with a finalistic one nowhere reducible in terms of any of the three-dimensional infinities of the explanatory quest. Gestalt psychology, as in so many other fundamental points, has been inconsistent also in respect to this particular issue: for example, the very concept of *time-Gestalten,* or Wertheimer's proposition concerning the "tendency of fields to assume meaningful order" imply finalism in fact, whereas Gestalt psychology in principle has continued to adhere to a causalistically conceived determinism of the nineteenth century type. While some future promise of clarification is held out by the rapid change in axiomatic parameter concepts going on in physics, within the fields close to human existence progress on the problem is hampered by two conditions: teleology, to the average scientist, is covered with a blinding, affectively charged, taboo, and teleology is misunderstood as implying such an abstruse proposition as a reversal of the causal order of mathematical time, with the causes operating from the future. Since the misunderstanding has been fostered by those versions of vitalism (Driesch, etc.) which proposed a special life agent (*entelechy*) as an entity acting in mathematical time within objectifiable fields of physicalistic observation, rather than proposing a questioning of the relevance of mathematical time itself[16] for understanding life's phenomena, it is important to recall that *telos* means no such thing as a future goal or cause but does mean the *ultimate whole.* The ultimate whole is inconceivable within the successivity of mathematical time. Any investigations of the problem which do not first suspend the horizon-like notion (underlying all explanatory cognizing) of mathematical time as a misunderstanding contingent upon the cognizer's existence therefore do not even stand a chance of closing in on its solution.

The stated hope for a reintegration of the universe of knowledge only can profit from what is proposed here, a sober realization of the obstacles in its way; but is it not in the nature precisely of such ultimate integrations that authentically they unfold from a situation of straight clash between the two positions in question, only afterwards to appear as evolutions, as "developments"? Considering the growing absolutism with which ever since Descartes the objectifying point of view has ruled, the completeness with which, in applying itself to human nature as its subject matter, it has by-passed the relevant data of human existence, the new phenomenological and existentialist opposition inevitably is radical, a clash situation inevitably the reality of our day. In exploring existence, the being-in-the-world of man, the first and most critical issue radical phenomenology meets with is the same that accounts, as we have shown, for the thematic gap in psychology; or, putting it more in the concrete, that most crucial problem is posed by the seeming disparity between the experience-transcendent *contents* of experience in their claim to be true regardless of the individuality of the experiencer, *and that individuality,* not in any immanentistic isolation from its experiential world context, but, on the contrary, precisely in as far as it represents an encompassing apperception of reality with its psychological irreducible but at the same time psychologically given claim to *truth.* The impossibility of a "pure" phenomenology of the Husserlian type, by-passing the existential sources of conceptual logic and ultimately failing to account for the being of either the self or the world has been exposed, and so has the necessity for a reversal of the now customary predication, untrue to authentic experience, of truth on "reality". But the latter argument has only been sketched in its contours; to implement it, a traditional and major preconception of objective psychology, the division between the cognitive and conative as distinctive functional spheres of the psyche must be examined.

Although inklings that something is wrong with that customary separation are no monopoly of phenomenological psychology,[17] it is not to be seen how its error can be tested except by being exposed to the testimony of what the named two notions somehow derive from, and without which no meaning at all can be given them, phenomenal experience. Since conation and cognition are ill-determined entities, even to speak of a possible influence of one of them on the other is to unempirically accept them as separate factors before knowing that they are such factors. But what are they? Abstractions, of course, but the customary separation between them would not have assumed such power over the minds of theorists, if what called for these abstractions were not a given order inherent in human experience: from the heaviness, the diffuse and inarticulate darkness of the "animalic", the "deep", the "unconscious", within, to the clarity and light of the valid and the true all events of orientation and decision run their courses. This justifies to determine the conative and cognitive as the static polar directions between which the whole gamut of experiential events is extended; it does not support their reification into factorial concepts of functions, as in objective psychology. Poles, abstracted from a unity that stretches between them, are not agents that enter into a compromise (that unity)—as though a unity ever *were* a compromise; the polarity between them vice versa is unfolded only by the events that then allow to abstract it *from* them. These events, then, have to be examined without an *a priori* recourse to the polarity they map out; otherwise, that polarity will never be comprehended. But do there exist polarities of a different kind? The answer, evidently, is yes, for wherever we speak of compromises, a mutual hostility, an exclusivity in principle, between the compromising parties is implied. Why was—as emphatically in psychoanalysis with its unquestioning counterposing of an animal nature (id) and a rational, reality-oriented ego acting under the tyranny of an again tending-to-be-irrational superego—the relationship between the cognitive and conative seen as a polarity of the exclusive kind, calling for a relative repression of one of the poles by the other in order to make existences *already determined as compromises* livable? If constellations of this kind did not occur, neither psychoanalytic theory nor its enormous success in our time could be understood. But if constellations of this kind, rather than being the rule only in typical modern existences, a rule induced, as we later shall see, by a type of self-reflection characteristic of one specific historical phase of man and his society, would represent, as Freud thought, the true law governing the relations between the cognitive and conative, uncounted basic phenomena of our living would escape comprehension.

But what is a true law? How can it be determined? In order to determine it, excluding "uncontrolled variables", that is, anything extraneous to the law, the phenomena that law is supposed to govern must be observed where they are purest: to determine the true relation between cognition and conation, we must look at them where their accomplishments are greatest. If we do this we find that where conation is most vigorous, in the pure phenomena of sexual love, it *becomes cognition*. It becomes an affirmation of the *other* the way that other *is*; it does not become affirmation of a need on the part of the lover, because, if it did, that need itself would neither be as strong nor as effective as it must be to be one with the person; where, destroying that unity between the lover and his love, the need as such moves into the focus of that person's awareness, where self-reflectivity, as the eternal enemy of love, already splits the psyche and the world, it is not in that central place (the focus of awareness) that the loved one can conceivably remain. To *be true* not accidentally means personal openness and fidelity as much as the "adequacy" of a judgment, and not any more accidentally does *to know* mean of old the love act; it does not mean that "in addition" to what else it means (and today has come to connote exclusively), but because the essence of the love act and the essence of knowledge *are one*.

A brief examination of the pure phenomena of knowledge confirms this from the side of "cognition". The inseparability between understanding and good will; between insight into the intrinsic order of a thing, and enough inner freedom to *attend* to it fully, to give it one's undivided attention; the already expounded experience of existential freedom in *emerging* into the truth about something, as which we discerned the nature of insight; the spontaneous *ought* character of compelling conclusions of thought: all these point to a hidden unity of the cognitive and conative, with our own abstractions of these, by causing us to confound different aspects and aspect-accentuations of psychic events with different factorial entities, serving in the role of the smoke screen. We later shall see that this smoke screen is not a product of psychological theorizing, unless our concept of psychological theorizing is wide enough to comprise an indecisive and unclarified type of self-conscious reflectiveness that man for a long time has seemed fated to nurture in himself. But psychological theorizing *qua* scientific thought about the psyche does not produce that smoke screen; the scientist's mind merely fails to see through it.

The interdependence between the misunderstanding here exposed and the one that concerns the subjectivity-objectivity dichotomy lies open at a glance. With respect to the implications of this dichotomy for the theory of cognition, the history of objective psychology has been a shuttling back and forth between positions alternately stressing the "subjective" and "objective" factors. Gestalt psychology accentuated the relative constancies of the objective. The more complex these constancies are in a material sense, the more individually restricted is their reign; the simpler they are, the more generally valid are they also, that is, no longer restricted by the experiential scope of an individual, a generation, a type, or group of whatever determining constituent, but by whole cultures, farther on by the human species, still farther on, where constancies of an ever-more primitive type are involved (and as far as the behavior of animals allows of deductions), by common biological organization. At any rate, the very research in the *Gestalten* of experience, if and as long as the latter are understood as immanent organizations of the physical universe, is fated to hit a wall after a while, from which it bounces back to the subjective. But what is that? An objectivistic proposition, that nowhere exceeds the status of a mere frame of orientation, since implementing it turns out to be impossible without recourse to the *what* of experience, the "objective" *Gestalten*. The shuttling, then, goes on.

Why must it? Why, for example, can such a proposition as Freud's concerning the "share" of a quite limitlessly defined projection mechanism in man's noetic shaping of his world[18] never conceivably be implemented by research, either clinical or experimental? Because *share* requires a quantitative determinant which is unavailable here: if "reality" is distorted by projection, of which the projector has by Freud's own definition no knowledge, how can one know the extent of the distortion without knowing (which according to Freud's definition one cannot know) what a projectionless reality picture is like?[19] It is evident that opposing metaphysics as a point of ideology is not enough; metaphysical being any statement about the "totality" of that-which-is (reality), "reality" (and all similarly *ultimate* concepts) must first of all not figure in specific psychological propositions and reports any more than is the case in propositions and reports of that envied model of the man of science, the physicist. Hegel's classic mockery about certain psychological "laws" understood, without regard to their objective unverifiability in principle, as *explanatory of individuality*, concerned exactly this issue; returning to the actuality of individual experience, what can we make out? Man experiencing nothing, as we saw, the experience of which would not have the form of a conviction,[20] it becomes obvious, 1) that not only there are more convictions in the human psyche than man's *focal* awareness is ready to spell out, but that the surest and deepest, most unquestioned, among them, being horizonlike to the whole scope and structure of his world consciousness, are just for this reason not likely to be a matter of his own conceptual attention (consciousness in Freud's far too one-sided sense), necessitating a more careful examination by the psychologist of the structure of attention from its focal centering to its dimming out periphery; 2) that the human unconscious, permitting only to be inferred in its infinite power and scope, never its contents, from experiences of inner articulation, as the wherefrom of a *becoming conscious,* cannot conceivably be thought of as either a wastebasket of censored impulses and memories (Freud) or a reified pool of images and strivings (Jung): the very concept of an image, or of the goal of a striving, cannot be constituted without reference to a beholder conscious *of it*; 3) that the phenomenal polarity of the cognitive and conative turns out as the best witness to the doctrine of experiential self-transcendence: the two concept-lines diverge *within* a horizon of unreflected existence *beyond* which, as only radical reflection can disclose to us, they must meet and merge in the infinite which this horizon connotes.

Without such reflection about the implications of existential horizons, how can the psychologist hope ever to find the Archimedean point from which to grasp anything even approximating the true order of his subject matter? His own self-evident concepts (such as the cognitive and the conative) *for* the comprehension of the psyche being themselves manifestations, events, *of* what he is trying to comprehend there, it is this self-evidence which he must question at the outset. His very resistance against doing so is the best conceivable evidence for a major implication of the radical phenomenological (existentialist) interpretation of the conation-cognition gap: it confirms the directedness of cognition by an existential decision of the cognizer. So, of course, did the presence of a choice which we discerned between the radical objectivistic and the phenomenological quests at the beginning of this study, so do uncounted other observations we may make in contemplating the historic totality of modern science—but does this existence-immanence of cognition imply its immanence in an objectified psyche? The distinction becomes important, for our argument will never pass without first inciting a vehement objection that what is being proposed here is a voluntaristic theory of knowledge.

In respect to their own cognitive operations, the functionalist and neo-positivist will deny such voluntaristic charges, as they deny any autonomy of the opposite pole of the experience axis—Truth. But just as we recognized that denials of an "absolute" truth (whatever this shall mean) do not protect from dogmatism which on the contrary they seem to foster, the claim to be nothing but objective conspicuously contrasts with the actual emotionality of the functionalist's attitude which our analysis of *technicalism* disclosed. The aspiration of the latter to an absolute objectifying sovereignty of rational operation we then found avenged by an invasion of this very rational operation by the very voluntarism it disavows, but by voluntarism of a literal kind, for its "operational" definitions and dispositions could hardly be more arbitrary. What works here is a mechanism which in substance was first discerned by Jung; according to Jung's far less satisfactory theory of it (which underlies his understanding of schizophrenia), tropisms of the *anima*, the goal images of which the *persona*, having cast them out, does not tolerate, warring against them wherever it encounters them in the outside world, will finally rise again from the unconscious, invade—in their lowest and crudest, most archaic forms—the precariously brittle structure of that far too narrowly self-defensive *persona*, and overwhelm its defenses. In essence this is not a new truth: Goethe had a similar perception when stating that the more one nurtures illusions of freedom, the more unfree one becomes. Awareness of the decisiveness of *existence* for *cognition* therefore at once protects from unconscious voluntarisms and asserts the inevitable truth of a voluntarism *itself rethought from the point of its inception.*

This new interpretation of the relations between cognition and the will may best be understood by focussing on the attitudinal change which it induces: the more one becomes aware of the inevitability of existential decisions in thinking as in any other *engagement,* the greater becomes the experienced weight of responsibility in finding oneself ever more compellingly referred to Truth as the never definable and yet, as we saw, never questionable—how could something be questioned without the question having reference to Truth? Truth, the only possible horizon of orientation for a decision of such magnitude and the common source of both ontology and ethics,[21] becomes the goal of volition itself: by an act of existential break-through that involves both aspects of phenomenal experience at once, the horizon of the conation-cognition dichotomy is widened to encompass the point-in-infinity where the intentions of the two concepts merge into one meaning. It is only in accordance with this ultimate invalidity of the gap between them that the experience of decisiveness—in the decision with which cognitive thought must necessarily start—becomes the stronger the *less* the unauthentic self, the person as a public subject, the ego, is involved in the decision: the *more* the decision involves an emphaticness of self-transcendent conviction, the more axiomatic and fruitful will cognition (*qua theory*) become.

Such a widening of the existential horizon reveals innumerable truths that before could hide from sight. The strict co-relativity with which typically horizon-blocked modes-of-being of man respond to psychological theories that generalize what holds true only for them is another case in point; the more explanatoriness they claim, the more telling that evidence. Psychoanalysis took off from a study of the impulsive unspontaneous, the hysteric personality, and we cannot help but notice how the actual immanentism of this self-observing, self-objectifying, self-manipulating existence-form, its deliberate and sterile preoccupation with the self, is reflected in the psychoanalytic image of the human person with its structural division into a perceiving and deliberating consciousness and a perceived and administered, "irrational" sphere of animalic conations: the very source of humanness in man, his *spirit* as manifested by such elementary states as enthusiasm, shakenness, devotion, enchantment, and dread, remains as ununderstood and unaccounted for in Freud's doctrine as in any but substitution forms it is missing from the experience-range of the original model.[22] Or we may inquire into John Dewey's consummation theory of aesthetic experience, which places aesthetic experience on a par with other need-fulfillments of the organism, such as food-intake.[23] The doctrine by-passes the entire gamut of relationships between existence and time: any inquiry into the phenomenal structure of either type of experience reveals that in organismic intake experiences, existence, according to its factual and acute self-definition, *is* a purely momentary state of the body in a purely momentary world; accordingly, no time-pervadingness of the experience becoming phenomenal, the person here exists as a nothing-but-spatial self (body) in a nothing-but-spatial world (phenomenalized as mere *materials* for the intake). In aesthetic, as in all spiritually oriented experience, contrariwise, time-pervadingness, that is, time*less*ness in the sense of an irrelevance of the momentary, turns out to be the determinant phenomenal characteristic, and accordingly spatiality is neutralized as well; neither—on the subject side of the experience—does the person's own body-sphere, nor, on the object side, the mere factualness, for example, of a painting (the painting as a mere spatially extended *thing*) show any phenomenal relevance in true art experience that would allow of the determination of this experience-type as a consummatory one. But does that make Dewey's theory inexplicable historically? Such phenomena as the attitude of the typical collector, by which art, in western civilization only a few centuries ago the most self-evidently living manifestation of the being-human, as deeply interwoven into the lives of the people as into the traditions of craftsmanship, has been turned into an isolated special sphere of production and interest and an object of much cultivated and deliberate emoting, are evidence for the fact that consummatory modes of art experience likely to respond to Dewey's thesis have indeed become more frequent in our day.

Returning to the cognition-conation theory already expounded, we can finally not help noticing an even further-reaching implication of the conceptual *whirl* in which man at first must encounter himself upon realizing at once the decision-nature of theoretical knowledge and thought and the conviction-nature of such decisions themselves and of the values that guide them. Not only is the gap in psychology finally overcome, but another existentialist reversal becomes due if once more we contemplate the notion of the being-in-the-world *qua* world-apperception. As long as this notion of apperception retains any implication of arbitrariness, as though it meant a standing in apposition of a psyche-object to a "reality" only thereby becoming *its* object, we not only have still not ventured beyond the Cartesian subjectivity and its objectivism but remain quite unable either to reconcile the differentiality of subjective cognitive claims with the axiomatic character of what orients them *qua* claims to truth; or, for that matter, this entire notion of subjectivity with what was found to implement it in the concrete, the "having" the world as conscious, and with what, in turn, was found constituent to the notion of world, its necessary phenomenal givenness to *someone*. Another step becomes necessary to overcome these difficulties: the work of exploding Cartesian dualism cannot rest at the point of a mere exposure of the nihilistic implications of the subject-object split as such, but must extend to calling into question the traditional distinction between being and thinking. At this point the necessity with which existentialist reflection springs from phenomenology becomes visible: if being no longer is primarily an object of thought but the horizonlike premise for the possibility of thought as such—if thought is itself a manifestation of being—must we continue to accept in science the scientifically never examined, always already presupposed notion of it as though it were a kind of behavioral adjustment activity of the organism? Phenomenological analysis refutes this notion: a thought *occurs* to the subject, and however much he may "systematize" his thinking, he continues to depend with every step of this activity on the necessity for truths to be intuited, which in the concrete of his experience means *to reveal themselves to him*. In a fundamental ontological interpretation of consciousness, therefore, the original order of experiencing discussed before in this text[24] is restored, a thought no longer is an event on the subject's part but is an event on the part of its own content, and the difficulties surrounding the notion of world-apperceptions that we noticed are overcome by one bold stroke of existentialist reflection: realities are not inasmuch as the subjects are who experience and think them—a derivation which could never account either for their being realities or for the being of the subjects—but vice versa, the subjects *are* inasmuch as *being,* in entering the horizon of time, enfolds its all-encompassing truth in multiple world-apperceptions, world *projects,* which are implemented as existences. In its *projects*—literally, *throws*—being throws existences into the realm of temporality.

The direction for developing an existential analytic suitable for the purposes of differential psychology is set thereby: the central tendency or idea of an existence, that particular existence as a project of being and as that project's own perpetual effort at world-realization, must be worked out. This finally implements the postulation arrived at with the end of our first chapter, according to which phenomenological psychology must strive for an essential account of the most comprising contexts of experience in their most axiomatic constancies discoverable. But how is this specification meanwhile attained to be implemented? How—already at this point finding ourselves drawn into a web of existentialist conceptions—can we hope for any consistency in applying the insights we have won to the aims of a science of man without first casting a glance at extentialism in its doctrinal cohesion? Much of its thought already had to be unfolded in exposing as fully as possible the *hysteron proteron* of objectivism in psychology and following up the inner necessity with which, once phenomenology is freely allowed its way, the challenge of the ever more radical questions is encountered. Much of it, in turn, can unfold itself only when those of its implications that more specifically concern the clinician are studied. But a fundamentally new way of thought of such incisiveness as the philosophy of existence must be discerned first of all in its own context, to protect its applications in science from the threat of facile misunderstandings, and no doubt, then, is left about the next step in our inquiry: while anything even close to an exhaustive discussion of existentialist thought would exceed our purposes by far, a separate brief presentation of its tenets may no longer be delayed.

NOTES

1. S. Freud, *Totem and Taboo*, p. 857, (in *Basic Writings of S. Freud*).
2. S. Freud, "Psychoanalytic Notes upon an Autobiographical Account of a Case of Paranoia (Dementia Praecox)", in *Coll. Works*, vol. 3, p. 453.
3. M. Heidegger, *Vom Wesen der Wahrheit*, Frankfurt a. Main, 1943.
4. Hans Reichenbach, *The Rise of Scientific Philosophy*, Berkeley, California, 1953, pp. 272-3.
5. It is to be noted that the functionalist, in order to implement this proposition, must be able to account for processes in animate nature on the basis of his ultimate conception of physical causality itself, i.e., in consistent terms of statistical probability. As shown by Dessauer (*Die Teleologie in der Natur*, 1949) the peculiarity of biologic events is that they nowhere either contradict in the least degree physical causality nor are sufficiently determined by it to account for their specificity (their particular, only "finalistically" comprehensible event-directions). On the other hand, their amassing of understandably related events in a distinctly purposive selection which, physicalistically, is never "impossible", to be sure, but about as probable mathematically as a spontaneous warming up

of one half of a body of water of homogeneous temperature at the expense of the other, shatters in principle all attempts at a theoretical account of them in any terms of a functionalistic probabilism. Attempts at solving the problem of a physicalistic explanation of organicity through further developments of applied quantum theory are in progress (Schrödinger and others) but involve changes in the parameter concepts of physics itself which far transcend the limits of a mechanistic world picture. In brief, while *classic* causality is valid throughout and without loopholes, in its appearance at least in organic nature it interpenetrates with event-orders of a quite different—irreducibly meaning-centered—kind.

6. E. Brunswik, *Op. cit.*, p. 60.

7. Friedrich Dessauer, *Die Teleologie in der Natur.* 1949.

8. Cf. Martin Heidegger, *Vom Wesen des Grundes*, Frankfurt a.M., 1929, p. 40. "Der Überstieg zur Welt ist die Freiheit selbst."

9. It goes without saying that the present argument is to be understood as a mere preliminary attempt to sketch the possibility of a genetic theory which might translate the essence of the being-man according to radical phenomenological inspection into the language of biological objectivism; the truth of the inspection itself, being more immediately empiric than any genetic theory *can* be, does not, of course, depend on it, any dependency relation here rather implying in an inverse direction.

10. Cf. Martin Heidegger. *Vom Wesen der Wahrheit*, Frankfurt a. M., 1943, p. 12: "Das Sich-freigeben für eine bindende Richte ist nur möglich als *Freisein* zum Offenbaren eines Offenen. Solches Freisein zeigt auf das bisher unbegriffene Wesen der Freiheit. Die Offenständigkeit des Verhaltens als innere Ermöglichung der Richtigkeit gründet in der Freiheit. *Das Wesen der Wahrheit ist die Freiheit.*"

11. K. Goldstein, "The Effect of Brain Damage on the Personality", *Psychiatry*, 1952, 15, 245–60. See also the same author's *After-Effects of Brain Injuries in War*, 1942.

12. Cf. *op. cit.*, p. 256.

13. Cf. A. Angyal, *op. cit.*, pp. 243–55.

14. Cf. pp. 113–17.

15. Either of them presenting him with arrangements of that-which-is; contrariwise, the "causal" certitude he is after is contained not in anything-that-is, but in *being*.

16. Cf. pp. 204–05.

17. Cf. D. Krech's lone voice at the 1949 symposium on the relations between personality and perception, "Notes toward a Psychological Theory", *J. Personal.*, 1949, 18, 66–87, esp. p. 82.

18. S. Freud, *Totem and Taboo*, p. 857.

19. For a more ample discussion of this impossibility, cf. S. Koppel, "An Inquiry into the Validity of the Concept of Projection", unpublished dissertation, 1954.

20. Cf. pp. 18–19.

21. Cf. M. Heidegger, *Was ist Metaphysik?* 1949, and *Über den Humanismus*, 1947.

22. The time does not seem ripe for an investigation of the possibility that the more recently observed relative statistical drop in classic conversion cases in better-situated big city populations (in spite of a constant spreading of hysterical personality patterns and hysterical tendencies in twentieth century culture) may be attributable to the greater facility which psychoanalysis as an attitudinal mass-fashion has provided to replace the soma as an object of manipulatory self-experience by an objectified psyche, itself assuming that role.

23. The problem may seem to be made more complex by the evident truth that "food intake" of the cultured cuisine—and other intake experiences—may be differentiated in the direction of aesthetic experience. But to the extent to which this is the case, such experiences cease to be merely consummatory in the Deweyan sense. Already at the most primitive stages of such differentiation, no one but the objectifying scientist of man, and even he only theoretically, will refer to meals as *intakes*.

24. Cf. p. 22.

PART TWO

The Spectre of Nothingness and the Janus Face of Reflection

CHAPTER 5

Origins and Themes of Existentialism—The Condition of Man in Our Age—The Problem of Time—Some Principal Features of Heidegger's Fundamental Ontology—Dread and Care and Their Fundamental-Ontological Implications—Being and the Naught—Existence as Being-toward-Death and as Resolution—The Ambiguities of Self-Transcendentness—Freedom and Determinacy—The Misleadingness of Categories—Being and Having—The Whirl of Self-Objectification—Existences as World Projects—The Place of the Therapist.

THE CRISIS OF KNOWLEDGE AS A RESULT OF THE expansion of knowledge in only one dimension of the cognitive quest has been analyzed. In its earlier appearance, as crisis of philosophy, it is rapidly on the rise ever since Kant's destruction of traditional metaphysics which according to Heidegger's analysis had preceded modern science in the tacit nihilism of objectifying world accounts. Then, during the whole nineteenth and early twentieth centuries, the fires of that crisis smolder; what prevents them from breaking into flame is the stunning success of research in physical nature in providing man with the tools for an exploitation and manipulation of that-which-is (extensio) as domain of his will, mistaken at this stage to imply also a satisfaction of the original *why* in him, of the quest for ultimate knowledge, the unanswerable part of which one increasingly relegates to futile speculation; since ontology, in misunderstanding its own fundamental concern with *being* as a search after the totality

of that-which-is—the search of metaphysics—only brings forth speculative accounts of what science seems to be able to account for without
recourse to such idleness, that attitude of the progressive mind in
fact seems supported by plenty of good reason. Signs of a growing
discomfort of man in the midst of what corresponds to this self-misunderstanding of his quest for certitude: his ever more utilitarian
civilization, begin to abound in the later part of that century. Significantly, as the first one in the history of the West, that century knows
no form of its own, no "style"; instead, it indulges in a more or less
imitative, more or less empathizing cultivation of by-gone modes-of-
being, historicism; in this process, objectification begins to extend its
claim to the axioms of existence, the "values"; as Heidegger aptly
states,[1] one begins to talk of values as such only in the course of the
nineteenth century, that is, after what one talks of has begun to become
shaky. The idea that objectification of the fundaments of existence is
only a form of their own disintegration presupposes a conception of
thought according to which thought is manifested by the contents
thought of. This existentialist conception does not as yet occur to the
first radical inquirer into historicism, Nietzsche. Instead, Nietzsche
bases his criticism of the nineteenth century attitude named on its
evident effects on the will: the sureness of direction of the will, its
spontaneity, the innocence of living, all these powers, self-evident in
man only as long as he continues to exercise them, are seen weakened
by historicism as the sterile and self-paralyzing form which the human
spirit, once it has been misled by objectivism, inevitably must assume
in encountering itself in its own past creations. Though Nietzsche's
analysis fails to penetrate to the core of the matter, it nails down an
essential constellational law of existence, and in doing so anticipates,
in dealing with phenomena on the social-historic plane, what individually and clinically applies no less to the morbid self-consciousness
of many of our typically psychoneurotic.

The crisis of knowledge is thus from the very start a crisis of man's
Dasein. The interweaving in this crisis of being and knowledge escapes
the grasp of naturalism, for no analogy between human and animal
existence can provide any place or explanation for the powerful role
in it of the notion of *truth*. The crisis in the nineteenth century, in
either of its aspects, is seen only by a very few radically independent
and prophetic minds—Hölderlin, Kierkegaard, Dostoyevski, Nietzsche

—able to look through the fallacy of the objectivistic claim, to discern the "growing desert" (Nietzsche), and to predict the twentieth century convulsions and catastrophes to come. Once, however, the Cartesian *whirl* has fully engulfed its own source—subjectivity—the crisis must manifest itself increasingly in the typical experiences of the average contemporary: man's spectacular gains in calculative and manipulatory power, finally changing his own self-image into one of just another object for this power to exploit, cannot but be accompanied by a loss of powers both more silent and more fundamental, possession of which the entire scientific and technological expansion had unknowingly taken for granted.

On the wider plane of historic evolution, this peculiar loss of tranquil self-certainty, this *mass anxiety*—so typical of our present industrialized culture—resembles the *reality loss* in the clinically schizophrenic in one conspicuous point: here as there, the nature of that which is lost becomes discernible only when the loss has become a fact. Whatever is most self-evident, or with the existentialist term, horizonlike in human consciousness, submits to the same rule: any fundaments of man's concrete existence, such as his true position in history, would not be fundamental at all *if* they readily occurred to him as objects of perception and reflective self-consciousness, as the "pale cast of thought". The reason for this is simple: since these subject-object dualities, perception and reflection, derive their sureness from the source of spontaneity—*being*—they can never call the being they spring from into question without its immediacy (spontaneity) getting lost in the act. Attempting to formulate the major implication of this condition of man, we rediscover—as all existentialists do— the forgotten supremacy of identity over duality at the basis of knowledge; or, straining this insight through a reflection of what identity means, what we rediscover is the supremacy of *being* over *being object,* for this very notion of identity would not be so foundational if it did not tacitly presuppose the even more elemental one of being.[2] But does not existentialism contradict its own tenet concerning the fundamentalness of being by the very act of turning being into an object of reflection? While its message is a determined exhortation of man to return, from the fallacy of a self-objectifying split in conscious experience, nowhere allowing of authentic existence any more, to the identity of the *I am*, that message itself springs from reflection.

But with what right can it have its origin there? Existentialism would seem to make itself guilty of the very existential untruth that historically it rose against.

But this movement has never been opposed to what it depends upon as a philosophy, reflection *per se*; its attack which, on the contrary, restores the sovereignty of *spontaneous* thought as a manifestation of being in front of an objective world of facts, is directed solely against the usual arbitrary and superficial substitute modes of pseudo-reflective thought, which in by-passing man's immediate awareness for the sake of a spurious objectivity (motivationally still to be studied more closely) only succeeds in blocking the authentic horizon of his own situation from his sight. This non-intrinsic reflection, as Heidegger has shown, is only a historic station along the tortuous path of the *logos* which man as a thinker is fated to travel; it would not lead to his radical remembrance in the end, his rediscovery of being as the forgotten ground of thought itself, if its first objectifying turns would not take man the thinker out of the context of being (encountered as the context of that-which-is) into the naught of self-consciousness.[3] Without seeking the compelling source of thought in being, with being thus "coming into its own" only in human reflection: without, for example, going behind logic in accounting for the *strictness*[4] of logic, existentialist philosophy neither would ever have circumnavigated the Husserlian cliff of the transcendental ego nor been able to interpret consciousness once more in the affirmative. Yet it is in its affirmative interpretation of reflective thought which most strikingly distinguishes it from the vitalistic and irrationalistic metaphysics of Bergson and Klages with which it is still habitually confounded by mechanists, even though it opposes the former no less uncompromisingly than the latter. This error can, to some extent, be explained from the Nietzschean part of the existentialist heritage, but exactly Nietzsche's power metaphysics is what the existentialists discard. Their attitude toward Kierkegaard is hardly less critical, notwithstanding their acknowledged debt to him: they discern the undissolved bonds of "dialectic" speculation that still tie the thought of this mentor of existentialism to the world of ideas he opposed in his day—the absolutism of historic time (*becoming*) of the then powerful metaphysics of Hegel.

In either of the two currents of thought to which the immediate philosophic antecedence of existentialism can be traced, radical subjectivism (Kierkegaard and Nietzsche) and Husserl's phenomenology, the idea of the primacy of being is present already. In a state of inarticulate diffusion in both these currents, its genesis in early phenomenology is the reverse of what it is in the thinking of the radical subjectivists: Husserl's theorizing, starting out where that most unauthentic world account, neo-Kantianism, had left off, comes to imply that primacy as a tacit postulation that it cannot utter as yet—as it has restricted itself to a pseudo-horizon set for it by the fictitious ego of pure logic. But once Husserl's method is taken over by the bolder thought of Heidegger, it is uttered almost immediately: existentialism, which is born at this point, recognizes no restrictions for thought other than those which his being-in-the-world articulates for man. Contrariwise, philosophizing in both Kierkegaard and Nietzsche begins with an inkling of the substantiality of being. But what is substance? Is it merely a comprising, however hidden, attribute of everything-that-is? Neither Kierkegaard nor Nietzsche yet abandons this traditional notion: their eyes have no reason to penetrate its fallacy, for the most destructive implications of the objectivism they oppose are still unrevealed in their time. Hegelian metaphysics, "in the shadow of which", according to Heidegger's verdict, Kierkegaard's "entire thought still is moving altogether too much", therefore not only provides the central objective for the Danish theologian's attack (who is the first clearly to discern that *aesthetic* character of all-out objectivism to which our study has referred before) upon the *Zeitgeist* of his time; it also sets the scenery for that attack, whereas Nietzsche, reflecting for the first time upon the Western mind as a whole phenomenon of history, is far too deeply drawn into its immanent tensions and conflicts (only ripening *through* his thought) to recognize the mainsprings of all Western metaphysics. In Heidegger's interpretation, Nietzsche's philosophy—which Nietzsche himself, only seeing Platonism and its like as metaphysical, understands as a counter-movement to metaphysics—remains stuck, like any mere antithesis, in the essence of what it opposes.

The solutions these two thinkers provide therefore cannot solve the dilemma of modern western man with its ever more naked clashes between his being and his knowing, existence and awareness, but only sharpen its acuity: Kierkegaard offering his followers a "leap" into faith to escape the "fear and trembling" of a nothingness that with the advances of scientific objectivity "flattening out" everything

authentic in man is seen growing in him like an all-devouring desert—
as though such a leap could ever be authentic, a spontaneous act of
faith ever be achieved by a deliberate self-coercive act that first silences
the cognitive self in the faithful-to-be[5]; Nietzsche overcoming metaphysics by pushing metaphysical thought to its ultimate consequence
of nihilism in his absolutization of the quest for power as an alleged
causa sui to which, wholly in the fashion of late nineteenth century
determinism, the entire orientative side of existence is reduced. Yet,
while Kierkegaard's philosophy, serving him only as a support for his
pragmatic ends as a writer of religious pamphlets, remains an un-
finished structure, whereas Nietzsche's ends up with a renewed non-
fundamental ontology, the *situation* of thought at this stage is already
the typically modern one. Thought, passionately bent on "warning"
and "protest", on smashing its way through the anonymous niceties
of everybody's notions to existential truth in its unembellished
authenticity, is already existentialistic in its style and in the direction
of its query in both Kierkegaard and Nietzsche, even though the
teachings of neither reaches to the destination of that query. Existentialistic, even though Nietzsche fails to follow it through, is his discovery
that we have no conception of being other than in analogy with living
(an objectivistic reversal, of course, of their predicative relation).
Existentialistic is his opposition to conformity, complacency, and
routine (the morals of the herd); existentialistic his notion—which,
as an ultimate attainment of his thought rather than the starting point
for radical reflection, becomes the basis for his immanentism and
relativism—of an unseverability both of the "values" and of truth
itself from the authentic experience of *somebody*. Existentialistic is
Kierkegaard's recall of modern "cipher man", the abstract *individual*
of modern societal doctrines, to the truth of his existing as a *person*;
his rediscovery of original dread as a phenomenon testifying against
the absolutistic claims inherent in the aesthetic attitude of both Hegel's
all-objectifying metaphysics and of the objectivism of science; and his
most fruitful hierarchization, on the basis, of existence according to
its levels of compelling *engagement* (the aesthetic, the ethical, and the
religious). In an age saturated with objectivism in philosophy as much
as ours is in science, Kierkegaard even more distinctly than Nietzsche
after him takes up motifs of thought which in the history of western
philosophy had only played sporadic roles before (for example, in

Augustine and Pascal, and though nineteenth century philologists
and historians still completely miss out on their presence there, in the
pre-Socratics)—to unfold again in full only in the thinkers of our time.[6]

From its inception, existentialist thought, in centering its focus on
man's situation according to its only plausible cognitive constituent,
his own direct awareness, finds itself referred to the problem of the
constitution of *time*, which in its first and still unauthentic version as
problem of the relationship between inner and clock time had been
broached by Bergson. But Bergson's philosophy of time does not
exceed the limits of a descriptive psychology of time perception: in
defending the primacy of inner over mathematical time, it retains
the latter as an involuntarily implied premise, as the tacit background
against which inner time is allowed to appear as a separate and special
intrapsychic datum, one not to be accounted-for in terms of our time
measurements (all applying spatial rather than temporal criteria to
time) but not comprehensible in its original phenomenal link with
conventional time either. Kierkegaard had recognized the peculiar
significance of the phenomenon circumscriptively referred to as *this
instant* (*Augenblick*) for the interpretation of existence, but had not
abandoned the conventional conception of time (with its notion of
eternity as infinity and of the *now* as a point) in determining the
this instant as an intra-temporal phenomenon, with temporality itself
remaining beyond his scope of reflection. Jaspers, in his early *Psychologie der Weltanschauungen* had first discerned the *this instant* as an
unfathomable paradox: if time is determined as a flow, no fixating
this (of any instant) has any basis in the structure of time. The *this
instant* thus implies a beyond-time phenomenally, while at the same
time hiding the implication behind its "obvious", that is, categorial,
intra-temporality, so that its conceptualization alienates it from itself.
Again in his *General Psychopathology*, Jaspers uses the expression
quer zur-Zeit (perpendicular to time) in referring to the non-temporal
(axiomatic) sources of the notion of reality, as reality appears according to the constitution of any unbroken experience of it, that is, according to faith in any of its forms.[7] Why, we may ask, unless existence
refers to a *beyond time* according to the phenomenal origin of the
notion of being, should it find itself referred to timelessness in encountering the essence of reality? With the insight that the concept

of reality implies the timeless in its origin, being and time move into a constellation of polar apposition.

Only once this apposition is disconcerned as inescapable, the enigma of the meaning of *being* moves fully into sight. Our ordinary time conception is instrumental in obscuring the meaning of being even as a *problem*—but what kind of a problem is this? To Heidegger's reflection in his principal work,[8] significantly titled, being reveals itself as the original but traditionally forgotten concern of all western metaphysics: the metaphysical quest, in misunderstanding itself, in habitually by-passing being (*Sein*) and replacing it by what only (and more and more remotely as objectification proceeds) implies being, the spatio-temporal expanse of that-which-*is* (*Seiendes*) and of what the mind can present to itself in an object-like fashion and hence in anology with that-which-is (*Vorgestelltes*; for example, the totality of *Seiendes* as metaphysics conceives of it), has constructed non-fundamental ontologies throughout its long history. This history Heidegger sees as fated toward modern nihilism from the start; the fundamental ontology he proposed thus from the very beginning was designed not only as a hermeneutic reclaiming of the "ground" but as a "destruction" of the history of all non-fundamental ontologies, that is, of metaphysics. Man's return from the nothingness in front of which his purely willful subjectivity—calculating and manipulating that-which-is and finally himself as one-who-is—has placed him, is conditional on such a readiness to remember being: without his willingness to listen back to the origins in him of the *I am*, he not only must dangle precariously over the bottomless naught of his ever flatter and more anonymous existence, but is delivering himself up to an utter and unprecedented peril.

With this fundamental interpretation of the situation of modern western man, Heidegger finds himself in close agreement with the mood and insights of existential philosophy as a whole. Most akin to his thought seems that of the French existentialist, Gabriel Marcel, whose reflection parallel's Heidegger's in its focal concern with the meaning of being. This concept Marcel sets off against that of the objective order by ascribing to man's relations with the latter the character of having; Marcel's emphasis on the distinction between being and having, in turn, is echoed by similar observations of Jaspers and Sartre and by Heidegger's poignant insight into what continually blocks being from our sight, the dead utensility character of much of what psychology would call our behavioral environments. Without objectivism being geared to a specific characteristic of existence (the power interest), modern technology as the form which science assumes in becoming historically effective would remain utterly incomprehensible; for example, if the technological slant of objectivism would inhere in the idea of science as such, it could never be understood why a more advanced technology failed to spring from the already highly sophisticated mathematics of the Greeks; the failure does not imply lack of intelligence on the part of the most spontaneously intellectual people in history, but only of cleverness, that is, of the readiness to outrage against the sacred order of being by resorting to the idea of exploiting that-which-is. As this sacred order weakens, such exploitation becomes conceivable; in the form of a conception of *Archimedean points*, it finally occurs in the Hellenistic period, but the impulses of Greek thought are already far too weakened at this stage to allow of its fructification. Yet, just as our analysis of *explanatoriness* revealed an impossibility to sever this mode of the cognitive quest from its moorings in understanding (intuiting), the pragmatic concern in the service of which explanatoriness operates in subjecting the fact world cannot do without an ultimate orientation to being—which, in objectifying judgments, still appears in the definitive use of the *is*.

While Heidegger links technology with the oblivion into which the truth of being has "retired", he distances himself from all romanticizing critics of this development by pointing out that technology itself is a "manifestation of truth" (*Gestalt der Wahrheit*), deriving its essence from a "destined mode of revealing that-which-is" and hence brought forth—since no arbitrary decision of man can be made responsible for technology as a historic destiny—by the hidden "history of being". It is thus a necessary stage which being has to traverse on its historic path and which must be followed by its ultimate home-coming in man through man's effort—to be aroused by his experience of the unthinkable present state of that-which-is—to rediscover being and find his way back into its truth.[9] It is not enough for this end to lament about symptoms; such lamenting is part and parcel of the "present state of that-which-is". Anxiety *must* be misunderstood as a fear by him who has it. As a fear it requires an object. The vestiges of technology, the atomic bomb, for example, may lend themselves

readily to such misunderstanding. Modern man in his anxiety is
threatened by the bomb as killing machinery; he does no discern in
it the manifestations of his own alienation from the order and truth
of being.[10] But the essence of the ultimate peril which he encounters in
his dread this superficial interpretation still conceals from him, for
even the conventional reply that death is the object of anxiety evades
the issue. What is death? Known only as an objective event that is
seen to happen to others, what anxiety means by it is inevitably *my
death*. As the *my death*, it not only is not known, it is the negation,
as of being, thus also of knowledge, and nothingness itself, the *no-thing*,
therefore remains the "object" (the phenomenal content) of anxiety.
Anxiety, its objectlessness notwithstanding, nevertheless is experienced
by man in such a manner that whatever is encountered in it (its
phenomenal reference) becomes just as real for him as do objects.
The objectivistic world account in its claim to present the mind with
the totality of the *real* is called into question by this fact; but
what questions the claim even more is the peculiar shakiness it imparts
to man's knowledge of what *is* even means. This shakiness, as we soon
shall see, becomes manifest in the source of our abstract concept of
anxiety, the phenomenon of *dread*.

Heidegger's early explorations in *Being and Time* center on the
main attributes of what he terms the thrownness (*Geworfenheit*) of
existence—*dread* and *care*. These, the two fundamental conditions
wherein existence encounters itself whenever daring such encounter,
lay the ground for the fundamental ontology he envisages, and dread
and care testify to being as that which throws existence into the
horizon of time by exposing man to the negation of being, the naught.
From the very first, Heidegger's thought diverges from that of all
other existentialists by focussing on the primacy of the problem of
being, rather than of "existence" as a mere descriptive one. A mere
description of "man's actual situation" (in Sartre's sense) must arbitrarily choose an unaccounted-for subjectivity as the priming point
for ontologies alleged to be phenomenological; but does describing
one's situation include the one who does the describing? The "subject"
in Sartre's subjectivity cannot but remain undetermined, and Sartre's
reflective search for the pre-reflective unity of self and world still
leaves it so since it merely replaces the Cartesian *ego cogito* by an
absolutized Husserlian consciousness arising with limitless freedom

from "nowhere". The self-transcendentness of consciousness toward its contents is seen by Sartre, but he wholly fails to recognize the primal phenomenal presence in consciousness of an awareness of *being* as the wherefrom of thought; the absolutely *first* transcendence which consciousness implies is not "in front" but already "behind" it. The primacy of the meaning of being which *Being and Time* therefore demonstrates first, is contended by Heidegger on both ontological and ontic grounds: inasmuch as no knowledge about anything-that-is can be valid without a prior exploration of the authentic mode-of-being of that immediate presence of the meaning of being which the *is* of our objective judgments conceals, a satisfactory solution of the problem of being becomes the condition for the legitimacy of both sciences and ontologies. In turn, the awareness of being *as* a problem is a constituent potential of one kind of existence, *human Dasein,* pointing to an analytic of *Dasein* as the only way to make ontology fundamental.

This is corroborated by Heidegger's subsequent outline of his proposition for a "destruction of the history of ontology", the central idea of which we already have sketched, and is implemented by the inquiries to follow. Their first objective is a closer determination of the methodological requirements of the task and of the being-in-the-world as the unitary topic it encounters; the latter is highlighted by a demonstration, wholly ruinous to the concept of world according to Descartes, of the contingency of the phenomenon of space on an *a priori* spatiality of existing.[11] In further chapters Heidegger first undertakes to illuminate such constitutive phenomena of the being-in-the-world as the conventional *I* (ego)—discerned as the primal instrumentality through which being, as the proper *who* of existence, hides itself behind a pseudo-foundational subjectivity on which the subsequent error of self-objectification, the failure of existence to obtain a hold upon itself, becomes contingent. Other such phenomena are the *being with . . .* (others), an "existential constituent of the being-in-the-world"[12] but "misunderstanding" itself as the "product" of an *a posteriori empathy*[13]; the impersonal *one* ("everybody"; the French *on,* German *man*) in orientation to which man, evading what calls him forth to his very own freedom to *be* (his conscience), establishes his position on the "outside" and hence in the *nowhere* of an implicitly projected and ultimately spurious *public* sphere (a "projection" inherent in all consciousness and comparable with the

mechanism operant in the *persona* formation of Jungian psychology) ;
the "small talk" (*Gerede*) serving the *everybody* and the self-obscuring
of being by putting at the person's continuous disposal the most facile
opportunities for a non-authentic but all the more objectively plausible account of his own situation according to always and already
evident public norms of self-comprehension; and common curiosity
as a self-deception inherent in the fate of the original *why*, which is
fooled by the mere extensivity of the world (*qua* spatial and quasi-
spatial infinities) into a policy of mere wandering, of gliding from
remote to ever more remote appearances, without daring to penetrate
a single one toward a full illumination of its own mode of being.[14]
Finally, the fundamental ambiguity characteristic of all experiential
encounters within the sphere of the social-communicative—the constitutive presence in them at once of a public mode of intersubjectivity
concealing the authentic being-with . . . and of the latter itself *in its
concealment*—is seen to imply the dread-inspiring seriousness and
decision-character of what the concealment in turn makes manifest, the
"fall" of existence (*Verfallenheit*). This term is used by Heidegger in
a double sense—which, as all such double senses of words, points to
one original meaning image; it connotes at once decadence, the being-
toward-death, and a *falling out* (of itself) and falling prey to a world
governed by the *everybody* and the "categories" (literally: common-
places) of the *everyday*. In its first radical self-encounter, existence
thus finds itself in a state of thrownness; of being thrown into a whirl
generated by its fatedness perpetually to be torn loose from its own
moorings in being and to be seized upon by the naught of self-
objectification. Self-objectification in this most elementary experience
requires no special act of the mind; it is subtly, unnoticeably suggested already by everybody's determinations of man's self inasmuch as
these are capable of creating make-believe notions of the what-am-I
that offer themselves as most plausible substitutes for the authenticity
that was by-passed, the *Truth* that was lost.

But the ambiguity of existence, by imparting an awareness to man
that at once it *is* his being and yet continually tears him from its
ground, implies being as the absolute contradiction to what it implies
also, its own untenableness (finiteness, temporality, dread). Existence
therefore cannot rest at this point in the sense of a mere passive
acceptance of this thrownness, fatedness, toward the unauthentic and

toward death; man, as both a project of being and a projector of world can accept himself only by not accepting himself as an object; a fleeting particle of that-which-is. The primal knowledge of which we spoke must therefore be seen as being what intrinsically it becomes in the medium of any *open* self-encounter of man, a challenge: the call of conscience (which this knowledge is) can neither be objectified at all, nor even be translated into words. The paradoxical silence of this call, which is what makes it so telling, refuses to be claimed by this or that definable content of the person's world relationships in their mere factualness (objectivity). From the latter no *ought* that conscience ever conveys could be derived; silence cannot be said to *hide*, but on the contrary, to *be* its message. Existence calls *itself* in conscience (Heidegger) and the call is heard by anyone who has an *ear* for its silence, anyone ready to be received back into what calls here—being. The "decision", "resolution", which the call when heeded arouses, is not to be the master of one's fate in the mistaken sense of a mere subjective *willing*; a mere subjective willing, while in actuality isolating man further, is capable only of nurturing illusions of power. What is meant by the call (and alone may still allow of a triumph over death and guilt) is on the contrary a completely open *willingness* (self-dedication to the immediately sensible order of being which the will's arbitrary subjectivism by-passes) in accepting the imperative-to-be which death and guilt, in connoting a loss *of* being, a being lost *by* being, imply—not as an alternative to *them* (for there is none) but to that loss: in man's freedom to be what most authentically he *is* (*sein eigenstes Seinkönnen*) and to which his conscience calls him whenever it does call, there inheres, like the *going-to-die-my-death*, also the *being-guilty* as a modality of all existence. Guilt, as the elemental presence to man of his severance from being, is factual before all facts; and a facing-up acceptance of that factualness of one's own guilt,[15] rather than either an unauthentic objectivism in deterministically talking oneself out of it, or a shirking avoidance of decisions, is thus the real message of the voice of conscience. The imperative-to-be which the silence of the call spells out is manifested in everyday life in a silent and constant tendency of *Dasein* that Heidegger characterizes as its *running-ahead-of-itself* and in the end defines as the very being of existence as such (existence as being-toward-death), the phenomenon of *care*; an analysis, in turn, of the existential structure

wherein care—as the key to an understanding of the temporality of
Dasein, on its part found to differ radically from the objective successivity of past, present, and future—is encountered, meets with the
phenomenon of dread as the most foundational of all. The characteristic
of a foundation is that it sustains what conceals it; *foundational* always
implies both characteristics at once. The ordinary and commonplace
notions of existential self-understanding, oriented toward whatever
public norms and slogans are available for an interpretation of the
fact "that one dies some day", must by-pass dread, and yet, it is in
the hidden image of death, in this peculiar "presence of an absence",
as which death is dreaded so much that the dread is fled from and
obscured from sight, that the very being of *Dasein* as a problem unto
itself is pre-designed.

   In his determination of dread as an encounter with the *naught*
Heidegger is preceded by such thinkers as Pascal and Kierkegaard;
his bold ontological interpretation of this finding, on the other hand,
owes more to Heracleitus and Hegel than to the direct forebears of
existentialism in a stricter sense of thematic lineage. Since the inquiries
of *Being and Time*, in reaching out for the goal of a fundamental
ontology, apply to this task an unprecedented analyticalness in enucleating the essences of such ordinary and therefore believed to be
known phenomena as the "I", the "thing", utensility, boredom, anguish,
guilt, and countless others, they in effect achieve the first phenomenono-
logical psychology of existence. The inevitability with which the subsequent explorations, by anthropological scientists, of existence in its
subject-to-subject differentiality had to base themselves on the results
of this feat becomes understandable even from a superficial reading of
Heidegger's searching text; with all its difficulties, its impact on the
human sciences was felt in Europe before his later writings supplied
long desired commentaries. Considering the central and generally
acknowledged role which anxiety plays in most states of personality
that psychopathology deals with, the necessity to present Heidegger's
treatment of it in as distinct an abstract as possible refers us to a
number of accesses of understanding in his work. Most of these are
contained in *Being and Time* (1927) and *What is Metaphysics?*
(1930–1943); the most poignant condensation, on the other hand, of
a great many elements of Heideggerian thought basic to a proper

understanding of his theory of dread is found in his more recent pamphlet that incisively sets off his thought from Sartre's.

The *Letter on Humanism* (1947) is a reply to a letter from Jean Beaufret which had raised the issue of the engagement (action) character of thought as implying a demand for a rather undefined "activism" as the result and justification of thinking. Heidegger here first clarifies how "action", which is superficially known only as an "effecting of effects" (the reality of which is assessed according to their usefulness) cannot be determined by these utilitarian *applications* of the notion of action at all. "The essence of action is bringing forth. Bringing forth means: to unfold something in accordance with what essentially it *is*, lead it to full bloom, *producere*. Brought forth, therefore, can properly speaking only be that which *is* already. Before anything-that-is *is* being. Thought implements the affinity of being to the essence of *being man*. It does not make or effect this affinity. . . . *Thought acts inasmuch as it thinks*. This action is probably the simplest and at the same time also highest because it concerns the affinity of being to man. All effective action is anchored in being and aims at that-which-is. Thought, contrariwise, *lets* itself be claimed by being in order to listen to and utter its truth. Thought is the enactment of this *letting*. Thought is *l'engagement par l'être pour l'être*. . . . Thought is not only *l'engagement dans l'action* for and through that-which-is in the sense of the realities of a present situation. Thought is *l'engagement* through and for the truth of being. The history of that truth is never past, always *to be*. The history of being sustains and determines every *condition et situation humaine*. In order for us even to learn to experience this essence of thought in its purity (and this of itself means to enact it), we must free ourselves from the technical interpretation of thinking. The beginnings of this interpretation reach back to Plato and Aristotle. . . . *Being*, in which thought is in its very own element, is given up and abandoned in the technical interpretation of thought. 'Logic', since the Sophists and Plato, has served to sanction this interpretation. One judges thought according to a norm wholly inappropriate to it. This way of judging is equivalent to an attempt to assess the nature and capacity of a fish according to his ability to live on dry land. Too long, too long already has thought been sitting there and drying up. Can one now really put the label of 'irrationalism' upon an attempt to bring thought back into its element?"[16] The content-receptive rather than content-"producing" character precisely of *productive* thought had been a discovery of the early phenomenologists; its ultimate implication—expounded before in our text—had crystallized in Heidegger's conception of thought as *an event on the part of its own content*; the *Letter on Humanism* now dissipates the last misunderstanding that, in Beaufret's (and Sartre's own) reactions to Heidegger's thought, still surrounded his notion of a "mere" receptivity of thought for being. This—masculinistic—misunderstanding continues a Kantian notion to the same effect: receptivity is mistakenly seen as *passive.*

Since authentic thought, being both the vessel and the guardian of the truth of being, is active in and through its very state of receptivity, it dwells in a sphere that comprises in one the origins of both ontology and ethics: their duality, which historically unfolds from its priming point in Greek enlightenment, is "self-evident" and, even to the most radical objectivist,[17] unbridgeable to our day precisely because of the ever-increasing distance by which modern man's thinking of the *is* and the *ought* by-passes their common root in authentic existence. In thinking the duality of ethics and ontology, the one dealing with what should be, the other with that-which-is, back to their common and tacit premise in being, a Heracleitean vista is recovered, and in its light the full extent of the cleavage between the two most famous versions of existentialism moves into sight. Heidegger's first step is a condensation of one of his fundamental tenets, according to which metaphysics—meaning any speculative system of ideas, regardless whether spiritualistic or naturalistic, about reality in its entirety—is inevitably operating with categorial images (*Vorstellungen*) of that-which-is; metaphysics thus by-passes the foundational problem of *being proper* (*Seinsfrage*) with which the metaphysical concern begins but which non-fundamental reflection conceals as soon as that problem emerges in the mind of the thinker. A purely formal concept of the *whole* lends itself to such concealment. The authentic world of the existential encounter is neither finite nor infinite, but open and all-encompassing; contrariwise, the world of the cosmologies, like any object-artifact, inevitably has the pseudo-eidetic finiteness of all objects of abstraction. A more intricate form of the concealment occurs where the unsatisfactoriness of reifying objectification for an account of existence is experienced within a context of metaphysical speculation; in this case the original metaphysical quest tends to be obscured by means of a wholly uncompelling additive attachment *to* the objective world account of just as objectified a soul, reason, intellect, or divinity. "This question"—of the truth of being and its constitutiveness for the essential nature of man—"metaphysics not only has not posed thus far. This question is inaccessible to metaphysics as metaphysics. . . . The aberration of biologism is not yet overcome in such a manner, that one piles man's soul on top of his body, a spirit on top of his soul, and existentiality on top of the spirit, and preaches louder than heretofore a high appreciation of the spiritual—to let everything then still fall back into the 'experiencing of living', with the warning that thought was disrupting the stream of life by its rigid conceptions and that the thought of *being* was a distortion of existence. That physiology and physiological chemistry can inquire into man as an organism from the standpoint of natural science does not prove that the essence of man is contained in this 'organic', that is, in the scientifically explicable soma. This is as little valid as the opinion that the essence of nature is bound up in nuclear energy. After all, it could be that nature just chooses to conceal its essence in that side which it lays open to man's technological appropriation. Just as little as the being-man consists in his being an animal organism, this inadequate determination of his essence is not removed or compensated by supplying him with an immortal soul or with the faculty of reason or with the attributes of a 'person'. Each time his essence is by-passed, and each time the same metaphysical design underlies the by-passing." [18]

Contrary to the use which the term finds in Sartre's publications, existence here is not to be understood according to what it means in scholastic tradition. It does not stand in apposition to "essence"; it is not an actuality, distinguished, as such, from its own potentiality, be the latter conceived as its idea, meaning, possibility, or whatever. All these notions objectify what they mean to connote and thereby lead away from the authentic phenomenal contents originally in their grasp. "Sartre, on the contrary, enounces the axiom of existentialism thus: Existence precedes essence. He therewith uses *existentia* and *essentia* in the connotation of metaphysics which has been saying since Plato: *essentia* precedes *existentia*. Sartre reverses this. But the reversal of a metaphysical statement remains a metaphysical statement. As this statement, it continues to be, with metaphysics, oblivious to the truth of being."[19] The essence of *Da-sein* (synonomous with existence but meaning literally *being-there*) *is its existence*: this quotation from *Time and Being,* which on the surface would appear as a tautology, is clarified by sketching anew a hermeneutic reflection on the notion of *Dasein* from the earlier work. The *da* does not imply an allocation of existence within an already "objective" space,[20] with man finding himself, as according to the Sartrean vista, tossed by an unintelligible vicissitude into the meaningless somewhere of a mute dimensional domain of "things in themselves", with only his evaluative mood concerning this fundamentally *unchanged* Cartesian situation changed from self-confidence to nausea. *Dasein,* on the contrary, means the *Sein* (being) of the *da*; means that man himself is the place where being comes into its own, its clearing—Truth. Existence, consequently, is to be thought of from the side of its meaning-origin, as a standing-*out* of being over and against itself, *ek-sistence,* in Heidegger's frequent spelling of the term. It means that, in man as the thinker of "it all", being surpasses as much as it encounters itself. Thought, as the coming-into-its-own of being, is man's own original destination (*Seinsgeschick*), a destiny into which being throws him and which determines his place among the all-things-that-are as one fundamentally undeterminable by any "objective", that is, object-comparing, applications of language. But inasmuch as man, the sole aware existent, may be oblivious both to the ground of his awareness and to the mission it imparts, this awareness in its negative aspect, as the standing-out (*ec-stasy*) of being, only takes him outside of being, into the more and more unauthentic existence of one *who has himself as his object* among other objects, who has everything only as an *ob-ject,* a "thing thrown against" him, with his own position as an individual becoming just as groundless as the being-object of the things that his arbitrary rationality subjects. The proximity of extreme terror as a documented implication of all human ecstatic experience is anything but accidental: what man encounters in the absolute dread of finding himself outside of being is the negation of being, the naught.

Nothingness being the phenomenal content of "anxiety", which in turn has a comprehensive and generally acknowledged "relation" to self-consciousness, both the experiential truth and the enormity of the psychological and psychotherapeutic implications of this insight are evident at a glance; only their precise contents are far from evident,

for exactly of the concepts "evident" here none as yet seems clear
enough, neither nothingness itself, nor "anxiety", nor "self-consciousness", and thus psychology would seem to have little to gain from the
discovery. Moreover, it would seem to remain unclear how, man being
destined to "encounter himself", he could escape his own loss of self,
that is, unless being should somehow "catch" again what it is "throwing", and finally we might ask ourselves whether, with such prospects
attached to its own most determinant characteristic—knowledge—
existence precisely as *ec-static being* (Heidegger) would not necessarily appear destined to cancel itself out. Returning to *Being and
Time,* we find, first, a demonstration of the inseparability, in the form
of an innermost (absolutely unobjectifiable) awareness on the part
of man himself, of the notions of Being and Truth. This already sheds
light on our problem, since it characterizes as untrue, or rather, as
in the untruth, any objectifying self- (as well as world-) awareness
that has severed its links with its own innermost sources of *understanding* (knowledge) sufficiently to assert the reality of the "object"
it alleges; since the assertion must be unauthentic and thus "against
itself" as an assertion, the truth which it misses is inevitably present
in it "in the negative", that is, it pursues its claim through the medium
of anxiety; in the mechanisms of neurosis, as we shall see, precisely
this is what is taking place. With the missing of one's authentic being-
in-the-world "world" itself must occur "in the untrue"; therefore *all*
objectifying notions are called into question once the return to being
has occurred to the person as an imperative of his existing qua ec-stacy.

Since *all* these notions hinge on the self-misunderstanding, obscuring
its own phenomenal structure, of *Dasein* "as the order of succession
of experienced events as they pass", the whole second half of the published part[21] of *Being and Time* is a phenomenological exploration of
the temporality of *Dasein.* Most of its clues are taken from the previous
analysis of the phenomenon of care as implying an ahead-of-itself of
existence as its most outstanding structural characteristic; of the many
results of this study, the one most important for our purposes is
Heidegger's demonstration of the experiential origin of "public"
time (with its mathematical attributes of infinity, measurability, etc.)
in an increasing differentiation and, finally, atomization of the
structure of experienced *space*: the "original world" is what objectively
we might circumscribe as an unbroken pragmatic experience-context,

comparable to the animal's instinct-locked inhesion in his environment
in everything except man's having a *hand;* indeed it is this very possession that implies a greater independence of man from his environment as a pre-given characteristic of his relation to his world. His
hand is what lends him the power to subject what he finds himself
embedded in and turn it into world (as the counter-pole to his
"sovereignty"), but world itself is at this stage *zuhanden* (at hand)
rather than *vorhanden* (before us in space, tangible, but not functionally referring to our hand; that is, factual, or, with Sartre's term,
in-itself). Yet this pragmatic context has nothing to do with a prag-
matistic attitude that examines things according to a—itself unexamined—criterion of usefulness or workability; what distinguishes it,
on the contrary, is a fundamental trust, an attitude of openness, ready
to receive the world as world. Phenomenally, this trust, as in the
unafraid infant, arises from the encompassing and everywhere meaning-
laden presence of the order of being; still holding united within its
own unreflected openness self as well as non-self, this order is the
ultimate and secure *per se.* It is this order *which is trusted*: nothing
and no one can fall out from it. Being absolutely horizonlike it is not
even seen as a horizon; no beyond, no *outside* of it can become even
thinkable. Time, at this stage, is all *Zukunft* (future; literally, that
which is coming towards) but not "future" in the usual unauthentic
and derived sense as one of the directions within an already abstracted,
dimensionalized time, but quite concretely *that-which-is-coming,* that
is, coming to be *present* in the sense of presenting itself, of coming
to be *here;* whatever has "absented" itself, in turn, is noticed only in
the negative, by the void it leaves, its absence from its customary place,
and thus the notion of the past is derived, subsequently to become
foundational to the entire mathematical conception of time.

Original time, then, runs from the future to the present; since it
precedes any possible reflection of it, since the perception of its "movement" originates as one of a *toward* the existent, he does not originally
conceive of its continuation "back" of himself. Forgetting, not remembering, is the fundamental experiential mode of the relationship between
self and past; forgetting is not to be understood as a blocking out of
parts of memory by no matter which on the whole healthy processes,
but is on the contrary the original background formed by all-that-is-
absent, which memory overlays with its images and which would not

otherwise even become "visible" *as a background*. The implications for psychology are now becoming far more tangible: the extent to which memory, a derived experience-form according to its constitution, partakes in present experience, is reciprocal to the immediacy with which the present as such is experienced. Whereas with aging the phenomenal content of the present wanes, thus making room for memory as a positive presence of images, a widely different constellation obtains wherever the *I* draws the person's attention upon *it* and thus away, to precisely the extent of this ungenuine "engagement", from the *present in its concreteness,* as which the present is constituted as the non-self, or *world.* The less—a determining feature of ordinary anxiety—the phenomenal content of the present is thus allowed to unfold itself, the less future, in the original sense of the term, can there be, and the greater must become the power of the past in its *negativity,* as an absence of being; consequently, then, the more feverish the *seeking* of the future in this case, that is, its construction by way of deliberate calculations and schemes, which in turn overlay the naught of the person's actual "anticipation": his dread of the future *because he has none.*

But in order to show the want of genuineness of that "time" which underlies the calculations and the schemes, their tendency to conceal a blocked-off absence of the *open* and *coming-toward* of original future, they themselves would have to be shown to depend on the notion of the past (that is, on what is only a derivative of original time) in their phenomenal structure; the manipulated substitute future, on which, as constructions, they hinge, would have to reveal itself as the projection of an image of a succession of past events upon the nothingness ahead as its background. Mathematical time, in this event, no matter to what future its concepts may be applied actually or only "logically", would phenomenologically turn out to depend on mental presentations of the past and the past only, that is, on something that is given to our consciousness only as the presence of an absence. Significantly, this dependence of mathematical time upon the image of the phenomenal past turns out to be the actual experience-content of any conception of processes *as such,* that is, as the fundamental eidetic presentation to the mind on which all objectifications hinge: no matter whether the processes are—either as ordinary or typical ones or else as process models which the mind can "visualize"—taken out of historic time altogether, or speculatively envisaged in the historic future, by an inevitable necessity they are "seen" from a vantage point projected to a time-locus beyond their completion and hence are visualized *retrospectively,* so that objective reality, yielded as it is by a conception of the world as *process,* remains bound up forever with the phenomenal past. The phenomenal past, in turn, is, *qua* past, unreal by definition: objectivism, therefore, must substitute a derived conceivability of that-which-is for the entire authentic (creative) fundament of reality. Only as far as man can still muster—with Tillich's term[22]—the courage to be, only inasmuch as he *has future,* can this fundament be restored to his identity as well as to his knowledge. The having of future, for its part—as no longer stands in need of exposition—is not an ego-centered possession that calculating can supply, but on the contrary is man's readiness (and ability to afford) *to forget about his ego.* As the objectified (and never the real) self, the *I,* phenomenally, belongs, at any moment, to the past, and thus man's having of future consists essentially of his freedom of engagement, his openness toward being, his willingness to allow future as the freely coming-toward-him to *have him first.*

While the original discovery of mathematical time is contingent on memory, both the link between the two, and the inner order of memory itself, would still remain incomprehensible without a disruption of the original pragmatic existence context of the unreflected being-in-the-world—which, in turn, gets under way with man's discovery of the "thing" as a separate entity, no longer "at hand" but "before us" (*vorhanden*): once it is seen that anything without follows a law or cycle of its own, observation of which allows of fuller and more sovereign mastery of that thing, its changes for the first time are seen in their order. The thing changes, yet can be followed through the changes in its nevertheless evident *sameness,* and thus the total transmutation of the being-in of existence which sets in at this point can be qualified by three main characteristics: 1) since the observation of the changes, for example of the structure of a seasonal or astronomic cycle, requires an active concentration on the degrees of remoteness from the present of the phases observed, the past as that which has absented itself for the first time is seen in the order of its successivity of events[23]; 2) the conception of space in its abstractness emerges as the unitary space-time context of pragmatic existence "splits"; simultaneously with the discovery of the past as an "equal" of the future and present, the ground for the abstraction of time, reversing the direction of phenomenal time (of the towardness of original future) is laid; 3) the notion of identity arises equi-originally with the notion of what identity, by persisting through it, resists, that is, with the notion of time. The observation that every-thing changes thus simultaneously implies, a) time itself, and b) the unfolding of reason and ultimate severence of reason from its own roots in the immediate awareness of the truth and order of being; as that unfolding proceeds, reason becomes unreason ("rationality") by beginning to determine itself from the side of its own *application* to the tasks of a purposive mastery of that-which-is, that is, in a direction counter to its true one.

While this immanent self-contradictoriness of time becomes apparent historically in the genesis of calculative and manipulatory rationality, it is open to inspection on strict grounds of fundamental-ontological analysis and critique. Since the concept of absolute identity as one of essential sameness, implying a notion of being which the changes observed refute throughout, underlies, as is readily seen, the whole structure of logic, any instrumentalist attempt to found logic on empiric observation (genetically; intrinsically on one of its own applications, mathematics) turns out to be groundless. The sources of its own strict-ness, compellingness, which logic as an operational system, always and already dealing with objects, must by-pass, can only be sought in thought as itself a manifestation of being, for no other explanation remains available: the awareness of persistence (timelessness, essence) which *identity* connotes, cannot even be derived from any experiential encounters with phenomena as such, since, on the contrary, this aware-ness must already extend itself *to* them in order to account for the fact that they maintain themselves through time.[24] The fact, in turn, that some changes are too slow to be noticed supports no objection to this argument: once insight into the universality of changing is gained, the self-evidentness of the notion of identity only becomes an object of philosophical reflection,[25] *as* that self-evidentness, however, it remains wholly as unshaken as before.

Man's discoveries of the world as objects and of mathematical time are therefore equi-original: they are one event. That event, in first alienating him from his world, exposes him, frees him for his danger:

his alternative between an encompassing awareness, a shepherdship of being that respects its ultimate incomprehensibility and restores his own unity with it through an act of existential homecoming in which thought becomes a listening to the truth of being (as revealed, for example, by the great poets); and what offers itself to him as the always and already available, an unauthentic existence anchored in the naught of the anonymous everyone and its limitless objectifications of both the self and the world. Heidegger reconstructs the constitution of the genesis through which being, in the phenomenal world-structure of man, withdraws from him by way of an increasing shrinkage of the sphere of the original *at-hand* to the mere range of the tools and utensils that make up the milieu into which he finds himself tossed and which surrounds him with more and more meaningless, that is, merely *useful* stuff (*Zeug*). Utensils—the more they become functional—*are* not (anything in themselves) but merely *are for* something else. Being thus withdraws in a triple fashion. Its original *toward-man* (the openness of the *at-hand*) is replaced by the dead submissiveness, handiness, of the *stuff*. The stuff itself is in a constant process of quantitative growth, crowding ever more densely around man and concealing his vista for any manifestation of being outside of himself. Finally, what still remains as chances for being to manifest itself in the outside world, instead is turned into a mere *before-us* (*Vorhandenes*), that is, into measurable and dissectible things, which as such become objects for the utilitarian exploitation of the utensils; in that process, in turn, the sphere of utensils finally comes to include man's reason inasmuch as, at this stage, reason notices the useful ones among its own categories and begins to select from them according to this standard. It now determines itself as a tool for "adjustment" or "mastery of nature" (instrumentalism); accordingly, the sphere of objects comes to include him, the subject and tool-maker, *as an individual*. As such, he is either openly manipulated as a mere means-to-ends, as in some societies, or, as in some others, undertakes his own calculative exploitation as an object of his striving for quantitatively defined "success".

Whereas in the first case at least his chance for an ultimate rebellion is retained, his very self-unity is increasingly lost in the second. Without making it explicit as yet at least in *Being and Time*, what Heidegger concretely succeeds in describing there is the situation of modern western man, which is elucidated by way of a descriptive laying-bare of one after the other stratum of the top structure of existence, one after the other of its characteristic and deep-seated self-misunderstandings. The latter feature is seen as existence-constituent and -pervasive, as immanent to man's ordinary dealings with his situations necessarily and therefore rightly: since this ordinariness inheres in the existence of the average person, Heidegger nowhere denies a certain legitimacy of the unauthentic notions that surround man's situations. Constitutionally thrown into man's existence by being, these notions succeed in hiding that which throws them, but the specific texture as well as relative importance of the concealment is subject to historic flux: if its magnitude were not so enormous in our day, its texture not so coarse, existential philosophy would never have arisen at this particular point in western history, and Heidegger's concrete phenomenological accounts, in turn, would not continue to find an ever more resounding echo in the humanities and the anthropological sciences alike if they did not discern, in its most telling features, the condition of typical twentieth century man.

But the farther down in our understanding we follow the ontological structure of existence, the more axiomatic, all-encompassing, and historically timeless become the phenomena. Modern anxiety is but a specific, flight-like mode of original dread, and an unauthentic one since it does not dare face its own content, the naught; rather, the individual beset by anxiety hides his face from the naught by attributing this experience either to genetic causes or to objects of fear. With his hermeneutic of dread—in which, in distinction from that other fundament of existence, care, nothingness is not present as a constant, silent, and invisibly challenging background but in its overwhelming immediacy, its proximity of annihilation—Heidegger's thought, recognizing with Kierkegaard's the constitutive character of the nothingness phenomenon for the entire dimension of religious experience in man, reaches its high point of acumination as much as of boldness: the naught as the one and only undeniably given phenomenon that absolutely defies—since it *is* not—any attempt to account for it from the side of that-which-is, is also the only one that implies being in its absoluteness. It implies it "at its earliest",[26] as the wholly attributeless (un-unfolded, undifferentiated) ultimate ground, fundamental-ontologically *anteceding time* and thus devoid—as besides it only nothingness is—of any kind and degree of individuation or structure.[27]

The definitive (logical) identity of being and the naught, both absolutely bare, as no other categories besides them, of any attributes at all, was expounded first by Hegel. But while logic can make this peculiar identity visible, it is itself not the source of the notions either of being or of the naught any more than of those of identity (or of otherness) : the very fact that logic, in its objectifying usage, can master the world of that-which-is refers both logic and that-which-is to a common and earlier principle from which both stem. While this has been recognized at frequent points throughout the history of metaphysics, metaphysics, as for example in Leibniz's conception of a pre-stabilized harmony, immediately concealed again the problem of the common principle just detected by turning that principle into another, if hypothetical, objective entity, such as an instituted order, a cosmological arrangement, "something", at any rate, within the reaches of the that-which-is. But man's encounters with either being or the naught are earlier than logic. Accordingly his notion of the reality of both the self and the world is earlier than either his object perceptions or the "I-talk" (Heidegger) of his ordinary self-understanding: the truth of being in its encompassingness—its reality—as one unfolding in a pragmatic polarity of self and world, is present already in his most primitive obstacle experiences of which, objectifyingly, we may say that they lie within the phenomenal spatiality of his being as the being of his body. In concrete experience, contrariwise, this *post hoc* abstracted spatiality, which only our reflection may discover there, remains just as much beyond the horizon set by the authentic content of such obstacle-encounters as the Cartesian ego and its objects lie beyond the horizon of original reality. If being thus transcends any *post hoc* objectifying accounts of its apperception by man, his experiences in their unadulterated immediacy remain as the only criteria of the real *per se*, and in this only authentic sense of reality the naught "is" real, for man encounters it in his dread: the paradoxical truth that it implements "unreality" *in the encounter* only points up, in turn, the existential challenge that its power to impinge on him imparts. But does man tend to face what he encounters? Anticipating annihilation, he may—availing himself of another opportunity for self-objectification—refer what he encounters to his own personal end in time (death) and thus turn his gaze from the presence of dread with its peculiar phenomenal message to a future that, as such, at least can be feared.

But since anxiety has no objects, what can be the object of an anxiety understanding itself as fear of death? Since objective knowledge of the fact "that one dies someday" may long have preceded the experience of dread, dread cannot have its roots in that knowledge; instead, the never yet understood phenomenality of death as the authentic *my death* of any anticipated termination of existence becomes itself a problem for fundamental ontology.[28] The more the phenomenal content of dread is objectified—that is, fled from—the more, with that innermost movement of flight itself now partaking in what experience here encounters, does dread become anxiety in the ordinary and clinical sense: an amorphous and anticipatory fear of personal annihilation. The less, then, with such turning of man's gaze from it, is it seen in its genuineness, as the naught on which the very notion of annihilation depends but of which nothing but the implication of a total menace and the anguish it imparts is left in that notion as it is elaborated into knowledge. This truth—about the *what* of the original encounter of his dread—the person himself will unsuspectingly utter once, discarding his experience as it occurs to him in retrospect, he will say without understanding what it is he is saying, that his "fear" was "groundless", that he has been afraid of *nothing*. It is evident that what he "means" by the "groundlessness" of his experience at this point is not the groundlessness of his own falling-out-of-being that the experience had actualized, that the "nothing" at this point is not the *nihil* of the inexplicable annihilation that he had met with anticipatorily, but is the "purely logical" negation of the *anything qua any objects*: and neo-positivistic critics of Heidegger indeed have not tired of pointing out this "difference".[29]

This reaction is precisely what would have to be expected in order to confirm Heidegger's interpretation of the naught as a *reality*: the "evident difference" common sense so insists upon is of course overwhelmingly great, but what is it that makes it so, since "logic" does not admit of any? In either "version" of the naught, the same negation of that-which-is is apperceived; but in the first instance the negation is encountered as an *event*, whereas in the second it is present in the person's experience only in its conceptual role as the means of thought to express the notion of an exclusion of *anything*. The "difference", then, is not one in ultimate content but in the acute existential situation, that is, in man's perspective *for* this content; as that difference, however, it is so radical as to conceal not only the link between the two beholdings of one and the same phenomenon, but to arouse vehement objections to the rediscovery of its oneness. The reason for this is that this rediscovery, by making visible the naught as the background of that-which-is, would endanger that very security of existence from the vantage point of which a "purely conceptual" use of the *nothing* is possible; but is the naught an object of "something like fear"? If it is, furthermore, what is the original meaning of dread as such, and why is it exactly to religious experience with its encounter of the alternative between life and death as one posed from *beyond* the boundaries of man's personal existence that dread has ever been so fundamental?[30] As always, the phenomenal conveyances of original language provide the answer: in English, it is the concept of *awe* in its authentic unity of meaning, not yet differentiated into the *sublime* which aesthetics may abstract from its encountered content, and the *fearful* into which the awe-inspiring only may turn as man already "determines" his relation to it in the image of flight, that connotes the highest *ec-stasy* of self-transcendence. This encounter with the presence of awe in the inspirational experience of the sublime as an over-and-beyond-all-limits is at least as much an unveiling of the naught before man's gaze as is "anxiety"; yet, as a making contact with the ultimate, the very ground where life and death are both suspended and provided for, the sublime only affirms *being* by exposing it to the absolute and naked peril of the presence of its own negation and thus exhorts man's *Dasein* to the resolution of its own freedom to be[31]; the pervading tendency of existence to "understand" itself from the side of *what it understands*—world—and to forget that its understanding of world can never genuinely extend its claim to its own sources in man's *being*, thus vanishes precisely in the beheld presence of the alternative of being—nothingness. The logical identity of being and the naught only reflects, therefore, their fundamental-ontological one, but the difference in existential "perspective" which has been pointed out must be understood on its part as the unfolding of an alternative which *Dasein is*: in man's existence, being "obtrudes into the naught" (*ragt ins Nichts*); seeing itself from beyond itself, *being* can therefore "see" itself as its own opposite, or *nothing*. The encounter that thus, in his dread, calls man back to being is *being,* but being as it intrudes on his reflection from "without", as the nothing-but-extended that-which-"is" (fact world) in its senseless ("unreal") side-by-side and point-for-point of things no longer meaning-transparent, and thus in the guise of the naught. At this glance of nothingness, man is faced with the alternative either of *standing* it and thus *understanding* the imperative-to-be which it both hides and spells out, or fleeing *from* it (the self-misunderstanding of dread as "mere" anxiety or as a fear of "something" in the "future"). But in fleeing from his dread, in shunning death even in his thinking, and yet with every dread-dissipating move only finding himself nearer to it and thus more absolutely in its power, man succeeds solely in implementing the annihilation-character of the "vague anticipation" which he had and which logic can by-pass or belittle but never disentangle for him since the constitution of the naught is set off from that of "anything" precisely by the peculiarity that it *is not.*[32]

A cognitive transcendence toward being from a mere descriptive reflection on the structure of existence in the Jaspers manner finds being implied everywhere only be negations of being. Conceptual language, as necessarily object-categorizing language, partakes in the self-alienation of being which existence in its temporality *is.* It is for this reason that Heidegger's first attempt at a fundamental ontology remained a torso; neither the second part of *Being and Time,* which was to implement the proposed "Destruction of the History of Ontology", nor the third section of the first part which, under the title of *Time and Being,* was to reverse the approach of the preceding studies by inquiring into *being* from the "horizon of time" (historicity) have been published to this day. While this gave rise to uncounted early misunderstandings of Heidegger's work either as immanentistic—an interpretation which such direction-setting features as the phenomenology of conscience contradicted from the start—or as a failure to carry out its own fundamental proposal, the more recent work has answered most if not all the questions which *Being and Time* had posed and still left open. The task of philosophy is to enounce the truth of being in the midst of what is constantly hiding it from our sight, the ever-growing mass of inveterate objective ("functional") determinations which, in alienating our everyday existences from their own home grounds, condemn their roots to wither. Not only the unauthentic and derived condition of the whole gamut of existentially unpenetrated, that is, unintuited, fact knowledge, not only the customary ways of forming opinions (*das gewöhnliche Meinen*) of both the layman and the intellectual, but already such ready notions form part of *existence in its untruth* as the usual self-objectifying *I myself* of a wholly arbitrary subjectivity that replaces by demonstrativeness what it has lost in genuineness of being. While philosophic reflection can make all this more visible, it cannot of itself restore being to its legitimate place in existence or man to his in being: only a spontaneous inner decision in man himself, his free reconversion to the abundant availability, the ever-presence of the truth of being in and around him, can bring about a change in his present status that would give his historic destiny, now headed toward ever increasing losses of both his world and himself, a new turn toward the wholesome.

Human *Dasein* is the only known manifestation of being in which, out of the absolute pragmaticity that ties the existence of animals into their "windowless" environmental contexts, "being comes home to itself", the only one that arrives in the "clearing" of Truth; hence, the keys to man's own homecoming must be recovered in the dimension which this self-freeing of being has set. While this dimension is language,[33] our accesses to its depth are blocked by the small talk that adheres to existence in its ordinary failure to obtain a hold upon itself and which no reversal of the direction of spontaneous language, no definitive analyses (themselves partaking in that small talk) from *beyond* language can remove: neither semantic nor psychoanalytic reversals of the direction in which spontaneity unfolds are possible any more than reversals of the direction of heat conduction according to the second law of thermodynamics. But once the access to the meaning background of language is blocked and its usages have become arbitrary, the arbitrariness at once is concealed by the discovery, occurring in one event with that severance of eidetic immediacy, of the operational role of language as a system of communicative significations: while the sources of language are no longer beheld, its power to categorize, that is, to turn presences of being into objects-that-are, becomes hypnotic. Language, at this point—the point to which all definitions of man as a "rational" or "irrational" animal or creature date back—thus turns into the very tool that converts the essences revealing themselves in it into terms which in turn obscure their own phenomenal backgrounds. It is evident from uncounted observations in our time that man's self-distancing from the sources of Truth does not stop at this point but at present threatens to go on to a loss of essential language: never has an age either been so powerless over the word as ours or so concealed its impotence behind the public talkativeness of the *word-as-coin* that the ever more facile facilities of communication are feeding. Does not man's replacement of the categorial order of logic by the relational context of mathematical "symbols" already signify an essential return to muteness? As a sphere of significations that radically presuppose *being* as *already unfolded dimensionally* (into that-which-is; a predicative relation that can nowhere be reversed), mathematics is all-analytic, but, unlike thought in its preconstituted verbality, most absolutely uncreative.[34]

This interpretation not only is in full accord with the phenomenal source of the notion of reality which originally has nothing to do with fact worlds as such but signifies the power of being to take effect, to *work* upon the beholder (*Wirklichkeit* connotes reality); it also is the only one that does full justice to the genesis of the schizophrenic's loss of reality in his dread, the genesis of those states of his in which reality quite literally goes to pieces, while his perceptions of the "pieces" (the objects around him of which empiricism has always tried to *piece* reality together) remain, as Jaspers has shown, wholly unaltered. To illustrate the similarity between the actual world of the schizophrenic and the theoretical world of the empiricist, the one in pieces, the other pieced together, we may refer to Dostoyevski's story "The Double", by far the best case history of an outbreak of paranoid schizophrenia available in the literature, although written decades before the beginning of modern scientific psychiatry. Nearing the acute climax of his anxiety, his world-alienation, the hero, Jakov Petrovitch Goljadkin, has a "perceptual" experience which Dostoyevski describes as follows: "Here, in his bewilderment, he cast his eyes to the floor and to his utter astonishment saw a white spot of considerable size on the boots of His Excellency. 'Could they really have burst?' thought Mr. Goljadkin. Soon, however, the insight dawned on him that the boots of His Excellency by no means had burst but were only reflecting the light with particular strength, a phenomenon wholly explicable from the fact that they were highly polished patents." Goljadkin, in other words, "knows" his world precisely the way empiricism postulates that the normal person knows his, as a senseless agglomeration of "light spots" in which some subsequent order may be introduced by past experience—that is, by something that in turn would never have come about and therefore been available to Mr. Goljadkin, if during the pre-psychotic part of his life his way of knowing had already been constituted in that fashion.

In the tendency of his thinking to be suspicious of categorial schemes,[35] Heidegger shares with all other radical phenomenologists, most distinctly again with Marcel. The latter's exceedingly subtle analyses center on such observations as the contradiction between the logical possibility for a eulogy to include a person's charm among his positive qualities, and the utterly personal (intimate and objectively elusive) characteristics of charm that would render such inclusion silly. A further analysis of the phenomenality of charm shows its unconscious quality (unconscious in a sense wholly different from the Freudian), namely, the non-participation in charm of the direction of the will of the person, of that which manifests itself in "virtues" in the original sense of the word. Virtues are directional, are what retrospectively is seen as having steered the life course toward the performance of a specifically shaped biographic whole. They therefore offer themselves to a eulogy as its authentic themes, whereas "charm" appears as a quality ever-present but non-historical, since its goalless constancy leaves it biographically uncrystallized; as a textural attribute of the very living of the person, charm depends phenomenally on this living as a presence. This holds for all characterological concepts that are aesthetically objective: they convey an external vista of the person in his every-day being, and they could not convey it if the qualities to which they refer had been objectives of the person's attention and will, for example, if charm could result from a striving for charm. Since "charm" (as a concept) rules the *now*, its disappearance (as a phenomenon) with the person's death is wholly different from the "disappearance" of his virtues. Virtues are abstractions from definable accomplishments of the person; "charm", though having its source in his innermost identity at least as much as does any volition, is, contrariwise, purely physiognomic. The former thus refer to his doings, to that through which his being has *become* existence, temporality, the latter to his *being* in the far closer and more timeless sense of a standing presence. This presence no longer coincides with the person's, an observation that only points up the refusal of being (as that from which a phenomenon such as "charm" most immediately unfolds) to let itself be claimed by individual existences *beyond their time.*

From any angle of observation, then, a merely "logical" approach on the part of our eulogist—one that in the quantifying fashion of the electric brain first accepts the inclusiveness (superordination) of the category "good qualities" for both the "virtues" and "charm", then mechanically operates on the premise of this datum of logic without conceiving of examining its relevancy—turns out to be, with all its exactitude, devoid of that genuine strictness of thought which no automaton or automatic way of "thinking" can duplicate. Already in our preliminary analysis[36] of the use which objectifying psychology— and psychoanalysis perhaps most uncritically—makes of the grammatical opportunity of conceptual reification that language grants, the peculiar blinding for the concrete phenomenal implication of a term, which this non-authentic use of grammar imparts, stood out conspicuously; in turn, our analysis of the "background function" in the exercise of which the dimensional infinity of abstraction appears to lend itself to the explanatory quest allowed us to ground this observation in a more comprehensive phenomenology of some fundaments of the structure of knowledge. The firmness with which this "logical" arbitrariness existentialism exposes has, under the enduring influence of Greek metaphysics, entrenched itself in modern anthropological science would be incomprehensible without a general demonstrability of the stated tendency in western thought toward an over-extension of "categories" beyond their own phenomenal confines, that is, to the— usually unnoticed—point where they cancel themselves out; the concept of egotism, for example, may be extended to a point where the pursuit of love interests can be construed as egotistical, as in many ideas of puritanism. It is evident that this expansion of "egotism" to include its own diametric opposite leaves no room for *any* "interests" that in a genuine sense still could implement the opposite concept, altruism; since, in turn, a concept of the constitution of "egotism" depends on its opposite as one that conceivable human attitudes and acts—of which the expansion leaves none—at least *might* implement, the concept of egotism becomes meaningless in that case. The consequence is fully visible in both a psychological and historic sense: since the error is not recognized within its own sphere—thought—it becomes an untruth *lived*, the priming point of an attitude of self-hounding scrupulosity in which we find altruistic justifications of actual egotism interlocked in an exitless circle with extremes of self-denial, that is, lovelessness. The entire conception, so fundamental to both puritanism and psychoanalysis, of sex as a blind "irrational" "need" which the person egotistically strives to satisfy, is possible only on this basis of a hypnotism of the *categorial,* yet the blinding for phenomenal contents which the hypnotism imparts is not restricted to the sphere of thought. Thought being itself a manifestation of existence, which in turn has the character of an engaging *encounter* throughout, the discovery we make at this point is that to the extent to which a certain mode of objectifying self-interpretation has gained power over the thinking of the person, inevitably the self will live up to the interpretation. Thus, where puritan (or psychoanalytic) self-observation, or any of its equivalents in pathogenic self-consciousness, has succeeded in turning the person's situation away from "world" (as the given locus, in which "outer" and "inner" world are still undivided, for the fulfillment of love interests) toward the objectified self as the locus of these interests (sex), the latter indeed *will* occur to the person in their "instinctual" isolation. As an existential decision, self-objectification only brings the isolation about; but as an act of knowledge it alleges all the more apodictically that the isolation is a datum that it finds.

Heracleitus' word, so far more modern now than nineteenth century instinct theories, concerning the unfathomable "reasonableness" of the soul is thus echoed once more by Heidegger's dictum that the ultimate *who* of existence is *being,* and in turn by his insight into the impossibility to perform a full transcendence toward being by means of the traditional categorial language of metaphysics. The wornness of that language, the thick historic patina of misleading connotations that has settled on its terminology, indeed had made impossible the writing of the proposed later sections of *Being and Time,* and thus categoriality itself was soon discerned to be what superimposed a derived rationalism on the concrete and sensible order of eidetic presences through which, in that status of man where concepts still behold their quiddities and the sources of *ek-sistence* still spring fresh, being unfolds its truth in an immediate transparence of meanings. To unblock again the dimension of language through which being sends the presences of its truth

into the concrete historic *Da* of existence, not only the single word as
a fountain of its own spontaneous significance but language as a
whole had to be *listened to* where it "spoke itself" with the utmost of
genuineness and compellingness, in the mouths of the great poets; an
exegesis of Hölderlin, of very visible effects on his own use of language, thus preceded Heidegger's more pithy presentation of his
doctrine in the later writings. In dissipating all doubts that the "subjective turn" of philosophy, in order to master the challenge of
deadening objectivism, had first to discard "subjectivity" as the commonplace misunderstanding of itself to which existence in its isolation
from being is prone, Heidegger not only refuted Sartre but those of
his critics as well who, like H. Kuhn,[37] had charged him with Sartrean
immanentism and agnosticism. The essay "On Nietzsche's Word: God
is dead",[38] elucidated as nothing had before both Nietzsche's position
in the history of ideas and the nature of transcendence as a constituent
characteristic of existence that of itself implies the "place of God."
Two closely interrelated topics of thought stand out from Heidegger's
discussion: from an objectified world that has become all facts, God
has withdrawn, so that in the actual experience of modern man as one
finds it, God's place is vacant; accordingly, the "supersensory", the
whole sphere of ideas and ideals *as such* no longer exercises any true
power or attraction. The reason for this is that the power and attraction
of the supersensory are contingent upon a beheld occupancy of that
place by a being accessible to experience in its *reality;* that this reality
has no qualities becomes understandable, as we may see, from its
position as the *ultimate* reality, that is, as an absolute background that
cannot at the same time be *Gestalt*. The situation of agnosticism
Heidegger here diagnoses is the *non plus ultra* of nihilism and the
terminal point of its history so far; it also marks the point where the
alternative must occur to man either to make his way "back"—which
authentically, the truth of being always lying *ahead,* is his way forward—into that truth, or to replace the position of God in the orientation of his *Dasein* by an absolutization of his own "subjectivity", his
own deliberating ("purely willful") ego in its already "given" apposition to a just as metaphysically absolutized fact world.

It is in the latter case that his self-loss becomes ever more total:
so total, indeed, that its being *totally ununderstood as such* becomes
the essence of the loss. This situation, according to Heidegger, is not

escaped by any theology that, in an already previously characterized manner,[39] "piles" a divinity (itself conceptualized in analogy with something-that-is) on top of everything-else-that-is (the objectified world) ; just as the paling object image held by this misleading notion of world no longer knows its own source in the original self-transcendence of existence into world as the open, encompassing, and immediately meaningful, just as the beyond-time must misunderstand itself already at an early point to connote *temporal* projections of temporality into speculative notions of a "before" or "after" time that then clash with the "facts" of mathematical time, thus also the objectified God image must more and more conceal its own *wherefrom*, the compelling presence of which thus gives way to an increasing self-distancing of God, a becoming vacant of His place in human existence. It is evident that this, as the description of an actual and typical modern situation courageously stated as what it is, has nothing in the least to do either with denials of positive religious experiences as noetically valid ones, which on the contrary and in distinction from Jaspers' and Sartre's teachings it affirms, or even with an undefined "agnostic attitude"; the gist of Heidegger's essay on Nietzsche is precisely to reveal the bottomless gap between the God-seeking "madman" in *La Gaia Scienza* who cries that "we have murdered God" and the shallow cleverness of the herd of the enlightened that mock him.

Nor can Heidegger's thinking be indicted of any equivocation concerning the reality of God; the real, as a previous analysis has shown, being the presently manifest and engaging that experience beholds, any way of categorizing that turns the presently manifest and engaging into the existing or non-existing (items of that-which-is or is-not) comes to notice double meanings where there is only one precisely because it has so firmly established its own vantage point in the ambiguity of objectifying notions that the truth of the one meaning is out of bounds for it. This holds true for many "multiple" meanings of words having one origin but several connotations, such as the *being true* of a statement and one's *being true* to somebody else. We tend to be at once distrusting and un-self-suspecting enough not even to ask ourselves whether it is not we who do the splitting, and we thus will assess the terminological situation in accord with our superficial notions of "cognitive correctness" and of "personal loyalty" instead of examining these notions in the light of the one concrete phenomenal content that the word *true* lays open. "Truth"[40] has been chosen here because the absolute horizon-likeness of that notion, bound up as it is with *being* in such a manner that both inevitably refer to one another, makes particularly transparent the necessity with which the notion must "split" once it applies itself to different relationships— if different only in terms of the objects which they relate to each other. The necessity, in turn, by which truth "becomes" untruth[41] in the encounter of that-which-is can be traced by reflecting on the essence of understanding as that original stretching-toward-the-open that existence *is*: the essence of understanding is freedom,[42] because without freedom as the condition of transcendence from the boundness of animal being in the immanence of a pragmatic context of mere "living" into the *world* of our awareness no conception of the true nature of a thing would be possible. The more the true is mistakenly identified with what can only (but less and less visibly as categorizing proceeds) be predicated on it, the that-which-is (facts), the more, with these facts and man's own factualness in the end crowding in on him, is freedom lost, and the more, in consequence, does he come to exist in *untruth*. But what is such untruth, the untruth, for example, of any objectivism that sees man as a herd animal—if not the phony renewal of a status that his self-transcendence left behind?

The problem of truth is thus linked with that of freedom—or, putting it in the terms of the traditional objectivistic turn which that problem has taken, with the question of determinacy versus free will. For a discussion of this problem, the facts of determinacy are irrelevant, because facticity *per se* is irrelevant here: the that-which-is in its very objectivity, its "determinacy", presupposes a freedom of cognition of man which determinacy as the law of the *cognized* can neither undo nor in the least "explain". Traditionally, through a gradual flattening of Kant's conception of the postulates of practical reason, freedom has been salvaged by the functionalist as a "subjectively valid" experience, whatever that shall mean, as a state of human will or feeling that "objectively, of course" is a delusion, but a nice and also very useful one and therefore sanctionable "practically"; but it is not to be seen either how a delusion which one knows to be a delusion can be maintained or what expediencies and niceties should have to do with the status of the *free*. If of anything, it is characteristic of the hopelessness with which objectivistic anthropology has

continued to limp behind what it attempted to take as its model—
physics—that the only sensible objective account of the freedom-
determinacy problem, so vital to psychology, has come from a physicist's pen: Planck, in his *Scientific Autobiography*,[43] assigns to these
paired opposites, freedom and determinacy, a merely perspectivic
significance comparable to that of the notions of *right* and *left* which
we apply to objects with the implication of our spatial position in
reference to them rather than of any qualities of the objects as such:
determinacy, in its psychological applications, thus not only applies
to the self as process but already *in its constitution* refers to an
observation post from which the self as process is encountered as an
object; whereas freedom not only *applies* to the actions of that self
(*qua its* actions) but already as a concept *refers* to the position of
that self as the premise of *any* object encounters: *as* that self acts, only
whatever is non-self is objectified,[44] that is, constituted as a field
governed in its structure and the changes of its structure by abstractible
(deterministic) laws.

Planck's solution, which in this manner can dismiss the freedom-
determinacy problem as a phantom, unquestionably presents an
enormous advance; no approach to the question below the Planckian
level, none that does not at least start out with a full insight into what
in his solution is true, should any longer be of interest even to
objectivists. The truth of determinism, which to the average scientist
of man has become as axiomatic as the power of his totem to the
Ojibwa, is called into question by Planck's analysis with far more
compellingness than can ever be expected from any uncertainty
coefficients and similarly transient by-products of research already
within the reaches of the objectifying world account of physics—which
according to his analysis is deterministic as a matter of *prior* necessity.
All the more significant, then, is what Planck's reflection exhibits
attitudinally: the creative physicist's freedom from such schematic
thought routines of objectivism as have continued to bind only the
ideologists of "determinacy", the late-coming imitators of physics in
the anthropological fields. A conclusive settlement of the problem
Planck's solution nevertheless is not. The essential difference between
the paired opposites *left* and *right* and the paired opposites *freedom*
and *determinacy* is precisely that the implication of dependence-on-
perspective in the former pair is itself phenomenal, whereas in the

latter only reflection can detect it. What this reflection *re-flects,* now, is a fundamental ambiguity that inheres in what the two named general ideas of humanity first emerge from, man's own situation as one that implies, not a primal alternative between the two perspective notions *qua* conceptions of logic, but one between two different and mutually exclusive modes of his existing as the basis for the duality of the perspectives. *Dasein is* freedom inasmuch as it can be authentic, that is, identical with itself, and *Dasein* "has" itself as determinate inasmuch as it tends to found itself on a commonplace self-consciousness that tacitly refers to an "outside of self" (Heidegger's "public" or "everybody", in other words, a substitute *who*) as the vantage point for its self-objectification. The two ideas, freedom and determinacy, therefore connote actual modes of existence before they even *can* come to connote different intellectual perspectives for one and the same event: their antinomy, whether reduced to an immanent self-contradictoriness of pure reason (Kant) or to a difference in observation posts (Planck), continues to hide what the fact of such hiding in turn makes manifest, the deep-seated equivocation of existence in which it is rooted.

Determinism, therefore, long before becoming an articulate principle guiding a theoretical determination of the world inclusive of the "self", is the determinate—unfree—actual mode of existing on which objectivism, only later to unfold from it *as such,* is predicated from the start. The *other* propensity of existence, its mission as the homecoming of being into its truth, its transcendence toward world, in one word, its freedom, is thus ever in danger of failing, man ever in danger of falling prey to his own "first", but actually least authentic reflections —least authentic both because reflection is first of all an abandonment of the authentic (existence in its self-identity) and because reflection as the specifically human imperative of *being* (*ek-sistence*) has, with this commonplace want of bold radicality, this self-by-passing failure to examine its own most ready notions, as yet not fulfilled its own inherent task of going to those outermost fringes of its legitimate domain where the naught is faced squarely and being once more can be "remembered" and "returned to". Non-radical reflection, historically at its peak in the nineteenth and early twentieth century deterministic theoreticians, is a self-abandonment of *Dasein* to its own untruth (its "past"[45]). Precisely because it has lost itself in these objectifying self-"determinations", lost itself as what it first and last *is*

—freedom—it no longer (or not yet again) commands, at that stage, the power of "overstepping" itself, of "stepping into the open" (Truth) ; following Heidegger's definition of freedom as the transcendence-toward-world, we recognize the exitlessness that determinism shares with self-consciousness, the exitlessness that must become the fate of an inadvertent metaphysics starting out, like all theorizing, as self-trans-cendence, but ending in immanentism. While the necessity to reunite the theoretical and practical roles of thought occurs to all those originators of non-genuine accounts of man's situation who follow in the footsteps of Hegel, no objectifying *Realdialektik* such as they more or less explicitly develop can restore this unity which remains lost as long and in as far as man is deprived of his immediacy of being— his original freedom to *exist in Truth*.

But self-consciousness not only leads him into the error; as a *first* manifestation of his destiny to come to grips with himself it is a genuine and even very necessary characteristic of his given form of existence. Remembering our earlier observation of the pervading *cognitiveness* of all events of the psyche, of its conviction-character down to its most conative levels (and in a sense *increasing* with the fundamentalness of the levels), we find no difficulty in reconciling that existentialist tenet with the facts of experience. What biologists have called the "symbolic self", the tendency of the human organism to "represent itself to itself"[46]—self-consciousness—starts out, like all awarenesses, as a still inarticulate *having* of its own phenomenal con-tent—the self—which content in turn is striving to elaborate itself, to take shape in *thought*. What happens, if this phenomenal content, which authentically is never the psyche[47] but the spatial and space-exposed *body* as "the others" are alleged to see it by this "representa-tion of the self to itself", begins to absorb its own attention to such an extent that attention no longer is free to be absorbed by the person's *world*—regardless whether "outer" or "inner"? Objective psychology has rightly discerned the character of *mechanisms* inhering in those types of neurotic experience and behavior in which, as the existentialist would say, world (and thereby self-realization) is missed, but objective psychology has failed to discern the predicative as well as genetic order of the underlying "mechanizations". As shown most brilliantly by Binswanger's case studies,[48] the neurotic's most horizon-like ideas do not ensue upon his mechanisms; vice versa, existence as a throw or *pro-ject* of being determining itself by *knowing* from the start, the neurotic's experience-behavior context becomes mechanical *in fact* because he is ruled by his own decision (capable only of engendering indecision) that he is thing-like. The decision, in turn, is the only possible implementation of his primal conviction (which, as holds for all convictions to the extent that they are horizon-like, is not to be misunderstood as one conceptually elaborated or otherwise focalized) that he should "have himself as an object" instead of that he should *be*. This decisive conviction, in centering the focus of his attention upon that in him which *should do the focussing*, cannot but disrupt the unity of the psyche; subsequently, in a full reversal of the genetic order as much as of the phenomenal, it is *to* the disruption—which it only brings about—that a doctrine like psychoanalysis will attribute that conviction.[49]

Knowledge, in the mechanisms of neurosis as they impinge upon an existence, thus undergoes a peculiar (psychological as well as noetic) "whirl": by its very occurrence *as an event* it turns into a fact what *as a conviction* it alleges to know *already*, that is, as being there quite independently of its occurrence as an event, and only in this manner, which shows the diametric opposite of the structure of all genuine (self-transcendent) *noesis* are its "anticipations" verified by the neurotic's factual experiences to ensue. While a closer analysis of this logically exceedingly intricate phenomenon must await its proper place in our account, three topics of existentialist reflection stand out from our analysis as of the most burning concern to the psychologist and psychotherapist. One is the inextricable interwovenness of being and knowing which our inquiry just showed; another the phenomenology of *being and having*, the trans-categorial, trans-grammatical direction of which is emphasized by Heidegger and consistently followed also— as previously exemplified—by Marcel in his descriptive explorations of most typical situations of man and of man's thinking. While the explosiveness of the issue of being and having for uncounted tenets of objective psychology, especially of psychoanalysis, will be shown in greater detail as we proceed, an example of wider representativeness than any from psychonalysis is likely to have may suffice at this point: according to Tolman's redefinition of goal[50] (as what phenomenally goal is *not*, the physiological quiescence ensuing upon reaching a *phenomenal* goal) a baby, when it cries for food, does not want food but to be rid of its hunger. That it should not be wanting food may be argued on the basis of its having no concept of food (since it has no words), but the counter point can be made that having no concepts at all he has none of quiescence either. The phenomenal structure of *wanting* remaining forever unexamined by molar behaviorists, the assumption that wanting presupposes verbal concepts of its objectives on the part of one who wants suggests itself only too readily to their audiences; and since the phenomenal structure of goal remains unreflected, goal is given the unauthentic meaning by the molar behaviorists of being that state which *objectively results* from a certain action of the organism that is acknowledged to be goal-directed. The observation that registers first at this point is this: psychological objectivism, in attempting to imitate physics, dissolves the phenomenal, but, as pointed out previously,[51] cannot help introducing concepts of phenomenal constitution into its accounts, for neither does physics—in the language of which the only truly *objective* account of the baby in his field could conceivably be given—have any use for such notions as "goals", nor is the notion itself severable from its phenomenality; in consequence of this, Tolman's redefinition of goal, in the concrete theoretical image that inevitably it imparts, cannot help substituting a fictitious phenomenal goal for the actual one of the baby. The hypnotic attraction which this manner of theorizing by substitution exercises is readily understandable from twentieth century man's intellectualistic weakness for the pseudo-sophistications of the unauthentic and abstract, in which he naively believes the more "real" reality can be found, as much as from the natural weakness of his intellect; but how can we understand that the substitution follows the particular direction which it does in this case? The baby, of course, does not truly *have* his craving; the baby, as his mother readily understands, *is* that craving at the moment when he cries, and very much is food his goal; but since according to the grammatical structure of language he can be said to *have* a craving (or "need"), the idea—which is but a shadow of categoriality[52]—offers itself only too readily that if this is what he *has* it may also be what he is aiming *to get rid of*. The assertion, in turn, cannot be said to be incorrect but merely, like most assertions of objectivism, to be *untrue*:[53] it misses out on the essence of the baby's situation in the only sense in which this situation can be determined *as a situation* at all, from the baby's own vantage-point, the position of his being. The likely objection that, in the absence of facilities of verbal communication with the baby, we have no access to his world and hence none to his inner person according to the rationale of existential analysis itself, is refuted by the factualness of maternal understanding, and the further objection that may be raised that maternal understanding is a function of empathy rather than of cognition, turns a correct observation into an untrue theoretical report: while *feeling* evidently and on many different accounts plays a dominant and even exclusive role in the relationship of child and mother, feeling itself is not—as such theorizations persistently seem to connote—an objectifiable something that somehow is "functioning" in the two persons, but is the occurrence *to* either of them (knowledge) of the unique import of the other.   Their worlds thus not only communicate but to a considerable extent come to form *one*, an observation that is in complete accordance with the existentialist tenet concerning the contingency of shared "mundanizations" (existences insofar as they refer to world) on the primal *certainty* of Truth toward the "light" of which they converge; for, if anything, the classic relationship here spoken of is truthful, and only the obscuring of the original meaning of *truth* by the genesis of connotation-splitting—categoriality—may block from sight the evidence that we are *not* using "truth" here in a "different" (for example, more "literary") meaning.

Since the *what* of experience is the only available key to as nearly full as possible a penetration of psychological subject matter, why has the scientist of today such inner difficulties to reconcile himself to this? Because concentration upon the *what* of experience presupposes an acceptance of his subject's self in its unadulterated identity, as the immediate referent of all these *whats*, and this is "unscientific"—but why is it said to be? Because having been accustomed to the fact that objectification promotes knowledge, the scientist cannot conceive of the possibility that there should be subject matters to which man constitutionally is given accesses of cognition more direct than those he has to objects. The problem posed by the alternative between receptive *identification* with a subject matter on the one hand, alienating *dualization* of the *ego cogitans* and its "objects"—a rapport capable only of manipulating what it lays hands on—on the other, thus is raised not as a luxury question of "pure thought" but as an issue which the realities of psychological theory and practice today articulate as the

most burning one of all. The third of the existentialist topics that were
said to concern the clinician most immediately therefore points to a
maxim of *Daseinsanalyse* on which psychotherapy, conceived as a vocation, must build: the situation between the clinician and his patient has
nothing in the least to do with that of the natural scientist at his
microscope. Their relationship, if anything shall come from it, must be
one between persons, and thought, in the psychologist's and psychotherapist's province of science, is not to be split into that which the
subject thinks and that which he himself may be inclined to think
about the subject's thinking on the basis of no matter what preconceived structuralistic or functionalistic scheme; thought is *one domain*
in which two subjects, such as the therapist and his patient, may meet
precisely because thinking is an engagement that refers both of them
to *world*. The psychologist of personality who is a therapist is not,
therefore, referred to isolated thing-like "psyches" within his own conceptual grasp of the world as that-which-is; his subject matter are
beings—projects and designs of *world*, each different, but mutually
communicable since all have access to Truth. The implications are,
first, that the psychotherapist must be true in his personal world encounter, including his professional task—that the powers of spontaneity
and inner freedom must abound in him as a precondition of his work,
a matter of vocational qualification; secondly, that he must freely
understand the necessity by which, spearheading any world design that
being "throws", authentic thought must ever spring from existence.

In brief, then, what he ought to revise as radically as he can is his
conventional conception—still dating from what Levinas terms the
philosophy of the professors—of philosophizing as the "Platonic" indulgence of some rather worldless specialists; articulateness itself, which
his vocation demands so imperatively, does not allow him to keep the
very element wherein all articulation is at home out of his field by
limiting the latter to wholly artificial boundaries for which the justification, while still generally accepted, reveals itself as curiously uncritical and vague. Ready-made theoretical schemes such as he is used
to from the customary objectifying theories he must not expect from
his engagement in the exploration of existence; like any other true
engagement, this one, too, consists essentially of a readiness to let oneself be engaged by the phenomena before one, a readiness that is
active inasmuch as it is an affirmation of risk. But has substantial

thought ever in its history been riskless, or been spared the necessity of some slow and dogged groping? Can man follow the recall to *being* that goes out to him in our time, and, before he does, insure himself against failures to attain his destination? Or shall we rather ask, can he ever attain it without already manifesting who he is *as a person*? A full break-through to being, as Heidegger rightly saw, no fundamental ontological reflection itself bound to categoriality can achieve; but it can prepare for it, lead into its element, and even lose itself in it like forest trails that, winding on, end "nowhere". Just this nowhere, as the huntsman and the forester know, does not mean failure-to-attain but means an entering into the midst of what "engages" the "trails"— in our case, the truth of being that by its very own constitution cannot ever be "defined", always and only be lived, thought, known, and realized, and to which man in our time once more is asked to return. Before the turn in man that this return connotes has become an event, how can even the possibility of a solution to the *Seinsfrage*, the "question of being", be conceived? An interpretation of being—as of the attributeless wherefrom of existence—can never be determination in the theoretical sense without first of all being a determination *by being* of the *who* of existence and the *what* of the world of the existent: ontic and noetic specification are one at this point. Does such specification, such determination, not pre-require the existent's break-through to the openness of a horizon on which at least the magnitude of the truth *that has lost him* becomes a clear and overwhelming vista? Does it not already request of him to remember his status? "The conflict concerning the interpretation of being"—as Heidegger himself had written in *Being and Time*—"cannot be settled *because it has not even broken loose yet*".

NOTES

1. M. Heidegger, *Holzwege,* Frankfurt a.M., 1950, pp. 209–210.
2. Cf. pp. 140–41.
3. Cf. pp. 133–35.
4. Cf. p. 26.
5. Implied as evident here is the necessity with which, according to its phenominal content, an act of faith is either spontaneous or nothing at all: the experiential structure of faith hinges on a primal occurrence *to* the subject of what the faith is in, that is, of the essence of the creed itself; it therefore can never be the product of any deliberation on man's part (nor of his subjectivity

altogether and in any form), no matter how spontaneous the despair itself may be that prompts the deliberation.

6. For a fuller account of the antecedents of existentialism, cf. J. Collins, *The Existentialists*. Since our own treatment of existentialism as a philosophic doctrine must necessarily be brief according to the different principal aims of this book, the reader not in command of German is altogether referred to Collins' introduction and survey as the best complementation for the present chapter now available in English.

7. Cf. p. 204.

8. M. Heidegger, *Sein und Zeit*, Tuebingen, 1949.

9. M. Heidegger, *Über den Humanismus*, pp. 27–28.

10. Cf. *Holzwege*, p. 271.

11. Cf. p. 10.

12. M. Heidegger, *Sein und Zeit*, p. 125.

13. *Ibid.*, p. 124.

14. *Ibid.*, p. 172.

15. It goes without saying that "guilt" here does not primarily mean the being guilty of this or that of a specific guilt experience, always already the self-implementing application of existential guilt to a certain act or failure, but the very phenomenon of the notion of guilt, on which the possibility of such experience is contingent and which, on its part, is constituted as an awareness of the *having-fallen-out* . . . characterized before.

16. M. Heidegger, *Über den Humanismus*, pp. 5–6.

17. Cf. H. Reichenbach, *op. cit.*, pp. 276–302.

18. M. Heidegger, *Über den Humanismus*, pp. 12–14.

19. *Ibid.*, p. 17.

20. Cf. p. 10.

21. Cf. p. 123.

22. Paul Tillich, *The Courage to Be*, 1953.

23. This is in complete agreement with the ontogenetic fact that earliest childhood memories, while testifying to the greater immediacy of the child's existence by their concrete and brilliant vividness, are vague concerning both their—even half-way—precise historic *when* and the order of their successive placement in mathematical time: the temporal (life-historical) self-ordering of childhood memories as they are retained by the adult never antedates a certain age level of childhood.

24. Inasmuch as phenomena—*qua appearances*—change, the notion of identity cannot be predicated upon them but only on the tacit presence within the existence-context as a whole of a "background" against which the changes *can* become conceivable as such and which therefore itself remains stable. Only the being-in-the-world can serve as such a background; it is axiomatic to the person as his own being (his identity), and it requires, as all experienced convictions, its realization as an encounter with phenomena of the world; since it succeeds in the latter in spite of everything changing, the foreground of phenomenal reality the changes represent must be thought of as transparent for what tends to hide itself behind it, the being of the things. Heidegger, significantly, restricts the term

phenomenon to such appearances only of which the structure, in its transparence for being, belies their semblance; phenomena, in his usage, have the paradoxical status—which is no speculative construct, but a demonstrable discovery of fundamental ontology—of being *appearances of the concealed in its concealment.* This concealment is characteristic of anything of which the meaning transcends its facticity. It is no absolute invisibility behind a sharply drawn boundary, but rather the tendency of all appearing modes-of-being (essences) as radical reflection follows them into their depths, gradually to withdraw into the dimness of their common ground (being).

25. Without this axiomaticity of the notion of identity, the whole imperativeness of the problem of timeless (unchanging) *substance,* as occurring to Heracleitus, and in a different form to Parmenides, would remain unintelligible.

26. Heidegger has used the term *Seinsfrühe,* dawn of being, to connote, not any historic period or event, but a characteristic phenomenon co-constitutive to all historicity and present in individual memory as the earliness of earliest infancy in its eidetic conveyance of an un-unfolded and unquestioned *one-ness*: the timeless "now and ever" *wherefrom* existence "comes" as though from the horizon of an absolute *being-at-home.*

27. M. Heidegger, *Was ist Metaphysik?* 1949.

28. Heidegger's ontology of death and of existence as the being-toward-death is bound up with his inquiries into *care* as the being-ahead-of-itself of existence as much as with those into *dread.* Existence is seen in the paradoxicality of its "thrownness", as something incomplete of which the completion itself "would be" the destruction, so that it exists as the "possibility of its impossibility", a formulation in which "possibility", as throughout Heidegger's philosophy of being, has neither the derived Aristotelian (*potestas* as the formal opportunity for a thing to be, that is, its conceivability) nor the derived scholastic signification (essence, as opposed to existence in the sense of actuality) nor does it imply any reduction of the objective certainty of death to an objective "perhaps", but connotes the faculty by virtue of which a thing can be what essentially it is and thus its power to partake in being; death, therefore, is "possible" inasmuch as in its genuineness as *mine* (of whomsoever) it is never yet *real,* its "realization" being the "unrealization" of existence and thus also of the entire basis of the *my* of *my death.* Existence is "ahead of itself" both as *understanding,* as which it "stretches toward" a future seen as constituted by the "openness" (*Erschlossenheit*) of the intelligible (*being*), and as *care*; in the latter mode, it is "ahead of itself" as *Entschlossenheit,* "resolution": in "mustering itself", finding itself called up to its very own freedom of *daring to be,* it becomes "resolution running ahead of itself" precisely in the ever-present proximity of its own alternative, that is, of death.

29. For Heidegger's treatment of the entire complexus of problems condensed in this passage, reference is made as much to *Was ist Metaphysik?* as to the pertinent chapters in *Sein und Zeit.* It goes without saying that what is investigated here is anxiety in its purity, not any fear of death objectively accounted for by illness, physical danger, etc. Whereas the latter type of experience must itself

remain ununderstandable without a prior understanding of what always is present as its phenomenal background—dread—the impossibility of reducing dread to an anticipation of death *as an objective event* also rules out the customary reversal of the predicative relation between anxiety and fear.

30. By reflecting the nature of *revelation* against the background of Heidegger's time philosophy, the conceptions of both the *original paradise* and the *hereafter* as well as of the *end of time* in their common interpretations disclose themselves as inevitable projections—inevitable because existence *qua* temporality must "understand" *even* the ecstasies of time in "temporal" terms—of the notion of *being* upon the plane of time. Thought back to their sources, that is, freed from their inauthenticity which any wording must impart to them, the truth of these conceptions is recovered: in their immediacy they connote an awareness of the timelessness of being. In their notion of a beyond-time, "misunderstanding" itself as signifying a "before" or an "after", the ground of existence is unveiled before man's eye in a standstill of time: in the timeless hence imperishable *standing* of an absolute presence (God).

31. For a verification, the reader is also referred to musical experience, for example, of many passages in Beethoven. Significantly, though Freud's theorization about man aspires to be a comprehensive account of the experience-behavior context of *Dasein*, it nowhere touches on the sphere of the musical. The refusal of the sphere of the musical to submit to objectification is only just as absolute, of course, as the refusals on the part of the *religious* and *poetical* spheres, but its non-conceptual nature renders unauthentic accounts of it more obviously implausible.

32. Heidegger's *"Das Nichts ist nicht, es nichtet"* is to be understood against the background of his fundamental hypothesis, formulated at the end of the published section of *Sein und Zeit* and concerning the horizon-character which time has for being. Time, in this connotation, is *original* time; rather than being the *wherein* of existence, it is *je endlich* (finite for whatever manifestation of being shows the temporality of *Dasein* as its constituent characteristic). But in its "publicity" (mathematical time) time is nevertheless a derivative of the authentic temporality (cf. p. 116) of existence (*Sein und Zeit*, p. 327) and thus a notion of limit by means of which—since time as *process time* and *identity* are forever incompatible—being "sets" its own opposite, the naught. The naught thus *is* not, it "undoes being", and inasmuch as this is so, objectivistic denials of its *being* are perfectly justified by the constitution of the naught itself, that is, so long as they stay aware of their own tautological character and of the limits of objectifying logic which the phenomenal concretization of the naught in the experience of awe and of dread irrefutably exposes.

33. M. Heidegger, *Ueber den Humanismus*, p. 16.

34. Cf. pp. 58–62. This constitutional restriction of mathematics is fully reflected again by the capacity of electric brains to perform more and more astonishing acts of self-regulation in solving tasks fed them by their masters and their total incapacity of either task-setting or of task-improvement (in the authentic sense of *betterment*; not of a functional "streamlining" of the task). Both would require

the "brain's" power of breaking open its own topographic confines, that is, self-transcendentness.

35. Concerning the first and already historical self-alienation of thought we spoke of, we may approximate its determination as follows: once language has begun to "understand itself" from *beyond* the sphere of its own eidetic beholdings, it is categorized throughout, that is, its concepts are operationally extended beyond their proper phenomenal scope. This procedure, which comes to rely more and more on the grammatical order of language, a structural characteristic of it that itself is *derived*, can (with Heidegger) be traced to Greek metaphysics: most of the pre-Socratics are still free from it. The complete misunderstanding during the whole nineteenth century of the pre-Socratic thinkers as primitive philosophers of nature can be attributed to some extent to the confounding effects of correct but untrue translations. Terms, still understood in their authentic conveyances by these early Greek authors, were translated into "corresponding" terms of modern languages that wholly fail to transmit the meaning of the original Greek.

36. Cf. p. 7.

37. Helmut Kuhn, *Encounter with Nothingness, An Essay on Existentialism,* 1949.

38. Cf. M. Heidegger, *Holzwege,* 1950.

39. Cf. p. 111.

40. Cf. p. 55, and M. Heidegger, *Vom Wesen der Wahrheit.* Heidegger demonstrates the definitive bottomlessness of the concept of truth, concealed by the notion of the *adequacy* (of a statement to its object, or vice versa) by means of which traditional metaphysical thought defined truth: "adequacy" presupposes the perception of an essential equality between a judgment and the thing it judges, which turns out to be absolutely undefinable without presupposing its evidence, that is, truth—that which is to be defined. The pragmatist definition of truth as that which works, we may, since a lie may work also, leave out of consideration at this point.

41. Cf. p. 196.

42. Cf. pp. 286, 321.

43. Max Planck, *Scientific Autobiography and Other Papers,* 1949.

44. Cf. pp. 29–30.

45. Cf. p. 116.

46. A. Angyal, *op. cit.,* pp. 116–21.

47. Cf. pp. 220, 224.

48. Cf. especially L. Binswanger, "Der Fall Jürg Zünd", *Schweizer Archiv für Neurologie und Psychiatrie,* vols. 56, 57, 58, 1946–47.

49. While the foregoing discussion may shed light on the problem of determinacy versus free will both from the standpoint of phenomenological psychology and as a modification of the interpretation of that problem by Planck, it does not touch on the question of the *objective* implementation of the postulate of strict causal determinacy by physical science in its dealing with organisms generally and man in particular; materially, however, the two complexes of problems overlap to such an extent that any clarification of one of them not bound to bear upon the other can be ruled out. Cf. p. 65.

50. E. C. Tolman, *Purposive Behavior in Animals and Men*, 1932.

51. Cf. p. 3.

52. It is indeed with the acceptance of this purely grammatical facility of categorial language as a proper theoretical scheme for rendering the order of one's cognitive object that a decision wholly prejudicial to that order is taken already: from here on out, the image of an organism principally "having" itself as its own object of perception and striving, in fixating *a priori* the eidetic setting for any task of thought to follow, becomes a shackle as invisible as it is hard to break.

53. Concerning the meaning difference between the notions of the *true* and the *correct* which are regularly confounded in their objectivistic usages, cf. M. Heidegger, *Vom Wesen der Wahrheit*, especially pp. 12–17.

PART THREE

The Peril to Man, and Psychotherapy: The Freedom to *Be*

CHAPTER 6

Binswanger's Criterion for the Therapist—The "Subjective" Turn of Psychology as a Recovery of Freedom—Existential Analysis vs. Jungian Objectivism—The Scope of Phenomenology—Being and Knowing (I)—The Central Position of Love—The Three Modi of Existence and Their Implications—The Hierarchy of Spheres of Existence and Its Bearing on the Differential Diagnosis of Psychoses—The Concept of the Clod-Worlds—Existential Psychology as a Normative Science—Existential Psychology and the Biologist.

In his essay "dream and existence"[1] ludwig Binswanger quotes Kierkegaard's word on Lessing: "In neither attempting an unfree devotion nor recognizing an unfree imitation, he—himself free—sets everyone coming near him in a free rapport to himself." This freedom of Lessing, Binswanger demands of the psychotherapist. A freedom thus defined is not an institutional right or privilege that society can bestow upon the individual, but freedom at its source: a spontaneous inner openness of the person, his readiness to let himself be engaged by the *true*[2] wherever it chooses to engage him; without such transcendentness of the self, no reality can emerge, and both the world and the self must remain shadows. A freedom of this fundamentalness man can strictly speaking never have but only be; the therapist, then, must *be* such freedom "so that his spirit may turn from dreaming to waking".[3] But why should, without or prior to the attitude which Kierkegaard discerns in Lessing, the therapist have been a "dreaming" spirit? Because only an unconditional readi-ness to recognize the *other* and share world with him, only an existence understanding itself in the light of intersubjectivity throughout, can truly be awake and hence self-realizing; without such openness of the inner horizon, the therapist, living in an *idios kosmos*, the "private" world as which Heracleitus determines the existential sphere of the sleeper, inevitably must turn the other into an object within that sphere, a shadow of that other's being. Such wakefulness is outside the reach of objectivism because the objectivist, however sober he believes him-self to be, is free only from what he believes are man's illusions about man.   But what *is* man? Since objectivism, like all non-radical reflec-tion, bypasses this question, it can not debunk answers to it without remaining ideological where it aspires to be scientific.

Binswanger's reference to Kierkegaard and Lessing follows his ex-position of a dream in the genesis of which he recognizes the three stages of the psychoanalytic process: the subject's stubborn and at the same time tormented dwelling in a dreamlike isolation with which the process begins, his subsequent egress into the "open" of a humble submission under the analyst's authority, and the final liquidation of that transference. It is characteristic of the complexity of Binswanger's position concerning psychoanalysis that the affirmation of a formal psychoanalytic tenet, such as Freud's axiom about the named succes-sion of stages, serves, as happens frequently in Binswanger's writings, as the starting point for what in substance is an anti-psychoanalytic argument. "That such a liquidation—about which so much has been and is being written—can come about *only* as a genuine inspiration, an ever more lucid wakeness in the sense of Heracleitus and Hegel—otherwise it is a fraud and a self-conceit—is being overlooked in inter-pretations either one-sidedly biological or even mistaking the spirit as an enemy of life. Only, as psychotherapists, we must not stop where Hegel stopped; for, as such, we are not dealing with *objective* truth, with the congruence between our own thinking and the being of ob-jects *as* objects, but with 'subjective truth', as Kierkegaard would say: with the 'innermost passion', by virtue of which subjectivity must work itself through objectivity (the objectivity of communication, consensus, submission to a superpersonal norm) and out of it again, as the third phase of our dream disclosed".[4] Binswanger's reflection on the situation of the therapist, which we quoted in the beginning, follows here; he goes on to say: "In Freud's doctrine of transference-on-the-physician and even more particularly of the liberation from it all these problems slumber; but they are not awakened there, because no one has yet succeeded and no one will ever succeed in deriving the human spirit from *drives*; these two concepts not only are incommensurable, but precisely their incommensurability justifies each of them within its sphere. A deeper penetration is achieved here by Jung's doctrine of individuation as the liberation of the self from the 'false veils of the *persona* on the one hand, the suggestive force of unconscious images on the other'. But however deep the insights may be that Jung gains from the contemplation of individuation as a 'process of psychological development', here, too, the fundamental problem of individuation is concealed by the fact that the contrast between dreaming and waking, suspension in one's 'private' and in the common world, is not understood as what it is: one between image and feeling (which always belong together) on the one hand, the spirit on the other. Since, however, this contrast is there, it cannot escape an explorer such as Jung. What makes the attempt to derive it from the 'function of the unconscious' and its 'compensatory rapport with consciousness' so unsatisfactory, is the disappearance of this contrast only from the center of the stage of problems; all the more it lives on in the questions of detail and in the fundamental concepts. That is especially true for the notion of the 'collective unconscious' which is both at once: a kind of eidetic 'race consciousness' in the sense of Schleiermacher, *and* the ethical reference to a *universal*, to 'the world' or 'the object'. It is clear that in this 'collective unconscious' our contrast continues undissolved. The same holds true for Jung's concept of the self, in which *conscious* and *unconscious* 'complement' each other to form a whole. The unconscious processes compensating the conscious ego are supposed already to contain all those elements necessary for a self-regulation of the total psyche; let alone, however, that that compensation harbors not less than what sets the entire functional dynamism in motion, the fundamental ethical agent of *conscience*, so that the compensatory mechanism does not, vice versa, regulate the total psyche, a problem is not furthered by shifting it from the whole to the parts".[5] We have quoted from Binswanger's remarks on Jung at some length, because the readily seen surface similarities between certain tenets of either make it imperative to bring the decisive divergence between their thoughts as sharply into

focus as possible. The gist of Binswanger's argument is that Jung's
concept of individuation only catches the process of psychical development as seen from without (objectification) and therefore—as our own
analysis of *process time*[6] had shown—in retrospect, missing out on
the phenomenal duality under the form of which this "process" unfolds from *within*, in the subject's own authentic experience; in his
own authentic experience it is precisely the phenomentality of the spirit
(Geist) that forever is uncommunicable *objectively* and therefore is
"bracketed in" rather than truly *accounted for* by Jung. What faces
us here once more are the limits of objectivism rather than of its aspi-
rations in their Jungian form: being communicativeness *per se*, the
spirit naturally has no use for "mediators" that would translate its
messages into the language of factual orders of any kind,[7] be they
Spenglerian typologies of cultures or Jungian ones of single personalities.

The many different forms in which the error of objectivism becomes
concrete in psychoanalytic theorizing will still occupy us; already, what
stands out from Binswanger's argument just quoted is the close link
that connects his own thought with existential philosophy as with that
movement of self-and-world-interpretation which restores the self-identity
of man as the priming point of *world per se*. In going out from subjectivity which already in its *unreflected* states (if not even more
securely in them than in the reflected; a point *Sartre* tends to overlook)
is knowledge of itself as a participant in *being*, Binswanger heavily
leans on Heidegger's method and findings but deviates from Heidegger's doctrine from the very start of his thinking by widening the scope
of the "fundamental situations" he contemplates. The one such fundamental situation or condition by which all true self-transcendentness
of human existence is implemented according to Binswanger, he recognizes in *love*; love is seen as the central, most direction-setting, phenomenon of the being-in-the-world of man, the one and only true
reality source around which Binswanger's entire conception of his phenomenological anthropology revolves. Had Heidegger's account left
love out of consideration? Had it, as some Heidegger interpreters have
wanted to know, debunked love as a mere manifestation of existence in
its non-authenticity—its commonplace "being-with. . . ."? The question is incisive for understanding both Heidegger's own position and
a recent tendency (within *Daseinsanalyse* as a movement in science) to
draw away from certain mainstays of Binswanger's teachings and

closer to *fundamental ontology* itself precisely for the sake of a better—
an even less debunking—understanding of *love*. How are we to comprehend this unless Heidegger's reversal of the traditional definition
of philosophy as love of wisdom into *wisdom of love* stood for an
otherwise silent implication of his entire thinking, too fundamental
indeed to be put in words? Whatever solution the question should
finally merit, any misunderstanding in its way is likely to involve this
given difference in *aims* between Heidegger's and Binswanger's queries:
Heidegger explores in the light of man's participation in being what
constitutionally imperils this participation, calls it into question, and
thus his attention is drawn precisely to those fundamental conditions
of existence—*dread* and *care*—where being is most drastically at stake;
contrariwise, Binswanger's attention as an anthropologist is drawn to
the general (normative) conditions under which, in the observable
spread of individual human existences, the "participation" itself (as
a certain personal way of existing) either takes form or fails to substantiate, and thus he comes to discern love as the one among all
elementary situations of the human person that allows of the fullest,
most engaging, *factual* transcendentness of the self.

The normative status of what Binswanger's research is after (and
which comprises the archetypes of Jung as much as the differential
existential premises of their encounter by the experience of man) is
contested by Jaspers and some others in accordance with Jaspers' general restriction of the scope of *reductive* phenomenology (which Jaspers scorns) to the "pure" eidetic sphere of categorial, logical, and
mathematical *Anschauungen* in Husserl's sense; the "typically" and
"typologically" human, the actual orbit of all that is intuitively understandable in interpersonal relations, is seen as possessing a high degree
of both immediacy and constancy by Jaspers, and its exploration is
supported by a purely *descriptive* phenomenology of subjective experience, but it is not acknowledged as representing essences in any strict
(that is, timeless) sense. The differences in compellingness, for example,
between an "idea" of pure eidetics and an anthropological idea such
as *Don Quixote* are, of course, evident: of man, as of a time-bound
(historical) being, no image in its inevitable specificity *as* one can
be conceived that, in the manner of the unhistorical phenomenality of
a cube or a triangle, would persist through time in the sense of a
timelessness inherent in its own constitution, independently of what-

ever genesis the experiential occurrences of such an image to historical
individuals or groups may sketch out. While this is obvious, the argument by-passes what all *reductive* phenomenology hinges on, the given
continuum of degrees of eidetic axiomaticity; what marks out this continuum, are the manifest differences with which, in the interpenetrations
of temporality and categoriality characteristic of all classes of ontological objects, categoriality may outweigh temporality to the point of
its exclusion (mathematical eidetics) while being more or less out-
weighed by temporality in such quiddities as are bound to historical
situations as the given horizons of their comprehension. A *historical*
situation, in turn, in this connotation, may be the situation of a single
person or a single generation as well as—if the archetype encountered
happens to represent an experiential content of relative historic constancy—of a millenium of generations: the degree of compellingness
which an image bound to that situation exercises on the immediate
experience of human beings *wholly outside* of its boundaries in historic time is not affected by this. Neither, however, does the degree of
mathematical compellingness of an idea or an image according to the
relative shares of "temporality" and "categoriality" in it determine
the degree of its immediate *convincingness*; whatever magnitude of
the former is given, the dimension these magnitudes stake out intersect at any point with another and wholly different one that is set by
the different degrees of immediacy with which phenomena are *plausible*. A story relying wholly on categoriality in the sense both of a maximum of rational construction in spinning its plot and of a maximum
of timeless typicalness of the human situations which the author weaves
into it without unfolding these situations from *within* their human
subjects may be forgotten after a very short time while Don Quixote,
so inextricably bound to numberless specifics of Cervantes' age, continues to be evident in and through the very "relativity" of these media.

The error behind Jaspers' restriction of phenomenology, then, is the
error of what explicitly Jaspers opposes, the idealism of Husserl which
in the Speusippian tradition confounds ideas with more or less mathe-
maticalized abstractions *from* them that it mistakes for essences; inevitably, abstractions remain only after the ideas themselves, already having
been buried in categories henceforth supposed to stand for them, have
ceased to be eidetically present. The dependence of this entire "rationality"—the rationality of all thing-ification, categorization, and ob-

jectification, of any mode of thought that replaces being in its authentic self-unfoldingness by a fixed succession of momentary structural exteriors of that-which-is—on mathematical time has been shown before, the contingency of mathematical time itself on an extension of the *past* beyond its proper phenomenal boundaries been pointed out. Since phenomenology, according to its own principle the reflective exploration of experience in its unreflected immediacy, cannot spare artifacts in its way any more than can any other genuine method of inquiry, not only must phenomenology go "behind" categoriality, logic, and the "pure" eidetics of geometry, but it is from this "going behind", which runs counter to empiricism just as much as to rationalism, that phenomenology must expect the richest empirical (psychological) yields: experience not only is "earlier" than what it is according to its own self-misunderstanding that arises from its tendency to reflect itself in categories, but it is earlier also than what the "tangible" ones among these categories comprise (sensory objects). Binswanger states it in this manner: "There are wide, indeed very wide fields-of-objects inaccessible to sensory perception, of which nevertheless we obtain as well as integrate *eidetic knowledge*; we may well say that for every field-of-objects a corresponding act of eidetic cognizance can be found".[8] While this statement is in full formal agreement with Husserl's conception of phenomenology, to which Binswanger refers at that point, it is the *every-field-of-objects* that implicitly leads away from the position of the founding father of phenomenology: the norms of existence, man's modes of being-in-the-world, which Binswanger explores, constitute a field of objects that would never have occurred as a worthy topic for phenomenological inquiry to *Husserl*.

In his conception of the being-in-the-world, which Binswanger takes over from Heidegger, neither the "subject" nor the "world" has priority in the sense of one of them objectively determining the other; according to the gist of Heidegger's own early analyses in *Being and Time* of the normal factual condition in which existence "encounters itself" one could rather say that what determines the whole "project" (the individual existence) is what in that formulation "connects" the subject and his world, the *being-in*. Inasmuch, as existence is temporality, this being-in, however, cannot be stationary: instead, it is "mundanization", meaning that the individual existence, as it "projects" or "designs" itself, is bent upon (*entwirft sich auf*) a certain world image ("reality"). As a specific phenomenalization of original Truth, as which, as we recall, Truth is not a condition of *judging* but of *being*, the world apperception in turn directs and shapes the self of the subject, a mode of interaction to be understood genetically as a constant and simultaneous mutuality of reference of the two (with their inherent *claims* upon the other) rather than as a successive alternation of objective directions of effectiveness. The entire pseudo-problem of genetic priorities ("nativism" versus "environmentalism"), so constitutive to the world of scientific thought dominated by the *idée fixe* of a split between "subject" and "object", vanishes at this point. In accordance with Heidegger's teaching—who determines existence in one of its aspects as *erschliessendes Verständnis*, understanding *unlocking* the otherwise mute contingency of that-which-is—being and knowing move into a relationship where one no longer can even be conceived without the other.[9]

This would seem to bring *Daseinsanalyse*, and the existentialist movement altogether, into the neighborhood of such deterministic doctrines as the Freudian, and indeed, from Freud's work, as Binswanger himself has often recognized, the new conception profited materially as from the accomplishments of no other of its precursors within the anthropological fields. But the tendency of existential analysis *to anchor thought in being* is the very opposite of naturalism and causal reductionism because being, very much in distinction from the objectified *id*, the objectified *subconscious* of psychoanalysis, is itself not a hypothetical construct within the sphere of that-which-is but, with Löwith's word,[10] the *transcendens per se*. Accordingly, the "existential" basis of thought has nothing to do with any objectifiable functional agents, and just as little can the existent's world in its *derangement* ever be—instead of an absence of truth—a "distortion of reality" (as though there *was* such a thing as a reality even conceivable as constituted without its reference to the experience of somebody). Since our Chapter Four has pointed this out systematically,[11] what remains to be realized most at this point is that no relativism is implied in this unification of being and knowing; the existentialist redetermination of Truth as the open and encompassing "clearing" in orientation to which being not only knows itself but unfolds its knowledge into the given differentiality of individual human existences allows of a measure for the *truth* of an existence as the extent to which

mundanization, the transcendence-toward-world of *Dasein*, has broken
through the barrier of the false self of self-objectification.[12] Since
the false self of self-objectification, in turn, is the self as determinism
understands it (the sphere of irrational animal instincts of psychoanalysis), the nineteenth century trend toward an anchoring of *thinking*
in *being* takes a significant turn at the existential-analytic stage: thought
and being not only are interdependent but are positively *one* where
self-transcendence as the self's engagement by the non-self is at its
peak of sustained *openness for the other* ("modus of we-ness"). Only
short of this optimal condition (and to precisely the extent to which
an individual case may show itself remote from its standard) can that
unauthentic state of *splitness* be said to obtain which psychoanalysis
prejudicially has turned into a theoretical model for the natural relationship between being and knowing altogether: once self-objectification, in
a manner already characterized, has positively dualized the psyche,
neither of these two, being and knowing, any longer is what it is
"meant" to be in any genuine sense. Instead, both quite literally enter
into an alternation of interdependencies (functional, that is,
"mechanical", determinations of one by the other), and it is this
alternation that shows the peculiar form of the "psychological as well
as noetic whirl" which our Chapter Five spelled out.

The problems that surround the new (and age-old) conception of
Truth in its application to concrete existences, the recovery of the
origin of that notion in an awareness of authentic *being*, will clarify
themselves as we proceed; Truth, at any rate, has already and tacitly
been understood as an *existential* condition before—as a "category"—
it can be defined as the condition of any *judgment*.[13] But which
existential status articulates itself of old in a spontaneous coming-to-
mind of just that notion of truth, if not *loving?* With his conviction
that love, or rather the fundamental situation of lovingness, is the
only possible implementation of maximal self-transcendence of the
existence of man, Binswanger's thinking, like that of many other
existentialists, follows the path of St. Augustine who is frequently
quoted in *The Basic Forms and the Cognition of Human Existence*,[14]
Binswanger's masterwork, which already in its subject and title contains a hint at the "transcendental" unity of being and knowing in
recognition *of* which as well as in accordance *with* which existences
require to be studied. Taking up suggestions which *Being and Time*

had supplied, Binswanger finds the link between being and knowing manifested most palpably in the tendency of man, observable in the structure of the *being-with* throughout, to "take" his fellowman "by" a certain of his interests—a general concern of human beings, a skill or talent, a line of private or vocational self-identification, or whatever may implement the true concept of *inter-est* as that which links together the self and the world; what completes this picture is, of course, the active readiness of the one thus taken to let himself be "taken by" whichever one of these may come nearest in his case to what Binswanger calls the central *tendency* of an existence. In human biographies, this existential tendency is made visible by what in them deviates from the typical yet shows an undiminished openness to intersubjective understanding in the very unity of the *personal* that such deviations mark out; as R. Kuhn[15] has pointed out in one of his contributions to the daseinsanalytic literature, not the road from the individual and differential to its categorization, but vice versa the road from a rough "objective" allocation of a "case" in any of the usual classificatory schemes to an understanding penetration of the structure of the patient's *world* is the road to pursue for psychology as a science.

Since Binswanger's conception of existential tendencies as specific implementations of a general principle of lawfulness (immanent to biographic structure independent of and beyond the person's own awareness of his "goals" in *living* his biography) moves visibly in the neighborhood of Jung's unconscious *tropisms* of the psyche, it again is in disputing an axiomatic claim of Jungian theory (as a shaky generalization from specific case materials) that Binswanger protects his own proposition from misunderstandings that would narrow and distort its scope. The chapter on "Existence and existential tendency" of his main work spells this out. "Incidentally, that Jung's contention, according to which we judge ourselves primarily according to the *wish-image* which we form of ourselves, cannot claim universal validity is already shown by the existence of persons judging themselves far more unsparingly and truthfully than others judge them. But even as a matter of pure principle one can hold against the Jungian skepticism what an equally profound knower of man, Marcel Proust, once uttered: 'Nous travaillons à tout moment à donner sa forme à notre vie, mais en copiant malgré nous comme un dessin les traits de la personne que nous sommes et non de celle qu'il nous serait agréable d'être'. (Le Côté de Guermantes, I, 168f). Nothing, then, is accomplished with a distinction between a 'conscious' wish-image and an 'unconscious' shaping of our lives; what is involved here are rather two contradictory views of man's essential nature. From this confrontation it appears that one can never penetrate to theorems of general psychological truth on the basis of purely discursive experience; as Hegel already had mockingly demonstrated in respect to psychological 'laws', every such 'empiric fact' can be confronted with one showing the diametrical opposite. Empiric theorems of purely discursive derivation must therefore be rejected as dogmatical in all those cases where they claim validity as keys to the cognition of the essential nature of man or of the *being human;* at best, their applicability extends to a limited human type but frequently only to a certain specific (normal or pathological) group of individuals. Cognizance and description of psychological *types* hence can never be understood as *cognitions of existence.*"[16] The reference to Proust, as a great narrator an immediately convincing, silently self-imposing authority on the situation of man, is paralleled by uncounted references to inspired literary and philosophical documents from all ages and cultures with which Binswanger's writings are strewn: a propensity of his intellect that can draw on an easy and universal command of history and the humanities as much as of the sciences. This sovereignty of orientation, self-evident for a scientist of man and therefore nowhere either stressed or postulated explicitly, reflects the general trend of phenomenology to "let things speak for themselves", to be radically empirical: the "speech of the things", in the case of documentary evidences supplied by the history of ideas and of letters, is not in itself already a theoretical account of human existence, but it is its only fully articulate alley of self-manifestation and therefore the *material* of psychology. So, in a wider and more basic sense, is its medium, man's *languages:* how, without being at home in them, can the psychologist have opinions on "the function of language"? He can not, not validly at least, and neither can his conceptions of past ages and their thoughts have any meaning whatsoever unless they take off from a radical absence of prejudice, an openness toward the tenor and content of ideas of the past as only the documents themselves—first hand—can convey to him at all.[17]

In its further ramifications, Binswanger's concept of *existential tendency* is interlocked closely with his perception of the manifoldness that inheres in the notion of *world* according to its universal norms.

This manifoldness cuts across the manifoldness of the existential worlds themselves: the being-in-the-world is, in one of its major aspects, seen as a being-in that knows itself (*is*) in three spheres simultaneously, as the *being-body* of the person, as his *being-with* (others; intersubjectivity therefore unlocks that "world" wherein the existent knows himself as soul, "ego", "personality", etc.), and as the *being-in* in its ultimateness, as a self-encountering rapport between the person and the cosmos. Further differentiations, for example of the local or systemic subspheres of the being-body (as first and incompletely pointed out by Freud) ramify from this core. Correspondingly, Binswanger finds both the imagery of his patients and the actual structure of their simultaneous experiences grouped in topical accordance with that hierarchy: "Generally I would like to draw your attention to the three forms which, in the main, the eidetic language of our patients shows, its tripartition into body images, soul images, and cosmic ones (either celestial or chthonic). Allow me briefly to exemplify in closing from the simple case of another patient how these *languages* run parallel not only with one another but also with the actual 'language' of body and soul: when the patient 'opens herself' in an existential-communicative step by wanting to communicate to herself and the physician something new that so far has been subject to repression, she experiences this bodily as a relaxation of the tonus of her sphincter muscles, body-eidetically as pregnancy and birth of a child, or of a melon which in turn opens on its part, psychically as the 'coming nearer' of an idea or a memory from the 'depth' of her soul, soul-eidetically, in close connection with that previously repressed idea, as a gap in the pavement of a betonized road, cosmically as a slow lifting and rising up of huge and heavy metal plates that cover the whole earth."[18]

A similar order (somatopsychic, autopsychic, allopsychic "central preoccupations") is applied by Binswanger to the understanding of the various ways in which, as in differently "preoccupied" schizophrenic biographies, the conflict giving rise to psychosis may center itself on the self as soma, the self in its "absoluteness" (its exposure to the cosmos) and the self in its *being-with*, as it stands in apposition to the social world, the others. Since existence as the being-in-the-world is constitutionally transcendence-*toward*-world, the "worlds" themselves and thereby, in turn, the existent's very identity hinge on the degree as well as on the specific where-toward of transcendence. *Dasein*, thus, since it is not just only "leads to", but throughout *exists as,* self- and world-understanding, knows a singular modus (I myself); a plural one ("I" *and* "they", as in the common social being-with . . . any number of other persons; *or* as the non-genuine we-ness of any explicit identification with a group, or any implicit one with the *everybody*); and, finally, a dual modus of existence (genuine we-ness of love, including its less "totally" engaging forms, such as friendship). The latter, in turn, is the modus most securely determined by self-transcendence in its capacity to sustain mundanization, that is, to unfold world[19]: a condition the dynamics of which, like the dynamics of all spontaneity, are pointing outward from within the existent, away from his self. The plural modus is the ordinary one; it determines the commonplace *who* of existence both in its normal conventionality and its more visible losses of self by way of submersion in the identities of groups.[20] Contrariwise, the singular modus is exposed to the sharpest, most extreme alternatives between a nearly complete "break-through" (authentic religiosity, philosophic thought, poetic and artistic creativity)[21] and that just as nearly complete failure of self-transcendence —autism—which is always and necessarily pathogenic, since according to the very constitution of the self as a world-referent it is the self that here remains unrealized. The phenomenological norm of this failure-to-attain can be determined as a veritable blocking-off of the beyond-the-self, a shrouding of the horizon of *Dasein*; since man's being-in-the-world is a *pro-ject,* a "throw" into the "clearing" of Truth, as well as a "stretching" (Heidegger) of his understanding towards the future, the very aiming of this throw as which existence "pre-designs itself" must already be drawn toward the openness of the existential horizon as which *Truth* and the *future* phenomenally coincide and which alone is capable of giving the "project" any sureness of direction. If Truth is missed in "aiming", "self-designing", in the most fundamental conviction of a person that determines his manner of encountering both *self* and *world*[22]; if the "opening" (Truth) is not attained toward which existences converge and which makes each one's truth a "different" one precisely because convergence itself is a coming-together of directions each different only according to its point of start (and thereby its route), the failing existence-project must become what in some psychoanalytic doctrines has been named a "supervalent" idea. It becomes the core of an ersatz world, a "clod world", with the daseinsanalytic term: perpetuating itself as what blocks the existence

from attaining its truth, the "idea" may at the same time so powerfully simulate the direction of attainment that around it the facts of
the person's position in society as well as of the objective environment
are ordered. Since, in such instances, no directing power is being exercised by an encompassing Truth as that which originally draws *Dasein*
"beyond itself", the dynamism of mundanization will finally reverse its
direction: man, helplessly exposed to his own petrified "conviction" of
yore, his supervalent *idée fixe*, is caught in and imposed upon by his
ersatz world like an aimless and furious animal amidst the steel bars
of his cage.[23]

Hardly the roughest presentation of Binswanger's principal building
stones in developing *Daseinsanalyse* as an orientation and method of
anthropological[24] normative science has been offered. Since this doctrine seeks to determine the subject matter of personality psychology in
terms of the gamut of experience-worlds to which human *Dasein* transcends and in which alone it encounters and articulates itself, it turns
into a normative (categorial) science of possible phenomenal world-
structures, with their different "spheric" centerings (as pointed out
before) and their different modi—developed in accordance with
Heidegger's ontology of transcendence—of "spatialization" and
"temporalization"; according to an observation of Binswanger still to
be presented *in extenso*, the latter two underly the specific constitution
of the very *who* of an existence, that is, of its identity. But existential
analysis, to carry out its proposition as we just defined it, must, as a
psychological theory, still concentrate on the categorization of some
general structural laws (if not of "psyches", all the more of "worlds") ;
without constant vigilance on the theoretician's and the therapist's
part, without their constant readiness to think categories back to the
experiential events they both represent and conceal, it is thus ever
endangered to fall back into the error of objectifying abstractions
that it fights. This danger not only has been pointed out by existential
philosophers but by recent voices from within the *daseinsanalytic*
school—the school of psychiatry that owes its origins to Binswanger's
teachings but with growing frequency seems drawn toward a fresh start
in interpreting existentialist thought in its psychological, clinical, and
therapeutic implications.[25] Criticisms from these quarters will be taken
up and followed later; at the present point in our discussion, more
importance may attach to the objection commonly levelled at Binswanger from the side of psychoanalysis and charging him, as far as its

gist can be made out at all, with a neglect of the "biological" side of personality and of its growth.

Since no other theory concentrates as frankly and intensely as his on the *being-body* that existence *is*, what can the criticism mean? Evidently, not the reproach of any neglect for, or even unsatisfactory rapport with, modern biology, which can hardly be contended, but the reproach of an abandonment by phenomenological anthropology of the allegedly "only solid basis", never yet shown in either its exclusiveness or its solidity, of biologistic *reductionism*, that is, "naturalism". That existential psychology knows such "spiritualists" as Scheler, Plessner, and Pfänder among its immediate ancestors, not to mention its less immediate ones from all historic periods of humanity, is itself a reason to nurture deep-seated suspicions; but if these suspicions seem to have difficulty to express their meaning clearly, what else can be the reason for this but the evident unbrokenness of the other line of ancestry of the new doctrine that legitimately connects it with the teachings just of biologists? Not only phenomenology, but such "functionalistic" conceptions as Üxküll's *Merkwelten* (the sensory-behavioral environments of organisms *as these environments occur to them*), Weizsäcker's *Gestaltkreise* (the unitary contexts of experience and action that bind organisms into their "worlds") have contributed to the theory of the being-in-the-world as self-transcendence; and if all these ideas had themselves to undergo a revision in the light of the existentialist rejection of the subject-object split of Descartes, *was* that gap in man's world ever itself a yield of scientific research?[26] The indebtedness—supported by pervading compatability—of existential analysis to the holistic biology of our time, which Binswanger himself has acknowledged as a debt especially to Goldstein's achievements,[27] is a matter of the record; and so only the position of existential psychology in respect to psychoanalysis itself remains for us to clarify before turning to more special questions.

NOTES

1. L. Binswanger, *Ausgewählte Vorträge und Aufsätze*, 1947, p. 95.
2. Cf. p. 85.
3. L. Binswanger, *loc. cit.*
4. *Ibid.*
5. L. Binswanger, *op. cit.*, pp. 95–96.
6. Cf. pp. 115–16.

7. For a comparison, see Heidegger's ontology of the mainspring of the "spirit" (*conscience*), *Sein und Zeit*, pp. 267–95. The indissoluble contradiction to which Jung's theorizing, in simultaneously recognizing the subjective autonomy of the spiritual in man and yet subjecting it, along with all the rest of the human psyche, to the most radical attempt at all-out objectification ever made in psychoanalytic thinking, must lead, is shown most poignantly by the conceptual dilemma of the "psychic realities" to which non-factual contents of phenomenal experience are reduced in his doctrine; according to the only empirical access to these contents which we have at all—according to man's *experience* of them—they are characterized precisely by this, that they do *not* form "part" of the subject's psyche but on the contrary are what—beyond its boundaries—the psyche *encounters*.

8. L. Binswanger, *Op. cit.*, p. 16.

9. Cf. pp. 91, 109.

10. K. Löwith, "Die Auslegung des Ungesagten in Nietzsche's Wort 'Gott ist tot' ", Die Neue Rundschau, 1953, 64, 105–137, p. 106.

11. Cf. pp. 54–58.

12. Cf. pp. 134–35, 188, 205.

13. Cf. p. 131.

14. L. Binswanger, *Grundformen und Erkenntnis menschlichen Daseins*, Zuerich, 1942.

15. R. Kuhn, *"Daseinsanalyse im psychotherapeutischen Gespraech"*, Schweizer Archiv für Neurologie und Psychiatrie, 1951, 47, 52–74.

16. L. Binswanger, *Op. cit.*, p. 457.

17. Concerning the objectivist's unscientific confounding of subjectivity (*experiencing* as such) as the exclusive form in which psychological data are *given*, with subjectivism (arbitrariness in handling them theoretically), cf. p. 15.

18. L. Binswanger, *Ausgewählte Vorträge und Aufsätze*, pp. 157–8.

19. In its fundamentalness to the phenomena of *understanding*, the dual modus of existence as a primal and constant (constituent) availability of man's being-in-the-world has been introduced before; cf. pp. 38, 85.

20. The implicit devaluation of the human *herd* or *mass* here (as an agglomeration of fundamentally isolated, "atomized" "individuals") has nothing to do, of course, with any lack of recognition by Binswanger (or any other existential thinker) of the organic and hard-to-overrate share with which a genuine *home*, a still integrated *society*, a *people* bound by common and spontaneous loyalties and values partake—as manifestations of *being*—in the *wherefrom* of existence as the ground in which the existent's very identity is rooted; the condition, however, for this share to be genuine and wholesome is its *silence* (relative unconsciousness), which already is broken once it is romanticized and subsequently politicized, that is, turned into a topic of ideology. As a topic of ideology (Cf. certain stages of romanticism; later, vitalism and irrationalism; finally, Nazism) it is "categorized", which means that it becomes a "self-misunderstanding" *remembrance* of man precisely *in his isolation* and therefore one of the possible characteristics of a form of existence occupying the extreme counterpole to what it means concretely.

21. It is to be noted that one of the most basic characterological attributes of the singular modus of existence, the very "fault" of egotism, may be "transfigured"

in this case. In pointing out the peculiarity of self-transcendent egotism, in which the ego is the "only one" only in a *societal* ("civic") respect while finding itself, like a child in rapport to his parent, bound into a "dual" modus of existence in which "the other one" is *God*, Binswanger takes up the Augustinian conception of *philautia*, "self-love", in which the *self* already no longer connotes the person as a finite biological and social entity (as in commonplace egotism) but connotes the person as the organon of "loving" (that is, of a limitlessly "stretching" *understanding*)—as the "child" to whom, in his own personal understanding, the world as a whole is being offered like a gift.

22. It is evident from many outstanding biographies (Tasso, Hölderlin, Van Gogh, etc.) that both positions within the alternative of the singular existence modus may appear in one life course. Ever since Lombroso, prevailing attention has been drawn to the more frequent sequence genius-insanity, which daseinsanalytically shows the tragic and at times lightning-like *narrowing* of the existential horizon that may follow its almost complete dissolution in the powerfully rising phase of some life histories. That this sequence is nothing absolute is shown by its complete reversal (if also lesser dramaticness) in the biography of the Swiss poet and novelist, C. F. Meyer, in which an early phase of almost schizophrenic autism was superseded by one of ingenious productivity bearing the characteristic marks of *philautia*.

23. This reversal of the dynamic direction of mundanization is connoted by *Wahn*, an untranslatable term of ordinary as well as psychiatric German which strictly speaking signifies an untruth in which the person is caught without knowing it as such and being able to help it. While *Wahn*, in English and French, has most frequently been rendered as *delusion*, its definitive scope is in one sense "narrower", in another "wider" than that of *delusion*. It is *narrower* inasmuch as an incorrigibility of the "untruth", an expansive-destructive power of it (seen as arising from the innermost being of the person caught in it) belong to the necessary phenomenal characteristics of *Wahn*, *wider* inasmuch as any existence-narrowing idea bearing the mark of futility and disproportion—existential *truthlessness*—but not necessarily clashing with either purposive rationality or the "facts" of an objective world-account comes under its definition.

24. Since "anthropology" ("Anthropologie"), in its more usual connotation in both English and German, has acquired the specialistic meaning of a comparative study of races and cultures, the term *Anthropologie*, in accordance with Binswanger's and the other existentialists' usage, is rendered throughout this and the following chapters in its original English connotation as science of man.

25. M. Boss, *Meaning and Content of Sexual Perversions*, 1949.

26. "Why do I bother you with these apparently complicated matters? For no other reason but because with the doctrine of the being-in-the-world as transcendence the cancer of all psychology up to now has been conquered and the road toward a science of man laid open: the cancer of the doctrine of the subject-object 'cleavage' of *world*." L. Binswanger, "Ueber die Daseinsanalytische Forschungsrichtung in der Psychiatrie", in *Ausgewählte Vorträge und Aufsätze*, 1947, p. 193.

27. *Ibid.*, p. 200.

CHAPTER 7

*An Inspection of Psychoanalysis—Existence and the
Mechanisms—Freud's Neglect of the Motor Sphere—
Some Fundamental Criticisms—Reason and Rationality
—The Nature of Symbols—A Dream and Its Interpreta-
tive Problem—Phenomenal Causality and Strict Explan-
atory Causalism—The Psychoanalytic Dissidents—A
Paradigmatic Error of Objectivism—Categoriality and
Time—Freud as Teacher.*

MANY OF THE PRINCIPAL PHENOMENOLOGICAL AND
existentialist criticisms of psychoanalysis have been voiced before in
this text. An impression may have been formed that the new movement
was oblivious to the magnitude and epochal significance of Freud's
achievements, or unmindful of its debt either to the revolutionary
course of his research or to the problems that his—less revolutionary—
thought had opened without solving; but nothing could be more
erroneous. That debt, which one of Ludwig Binswanger's most brilliant discourses, conceived in the spirit of the close personal friendship
that bound him to Freud, freely acknowledges,[1] is being paid in the
only legitimate form in which such debts are always paid in the history
of science, by integrating the whole of Freud's factual (especially
psychogenetic) discoveries and rediscoveries as modern physics has
integrated the factual knowledge of the physics of the time of Helmholtz. This does not prevent physicists nowadays from opposing the
doctrines of Helmholtz: inasmuch as scientific theories, in trying to
climb the wall of man's original ignorance, must stand on each other's
shoulders, no theory reaching the edge of that wall and for the first
time discerning what stretches beyond it will find even the vista accessible to the one just below its own position binding in any but the
literal sense in which it binds that other's eyes to the horizon-blocking
proximity of the obstacle before it.

A full evaluation of the way in which the truth and untruth of
psychoanalysis shapes up in the light of existentialist reflection must

await the results of the closer analysis to be undertaken in the present chapter; the psychogenetic gains of Freud, and their acknowledgment by existential analysis, have been spoken of. Already we may say that it is not so much the correctness of Freud's theorization of whatever in the psyche *is* objectifiable in terms of processes—its "mechanisms"[2]—as the truth of the psychoanalytic interpretation of these findings and the use that is made of them in therapy that existentialism contests: just as a trick mirror will give the cohesive yet distorted picture of whatever object it reflects, it is not the overall arrangement of psychological data but the essence of what they constitute in their togetherness that psychoanalysis misses. But just as the distortions inherent in the reflections of a trick mirror can be determined at closer range as specific failures to render proportions correctly, so also the correctness of the psychoanalytic data arrangement becomes less impressive under scrutiny. One of the observations that restrict it in psychogenetics is that Freud, in attempting to trace the structural development of the adult psyche to its infantile beginnings, nowhere founds his theorizing either on the entire normal topology of memory data from that period or on an unbiased observation of the behavior of infants; of the implications and consequences, only the one most vital in a factual sense may be mentioned at this point. We are speaking of Freud's obliviousness toward the entire motor sphere of infantile body as well as world experience: in distinction from actual children with their conspicuous primacy of muscular interests in *acting into* their environments, exploring and mastering them, Freud's infants, condemned by an immanentistic preoccupation of his thought to exist in a worldless ("precathectic") status *a priori*, appear to be worldless also in this respect that instead of bodies they have only body holes. Yet this "orificial" status of existence is nowhere denied by existential analysis as one of the normative *possibilities*, the possible forms of *Dasein*, which Binswanger's own research is after: what is contested is rather the cognitive legitimacy of the psychoanalytic hope ever to understand, with a paraphrasing of Freud's own word, the normal in terms of the sick rather than the latter in terms of the former.

As any such undertaking as tracing the immanentistic and objectivistic errors of psychoanalysis throughout the maze of movements of circular reasoning of which the doctrine is woven would require a

separate volume, only clues to the gist of the existentialist critique—
arranged according to the main observations and whole themes on
which they are centered—are given in the following section. In this
presentation, certain previously developed lines of argument had to be
briefly sketched anew in the mere interest of systematicness, necessitating repetitions for which the reader's forbearance is sought.

1) There is, in Freud and with less explicitness in all the dissidents
from his doctrine, an aprioristic view of the human psyche as though
it could be understood in analogy with causally reducible (mechanical)
processes observable in a field of which the observer's vantage point
is independent. This already dictates properties to the subject matter
of which, empirically, it shows the direct opposite; it also misjudges
the given relations between the observer and the field. In distinction
from events in physics, not a single psychic event can be observed that
does not refer to something beyond itself, or rather, *is* that reference.
Its object may be diffuse but there always and at any stage of the
event is one. The modus of being of the psyche, of "subjectivity", then,
in distinction from the modus of being of physical objects, is a unity
of self and world which makes it impossible to turn subjectivity into
an object of inquiry without already stating it in terms of its own
experiential sphere—its world. This world, which is given only to the
subject himself, is not a standard reality which the observer can easily
undertake to describe, as such description will come out in terms of
the observer's, not the subject's, world apperception, within which
the subject's psyche has become just another object. As given to the
subject, unless there is already disintegration, the world neither depends
on his drives, as Freud's later extension of his projection theory has it,
nor does it resist his drives, nor gratify them to some extent, as he
states elsewhere—all these topological characterizations already refer
to the observer's perspective. The subject, unless he observes himself,
is not concerned with his drives and impulses; he does not "have"
them, he *is* them, and the more so the more he is motivated by them;
his world has properties and values whose significance, to his
experience, is independent of the fact of his experiencing. Experience,
then, is a self-transcendent act which cannot even be stated in terms
other than of what it transcends itself toward. In distinction from the
situation of the physicist, the psychologist is caught with his subject
matter not in a simple polarity, which would justify Freudian immanen-

tism, but in a triadic constellation, subject-phenomenon-observer. Of the three corners of that triangle, each is just as real as either of the two others, so that a phenomenon encountered by the subject's experiencing can never be understood with any claim to truthfulness as a function or product of his psyche.

Experience processes are intercommunicable, for example, between a patient and his therapist, *only* in terms of their transcendent objects; a model, although insufficient for therapy because it does not ask sufficiently radical questions, of such communication is the Socratic method; any other "communication", as in terms of his introspection into his own psychical "processes" (which, of course, are not identical with spontaneous dreams or meditations faced with inner transcendent phenomena such as images and ideas) places the subject outside of himself as an observer of himself. As an observer of himself, his perspective for his own experience *as a process* is a radically different one from his primary perspective as an experiencer; the original (phenomenal) object is gone, the two perspectives, the spontaneous and the self-conscious, pertain to different things, and "re-evaluations" of the experience, "insights" into it other than in direct orientation to its transcendent object, are therefore displacements of focus. This is stating the cognitive inadequacy of self-perception; the same can be stated in terms of what is being perceived. As the subject observes himself, he diverts attention away from any possible transcendent objects and toward his own psyche; simultaneously, this new object, his psyche, is by this very diversion reduced in spontaneity, in self-transcending strength, since it is left with much less attention than before for its own whole sphere of primary phenomenal objects: the process of self-cognition, as some cognitive events do in physics also, thus changes the properties of that which is to be cognized, the psyche. The psychological result is a form of decomposition characterized by multiple and variable inner sets, a libertinage of single impulses and a lessening of total spontaneity and freedom, of *character*, very similar to hysteria. This symptom picture, significantly, gave rise to the whole immanentistic doctrine, was understood best and treated most successfully by Freud, but in its total structural deviation from integrated states, which are integrated always and only at the price of transcending themselves toward *world*, remained—as will be shown under 5)—uncomprehended as well.

2) The subject's world, in the particular way in which it *matters* to him, is structured by values—valences, demand qualities; but all these expressions are already abstractions referring to the theoretician's perspective rather than the subject's. What, in the therapeutic situations, they mean concretely, must be distorted by immanentistic confounding of perspectives unless a complete retranslation is constantly made of the therapist's theoretical (psychological) insights into the subject's existential world-context constellated triadically with the therapist's position. This is impossible unless the therapist is able to identify with the patient's value experiences in their transcendency: ecological "facts" to the therapist as a theoretician, to the subject himself his values have no *facticity* (unless he is self-conscious, he is not even aware of them as values) but *validity*—not *they are,* but *he ought to.* This "ought to", which is wholly different from any *must,* is a radically different experiential category altogether from any that fits into Freud's system with its view of a police-state-like role ascribed to the superego. Conflicts in the patient, then, which at their root are always value conflicts, can only be helped toward solution by phenomenological clarification, never by reduction to needs and drives. This, in turn, presupposes that the therapist is guided by vigorous but also—considering his special role—sufficiently *explicit* values of his own, which allow of direct communication with the patient's. "Full psychological understanding", then, is never full enough psychological understanding, if it strives to be merely *that*; the "value problem" is inescapable and occurs at practically every step in theory and therapy. Freud avoids it, as he avoids (and opposes) "philosophy", yet he evaluates as well as philosophizes constantly and not even implicitly: both are done quite in the open, yet apparently without any awareness on the part of Freud of the tacit metaphysical premises— of which an antimetaphysical ideology is just another one—from which his thinking takes off.

This is an inarticulate position: empiricism, rather than being the operant principle of inquiry, becomes to a large extent a dogma preached to others. Perhaps Freud himself could hardly be aware of this, as against the background of what psychology there was in his day his factual discoveries were so enormous that there was little obvious reason for him to be suspicious of the limitations on empiricalness which his own thinking imposed. It is evident, however, that under the protection of his ideology as characterized, Freud's personal prejudices determined blindly which properties the subject matter was allowed to have, which not. Whatever he could not re-experience, therefore, was debunked, and it is this debunking indeed which, like most of late nineteenth century deterministic thought, was bound inadvertently to turn into nihilism through its destruction of the very basis for theoretical interexchange altogether, a development for which Freud's statement in the Introduction to the *Introductory Lectures* may be quoted as the perhaps most representative example: "Society therefore turns the unwelcome into the untrue, contests the truths of psychoanalysis with *logical* and *objective* arguments but from affective sources of motivation, and maintains these doubts and *prejudices* against all attempts at disproof."[3] This, of course, is the old *argumentum ad hominem*. Only that, in this its new, deterministic version, it no longer alleges, as in the older ones, an untruthful intent on the part of the opponent but in accordance with Freud's immanentism has already turned the opponent into an object, a *thing* closed to truth, as it shifts the debate from the cognitive level on which science stands or falls to the conative: who cares if what my opponent says is true; *why* does he say so? This debunking intent prior to any noetic analysis of a counter-argument to one's own is, of course, not only all over Freud; it largely characterizes the specific dehumanization of the *Zeitgeist* of Freud's age, out of which present world realities have grown, a collective state of mind of which the central peculiarity is just this that its sharers no longer are capable even of *expecting*, before having listened to them, counter-arguments to their own to be anything but either an ideational superstructure erected by unconscious interests of their adversaries, or simply "propaganda". The logical consequence of Freud's philosophizing as implicit in the sentence quoted can thus be stated in this form: every belief, including this one, is a disguise of some ulterior motive; only the middle clause, peculiarly, never seems to occur to the *anthropological determinist*. The search for truth, monopolized by him and denied his opponent, is usually—as in Freud's own case—a matter of particular pride to him, which is inconsistent with his theoretical tenets, since truth is a transcendent value which in an immanentistic theory of man has no place: Freud's theory, for mysterious reasons, fails to apply to him, the theoretician.

   3) The stated confounding of perspectives is not onesidedly a sub-

stituting of analytical-theoretical for phenomenal data; it also works in the opposite direction, the theorization being incomplete. Plenty of concepts which have none but phenomenal reference make their way into theoretical statements of processes, with a kind of conceptual sea-sickness as the inevitable result. We are touching, of course, on the characteristic phenomenon of the clinically applied as well as popular verbiage, the conceptual and terminological mass fashion that the psychoanalytic way of thinking-about-man has led to. This thinking harbors a two-way confusion: statements to the effect that the "id" and the "superego", instead of being objective abstractions, were phenomenal manifestations within the subject's existential life sphere, which he "handles", and statements such as "the patient wants unconsciously . . ." (which is out of keeping with the phenomenality of wanting without which "wanting" could not even be *understood* as a concept, hence not be used as one either). This insufficient separation of perspectives leads to a reductionism which, as has often been noted, reduces whatever it hits upon into its own opposite: thus, dependent on the theoretical or not-so-theoretical moods of the analyst, aggresiveness can be "explained" as the overcompensation of an unconscious timidity, or timidity as the overcompensation of unconscious aggression. But what *is* an unconscious aggression (or timidity)? What, altogether, is an unconscious feeling? Feelings, from whatever unconscious strata of the personality (as we follow them "down" in the direction opposite to that of their emergence) they are experienced as *coming*, have the character of convictions, of knowledge; their role as messengers of an existential state *is what defines them as feelings,* and no concept at all in any authentic sense, then, only a terminological shadow, can accrue from designating feelings as unconscious. If, in turn, we assume—as is truer to Freud's own teachings but increasingly untrue to their effects on the thinking of the disciples— that, for example, an "overcompensatory" aggressivity is assumed to result from the repression of a (conscious) impulse toward timid behavior, the problem still is merely shifted: we are now at a loss to understand how the ego's decision-for-aggression (rather than for timidity) can be accounted for without involving the *merits* of the aggression in the account, a question that involves the subject's, not the analyst's, "values" as pre-given constituents of his world. Since the very *who* of existence already is dissolved into conflicting elements in the psychoanalytic account, elements of which it never becomes quite clear whether they themselves are protagonists of certain *interests* of his (versions of his subjectivity) or are *objective forces*, this question in principle remains unposed by psychoanalysis. The analyst, nevertheless, cannot escape it. His pre-given orientation to his own "values" is what shows up in the *nothing-but* of a debunking procedure that explodes the subject's "overt" aggression as an *over*-compensation— leaving unanswered the other question, according to which criteria (since the only conceivably valid ones can nowhere be derived from a mere structural and functional inventory of the psyche) the differentiation between compensations and over-compensations is made in the first place.

Thus any manifest phenomenon that happens to be noticed by the analyst may "in reality" be declared to be something else, of which it is the sublimation, substitution, projection, displacement, and so forth. Logically and epistemologically, the most important observation that registers at this point is that this "reality", in turn, not only is postulated, but that it must forever *stay* a postulate in order not to conflict with its own definitive implication—"unconsciousness" in the Freudian sense is *unphenomenality in principle*. The peculiar *whirl* of anthropological determinism, as both an existential state and a theoretical attitude in psychology, which has been noted before, thus raises problems for the theory of knowledge and of science that far outshadow in incisive significance whatever problems concerning factual points of his doctrine caused the dissidents from Freud to break away: the postulation, as is readily seen, turns out to be a *correction* of the "irrational" phenomena of the psyche by Freudian rationalism. For what, now, is this rationalism rationalizing on its part? Or, if it is not rationalizing, from whence does it derive its claim—which seems its monopoly among and in front of all mankind—to authentic reason?

4) The extension of categories beyond their phenomenal scope, peculiar to all objectivistic doctrines about man, has been investigated before. In psychoanalysis, it becomes crucial most of all in the conceptual treatment of the unconscious. In the instance of the problem of guilt versus innocence (in their application to childhood existence[4]), this has been shown before; attempting a *resumé* of the argument, we may state once more the illegitimacy of speculating about the genesis of such an entity as *guilt* without first of all exploring—as no psycho-

analyst has yet explored—what guilt *is,* a question that concerns its being (its phenomenal structure), not its becoming. The ways, however, in which categoriality at once traps rationalism and in turn conceals this feat are more manifold than a surface glance may betray. Turning to Freud's dream theory, it becomes readily visible how the original truth of psychoanalysis, the rediscovery of an underlying unity of all manifestations of the psyche, almost at once is denaturized into a fundamental assumption that the proper meanings (the "reasons") "behind" the "irrationality" of such phenomena as dreams are necessarily such that they *would* satisfy the demands of a wake rationality to which the analyst is oriented. As a particular version of the more general objectivistic confusion between linguistic meanings as *tools* and as *materials* of psychology, this observation may be referred to a previous discussion in this book; what makes it important in its particularity, however, is just its rationalism, namely Freud's obliviousness *as an objectivist* to the necessity for including his own thinking among the *object* materials in demand of an account. Indeed, so complete was this obliviousness that he never considered that dream "substitutions" or "displacements" might not be any such things at all, but—as the dream itself tells the dreamer as long as he is dreaming it—discoveries of relevancies, overlooked by the subject in his wake state, of the things manifestly dreamt of. Yet, it is this difference between the dream and the being awake as *states of existence* that readily explain Freud's need for postulating "latent" meanings behind what phenomenally is *already* revelation-of-the-latent: hypothecating in a wake state as he did it was natural for him to find the manifest themes irrelevant in their literalness. The overlooking of dream relevancies in the wake state can be shown to be a function of motivational set that cognitively is always more or less selective. It selects according to what fits its purposive attention set: the stronger the motivation—for example, a preoccupation with making dreams talk "rationally" after all—the more will be overlooked, until observation, however sharp and concentrated for what it chooses to see, becomes blind for whatever it does not. In the end the theoretician tells the phenomenon: "Actually, what you mean is . . .", and this indeed we discern as the paradigm, in and outside of Freud's school, of psychoanalytic interpretations.

But it is time to forestall the likely misunderstanding that Freud's magnificent if partial insights into the symbolisms of dreams, of insufficiently "censored" phenomena of the psyche altogether, were being overlooked. It has been said before that categoriality conceals its traps as much as it sets them, and the statement may now be implemented: what conceals the trap of categoriality in the instance of the Freudian theory of dreams is Freud's inconspicuous misunderstanding, made more inconspicuous by the very truth of his interpretation of certain dream materials as symbols, of the nature precisely of the *symbol*. The implicit connotation which this concept finds in its applications by Freud is the now conventional and colloquial, not the authentic one: throughout, it is used in the sense, not of *sym-bols,* but of allegories, that is, of something *substituting* for—or replacing, representing, signifying—something else. A symbol, however, is originally nothing of the sort; it is, indeed, the very opposite of all that. It is not that which stands for but that which is stood for by whatever it "symbolizes"; the *sym-bol,* literally, is that in which a meaning "shoots together", in which it crystallizes. This means that symbolizations manifested by the psyche must be traced by thought from the side of the symbols themselves, not of the unauthentic categories of a rationality no longer aware of either its origin or its mission: *the more real reality, that which gives the things symbolized their very sensibleness by making them transparent for the truth of being, is the symbol, not the symbolized.*

5) That the language of the unconscious should become expressible in categorial forms of Freudian rationalism is perplexing on still another account: a definitive constituent of any *conceivable* unconscious (and the more so the deeper we follow it down, which we can theoretically only) is increasing absence of differentiation, articulation, and form; in this respect, the perennial intuitions of humanity (Heracleitus!) are in perfect agreement with the tenet of such modern holistic systems as Angyal's. Freud's concept, though widened in its expanse and its relation to the ego, also differently evaluated, is taken over by Jung, whose unconscious is capable of such feats as adding correctly six or seven multidigit figures. Theoretically, the psychoanalytic concept, in Freud and in the dissidents, has the unconscious as a stratum or strata of the subjective psyche; practically, as used in the concrete interpretations of the analyst, the concept in most cases turns out to embed properties of the whole personality of which the

personality for this very reason is not aware while the analyst is (the same holds for structural and directional features of acute processes); all these objective data, then, are interpretatively turned into "unconscious" ones (of the subjective unconscious), into—secretely active—unconscious elements in the first sense. While the logical illegitimacy of this procedure, with its already familiar confounding of perspectives, is evident, this evidence is easily obscured by the patient's readiness in many instances to re-experience self-consciously what the analyst more or less suggests. The consciousness-unconsciousness problem awaits clarification—which has hardly begun—of the laws governing the fluctuations of attention, shifts of attention-focus, and simultaneously operant *levels* of attention, as well as a rather enormous job in shapening terminology so that the mentioned sleights of hand become impossible. All this being basic to an understanding of *consciousness*, yet virtually uninvestigated to this day by analysts and non-analysts alike, the fogginess that has continued to surround the psychoanalytic conception of the unconscious gives small reason to wonder; but however far we may later advance on the problems of consciousness and of its opposite, for Freud's particular conception of the unconscious we already can detect two origins that seem to have converged toward its rise.

One is his observation of the—once aroused to "consciousness"—crystal-clear contents of previously repressed experiences in his hysteric patients—never in any others. Indeed, Freud's whole theory of the unconscious begins with this discovery; but is the kind of organization of the psyche which he then concludes as a generally human one not already a specific one holding true for hysterics and other paroxysmals only? A "horizontal" rather than "vertical" segregation or displacement of experience materials, similar to the splitting of the psyche into multiple competing whole sets of the self as in hysteric fugues, indeed would cover that original discovery of Freud's with far greater theoretical satisfactoriness. The split itself, in turn, would not be *through* but *along* the dimension of depth, and the entire conceptualization offered here would account for the articulateness and perfect preservation of the "repressed" materials in a manner more adequate to biology's need for an at least *circumscriptive* objectification of the structure of personality, yet without ascribing to the unconscious what, phenomenally, are conscious contents.

The second of the two origins reveals itself as a phenomenological misunderstanding of the founder of psychoanalysis that is closely akin to the structural one just stated: of two conflicting whole sets of motivation, both operating simultaneously and *consciously,* the spontaneous one, with which the subject is motivationally most identified (which rises from the dimension of depth) is for no good reason termed unconscious; the other one, which phenomenally is marked by *deliberateness,* that is, anchored in momentary external purposivity (dimension of progression according to the structural system of Angyal) is termed conscious. Freud almost constantly says *conscious* where phenomenality itself says *deliberate, unconscious* where phenomenality itself says *spontaneous.* This restriction of "consciousness" to what essentially turns out to be outer control has much to do, of course, with what has been called Freud's distrust of "inspirationalism", or as one might rather say his blindness for the empiric fact of the existence of inspiration in man[5]; there nowhere in his writings appears any understanding of full, spontaneous, unifying engagements of motivation in its transcendent goals.[6] As to a most striking example of this we may refer to his interpretation of the famous Portia slip: that of which Portia is most conscious, more so than of anything else in the world—her love—succeeds in breaking into her labored deliberations, but according to the theory of slips (for which her case is used as a building stone by Freud) the "unconscious" did it.

6) A theoretician who purports to develop objective laws of generally human application, cannot do without at least attempting to make himself independent of his own position in his society, generation, culture, group, his locus in history altogether as a determinant of the way in which all these conditions "unconsciously" reflect themselves in his own thinking. As already stated, Freud never conceives of turning the knife of analysis against that consciousness which wields it. Contrary to a superficial, if popular, view that dwells on the conventional shockingness of the mere fact that sexual matters are important in his teachings, there is in these teachings a demonstrable core of puritan resentment, understandable perhaps from his opposition to *fin de siècle* Austrian society in his youth. The value accent on sex is—if only superficially—reversed, the experientially given alternative-for-evaluation the same as in puritanism.[7] This affinity—which may explain Freud's outstanding success just in puritanistic societies caught in a

growing crisis—has its roots in the aprioristic view of the human person with which Freud as much as his theological predecessors start out: one of fundamental and inevitable conflict between the intellect (*ratio*) and the animal underneath. This view prejudices the mode of being of man including the mode of being of man's reason; for where should reason itself find its origin unless the psyche tended to be reasonable from the bottom (or bottomless) up? Heracleitus, altogether the most rediscovered thinker in our time, appears, with this tenet of his as with so many others, more modern than nineteenth century instinct theory; what makes his truth so hard to grasp, is man's inclination (as examplified by the devinization of Reason by the Jacobins) to *believe in* his reason rather than to allow it to apply itself freely. Precisely whenever the psyche is not "reasonable", the intellect, however rationalistic, will be just as unreasonable as the blind animal within that it purports to "tame"; but in order to see this, in order to understand reason itself in its unfoldingness from the very ground of our being, the primacy of its transcendent (rather than reflectively controlling) task must be discerned *already,* and it is this perception that to our day has remained intolerable to the rationalist's pride.

7) Freud—for the first time in modern psychology—thus sees the whole subject matter that the psyche *is,* but misses out on its most constitutional characteristic, its quality of self-transcendentness. Oblivious to the one and only source of *integration* from which this "object" entity itself can draw, he cannot possibly yet see it as a true whole, for precisely what characterizes *wholes* is the appearance (in the medium of their component parts *as they refer to one another*) of a meaning content that their factualness refuses to account for. While giving a unity to them that no longer can be reduced to any of them or to their sum-total, this meaning content refers, on its part, to a non-factual sphere of pure identities: to that counter-principle to time, as which we previously have been able to discern *being.* Since the nature of the *whole* that human existence is and to which its being-in-the-world constitutionally belongs at any point already is not seen by psychoanalysis, the very concept of *insight* is prejudicially restricted to those self-perceptions of a subject in which the self has already been objectified—to manifestations of self-consciousness; true insight, on the contrary, while necessarily involving the self, assesses it in the light

of norms transcending the self (religious, erotic, ethical, aesthetic), viewing it against a background inaccessible in principle to psychoanalytic objectification. In accordance with observations already formulated in the last paragraph of 5), this raises the question more explicitly whether what is missed out on at the start of Freudian theorizing is not the very *who* of existence, the psyche in its original self-identity: in one of Freud's formulations of his theory of projection[8] it is taken for granted that the subject (whatever ego of pure deliberateness here remains as "subject") stands in a relationship of perceiving (cognitive) duality to impulses which he *has*, rather than in one of identity to impulses which he *is*—so much so that he "perceives", rather than these impulses themselves, their phenomenal objectives. It is evident, in turn, that what facilitates a concealment of the error is the inveterate "self-by-passingness" of existence: man "naturally" (as has been pointed out) inclines to be self-conscious, whenever (as in those conditions which would cause him to consult an analyst in the first place) his being-in-the-world is conflicted. Remembering, further, the increasing *conceptual* equivocality or rather multivocality[9] of the psyche as we follow its structure downward through its pre-verbal ("subconscious") strata, the convincingness to the patient himself of psychoanalytic interpretations no longer will be found surprising: since what an impulse arising from unconsciousness "means" *is in fact decided by consciousness* according to the constitution of "meaning" as much as of existence, no reason is visible, either why such a decision should not be brought about by the suggestion of an analyst just as much as by any other *existential encounter*, nor why from such a "success"—from the "insight" of the patient— the inference should be drawn that the content of the interpretation, before becoming just that, has been one of the subject's psyche at whichever of its strata.

The psyche, rather than speaking the language of symbols, is itself the language symbols speak, and thus it is in instances in which the manifest conveyances of symbolic experience clash with its allegoristic interpretations by psychoanalytic rationalism that such interpretations not only may fail to be echoed by the subject's "insight" but in fact may be exploded at the very touch of said conveyances; an exemplification may follow. A girl is passing from a depressive state of uncertainty and indirection into one of greater freedom, courage, hope, and joy. At the beginning of the transition she has a dream: winged as she knows herself, she flies to the top of a snowy mountain, where the stone tower of an observatory cuts sharply into the sunlit blue sky, is about to land there but, frightened by the piercing shape of the tower as well as its *observingness*, hesitates. At this moment she discerns the blue of the ocean that, invisible to her before, stretches beyond the mountain on its other side, and a white sail boat in the midst of it from which someone, a sailor, is waving at her with his *leg*. She flies down to him, lands on the boat with a feeling of intense bliss, discovers that she has been mistaken by the waving of a piece of cloth in the wind, that no one is aboard, but that the boat *and where it sails toward* is now all hers, and wakes up with the experience that knowledge of something critically essential to the whole, a knowledge that was coming toward her this very instant, is withdrawing inexorably. Interpretation of her analyst: the flight is a substitution at once for the new expansive tendency and for her habitual flight from the earth (reality), by which she meets that impulse in a characteristic neurotic manner. The mountain with the sharply shaped observatory tower is the male sex organ; reality, in the earth's rising up even in front of her flight, thus invites and exhorts her to return to it by making concessions to her very unrealism, offering to accept her in the lofty spaces of love; but even there she does not heed its call, as her genital fears forbid her to get down to earth. Rather she follows a phantom that allows her at once to rationalize for her avoidance of the "observatory" by way of a different new goal formation, and to give in, once having reached the semblance of that goal, to her narcissism (complete isolation, in the midst of the ocean, alone on an *empty vessel*), to her directionlessness (sailing into the blue), and, finally, to her illusionism by way of which she tends to cover up before herself both her narcissism and her lack of direction, as the boat and *where it sails toward* are seen as being "all hers"—but what about possible storms, and what is she going to subsist on? The dream, as wish fulfillment, thus throws her back into the aimlessness, the frustrations of her former way of life that had caused her depression to start with: that circle threatens to close, and what is withdrawing "inexorably" from her in the end is thus reality *per se*. One notices at once the analyst's unfounded sureness concerning the most crucial category of this account—"reality" —and the corresponding *naiveté* with which, evaluating by the presumable standards of his own existence as his existence understands itself, he takes it for granted that "flying from the ground" is *fleeing reality*, that "having a direction" depends on *steering toward a definable objective*,[10] that "sailing into the blue" is altogether *bad*, that "being on one's own" is synonymous with *narcissism*. The sailor is conveniently overlooked because upon landing he turns out to be a phantom; but who hung the piece of cloth there? and is a stone structure (even an oblong one) any more alive than a piece of cloth waving in the breeze? Rather than observing what was dreamt in the actuality of both the dream's specific phenomena and its mood or climate, rather than determining the meaning of what was dreamt against the background of the patient's existence as transparent only to *her*, the analyst relied on an itemized vocabulary, chosen from and weighted according to his own associations, his occupational or pre-occupational habits rather than those of the patient, of allegedly fixed object meanings of which he pieces the meaning of the dream un-self-suspectingly together. But is his logic any sharper than his perceptions? At the beginning of the interpretation, we find that he allows himself a gross confounding between phenomenal and objective perspectives: the *flight* is said to be a substitution for the "new expansive tendency", for that which psychologically-theoretically comprises the changes going on in the girl around that time. But, as is readily seen, this expansive tendency following the patient's depression is in actuality by no means *substituted* for by her flight; the flight, as a true symbol, with its literal connotation of a state of *rising* in which the patient's existence encounters itself in full accordance with the biographic truth, contains, on the contrary, the whole idea of the new expanding life as a seed does the tree. The impulse that determines that tendency (much less this tendency itself) is not even an original object of the subject's experience, as in succession of a characteristic misunderstanding of Freud our analyst believed; the stronger that impulse (or whole tendency), the more is the patient's psyche identified with it, unified with it, consequently, the less in a state of this kind *can* it occur to her as experiential *object*. The assumption that the actually "meant" object of experience should have been that tendency rather than the flight actually dreamt of thus overlooks the phenomenality of motivation as much as the demands, not of rationalism, perhaps, but of logic: that tendency was "operant" in the experience in an objective sense, but just for that reason was not its *object* in *any* sense, including a "latent" one; the conception of that new tendency which abstracts it from the experience-behavior context of the patient, thus coming to include its subject pole as well as object pole, is itself the result of a subsequent retrospective observation (or self-observation), a reflective discovery. While this discovery was actually the patient's own in our case, it referred, as such, to her vantage point as a chronologist of her own experiences *qua psychical processes,* a perspective radically different from that which was hers while being "in" the experience. Summing up, we find that "substitution" (as well as conceivable "displacement") charges can be reversed: in theorizing about an experience she had, the retrospective self-observer, standing "outside" of herself, has *displaced* her focus from the transcendent content of her experience to her experience as a psychical process, an *objective event;* this being the case, a reflective abstraction in which her analyst shares is *substituted* by him for the thing actually experienced.

In the present case, the core of the rationalistic misunderstanding that had muddied its interpretation by the analyst was, however, refuted by the dream itself, rather by its continuation, when the girl a few nights later found herself returned to the same situation with which the first dream experience had closed, her situation in the midst of the emptiness, the horizoned openness, of the blue sea, after landing aboard the moving sailboat. This time the dream was brief: it consisted in substance of a sharper look at the "piece of cloth waving in the breeze" and the discovery that, in confirmation of her original vista from midair, there indeed was a *leg,* if only one belonging to a certain human garment on a laundry line. This was followed by a short moment of paralyzing anxiety at the detection and sudden insight that her wings were gone; then, what took over almost immediately was a new and more intense—much "warmer"—experience of "expansiveness"—of bliss—in understanding that the discovery of the garment meant that she was not alone on board, that it pointed her way into the inside cabins of the boat to search there for her mate; with this knowledge, she woke up. The dream now made immediate sense to her in the entirety of its two parts, for the first one of which she was able spontaneously to account throughout in terms of such specific biographic features and events of her past as a state of frigidity which only now she understood in its dependence on the mortifications of

being "outside of oneself", of observing oneself (the *observatory*, besides having the connotation ascribed to it by the analyst, also had
the one of a watch tower, and the two connotations were but conceptual facets of *one symbol*: the tower, as the essence of a phenomenal
content from her *past*, was divided against itself in its meaning as her
past itself had been, but as her *present* was no longer so divided, the
tower, dead as any stone thing, *was* her dead past in which the male
genital had in fact been "mute", namely shut out from her spontaneous understanding of her world in its *belongingness*). On its part,
the dream sequel depicted the situation in which she found herself
at present but did not long continue to find herself: with her new
anticipatory knowledge, which the dream itself in its primary status
as an event of existential metamorphosis had left her, an attitude of
going out of herself and inside *her world*, of joyous and calmly attentive receptiveness for her future was assumed, and it was this more
genuine *search* that, in turn, in a matter of months, brought about in
actuality what the last sudden insight of her dream had held out.

Referring our criticism of Freud's doctrine, of the world of psychoanalytic ideas altogether that have been formulated here, to as few
common denominators as possible, we recognize the well known central
errors of objectivism: conceptualization of the being-man in the
image of a functional and noetic duality in which the psyche as an
itself irrational object stands in a self-conscious apposition *to* itself
in its capacity as the "one" (the *ego*) who can match its blind stirrings
with its own "rational" deliberations, its worldless impulsivity with an
"illusionless" severity that acts in the name of *everybody's* standard
notions of "reality"; a corresponding failure even to consider the
possibility that the derived and unauthentic rationality of this self-
conscious ego, which as a phenomenon of the psyche stands itself in
need of an account, may not be adequate to comprehend and express
in its own terms that lawfulness, reasonableness, of the psyche as a
whole that pervades every single one even of its "irrational" manifestations; an uncritical expansion, wholly understandable on the basis of
the failure just characterized, of categories beyond their proper phenomenal scope and to the very point where they themselves become
meaningless in a conceptual sense while their clinical applications
remain forever unverifiable in an empiric one; and, finally, the confounding of phenomenal causality as a nexus of understandability

between data such as a childhood trauma and an adult neurotic
symptom, with causality in a strict (quasi-physicalistic) sense, as
though not vice versa the childhood trauma would owe its entire understandability to what the pattern of adult existence made of it. Starting
out as an *understanding* approach in Dilthey's sense as psychoanalysis
does in Freud's *perceptions* of the psyche, it mistook its own quest
for an *explanatory* one,[11] and thus, in its way of comprehending its
cognitive achievements, it reversed their direction; yet, in so doing,
it has been neither able nor prepared to meet the one and only criterion of proof to which explanatory cognitions would be subject
just as much in a science of man as to analogous standards they are
expected to submit in any other field of scientific knowledge: the test
of accuracy in predicting behavioral and symptomatological events.

The historic importance of psychoanalysis is not lessened by such
material shortcomings of its tenets as the meanwhile recognized lack
of universality of the Oedipus complex, or of the penis envy of little
girls, and of similar contentions of its founder that came into being
by way of uncritical generalizations from individual case histories;
a rather primitive conception, colliding with any even half-way cautious survey of the anthropological facts,[12] of *primitive man,* a conception that entirely without Freud's awareness followed in one line
of succession the theological notion of the pagan and the "savage",
assisted, as first was recognized by Jung, these generalizations. If the
historic importance of psychoanalysis is not touched by all this, the
reason is that most of the questions that engage the thinkers of our day
are indeed posed by psychoanalysis—posed not by its own quest as
a system of inquiry and of thought but very much by psychoanalytic
theory and practice as a human phenomenon and thus as material-for-
psychology rather than as a psychological doctrine. However Freud's
primitive man may be spurious historically and anthropologically, like
the *Urpflanze* ("original plant") of a famous conversation between
Goethe and Schiller it retains its truth as a pre-given regulator of
thought: as the (mistakenly temporalized, historicized) image in which
man, in one of his possible self-interpretations, discerns his own *wherefrom,* and which hence is valid wherever it arises spontaneously, but
is invalid precisely where validity is claimed for it[13] by psychoanalysts, in science.

As human history moves by the force of the immanent contradic-

tions of ideas that, unseen at first in their contradictoriness, enter into
time, so does the history of psychoanalysis and of its ramifications in
the dissident systems of Jung, Adler, Rank, Horney, and so on.
Throughout, if to a large extent unknowingly, it feeds on those errors
of Freudian thought and the need for correctives which they generate
that the foregoing discussion exposed in an outline; somewhat simplifying, we may say that each of these dissidents was captivated by the
sight of a sector within the spread of specific theoretical absurdities
that result from the *visible* collision of the unseen fundamental errors
of psychoanalytic doctrine with the equally unseen truths of existence.
Failing to trace the tenets which they attack (or are trying to modify)
to the common roots of all of them—to that handful of entirely tacit,
and just as shaky, *a prioris* which our analysis identified as *objectivism*,
immanentism ("naturalism"), and *categorialism*—their criticisms were
bound to prove weaker in the end than the doctrine from which they
dissented: the long leash woven of the named three fundamental beliefs
and held firm by the hand of the master was invisibly restricting their
movements even as they turned against him.

In combining a loss of the truth of psychoanalysis with a failure to
get out of its untruth, their doctrines thus are true only as witnesses
to the previously sketched dilemma that Freud's thinking and teaching
conjured up: Jung—to name the by far most important of the dissidents first—*does* see the sphere of the spiritual in man as a reality
of the psyche reducible to other realities of the same psyche only in
the dynamics of its "guiding" and "compensatory" interactions with
them, never in its *contents*,[14] but does not see the reality of the spirit *as*
the spirit, and thus misses out on the trans-psychological, altogether
trans-factual, sovereignty of phenomenal truth. The consequence is that
objectification only reaches its climax of uncompelling relativism in his
teachings, as it comes to extend its claim to that in man which is itself
the premise and ground, the possibility-to-start-with, of all objectifications. As implied before, Jung also sees the creative aspect—the
fathomlessness and personality-sustaining power—of the unconscious,
but continues in an even more insistent manner, if one also testifying
to his wider historical and humanistic horizon, Freud's never-tiring
efforts at *categorizing* its contents—thus competing with the heroes
of an old German tale, the denizens of Schildburga, in their attempt
to catch the dark in barrels. Adler, on his part, starts out with a full

recognition of the peculiar worldlessness of *Freudian man* but stays oblivious to the immanentism that gives rise to it. The consequence is a mere shift in the focus of objectification: instead of the sexual urge, the drive for power here becomes the metaphysicized absolute to which all human strivings are reduced, and, as in Freud's account the phenomenal essence of the sex "function"—love—must be by-passed owing to a prior misapprehension of drives themselves as blind (worldless), so Adler by-passes what alone could implement his abstracted concept of the power drive in the phenomenal experience-medium at least of any sounder human being: the imperative ever ruling over the person's existence to realize ("mundanize") its *truth*. Overlooking (with Nietzsche) that power primarily is *exercised*, not sought for, and that the goal of gaining more power, as an explicit phenomenal one, is already restricted to subjects whose powerless existences are always and first of all *truthless* ones, Adler abstracts a universal human drive for power from what in the reality of man's experiencing is his striving for his freedom to *exist in truth*.[15] Adler thus misses the "self-", Freud the "world" pole of *Dasein*; or we may say that, as the *truth of love* escapes the latter's thinking, it is to the *love of truth* that the former's fails to penetrate.

The original phenomenal implementation of the power drive is overlooked by Adler owing to his initial, if tacit, decision *already* to consider man—and also, to let him thus consider himself—from the standpoint of "society". But society, in this connotation, having little to do with actual historic societies still held together by unbroken loyalties, rather is an abstract standard environment, a *milieu* deprived of its spirit and belongingness, to which to adjust himself here becomes the central life problem of the individual; significantly, then, the theme of *adjustment* takes over completely in the Rankian version of psychoanalysis. What it leads to at this stage is that explicit *robotism of adjustment* that debunks ununderstood (experientially unshared) human beliefs as illusions while at the same time teaching the necessity of maintaining them in the individual concerned in the interest of their better fitting-in, which in essence means their manageability from the standpoint of a human zoo or farm director. In its blindness for the nature of Truth, both in its incorruptibility and as the very home of man's existing that Truth *is*, Rank's line of reasoning represents what is perhaps the extreme of psychoanalytic immanentism, as it could equally well be applied to the problem of how to keep a herd of cows as "happy" as the interests of the milk and meat markets may demand. A "humanistic" revolt had to break loose in the very interior of the psychoanalytic orbit of thought, and break loose it did; but what, meanwhile, has become of that upheaval—what indeed, confined by objectivism as it has been with every single one of its steps, was its fate-line from the start?

Operating within these confines, all it could do was conjure up the— actual or alleged—factual power of given societal authorities, authorities other than the Freudian *instincts,* rather than any truly authoritative imperative immediately engaging man in the self-transcendentness of his being. The genesis of Karen Horney's teachings cannot here be traced to their origins in the revolt of a woman against a doctrine untrue to feminine experience not because of its pan-sexualism, whatever this popular indictment may mean, but because its peculiarly neutralized conception of sex turns out to be—as shown frequently in the literature—a generalization, undertaken by the intellect of one man, from male sexual experience only. But the representativeness of that rebellion (and of the resulting theorems) for the "leash" situation which we stated can be shown here, and for this end we may restrict ourselves to the example of Horney's notion of humanist culture, in which she embeds the goal concepts to serve a therapeutic reorientation of the "neurotic person of our time". Is it not paradigmatic for the way in which anthropological objectivism misses the original order of existence from which it derives its abstractions, that these abstractions always are reapplied to disordered existences in a manner wholly oblivious to what in the model order was the actual inner pattern, as well as the successivity, of its growth?[16] It is easy to see that none of the great manifestations of the human heart and spirit that make up Horney's "humanist culture of the West" ever was produced with an eye on accomplishing what they *succeeded* in accomplishing, namely on bringing forth that culture as what it is *also,* but never intrinsically, an at any time-point "factual", at any time-point finite historico-sociological entity submitting to retrospective abstractions of a scientist. For intrinsically it is not that at all, but is what it tends to be to its creators and contributors: the horizon of a still continuous growth going out from among their midst and from the midst of the being of each one of them, a growth of which western man, in as far as his relations to it have any degree of genuinity, can only be the medium and the carrier, never the operator. This means that—as medium and carrier of his culture as a historical growth—he necessarily must be "unconscious" of it at least far more than "conscious"; otherwise the well-known and pitiful *cultural policies* of twentieth century deliberators, strategists, and programmatizers, in replacing that growth, would soon condemn it to a halt of inexorable finality. The intrinsic nature of western humanist culture therefore escapes the grip of the objectifier just as much as does any other authentic manifestation of being, and what remains of it in Horney's usage of the concept is precisely the finite (historico-sociological) agglomeration of historic facts-for-analysis as which it can readily be categorized but just as readily killed—what, if not a leaving-behind of dead facts where before were beings, has categorization ever achieved? In the actual existences of the men and women, the peoples and the generations, who built the humanistic culture of the West, what compelled the growth of that culture has been faith—a faith of many contents, yet unified by one hard-to-define theme, one destiny of experience and action, one horizon of thought; it has *not* been compelled by its own mere factualness, endowed with a borrowed compellingness by Karen Horney. As though Nietzsche's *Of the Use and Misuse of History for Life* never had been written, historicism as an anti-spontaneous force *per se* never been disposed of,[17] the entire creative tension, underlying the birth of any of the documents of humanism and itself only *making* its history and *bringing forth* its culture, between man's factual and time-bound self and that timelessly valid Truth of his primordial ideas that alone can draw it "out of itself" and into the openness of a comprehensible world, is missed by Horney; for how can a reflective consideration of mere historical facts ever replace those authentic imperatives of the spirit that demand to be experienced *first* in order for western humanist culture to be understood once more in the genuine? If it shall not turn into what according to its own essence it is *not*, an exploitable, apportionable ingredient for the manipulation of psyches, precisely the neurotic person of our time (and of the present state of western culture) must be led by the therapist as much as the educator into a confrontation with *his truth*; to sustain him with handouts of shadows of the truths of others will improve matters neither for himself *nor* for his culture.

The paradigm just sketched applies to the teachings of the "dissidents" in their entirety. Just as the creative mind from which western humanism has ever drawn the forces that sustained it through the vicissitudes of history is most unconcerned of all about any of the cut-and-dry standard digests of that same humanist culture into which schoolmasters feeding on second- and third-hand presentations of its fact materials are ever busy turning it, so the authentically religious, the model for Jungian ways of treatment, also never is motivated toward the contents of his faith by any *already therapeutic* concern over the integration of his own psyche as an objective process.[18] The subject of whom *abstractingly* we could say with Rank that he is a model case of inner and outer adjustment (in the sense of a fruitful give-and-take between him and his neighbors) never sought adjustment as his goal, for no concept that according to its own constitution is but a name for observable objective events ever can generate that power-to-engage which freely beheld phenomenal goals must exercise in order to implement that same concept as a *post hoc* objective abstraction possible, as such, only from the viewpoint of the theoretical observer, never the subject; the shibboleth of "environmental adjustment" according to which, in some applied sections of the social sciences, field workers now tend to manipulate existences, thus is as superficial as it is untrue to the nature of adjustments that spontaneously *occur*. Is it different with certain Adlerian notions such as that of the "contributions to society" by way of which the individual is supposed to reconcile his power drive with the interests of the public? When *have* "contributions to society" ever been made by any mind intent on making *them*, when *has* the public and its typical representatives ever understood at the actual moment of a "contribution's" historic emergence—the more liberating and fertile they come, the more startingly *abrupt* do they come also—what only afterwards then turned out to have enriched the public good, and how often have individuals had to act diametrically against the standards of their environments, against what these environments believed (and expected them to act in accordance with) would be "contributory" behavior on their part, in order to gain the very freedom to make *their*—contributions? Why, then, should an Adlerian psychotherapist or educator, a theoretician seeing the individual already from the vantage point of an environment evaluating individuals according to their ability to fit in (namely with any presently given state of "society"), be wiser? The shadow that lies most heavily on the entire psychology of our time has been said by some to be the relative ignorance of history and of letters that his one-sidedly natural-scientific education has fostered in the individual psychologist as much as in the individual physician specializing in psychiatry. This may be a truth, at least it may be close to one; but it is evident that the essence of the charge itself is missed if it is understood just to mean a deficit in however desirable historic or literary fact knowledge. Rather, what has been lost since the humanistic orientation of advanced and higher education altogether was superseded by programs and systems geared to the all-out purpose of manipulating nature, inclusive of human "nature", and of a fitting in of the person with the vocational requirements, the technological mass organization, of a more and more robotized collective gradually replacing grown society itself, appears to be that inner freedom of the mind which perennially inheres only in its spirit-centered—its emphatically *non-utilitarian*—education and cultivation. Without such inner freedom, no sense of divine historic irony radically free from resentment, none of the playfulness of *being* altogether: of those time-less delights of the original skepticism of the spirit that precisely the paradoxical and witty side of existence lays open to man, can grow any more in him than, on its part, can original faith.

Objectivism nowhere escapes these ironies of existence; for they testify to man's freedom to be always a step ahead of any *post hoc* deterministic accounts of either his experiences or behavior, and thus they lead the objectivist's formulas inevitably *ad absurdum*. This is verified even by a glance at that particular break with Freudianism— the secession of Erich Fromm—that stretches and strains the leash of objectivism-immanentism-categorialism to the utmost endurance of every one of its fibres. Fromm's rediscovery of the forgotten phe-nomenon of *spontaneity* in man (as itself an objective datum) had pointed his way in theory and therapy, and already may his thinking finally have torn loose even from the most axiomatic, and most tacit, presuppositions of psychoanalysis at the time of this writing, but the "leash" at any rate still constrained his theorizing when Fromm, in finding his focus drawn to the motivating power of *values* in their irreducibility to any objectified "psyche", yet attempted to categorize values *objectively*. It is evident that such an attempt, as though values *could* be rendered theoretically on one plane of analytic fact-presentation with all other facts without violating their authentic experiential prerogative, must fail to do justice precisely to what makes them values in the first place—their *validity* as it occurs, prior to any factualizing abstraction *from* them of the very concept of "values", to the human beings they *engage*. Heidegger's analysis of the "talk about values" has been cited before in this text, and rather than repeating the fundamental argument we may contemplate the way in which it applies to a theory of values that adjudges values according to a dichotomy between those of them that serve the interests of individual or group egotisms and those that serve the interests of "humanity". The often cited dilemma of anthropological science, in which anthropological science is supposed to be thrown by its duty to be "objective" on the one hand, its inability to be radically non-evaluating without at the same time being radically deaf and dumb, on the other, is only lessened, not escaped, by a theory of values that itself frankly *evaluates;* for what can possibly be the criteria for the distinction of Fromm that we cited? The history of humanity has been a succession of ceaselessly clashing ideas about what *serves,* even what *are,* its "interests"—from where, inside or outside their own souls, do the psychological theoretician and the therapist derive authority to decide that question? It is evident that the dilemma is just as great once we consider the actuality of "value" experience in the concrete, namely in any subject's spontaneously motivating action impulses: when, in jumping into a river to save a drowning child, a deed unquestionably serving the interests of humanity in the Frommian sense, did humanity ever even enter the scope of that subject's consideration, and, in turn, if it had, would not just his spontaneity have suffered, the action itself been slowed down, its success been imperiled? In the error, which was recognized as a paradigmatic feature of anthropological objectivism *per se,* of reapplying objectified abstractions from the observation of past behavior in its factualness to the experiential actuality of motivation from which behavior *springs,* the value theory of the earlier Fromm turns out to be caught almost as much as the comparable turns-of-thought of Jung, Adler, Rank, and Horney.

Underlying that paradigm, as underlying all theorizations of man that do not accept the paradoxical status of his existence *as an empirically given state of self-transcendency to start with,* we find the reversal of

phenomenal time into process time, the replacement of the openness
of original future by the closedness, finality, of a projectively "visualized" past that *poses* as the future. Our earlier analyses had shown the
concomittance of this replacement not only with more drastically
self-conscious losses of spontaneity, but altogether with what this
shifting of the subject's experiential focus, away from its authentic
centeredness *in* his *being* and *on* his *world* (as which shift the be-
coming-self-conscious has been discerned), begins as: the conversion
of original *world* into a dead domain of *facts before one.* The observation that such "objectivism", "determinism", is more than a philosophic
tenet in the theory of knowledge and of the sciences, that it becomes
just that only because it is first of all a possible modus of the knower's
self-understanding and *thereby* of the manner in which he is-in-the-
world, has been stressed, and it may now have become evident why
the attention of such explorers of the being-man as Binswanger has
time and again been drawn, past the compromises of the dissidents,
to the work of the master—why, by the existential-analytic movement
as a whole, Freud himself is recognized (if allowance may be made
for the instructiveness, the unique teaching value, precisely of fundamental errors consistently upheld and followed through) as *teacher.*
With the characteristic one-sidedness of all true geniuses of theory,
Freud ignored the contents of existence, the very *what* of the being
of man, concentrating, instead, on the objective process-structure of
man's psyche, on its *mechanisms.* Far from exhausting the essence of
the being-man, these mechanisms do not even touch its core, which
on the contrary they are instrumental in by-passing; yet, in giving
them his sole attention, Freud, as he himself never knew, succeeded
in first bringing to light what the being-man has ever to stand, probe,
and vindicate itself *against*: the "animal within"—or rather, forever
unreal as we know that "animal",[19] its formless shadow, which only
reflection calls forth and lends a semblance of reality. But may a
semblance of reality not become real in the highest degree *as a semblance?* The spiritless, history-less, anxiety-persecuted *homo natura*,
with Binswanger's definition of the gist of Freudian man, do we not,
all of us, know him, and do we not at last know also *what* he is? He
is, as our analysis has shown, the observable, dissectable, calculable *self*
of the drives, the repressions, and the complexes, which the observing,
dissecting, calculating rationalisms of the *ego*—its deliberation ever

trying to outsmart its prisoner's stirrings—have beforehand driven into that very state of isolation and bewilderment in which, half dreading it and half triumphant over it, they will then find it.

NOTES

1. L. Binswanger, "Freuds Auffassung des Menschen im Lichte der Anthropologie", in *Ausgewählte Vorträge und Aufsätze.*

2. Cf. p. 134.

3. Translated from the original: *Vorlesungen zur Einführung in die Psychoanalyse,* Vienna, 1930, p. 17. Italics supplied.

4. Cf. p. 44.

5. The biographic fact that Freud was completely unmusical intimately connects with this peculiarity; it also poses the question in principle whether a theoretician so handicapped—cut off from an innermost power and propensity of the psyche and therefore from understanding that power and propensity—is in any position to work out a true psychology.

6. For example, it never occurred to Freud that free association, which worked so successfully with his hysterics, may have done so because it corresponded with the given organization (or disorganization) of their psyche as a differential clinical fact, by no means with that of other patient categories and many normals. For these, he attributes to unconscious resistance-to-analysis what may in actuality be resistance to the unnatural task of momentarily suppressing what in *them* is the most spontaneous, most "unconsciously motivated"—the formative syntactic urge for well-ordered, self-steering, concept-directed speech, as well as for world-centered behavior altogether.

7. Cf. pp. 127–28.

8. "The projection of inner perceptions to the outside is a primitive mechanism which, for instance, also influences our sense-perceptions, so that it normally has the greatest share in shaping our outer world. Under conditions that have not yet been sufficiently determined even *inner perceptions of ideational and emotional processes* are projected outwardly, like sense perceptions, and are used to shape the outer world, whereas they ought to remain in the inner world." Cf. S. Freud, *Totem and Taboo,* in *Basic Writings,* 1938, p. 857. Italics supplied.

9. From the vantage point of the unreflected *being* of the person in his self-identity, this "multivocality" is, of course, the very opposite of one, namely the original unity of any genuine symbol that only categorization then divides; cf. p. 130 and p. 171.

10. Goethe's dictum, "One never goes farther than when one does not know where one is going", exposes this fallacy most pithily.

11. Cf. K. Jaspers, *Allgemeine Psychopathologie,* pp. 299–302.

12. For the end of such a survey, cf. W. Koppers, *Der Urmensch und sein Weltbild,* Vienna, 1949.

13. The peculiar lovelessness—implying lack of understanding—that characterizes psychoanalytic studies of "primitive" cultures is a case in point; in order to

understand such cultures at all, their worlds of values and beliefs must first be seen from their own vantage points. Only in this manner can the unity of the perennially human that connects them in their roots with the culture of the explorer be discovered at all, whereas any imposition on the "primitive" culture, for example, of what a psychoanalyst may believe to be "western" standards, while alleging to stay clear of relativism, is relativism at its extreme inasmuch as its very intent must be one of debunking.

14. Which he rather lets emerge from a meta-individual underground of unconscious collective awarenesses, strata within a universal hierarchy of the animate, and thus still from an (however hypothetical) *objective* entity.

15. Cf. Goethe in the *Nausikaa Fragment:* "So you want power? The powerful has it."

16. This, of course, appears to be the general fate of abstractions occurring on that medium level of reflectiveness (cf. p. 133) on which modern man in the characteristic phenomenal impoverishment of his existence and his thought has come to vegetate; a similar error can be found in the case of all *type* concepts *originally* beholding a one-in-the-many, a unitary essence not only admitting of, but *requiring* a manifold spread of individual "elaborations" to manifest itself. Invariably, the unitary essence, in the categorization of the type concept and its subsequent reapplication to "cases", turns into a mechanized standard formula of superficially seen factual traits that a case may fit or may not but that in many instances may no longer have the slightest intrinsic relation to the original perception that underlay the concept. Cf. also pp. 317, 318.

17. Historicism, of course, is only one of the possible attitudes of man as he faces the "historical", and its condemnation by Nietzsche (as a thinker himself having history so-to-speak in his bloodstream) does not lend the slightest support to a pragmatist theory of education relegating historical studies to the attic of the house of learning.

18. Cf. pp. 100, *139–40.*

19. Cf. p. 69.

CHAPTER 8

Consciousness, Unconsciousness, and the Structure of Awareness—The Paradoxicalness of Transcendent Order —The Who of Existence—Spatiality and Temporality— The Modus of Love—The Problem of Identity— Dionysos and Apollon—Binswanger's Existence Modi— The Truth of Mythology—First Inquiry into the Dream: the Dream as Knowledge and as Situation.

It is time for us to study the structure of awareness more closely; thus far, we found reason both to affirm the reality of the unconscious and to question the objectifying conception of it of psychoanalysis in any of its versions. The unconscious *per se* can be inferred from any experience of the emergence of our minds into a state of awareness, because the phenomenality of *emergence* as an event implies it: that state from which our minds emerge, relative to their subsequent states, is one of unconsciousness. It becomes evident that "awareness" as we used it as well as "unconsciousness" as we used it both require qualifications in the form of a genetive, linking them with a content *of* which the subject is aware or of which he is unconscious; the habit of conceptual reification (*the* conscious, *the* unconscious), which is a convenience of thoughtlessness unless the reification stays aware of that requirement, became possible only at a moment in history when language, as was its specific fate during the nineteenth century, had sufficiently been flattened out—abstractified— to dim its phenomenal references so much that the tacit but constitutive "of what" inherent in both concepts ("aware" and "unconscious") could become relatively invisible. Since the statement, as well as its comprehension, of any allegedly unconscious contents presupposes an awareness of them on the part of him who states them or who comprehends the statement, the event of emergence inevitably precedes either the statement or its comprehension; consequently, the contents of

191

unconsciousness as such could by definition never be cognized *even* if
that emergence which our concept of insight connotes would be one
of a mental content rather than being, as in actuality, a coming-into
the truth about that content of him who is having the insight. The
being-unconscious-of is by definition an absence of a specific awareness; since a reified unconscious would accordingly be the totality of
such absences, it can never be determined by characterizations involving the presence of any particular content. The unconscious, on the
contrary, to the extent to which it *is* the unconscious, exists as a blank;
but it is time for us to remember that a blank, since it calls for
differentiation and structuring, for "something", namely something
definite and actual (concretely historical) to be "written" on it in the
unfolding of time, is nothing onesidedly negative; it is negative only
as the absence of the *actuality* of such a content or structure but very
positive as its *possibility*, which it is as well. The status of the unconscious, then, is that of a potential that actualizes itself in the events of
psychic emergence. This logical analysis of the consciousness-unconsciousness relation confirms its phenomenological: according to the
structure of an experiential event such as insight the dimension of its
wherefrom is not its successivity with a state of the psyche preceding
it in (outer) historic time, for if it were, insight would have its origin
in lack-of-insight as that which, in outer historic time, precedes it;
as an event in outer time (emergence), insight indeed proceeds from
a state of its own absence. But the starting position of a movement is
not its origin *as a movement*, the quasi-local *wherefrom* of insight as
an objective event not the *wherefrom* of insight in terms of its contents.
The dimension of the wherefrom of the contents of insight, instead, is
set by the availability of what the *in-sight* is *in*. Since the contents of
the insight are phenomenal, not objective-psychological, this availability
is not to be understood as a lying dormant *in* the psyche of one of its
actual contents, but as a lying ready *for* the psyche of a *possible*
manifestation of Truth: the *wherefrom* of insight, then, is Truth itself.

Since the status of the unconscious as a potential calls for an image
yet allowing it to be visualized as an entity, objective psychology where
it comes nearest to the truth about the unconscious without yet daring
to think it, resorts—as Jungian psychology does—to the image of the
pool. Since this image would not offer itself to the conceptual needs of
so perceptive and thoughtful an explorer as Jung if it were not, first of

all, true, it is not the emergence of the image of the pool from the
mind's awareness of the reality of its own recesses, but what becomes
of it in Jungian theorizing that phenomenology must distance itself
from: the fate of categories to lose their phenomenal moorings—of
which we have spoken—here means in the concrete that the eidetic
image of the pool, in which invisibility and lack of structure of the
submerged inhere, is replaced, in the abstractions of Jungianism, by its
facticity as an object among objects, a status in which a pool can of
course contain any number of actual items. The determination of the
unconscious which we gave is in better agreement with the phenomena-
circumscriptive objectifications of such a holistic biology and personality theory as Angyal's with its differentiation of the dimension of
depth according to levels of specificity and articulation vs. generality
(axiomaticity) and diffusion; generality there means pervasiveness of
potential tendencies of experience throughout the person's life course,
diffusion a relative absence of that definiteness (distinction) of experience and behavior which only actualization brings about. The agreement between this circumscription of what phenomenally is the potentiality character of the *wherefrom* of psychic events and our own results
in studying just this phenomenality is evident; the question that
remains is how the now customary (psychoanalysis-derived) application
of the term *unconscious* fits in with this picture.

The necessity, in order to advance on the problem, of studying the
dynamics of *attention* has been emphasized, and in Chapter VII we
pointed out the illegitimacy of assigning what in fact is spontaneity to
a reified unconscious: Portia, if of anything, is aware of her love for
Bassano. But reflecting a little longer just on her case seems to com-
plicate the consciousness-unconsciousness problem again and render the
solution just offered at least incomplete. True, the structure of the
being unconscious *of*, the becoming aware *of*, refer the problem in
substance to an analysis of presences *to* the mind rather than to the
mind-as-object, but the tacit premise for that reference is that at least
the mind itself (if not what may be "on" it) is *one*, whereas in Portia's
case we found it split in two different sets of her momentary *attending-to*
(which is at once what objective psychology calls motivation and
what it calls attention), two different modes of her being-in-the-world—
two *selves*. Since the split, in Portia's case, is less inveterate—less
stable—than it can become in many others, it is important to realize

from her slip of the tongue that splitness of mind is a paradigmatic possibility of the being-human that begins in normalcy long before assuming pathological proportions; further, that the plurality of the phenomenal contents of experience finds its counterpart in a possible (self-conflicted) plurality of the acute self of a person, posing the problem—to which we shall return—of the ultimate self, the true *who*, of an existence that this plurality may obscure. But while Portia's case shows no inveterate self-dissension, it shows splitness nevertheless and therefore is already too specific a material to illustrate the general laws under which the human person can, without splitting his self in the least, *simultaneously* be "conscious" and "unconscious" of the same identical content of experience.

Paradoxical though this may seem, it is not, like what happened to Portia, the (however frequent) exception, but the rule; it applies to every ounce and hour of man's experiencing as it shapes up under reflection. The person who expects hopefully what has only a negligible probability of becoming event, is he conscious or unconscious of what an other person may call his optimism? The person who raids the ice-box at night, is he conscious or unconscious of what an observer may term his voraciousness? We are purposely choosing simple examples in order to demonstrate that the complex of questions that surround our central problem does not begin at any particular level of complexity of motivation; vice versa, the pseudo-complexity of many theories of motivation is due to a prior failure of theoreticians to realize the primal ambiguity of *conscious* and *unconscious* as *concepts*. To be empirical here means as always to be descriptive; and describing the optimism of the one, the voraciousness of the other, from *within* their experiencing, first of all encounters their unconsciousness of either of these traits, *if* consciousness means a conceptual presence-to-the-mind of that content *of* which it is consciousness; for only upon reflecting (or being told) what they must already *be* (optimistic, voracious) in order to be able to reflect it, can either of the two come to focalize conceptually his condition as an objective one, as which, like all objects, it refers to an outside observer. That would seem to restrict consciousness to conceptual focalization, and much of the psychoanalytic application of the term to a person's motivation as psychoanalysis understands it is explicable, as already we have seen, from that restriction; but is the restriction legitimate, or simply, is it *true?* In order for it to be

true, optimism and voraciousness would primarily have to be concepts;
but is there such a thing as concepts—that is, words, that are more
than words—that are concepts *primarily*—concepts arising from
nowhere? Once we "think back" the two categories of characterization
named to their origins as manifestations *to* the mind of the contents
of experience they describe, who, if not the optimist *in* his optimism
(*not* upon reflecting it, which must first of all lessen the immediacy of
his knowledge) is completely conscious of this state of his? Who knows
the *meaning* of that other concept better than the one who is *being*
voracious? Their attention is gathered, in the one instance on the
object of the expectations, in the other on food, consequently it can not
be gathered on a parenthetic category for their own psychological states,
but does that mean that what these categories so to speak bracket-in
escapes their—consciousness? On the contrary, their conditions are so
self-evident, so near to them as knowers, that precisely as long as they
are *in* these conditions their conceptual focus, always requiring a certain
distance between the mind and what it articulates, must by-pass—shoot
beyond—these conditions as possible beholdings of their thought. This
does not render the conditions unconscious to them, unless we already
decide to define as unconscious what turns out to be a *horizon of
consciousness* in the actuality of experience as the person has it.

But we hear an immediate objection, accusing us of self-contradictoriness, to our determining the acute contour of a set of attention (or
motivation) in its engaging entirety as the momentary horizon of consciousness; for a horizon is far away, whereas the actual conditions
spoken of were characterized exactly by their nearness to the self-as-
knower. Horizonlike, however, is not only the contour of the field of
vision as our focus encounters it (phenomenal horizon) but its lateral
contours in their remoteness from the focal axis, toward which the
field of vision gradually dims out, as well. The horn rims of our
glasses, which our focus by-passes, are, in this sense, horizonlike precisely in their nearness; even more horizonlike (as well as nearer)
to our vision is the contour of the eye itself. We learn more here
than the surprising self-consistency of the image that underlies the
concept of horizonlikeness as phenomenology applies it (namely in
most instances where psychoanalysis will speak of the unconsciousness
of a certain experiential content) ; we learn more, because the distinction between the two kinds of "horizon" spoken of implies the dis-

tinction between sound and unsound attitudes and acts of consciousness. The person whom psychoanalysis charges with an unconsciousness of his own motivation is "unconscious" of his own motivation because his consciousness is directed toward its phenomenal, not its lateral, horizon; in order to become conscious of the latter, an attitude of reflective cross-eyedness must be assumed—that attitude of self-consciousness indeed which is most conspicuously troublesome for the person where phenomenal horizons are still accessible to him, but much less so if they are shut off. Directing, in the manner of psychoanalysis, the already self-conscious person's attention toward the self as a legitimate goal of his inner focalization (and thereby relativizing his *world*) will shut off phenomenal horizons still accessible to him; the patient will become more "relaxed", more reconciled to his psychological cross-eyedness, but will his existence be sounder?

The conceptual polarity of *horizonlike* vs. *focal*, in its application to existences, inasfar as they are unities of *knowing*, will become ever more important for us as we go on; but in order to round out the theorem, we ought to realize also the acute—and entirely normal—invisibility to the person of his own *phenomenal* horizons where the focalization point of his consciousness is short of them, as well as the visibility to him of a phenomenal pseudo-horizon where the genuine and original available one is blocked by a psychotic fixation. Such a fixation develops where a once focal conviction of the person is misunderstood by him, that is, is shut off from its own truth and from Truth altogether as from that which had first manifested it to him; subsequently, it petrifies into the formula-like materiality, the no longer truth-transparent literalness of the version in which it happened first to dawn on him, a possibility for which Binswanger's case studies of schizophrenics (to follow later in our report) are excellent illustrations. The law they map out, is nothing, however, that we could confine to psychosis, which shows the possible implications of its rule over human existences only at a certain (and specific) extreme; that ideas *emerge* as truths and *become* untruths by being—inevitably, if mistakenly—identified with the literalness of the formulations into which their genesis in the individuals and societies then freezes them, is a pervading axiom of history itself. Its implication is nothing less than a demand on the historian and the biographer to understand ideas of the past from the point of their historic take-off (situation of their emergence) rather than from any that followed and became of them, such as his own; in order to understand the past in its own phenomenality (which is not identical with the phenomenal past), the historic present (from which the phenomenal past cannot be extricated) must be suspended first by an active effort of thinking a human event back to its sources in a different world apperception, then from the sources outward to its actualization and appearance. What—among psychologists—blocks even the readiness for such an effort today is an unsuspectingness of the limits of one's own phenomenal horizon that the reign of objectivism fosters; it fosters it because it offers the psychologist an *ideology* of suspiciousness—of the debunking of other world apperceptions—rather than an incentive for *first* widening the contours of his own. Instead of such widening of phenomenal horizons, he has come to preach as well as practice the objectification of *all selves,* including, in many cases now, his own; but only that inner cross-eyedness of which we spoke, never more truth can result from such an attitude, for just *objectively* truth is always paradoxical—and what, if not the paradox, is intolerable to the objectivist?

Psychotherapy, contrariwise, must be an affirmation and utilization of what only the objectivist finds paradoxical: of the order of human existence as it eludes his grasp. For his grasp no longer is what it should be according to the native meaning of *understanding,* a standing-under, a becoming one, identification with the thing cognized, an entering into its being; his grasp, rather, has become a grabbing of the thing, an insistence on manipulating it, organizing it willfully, that precedes and precludes any coming-to-light of its own inner order. What happens if its own inner order conflicts with such willfullness in its respect? All human beings strive for happiness. Happiness, consequently, is a goal. The harder one strives for a goal, the more chances one has of getting there. How is it possible, then, that A, a man of health and wealth who does nothing all day long but strive for his happiness, is visibly unhappy, whereas B, a writer who not always knows quite how he is going to pay his rent check the first of next month, yet manages to radiate an unabatable buoyancy, not only seems unconcerned about his happiness but seems to find it in burdening himself with his lonely, dogged, and doubtfully remunerative labors that may devote hours to give perfection to a single passage in his books? A, our objectivist tells us, is suffering from a childhood trauma, while B, motivated by psychic masochism, is caught in an illusion. But how can we determine the meaning of the childhood trauma other than from our contact with what that trauma is supposed to have determined on its part, the adult Mr. A, and how can we say at all that B's preoccupation is an illusion, if it not only serves the integration of his world, and his in it, but succeeds in bringing forth a new *reality* that people may know and be stirred by decades after A, his name, health and wealth, have turned to dust? The problem throws us back on the never examined premise with which we started and according to which happiness is something that one strives for, that is, *seeks;* it is evident that everything here depends on the meaning that we give to the term *seeking.* Since it is just as evident that no one can sensibly contend the opposite of the premise, a closer determination of *seeking* is due as it relates to happiness: obviously, the gist of a successful seeking of happiness is that it is not concerned with happiness as a *focal* goal but as the horizon of seeking *per se* within which all focal goals are located and which makes them what they are. B can be said retrospectively to have sought happiness because he has *found* it and he never would have found it if he had sought it (that is, specifically or "focally"). According to the phenomenal structure of B's engagement in his work, the *seeking,* in turn, of perfection in his writing is first of all a *serving:* his efforts serve the being of an "unreality" (his work to be) that this service *can* make "real", that is, actual. This presupposes B's communication with *being,* which is man's only chance to partake in it, that is, to be; A, contrariwise, is one who *is* not (that he is not *happy,* is a redundant if customary expression for the same), therefore his preoccupation with having, taking-in, getting. It appears that our distinction between focal (purposive) and horizon-like ("unconscious") goals which stated the difference between being and having from the side of the phenomena of striving sheds light on a large number of absurdities characteristic of contemporary man and his civilization and illuminated, as pointed out before, by both Heidegger and Marcel: our examination of the paradoxes surrounding the concept of the pursuit of happiness could stand for uncounted others. A society, a culture, according to their intrinsic constitutions phenomena of pure historic growth, are horizonlike premises of the ideas as well as political forms that arise in their midst, yet since the middle of the nineteenth century we have seen, first political ideologies, later "cultural policies" founded on them that were oblivious enough of the trees of which they themselves are the branches to teach and undertake a purposive steering both of the "social process" and of "culture". All totalitarianisms, like all neuroses, are held in secret bondage by the idea of limitless manipulation; and however different the object of the totalitarian manipulation is from that of the neurotic, that idea is but the form in which the image of the *mechanism* attains virulence in thought.

But how can we hope to help the neurotic recover that in him—his being—that the mechanisms conceal as they by-pass it and usurp its position? We recall our composer whom a "progressive" education had led to shun the intrinsic order of things, their being, their *obstacle* nature, and seek self-expression instead, and who, abandoned to the world as a vacuum filled with nothing but objects, never was able to express anything at all in his music—until, unconsciously at last, he *succeeded* in expressing himself, which he did once he was persuaded to *seek* to express, not himself, but the intrinsic order of the world that he had shunned; the cardiac neurotic and former student of biology who could not get rid, either of the conviction that his heart was a precious and rather vulnerable machinery, or of the evidence for it which the behavior of that organ kept on supplying—until, no longer satisfied, apparently, with the false identity that his conviction had imposed on it, it assumed its true one when he lost it to a girl. For upon this event, which his convictions before would have relegated to the illusions of poets, his symptoms ceased completely, so completely indeed that he soon could not understand himself any longer how anyone in the world should be preoccupied just with his heart. Or the homosexual who could neither shed nor bear the idea of being one, but discovered an interest in women that soon set a new direction for his life once he had become reconciled to his being and no longer was *forcing* himself into heterosexual contacts. In all three cases, a hard to defeat pseudo-identity conceived in the image of the self-as-mechanism and inviting its manipulation by a deliberating rationality stood in their ways, and in all of them it might have continued to stand there if its correlate in *theory*—objectivism—had shackled their therapist's mind. We first, then, must explode the *theoretical* claim of the mechanisms of the psyche to represent anything like the essence of what man *is,* a topic that was touched upon before, at the end of our last chapter, and even earlier, when Reichenbach's psychological equation was examined. The testimony is now abundant, the core of what man *is* is not in "space and time". It is unobjectifiable *in fact*—but this "core" itself, what is it?

"In any psychology that objectifies man *at all*", Binswanger writes, "but most of all in such naturalistic psychologies as those of Freud, Bleuler, von Monakow, Pavlov, and some others, we find a crack, a gap that makes it visible at once that what is processed here scientifically is not the entire person, the being-man as a whole. Everywhere we find something that bursts and spills over the frame of a psychology of such kind. (This something, which the psychologist investigating human "nature" does not even have an eye for, is precisely what is decisive for the anthropologist.) To limit ourselves to Freud, we need only turn to any page of his work to find this something. To cite an instance, we hear him discuss the structure and order of functioning of *our* psychic apparatus, or *our* psyche as that precious instrument by means of which we maintain ourselves in life, or *our* emotions, *our* wishes, *our* thoughts. In all these possessive pronouns the talk is of a *being* that is pre-supposed as self-evident and just as self-evidently is bracketed out, namely the *being* of *existence as ours*. The same, of course, holds true for the *personal pronouns* such as: I mean, I incline, he alleges, he reports, he remembers, he has forgotten, he puts up resistance, I ask him, she is answering, we stated, we trusted in the future, we were agreed, and so on. Here too, the talk is of existence as *mine, hers, theirs*, etc., and of an existential communication, a fellow-human or we-relationship, that is, a relationship between a person and *one like him*, namely another person. Bracketing out that *mine* or *ours*, this *I* or *he* or *we*, results in this, that psychology, certainly, becomes 'impersonal' and 'objective' but also loses the science-character of a psychology in the proper sense and becomes a 'natural' science."[1]

The impossibility for anthropological objectivism to eliminate or dissolve the unobjective *my, your, his, hers* of whatever existence it sets out to analyze, has been demonstrated.[2] As Boss has rightly pointed out,[3] the *who* of existence is missed even in such holistic conceptions as the psychophysical unity of the person unless they are implemented by phenomenological accounts of the authentic mode-of-being of such a unity or whole; this mode of being, this *who*, then, which objectivism by-passes without being able either to account for or dissolve it

analytically, must be made the focal center of *psychology*. Such a
re-determination of the subject matter of psychology, in turn, demands,
as has been shown,[4] an inspection of the spatiality and temporality of
existence, as without it not even the first step toward an analysis of concrete existences can be taken by either the ontologist or the clinician:
the continued availability of the customary Cartesian notion of space
and of the customary Kantian notion of time still keeps working—as a
glance at Binswanger's case studies of schizophrenics, which almost
continuously have to ward off the very readiness of these notions, will
demonstrate—against the task of any true understanding. Spatiality in
the Cartesian sense is a modus qualified by divisibility, compositeness,
and movement.[5] As Heidegger has shown in *Being and Time*,[6] the
underlying apperception of space as a side-by-side (*Punktualität*, with
Hegel's definition of space) of things extending and displacing one
another "before one"[7] (before the "merely observing", actually rather
unobserving, cognizer) does not itself derive from observation but
from an interpretative conversion of *being* into *facticity*, an idea that
both the notion of identity and its empiric successfulness refute, as
shown before.[8] According to Binswanger,[9] who bases his position on
Heidegger's critique of Descartes, this entire conception of space in the
image of a universal *ôte-toi que je m'y mette* cannot behold the possibility that its own tacit existential premise—spatiality as a notion
nowhere reducible empiricistically—may mean something wholly different *empirically*. Yet, as we shall see, the original "empiric" (experiential) modus of spatiality indeed is different: its Cartesian, and subsequent objectivistic, theorization can be contested on the basis of human
experience not less but *more* immediate than that of space as a side-by-
side of mere abstract (phenomenally unreal) "points". Implicit in the
latter is the abstraction of facticity itself, the unreality of nothing-but-
objects inasmuch as de-phenomenalization has reduced them to mere
occupants of such points. Since such concealment of their being is
correlated with one of the observer's own that shows up in his losses
of "intuition" (phenomenal understanding), it is the aforementioned
"detached" mode of observation that is at fault here: its very detachment, rather than being what it ought to be, a restoration of the
primordial *openness* of world-experience, is its coercion from the
start.[10]

Man largely existing in that very isolation to which his thinking on a medium level of reflectiveness condemns its "objects" (himself as an object included), the unauthentic apperception of space as *Punktualität* —as the domain of mutual displacements of "things"—carries well into those analogous applications of space concepts to existential situations which the primary spatiality of man's existing brings with it.[11] Thus it is in situations of clash and strife that the appercepton of space in the image of the "get-up-that-I-can-sit" becomes emphatic even in such garments of politeness as one discussant *conceding a point* to another,[12] or in such psychosomatic phenomenalizations of inner conflicts that isolate man from his world-horizon as an anxiety-neurotic patient's physical sensations of pressure on certain strategic *loci* of his body, zones of a space precariously "had"—appropriated and defended— such as his stomach or heart. It is evident that any "room" that merely is "had", that is, owned in the sense of being possessed by an ego, admits (as all *loci* of abstract space do all objects) this ego only temporarily, as a kind of *paying guest* who may be evicted at a moment's notice; under existential analysis, it is indeed this unfathomable homelessness of being merely tolerated in abstract space as in a domain absolutely heterogeneous to a just as abstract ego that turns out to be the self- and world-experiential state of cardiac neurotics. The "eviction" danger here reaches its high point of terror, threatening quite literally the *ground* of existence; in a "whirl" of being and knowing that we explored before, these patients *know* that they will have to vacate whenever the notice terminating their "leases" comes through. The most absolutely opposite, most "anti-Cartesian" structure of experienced spatiality we would, in consequence, expect to find wherever existence has established that hold upon itself which according to its ontological structure only its hold upon "world" can lend it, in other words, where it is fully transcending and only thereby fully realizing itself, a condition which, as we remember, Binswanger recognizes in the phenomenon of love. The phenomenology of love—or rather of its premise, the existential status of lovingness—confirms this expectation in full:[13] it presents a merger of the "mine" and "thine" in their actual occurrences to the subject, a merger which no objectivistic "translations" of these possessive pronouns into the language of Cartesian spatiality can account for, since, for that medium, the mutual exclusiveness of objects, and their impenetrability by one another, holds axiomatically.[14] By strikingly suspending dead facticity

(the side-by-side of points in space) in that characteristic interpenetration, that "swinging" transparence of things for one another and for
the all-encompassing and -pervading truth of being with the testimony
of which, in poetry and in prose, the utterances of lovers have since
time eternal been replete, love achieves a maximal self-transcendentness
of existence; with perfect consistency of methodological principle, the
space conception of objectivism thus is attacked by Binswanger from
the side of love as the one phenomenon referring at the absolutely
highest level of immediacy to what objectivism *a priori* by-passes—
being. In the experience of lovers, *eternity* is neither a nebulous lyricism
of speculating metaphysicians nor a cut-and-dried article of no longer
understood religious creeds,[15] but a reality, or rather *the* reality, since
all other, factual "realities" are here encountered in their dependence on
this one, while precisely what calls *their* reality ever into question loses
its. What calls their reality ever into question, is, of course, the opposite
of eternity: time, as the principle of fleetingness (mortality) vanishes
so much in the beholding of a standing present that death itself must
lose its terror, its claim to be the end; the much-observed affinity
between the existential themes of love and of death thus reveals itself
as grounded in the lovers' awareness—which the petty rationalism of
psychoanalysis "corrects" as it corrects the phenomenal throughout[16]—
that the gist of their existence has come to be the beheld endurance of
its newly won status, the *being-with*. As a *Gestalt*-like (transposable)
phenomenon, as independent as any other true whole of the fleeting
materiality of whatever media it may temporarily occur in, that endurance, to probe and prove itself, may demand to be tested by what
everybody thinks will shatter it, the disappearance (death) of each of
the lovers in his mere factualness as part of that whole; since the
whole here is existence as an absolute *being-with*, the perishing of its
parts, as is generally the case with *Gestalten*, becomes the token of its
own endurance. This explains the frequency in lovers of the notion
of a finiteness of death;[17] instead of what the public supposes death
to mean, a finiteness of existence, it is existence itself which here
questions and challenges time. The identity "between" the ultimate *who*
of existence and *being*, which has been expounded in multiple connections, is not, therefore, a speculation of existential ontology but a
datum of possible human experience to which many clues are given
but which becomes nowhere quite as drastically evident as in the

existence-status of love.[18] It is therefore a fact—as factual as any other psychological datum; ontology, precisely if it abstains from speculation, can no more than nail it down.

Rather than by divisibility, compositeness, and movement, the authentic space of existence is characterized by a phenomenal *here* and *there*, by *widening* and *narrowing*, *centering* and *re-centering* on the possible identities (*whos*) that can be abstracted from the plurality as well as, within that plurality, from the shiftings of the *here* of existence; likewise, instead of the linearity, divisibility, and infinity of abstract time, the original temporalization structure of existence reveals expansions as well as shrinkings, in both the length and breadth of the ever death-bounded stream of time—of the "horizoned finiteness" in the midst of which existence "dwells"—of an indivisible *present* which the very directedness of existence, being constantly "ahead of itself", has always and already turned into that retrospectively beheld *absence* (the "past") in the image of which it shall then build its time concept. The peculiarity of horizons being that they can never be reached (never, that is, without losing their horizonlikeness), *being*, wherever it speaks with the authentic voice of experience, so much knows itself as bound to stay within the horizon of time that this horizon must widen beyond its initially beheld mark—the *my death*—so that not only the *my death*, owing all its terror to its claim to be the end, must lose it, but that time itself decidedly ceases to be a fleeing successivity of past, present, and future; the "transfigured" time apperception that the existence-status of the *being-with* knows as its own particular form of temporalization thus is identical with the *beyond-time* that in certain ecstasies of existence may phenomenally be beheld.[19] The quality of the "timeless" which is the immediate common denominator of the phenomenal contents of either experience-type, indeed has nothing to do with the schizophrenic's breakdown or stopping of time.[20] It rather lies in a direction diametrically opposite to that, for whereas the phenomenal content of the schizophrenic experience is a blocking off of *original future*[21] (of that which in coming-toward one ever turns into the *present*), the timelessness of radical self-transcendence means on the contrary a cleansing of time from the negativity of its ordinary power to destroy (in the sense of undo) by its *passing*; it is therefore a suspension of the past as such, a state which phenomenally occurs as a unique simultaneity of the future and the past and hence as a widening of the present. "Simultaneity" and "widening", of course, do not refer to clock-time, not even to its inner experiential organon, the faculty of clock-time estimation; the type of experience here under discussion therefore involves no suspension or confounding of the objective successivity of events. Its content is rather a perceptual one, namely *the presence in time per se of being as a standing center*. This discovery of its phenomenal content explains at once the vanishing of all anxiety so inherent in the experience: as the "standing center" of the horizon of time, *being* "knows itself" as just as little subject to the power of time to *undo* as dependent any longer on what corresponds to that power on the side of the "subject". What corresponds to it on the side of the "subject", in turn, is nothing "real", but only the most persistent of *images:* that perishable little *ego*, in one word, which existence in its unauthentic if most ready self-identifications of the everyday alleges obstinately, if never quite satisfactorily, to be its *who*.

It becomes increasingly evident that *identity* harbors problems of which psychology hardly yet has dreamt, although one of its entire subdivisions, personality theory, is built upon the premise that psychology knows what identity is to start with. For precisely what is this "ego" which so self-evidently seems to claim to be the content of what in the inner time of experience always *precedes* it, the notion of self-identity, itself arising from "nowhere"? We understand that something that *is* may be reflected, but what can something be that needs to be reflected *in order to be*? What *is* something that at any time at which it is encountered is encountered already as a memory, something that, first of all, *is* not, always and only *has been*, if no longer ago perhaps than that tiny span of time which it takes *attention* to turn from the world to the self, from a future *present*ing itself to the eidetic shadow of a past posing in the role of self-presence?[22] As Heidegger has shown,[23] the self-concealing tendency of once phenomenal concepts, their fatedness to lose, as they are turned into object categories operationally, their original meaning-contents, finds its earliest paradigm in the conversion of the phenomenal *here* into the *I;* as already the elder Humboldt had found so remarkable,[24] the *here* still takes the place of the *I* in some "primitive" languages that, significantly, know no other means to convey it. Any objectification of the noetic condition of *all objects as such*, the self, can only mean its phenomenal emptying: the conversion of the *here* of existence into any kind of "entity" thus is

bound from the start to lead to the ever-emptier *ego* that becomes the
conceptual backbone of the psychoanalytic account. As an immediate
"function" of memory and thus the *first* reflective counterpart to self-
identity—its self-conscious shadow, so to speak—the *I* easily mistakes
itself for the substance of the self that somehow appears to endure
throughout its manifold specific identities (inner existential conditions)
in remembered time, all so different in their contents, their orientations,
their "interests", in the concrete *what* of what the person *has been*
when finding himself in any one of them from what he found himself
to be in many another.

Yet it is, as always, only a "radicalization" of reflection that at once
lays open the threadbareness of this claim of the ego. Often enough,
the experience-ground which such radical reflection illuminates, reveals
itself to it without the slightest trace of introspection even getting a
chance to partake in the event, and this is what most drastically happens
in such actual and stunning changes of inner identity which, shaping
up in retrospect, may leave the person aghast, as from within an inner
"Dionysian" situation, a state of "driven" engagement dominated by a
passion, a supervalent idea, to the circumspect detachment of a cooler,
more "Apollonian" hour. Having been obeying an interest that no
longer claims "one" right now, the *one who one was* is positively seen
as a different *who* in such moments: a *who* that so unfathomable an
abyss separates from the subject's present one that his ultimate identity
as the common ground of all of his various "existences" is bared in
the "form" of precisely that unfathomableness that is beheld in his
shudder.[25] Neither of the two principles of Nietzsche's famous dualism
of human existence, the Dionysian or the Apollonian, representing the
core of his identity, the person inevitably must misunderstand either
of the two; in the neurotic's inner disorder of experiences, this misunderstanding only attains a particular depth. As though not precisely
the self in him, in that previous state of chthonic excitation, had found
itself challenged most perturbingly *beyond itself*, the neurotic self-
analytically tends to misidentify the Dionysian in him with the mere
forces of an objective inner *id*, while the Apollonian principle governing
the *now* of his existence may no less be misunderstood if identified,
vice versa, with the tenor of any possible self-objectification based upon
an outside-and-beyond-the-self as the locus of its vantage point. As one
of the possible authentic identities which the ultimate *who* of existence

can assume in elaborating itself in biographic time, the Apollonian interest of man is just as much an *inter-est,* a demand for engagement, for *being-in* one's world, as is the Dionysian; engagement, however, is always engagement *of* the self. Consequently it is not what would *refer* to a beyond-the-self as its *vantage-point* rather than *transcend* itself into such a beyond-the-self as into its *world:* the "mechanism" of self-objectification, what the Apollonian engagement *means at its source.* What makes it differ from the Dionysian, on the contrary, is in any genuine sense not its "objectiveness", into which only the utter self-misunderstanding of neurotic existence turns it by way of the inveterate self-consciousness, self-splitness, of the subject, but that the *self,* in each of these two so radically contrasting engagements, *is in fact a different who.* In distinction from the *who* of his Dionysian situation, by way of which *chthonos,* the earth, may have claimed the person's identity in an unconditional manner, he just as unconditionally *is* the spirit, *pneuma,* in his Apollonian engagements; the latter, therefore, are detachments only from the "earth", not the self. What is this *earth,* the depths of which the Apollonian engagement so shuns, if not all that which from the general direction of *below,* as inherent *a priori* in the spatiality of existence, pulls and weighs its structure down, threatening to destroy its very form and, with its form, the condition of inner freedom? As is readily seen, neurotic self-consciousness not only feeds on interferences—by an untrue existential decision[26]—with spontaneity in its role as openness toward the chthonic (psychoanalytically speaking, on repressions of the id) but equally as much on what such untrue existential decisions involve just as inevitably: a blocking off—the superego of psychoanalysis, wherever its effect is repressive, is from the very start precisely and only *that block*—of the pre-given accesses through which the spirit ever seeks to enter the soul.

What, then, beyond the shaky hold of that obstinate continuity-*substitute,* beyond the hold of an ego ever unrepresentative of man's spontaneous being, ever and already defining itself from the vantage point of the "public" as a general locus within the subject's sphere of inner orientation,[27] remains of the self? *Who* is the one that exists in all existence? *Being,* as we know;[28] but just the definitive lack of attributes inherent in the concept of being imposes on our thinking a quest after "something" that would implement this concept in such a way that precisely what constitutes existence empirically could still be accounted for: the individual and specific, the spread of biographic and characterological differentiality in its full observable breadth. The picture of the self as mere visiting ground for powers and principles themselves never definable in terms of the personality as *individual*, which we derived in this chapter, is first of all, as it appears, a telling confirmation of the world-picture of mythology. But mythology itself, that mythology at least, the Greek, that set the scene in which our own memories in the West, as enduring images of inner, not of course of "factual", historic time, originate, offers something better than the *impersonal* of calculable or incalculable forces; for what other body of archaic beliefs knows divinities so humanized, personalized, as just the Greek? The self, moreover, while ever receptive for the clashes and reunions of these powers, yet is anything but passive, anything but unselective: consistently, it seems to challenge or invite them, choosing among them in accordance with the fundamental world-idea which it *is*[29] and which to implement and realize they are ever called into its limelight. Its ruling principle, therefore, in the truth of mythology as much as of the existence of the actual person of history of no matter which of its eras, is that first and most immediate manifestation—that specification—of *being*, that guarantee of the personal throughout the individual's life, which is his *daimon* or *genius* and the ever-present *who* of his dreams.

This may appear paradoxical as it is in dreams that existence knows itself as most unreservedly exposed to the "powers", dependent on their good graces, without that-which-knows here (the dream subject) ever being free to act in that special and limited sense of "free" in which it understands its action-freedom in the wake state, as the power of analysis and deliberate choice. Even in dreams where the action of the dream consists to a larger extent of actions of the subject, the impulses from which the latter spring are phenomenally characterized by a peculiar sureness and unquestionableness, which does not focally enucle-ate or weigh its own motives as *reasons* but on the contrary is self-evident enough *already* to let the subject's action appear only as par-ticipant on equal terms with everything else there that "happens". The dreaming self, significantly, is reduced to the self of *noesis,* which means that it is all knowledge and no willfulness. This already seems to allude to a possible dissolution of the paradox, for *knowing*, as we saw, is that status which *being* assumes, or is ever striving to, in human existence; the self as pure knowledge, then, the self of the dream, is indeed a closer realization of the ultimate *who* of existence than any other we "know". All knowledge and no willfulness does not mean that the dream has no uncertainties, which on the contrary we know can be tormenting, or that the self in it has no will, which on the contrary can be exceedingly impetuous as well as persistent: what it does mean is that whatever uncertainties there are, must be solved, if at all, by the action of the dream itself *as it occurs*. The subject, here, is so perfectly identified with what precludes "willfulness"—his will as *existential tendency*,[30] as that which actually "throws" his existence, and which in the medium of the dream must therefore appear as one of the wellsprings of the characteristic necessity inherent in its actions as a whole—that it cannot possibly occur to him as *object* of any "inner" experience. His own vantage point occupying that position which in the "inner" experiences of the wake state is occupied by what only *they* encounter as phenomenal *objects*, it is but in the concrete action role that he is playing that he can "find" himself at all in his dream. Being all *knowledge*, the self here cannot help being self-knowledge also and hence, in a sense, self-objectification, but evidently one of a kind very different from that which inheres in any introspections of the wake state: his "acting" self, first of all, occurs to the dreamer without the occurrence itself being induced by any deliberation, any manipulation of the direction of attention on his part; his dreaming self, on the other hand, as the now exclusive *self of noesis*, stands in a relationship of polar apposition *not* to an abstract shadow of "itself" as "psyche" but to the dreamer's existence as a whole, namely as the whole of the actual person who he is in his *world*. In consequence of this greater radicality of "self"-dualization, the gap which it opens cannot, as in the orientative and motivational conflicts of the wake state, as altogether in the self-*disputant* awareness of self so basic to that state, split the self of the person in *either* its status as "orientation" *or* its status as "motivation", but *succeeds* in "splitting" the self in this manner, that it severs the whole of orientation (the dreamer) from the whole of motivation (the—"objectified"—course of action "actually" taken: the person himself as the one "found" acting in his dream). Instead of there being apposed—not necessarily opposed—to one another, as in the typical conflicts of the wake state, the two *knowledges* of feeling and of rationality, the two *wills* of authentic inner *wanting* and of deliberate

intending-proposing, the radical "self"-dualization of the dream, brought
about by the complete withdrawal of the experiencing subject to the
position of his true self, his self as knowledge, paradoxically succeeds
in unifying the person: even where the dream situation encountered is
at an extreme of adversity, unsafety, or strangeness, there never occurs
in it an ego that would *clash with itself.*[31]

In view of the freedom (in the sense of a relative absence of control) of the dream as much as of its phenomenal quality of revealingness,
this, at first glance, may seem to cancel out the argument with which
our whole study began and which called into question precisely the
cognitive validity of cognitive self-dualization (if seen then only in its
introspective, that is, self-reflective, form). This seeming contradiction
is not altogether new, since in spite of what that first tenet may
superficially have appeared to connote, the necessity, so much recognized just by the existential thinkers of our time, of a *radicalization*
of reflection—in order for self-consciousness to find its way back to an
authentic existence—rather than any Klagesian submersion of "consciousness" in the "unconscious" was argued. The gist of the argument
was that knowing, as the unique and precious *human* existence-form
which it is, not only is *per se* nothing life-inhibitive but that, where it
does inhibit "life", neither the inhibiting "knowledge" itself can be
valid *as knowledge,* nor that which it actually hampers (and which at
times rebels against it) be more than isolated and already directionless
impulses severed from their world-poles by a particular kind of self-
reflection. Not spontaneity, then, is *acutely* repressed in that process,
but that process as a *chronic* constellation of self-concern, a constellation that isolates the self by having it turn its "back" to what otherwise
would be its world, eliminates the very possibility of anything authentically spontaneous: spontaneity has no chance to become manifest here
because its constitutional prerequisite *is* that freedom of focussing
one's attention on one's world, "outer" as well as "inner", which introspective self-dualization precludes from the start. Contrariwise, the radical reflection of existential thought, in acknowledging the "self" only
and already as the irreplaceable referent of "world", 1) affirms the
essential character of the "subjective" in man as self-transcendency (or
simply as *knowledge,* in restoration of an oldest and most comprising
connotation of that term), postulating an ultimate identity, both as
the "origin" and the "aim" of the "throw" of human *Dasein,* of *being*

and *knowing*, 2) verifies the affirmation empirically by restoring to man precisely that primordial *spontaneity* which, to implement it, ought once more to be his; restoring it first to its own "home", the thought-springs of philosophizing, which before its time had virtually run dry under the sands of professorial residues from philosophies of the past, then, with its entrance into anthropological theory and psychotherapy, to those in our day who most drastically suffer from its shortage.

What else, then, if not that radical self-dualization of the dream which we recognized before as its constitutional premise, characterizes that existentialist imperative to go to the very end of reflection which insists on seeing the whole of man in his world? Indeed, the dream would appear as a paradigm of the type of noetic orientation which all theorizing about *existence* must seek; but the danger in this similarity is clear, for only an even more complete understanding of the status of dreaming than we have yet reached can protect that theorizing from the evident pitfalls just of *dreaming*. Is it not significant for *that* identity of being and knowing which the dreaming situation actually achieves that its "pitfalls", too, are pitfalls in the most literal sense conceivable? In any typical nightmares of the "fixed" variety, the dreamer, finding himself "glued" to his spot and, in his intolerable immobility, pressed in by obliterating forces of an anonymous and hostile universe, yearns for a liberation which only his *awakening* then brings him—a freedom which *is*, as he shall only learn upon awakening, the wake state itself. If the dream *is* essential knowledge, as except in the brief period between the first halves of the 18th and the 20th centuries has never seriously been doubted, and if the essence of that knowledge is freedom,[32] how is it that *awakening* may free the dreamer from the dream as from a bondage? It becomes evident that only one side of the dreaming situation has been explored thus far; but the clue to the contradiction appears to lie exactly in that literalness of the dream that raises the vastest of problems since it confronts our thinking (necessarily articulating itself in the categorial idiom of our verbal concepts, if never originating there) with what forever seems to defy categoriality *per se*, if only because of its greater proximity[33] to our being.

The way to break that defiance can never be found in a rationalism that "corrects" the phenomena of the dream by substituting categorized allegorical meanings for its authentic contents. The "defiance" of the dream can, strictly speaking, not be broken at all, it can only cease "voluntarily", and it never *does* cease unless the dream is first of all "befriended", a possibility of inner attitude that very much was actualized by the wake contemplations of the dreamer of the mountain-and-boat-dream that was reported in Chapter VII. "Befriending" means an as near as possible restoration of the attentive "perceptual" receptivity, so regularly mistaken for passivity, of the dream state: we have to be able to visualize again what we dreamt the way we dreamt it, and re-experience ourselves as the referent of its presence, a focus which discerns the self only in terms of what happens to it, as the obvious and tacit implication of the person's situation in his dream. Succeeding in this, we at once recognize a peculiar structural trait of the dream situation—of any dream situation—which we will have to try to reconcile with those already brought out: though the happenings of the dream, including the person's own actions as part of them, are seen as events independent of his will *qua his choice*,[34] these "independent happenings" nevertheless do not in the slightest have the character of any objective process. Dream *time*, in distinction from public time, in distinction most of all from what would seem its polar opposite, the temporalization-modus of the wake compulsive neurotic,[35] emphatically centers on a standing *now* and just as emphatically is discontiguous in terms of the *scenes* of the dream action. Correspondingly, dream *space* is never a neutral domain wherein the "things" and the events perceived can be localized; throughout the dream, it quite literally *is* the *there* of each one of those things and these events as referring to the *here* of the dreamer. This quality of the dream contents, their *referring* to the existent—in Heidegger's term, their being *at hand* rather than *before him*—finally is confirmed by their structure, which only the wake state with its itemizing recollections, by first isolating these contents from their authentic time space, then categorizing what it already mistakes for their phenomenality, will discover in their "independence", their "topical neutrality"; in the dreamer's experience (which wake memory *can* restore) as he dreams them, it is precisely this, that they incisively pertain to *him*, which most undoubtingly is *known* to him, if just for that reason never thought of, let alone perceived as posing any kind of problem.

This quality of the dream: this coincidence *in substance* between

"being referred to by everything" (having everything at one's *hand*)
and yet "seeing everything as it is in itself" presents, first of all, a
clue to what, in the "parallel" structure of radical self-transcendence as
existentialist reflection seeks it, the "identification" of *being* with
knowing spoken of would mean in the concrete: an attitude of unconditional openness, of true *inter-est*, of concern about the "things" of
the world for the sake of their being. For the neurotic self of the
ordinary ego-preoccupation can never be overcome by a self-imposed
"altruism" caught—with "egotism"—in one of those false if stubborn
alternatives which the old dictum has in mind, that the opposite of
an error is unfailingly another one; what can overcome egotism is on
the contrary the true selfishness of love, emphatically beginning in the
area of its existential core phenomenon, "sexual" love, and radiating
from there, but precisely *not* misunderstanding "sexual" love in the
sense which that term has taken on since Freud, as a matter of functional satisfaction of an objectifiable psychophysical "need". But the
stated quality of the dream, usually experienced as its "literalness",
implies something more, namely that revision of the objectivistic theory
of knowledge which Heidegger's demand to understand the events of
thought from the side of the *contents of thought* postulates likewise.
If the "knowing" self of the dream would actually, in the manner of
the ego of wake deliberation, set itself apart from the "known" (the
witnessed happenings of the dream), as our own first and tentative
formulation inferred, the "process" watched by the dreamer would, in
its entirety, have to be a matter of concern to what first must arise in
the "subject" in order for any "object" to be encountered *as one:* it
would have to be the object of a curiosity[36] explicitly aware of its
"mazes", an object of *amazement*. Such amazement is notoriously
absent from the dreamer's experience even of his most amazing dream
as he dreams it: the "duality" of the dream of which we spoke turns
out to be, not any splitting-apart of object and subject, world and self,
but, as in the existence-state of pre-reflective man,[37] their polarization
within one context of being.[38]

Since the "paradise" of this pre-reflective unity of existence does not,
as an exclusively "pragmatic" one, allow man to come "into his own"
(thought), it must be lost, and with that loss—the biblical eating of
the tree of knowledge—that genesis begins which first leads man to
discern only more sharply the identities of things as their modi-of-

being, then, with the distancing of the "world" from the "self" taking
on the character of an abyss, leads him to dissolve them into that dead
nothing-but of the deterministic debunkers, that growingly unreal
atomar facticity which characterizes his present existence-world in its
most typical versions.[39] As a determined effort at overcoming that state,
not by turning back romantically to the unity that was lost, but by
going forward along the line of reflection as the very fate-line of man,
existentialist thought can realize at once the two "sides" of the original
existence-context that the dream state parallels: the secure openness-
toward-the-existent of *all-that-is* (is *at his hand*) and the terror into
which that same condition of being absolutely "secure"—now suddenly
meaning absolutely *caught*—must turn, once the negation of all-that-is
—the naught—occurs to the subject, as most emphatically it does in
the pure anxiety dream, the "fixed" type of nightmare we spoke of.[40]
The power of the naught—according to Heidegger[41]—to convert into
nothingness everything that "is" and that it touches, is peculiarly
confirmed by the dreamer's experiences here, more conspicuously perhaps than by most anxiety states of the wake person, since the condition
in which existence finds itself in this shaking *notturno* is one of an
unwilling compulsion precisely to "stand" the approaching formlessness of the *dreaded*—without, in many instances, the dreamer being
able to stir. If everything-that-is, and that before gave so much security
to the existent, turns into nothingness—without, for that matter, vanishing as mere *things*—existence inevitably must find itself referred for
the first time to a beyond-all-things-that-are: breaking through a *horizon,*
one that before had been so "horizonlike" indeed that it was never and
in any fashion even *perceived,* becomes a necessity of existence, and this
existential imperative, by which pre-reflective man, having first discovered the naught as an implication of the discovered *past,*[42] is literally
pushed into reflection, also succeeds, in otherwise vastly different circumstances, in finally "pushing" the dreamer through that "horizon"
of his nightmare which is his acute condition of *being asleep.*

This "double nature" of the dream, to have at once the openness
of original knowledge, the security of original being; and to turn—
upon the mere touch of the *naught* with the frightening imperative it
engenders[43]—this same state of original freedom into one of intolerable
imprisonment, so that only the alternative between *this death* and *that*

freedom, is left, evidently does not in the least detract from the essential knowledge-character of the dream; on the contrary, the "imperative" of breaking through, waking up, with which the nightmare closes in full consistency with the message of its own "interior" content, rounds out the picture of a pervading representativeness of the dream, its representativeness not for the dreamer's needs and wishes in their "objective" isolation as Freud's immanentism believed, but for his situation in his world, which consists of more than needs and wishes. The latter tenet is the core principle of the phenomenological theory of dreams which Binswanger evolved most of all in his paper on "Dream and Existence"[44] and for which many passages of his essay on Heracleitus[45] provide supplements and supports from the dawn of western thought. As so many elements of existential reflection find their precedents in pre-socratic thinking, the seed also of the conception of a "double nature" of the dream, its freedom-to-reveal on the one hand, its nihilism when analogous to a "self-imprisoned" existence on the other, already is contained in Parmenides'[46] reference to the "palace of the night" with its two gates, but it is a preserved handful of Heracleitean [47] words that bring the nature of that duplicity most sharply into focus: in the main, the one on the sleeper as *participant* in the "works of the world", and that other one that divides humanity into those truly awake—making their *worlds* a common one by sharing in the *logos* as the all-obliging and -pervading law of Truth—and those turned self-ward, as a man in his sleep, to what the Ephesian calls their "private" worlds, the ever-sterile *shadows* of their selves. The peculiar discomfort of a *guilt unfaced*, of failing in one's world-responsibility, one's world *response*—which not always even *can* occur to the "dreamer", whose face is here neurotically turned "in"-ward, in the *open* of a naked dread—yet recognizably inheres in the status of the untrue "private" dreaming that Heraclitus' existential analogism plainly has in mind: a "dreaming" the agent of which is "glued", not to the horrible *here* of the dreamer of the nightmare, the mortifications of which at last *compel* an awakening, a breaking out, but to the *now* of an anxious holding-on to the "dream" as to a hiding, its worried and futureless self-perpetuation without happiness or hope; having first missed the *gate of life* of the dream itself as it opened, then ignored the insinuation of his conscience *that he might still break its spell.*

NOTES

1. L. Binswanger, *Ausgewählte Vorträge und Aufsätze*, pp. 179–81.

2. Cf. pp. 57–58.

3. M. Boss, "Beitrag zur daseinsanalytischen Fundierung des psychiatrischen Denkens", *Schweizer Archiv für Neurologie und Psychiatrie*, 1951, 47, 15–19, esp. p. 16.

4. Cf. pp. 101, 113–18.

5. L. Binswanger, *Grundformen und Erkenntnis menschlichen Daseins*, p. 23.

6. Cf. Par. 22–24.

7. Cf. pp. 60–62, 114, 116.

8. Cf. p. *140*.

9. L. Binswanger, *Grundformen und Erkenntnis menschlichen Daseins*, pp. 23–24.

10. We are, of course, only repeating at this point the argument with which, contrary to the nineteenth century methodological errors that trace back to Hume's notion of radical detachment and to English empiricism altogether, the phenomenological method was introduced in such "basic" areas as the psychology of perception: a step by which—a merit of early Gestalt psychology—objectivism was beaten on its own ground, as experimentation since has verified the argument beyond doubt.

11. Cf. p. 10.

12. L. Binswanger, *Op. cit.*, p. 25.

13. *Ibid.*

14. The absolute validity of this principle as governing Cartesian space is verified by the fact that natural science throughout is able to "debunk" not only molecular mixtures but atomar compounds (as well as elements and whatever follows them along the dimension of the ever-smaller) as combinations of entities each occupying its own "space". At the quantum-theoretical stage of the display of this power of natural science, that notion of space which itself underlay the entire atomistic analysis becomes shaky; but the implications of this event for all other tacit premises of objectivism have as yet been discerned only in their roughest contours by physicists, and only by such most pioneering thinkers among them as Heisenberg.

15. It may hardly be necessary to point out the differences between the unauthentic notions of eternity conveyed by any watered down "cultural memories" and the true eternity-encounter to which historically they themselves trace back: original religious experience with its striking resemblance to the timelessness experience of lovers. At no lesser level of immediacy, the latter type of experiential content only is reversed in the authentic situation of the original metaphysical quest, which non-fundamental ontologies then by-pass but which at its point of first awakening is characterized precisely by a beheld absence of eternity, a want of it that phenomenologically implies an axiomatic possibility of its becoming *present*.

16. Cf., L. Binswanger on the psychoanalytic treatment of the theme of incest: "Its inability to see the authentic structure-of-being of love, psychoanalysis already

has demonstrated by its conversion of the fundamental characteristic of love, its power *a priori* to transform the essence of temporality, into a causal-genetic process. . . . We do not, of course, by any means deny the factual biographic evidence that the sister or mother, as Kant already had conjectured, remains the 'arche-image', 'which in the future must determine all idealizing conceptions of the female able to arouse a fantastic nostalgia'. This historico-genetic nexus has been secured a thousand times, but it is something wholly different from the constitutional inherence *a priori* of the eternity motif in the whole of the structure of the being-with of love." L. Binswanger, *op. cit.*, p. 41.

17. Cf., the lines from Elizabeth Barrett Browning's forty-first sonnet:

> "Oh, to shoot
> My soul's full meaning into future years,
> That they should lend it utterance, and salute
> Love that endures, with life that disappears."

18. A similarly emphatic self-transcendency characterizes any specific status of existence that at least approximates the peculiar "deathlessness challenging death" of *love*, such as authentic courage. Authentic courage, mythico-historically embodied in the image of the *knight*, is encountered in historic biographies most of all in the form of that self-transfiguring state of inspiration that readies a subject to sacrifice him-"self" (his life) for "his" own truth and hence, if we reflect once more on the constitutional links between *being per se* and *knowing per se*, for *Truth itself*. Authentic courage, therefore, is neither the self-coercive acting despite and against one's fears, which is only its closest and on the whole legitimate substitute, nor the usual submersion of the self in the identity of a collective (plural modus of existence) which most frequently enables man to be "courageous", but a resolute self-affirmation of *being* in the face of "itself" as the *horizon of horizons*—as that *absolute* (the ultimate content of all true spiritual experience) which is spelled out by the beheld presence of its own just as absolute *alternative*. This "alternative" of being can only be the *negation* of being; the essence of authentic courage, therefore, is a facing not of death as one's "own", but of the "background" of being *in its entirety* (and therefore also of any resolute *affirmation* of being) : the naught. Cf. also pp. 67–68.

19. Cf. pp. 122, *142*.

20. K. Jaspers, *Allgemeine Psychopathologie*, pp. 69–74.

21. Cf. pp. 115–16.

22. Cf. p. 253.

23. "The *public* 'self' says I, I, loudest and most frequently precisely because *it is not itself* in any proper and fundamental sense and keeps evading its authentic power *to be*." M. Heidegger, *Sein und Zeit*, p. 322.

24. W. v. Humboldt, *Über die Verwandtschaft der Ortsadverbien mit dem Pronomen in einigen Sprachen* (1829). Gesammelte Schriften, Vol. VI, section 1, pp. 304–330 (ed. by the Prussian Academy of Sciences).

25. As a characteristic example for the naiveté with which objectivistic psychology has continued to by-pass the foundational problem of (inner-personal) identity, the fact may be cited here that in all experiments in personal recognition

reported in the literature it has to this day been taken for granted that the problem is at least primarily one on the part of the perceiver, not the "object" (though different *external* settings in which that "object" may occur or be presented at different times are acknowledged to make a difference worth their study as a controlled variable). That the one to be recognized "is" (whatever this shall mean) the same as when he was "known" first is never even questioned.

26. Cf. p. 134.

27. The constant experiential presence of this "locus" of inner orientation is, of course, the condition of the awareness of the being-one-among-many. This awareness, never lacking in the singular and dual modi of existence, becomes decisive in the plural one. Cf. pp. 157, *160*.

28. Cf. pp. 29–30, 113.

29. Cf. p. 156.

30. Cf. p. 154.

31. The ego-"fissure" of schizophrenics, significantly, does not carry over into their dreams, which seem characterized by the more unitary identity of their acting as well as their experiencing selves the more a tendency toward multiple personifications dominates their wake states.

32. Cf. pp. 131–33.

33. Cf. pp. 124–25.

34. Where in dreams he "chooses", he already encounters his choice as *execution;* the reflective freedom-awareness of the wake person in a situation of *choosing* fails to arise because it is itself the essence of the *being awake.*

35. Compulsivity insists on a clock time *contiguity* of all-that-is because it has lost the *continuity* of inner time (the phenomenal presence of *being* which the rites and the magics then conjure) ; cf., Max Picard, *Hitler in uns selbst,* 1945.

36. Cf. pp. 116–17.

37. The often observed "weakness", in man of the pre-reflective (myth-bound) cultures, of the limits between "dream" and "reality", the ease with which they interweave and experientially can replace one another, may be cited for confirmation.

38. Cf. p. 114; this unity of the dream, which precedes and escapes any interpretative categorization of its symbols, was already recognized by Stekel.

39. Cf. pp. 96–104.

40. The "chasing" nightmare, contrariwise, is not *centrally* characterized by true anxiety but by a fear only approximating anxiety in its phenomenal quality of *engulfing:* in the direction of the flight itself, its space is open.

41. Cf. pp. 123, *142.*

42. Cf. pp. 115–16.

43. The "imperative" is to find *being* again by going beyond what one *has been* up to now.

44. K. Binswanger, "Traum und Existenz", in *Ausgewählte Vorträge und Aufsätze,* pp. 74–97.

45. K. Binswanger, *Op. cit.* "Heraklits Auffassung des Menschen", pp. 98–131.

46. *Ancilla to the Pre-Socratic Philosophers,* ed. Kathleen Freeman.

47. *Ibid.*

CHAPTER 9

The Dream (Concluded)—Narcissus and His Problem—
Symbols as Timeless Realities—Fundamental Ontology
and the Dream—The Sexes and Their Modi of Being—
Worlds and Ersatz *Worlds—Binswanger's Schizophrenics*
—Inwardness and Self-representation.

THE DREAM, AND WHATEVER IN EXISTENCE IS
dreamlike, as a truthless world substitute and a true world reflection,
narcissism and extra-polarization, in one—how can we reconcile that
contradiction? It is at points like this that objectivism unnoticeably
slips into error by taking it for granted that the contradiction, instead
of inhering in the phenomenon being explored, is a theoretical-
explanatory one, a contradiction posing an alternative of conception
and obliging the scientist to take sides. Yet what appears contradictory
here calls no more for any *explanatory* solutions than does the mythical
paradigm of narcissism itself: the self-perception of Narcissus in his
water image with which he falls in love. The truth of this mirror
image *as what it is*—a likeness—is turned into an untruth by the
ensuing existential decision, as Narcissus soon comes to mistake a
reflection of reality for the reality reflected, the self's shadow for the
self. More subtly, if we re-experience his enchantment in the successivity
of its phases, the myth informs us about the existential origin of
autism: the "accidental" self-encounter is at first an encounter of the
youth *not* with the image of his body but with the reality of his soul.
In its objectivity, its standing against itself (his soul, significantly,
occurs to him from without), Narcissus' soul takes on the identity of
the most changeably and plastically receptive of the elements—water,
which as a world-wide and perennial soul-symbol needs no introduction at this point.[1] What the myth thus confirms is the necessity with
which, at the root of all reflectiveness, existence ever has met itself
already,[2] but moreover we are granted insight into the genesis-structure

219

of the existential error of self-objectification as the never missing starting point for hypertrophic ego-images that the encounter may bring forth.[3] In accordance with the common principle of Gestalt and phenomenological psychology that—in illuminating the inner order of anything whatsoever—its phenomenally evident structural analogy (as essential *identity*) with another thing of different materiality must be followed to precisely the extent which both phenomena justify in the way in which they are *given*, the shift in Narcissus' focus from the *water* to *what it reflects* is a shift of attention that replaces the true three-dimensionality of the water (in Heidegger's language, its being-to-the-ground) by the projective three-dimensionality of the external presence in it of Narcissus' body image. Only the soul-encounter of the first instant, since it occurs spontaneously, is thus a true confrontation of the self *as knowledge* with the self *as immanence*, pretty much as in the dream, but with the "eye" here *not* submerged in the "water" and thus able to discern what it beholds with the free clarity, comprehensiveness, and distance that distinguish the true space of *wake* existing[4]; already Narcissus' next look will have by-passed this perception of the ground (himself as soul), centering itself on the externality, only *appearing* in this medium, of his body. What else—in confirmation of a previous argument[5]—but the starting position for the ego of self-consciousness to arise, the authentic inner identity of *being* one's body (an existential *a priori* of all action-seeking spontaneity) to be lost, *is* this perception of the image of one's body as though seen actually from "without"? The one and only primary condition of existence, under which (if in a widely different manner) this focus would itself be legitimate, be "biopositive": the itself *phenomenal* "immanence" or "centripetality", the "demand" for attention, for being acted-toward, for care, inherent, according to Simone de Beauvoir,[6] in the structure of the female body, is not given in Narcissus' case,[7] and considering the inner imperative of all love to seek the *other*, the early dying of the self-lover—the conceivable self-hater of his later hours—which the myth recalls, assumes an utmost of compellingness.

The cited contradiction of the dream, then, inheres in the double role which it plays in existence all at once—to be, as *noesis*, the most immediate knowledge of the dreamer's situation in the world, whereas as an *existential state* it is the very incarnation of the peril of world-loss (also of "wetness") in the Heracleitean sense, a submersion in immanence, a blurring of direction and a dissolution of form, a loss, despite all the nearness, the "transparency" gained, of the focal freedom of *decision*. What stands out from its *noetic* accomplishments are such most "general" qualities as the mood, color, and temper of dreaming, its particular modi of temporalization and spatialization, which further differentiate *dream time* and *dream space* as qualified before; to the wake memory, all these characteristics stand out more, on the whole, than do specific elements of the dream action, but since the former are marked by a far greater "closeness", concreteness, of their acute presence in the dream than is its action that the dreamer "witnesses", they are far less readily accessible *verbally* to any retrospective account. In full consistency with phenomenological principle, then, it is on these characteristics of a dream *situation*, which with drastic literalness tend to chart the actual biographic situation of the existent, that Binswanger's clinical studies of dreams center; the link between the dream and the wake state is never objectifiable, it is only *evident;* the common denominator of the actual biographic situation and the dream is, with Binswanger's term, the inner life history of the subject, as distinct from a "history" of his life as an objective "functional" process.

The situations, in this sense, in which, in the dream, an existence finds and knows itself may represent its spatialization modus by way of such most comprehensive data of experience as *rising* or *falling*—that rising or falling which without exception turns out to be the factual phase of the subject's biography at the time of the dream and his own surest and most intimate but also, for just this reason, usually most tacit knowledge in his wake state; carrier of this knowledge is the dreamer's existence rather than his "subjectivity". What such attributes of the dreaming situation signify in the concrete therefore determines itself according to the qualifying specific circumstances of the "fall", the "rise", the moving in a plain, or whatever directionmodus of movement is met with; the rising upward within a wellstructured mountain scenery, the lowering oneself—"falling" can be a movement of *settling down*—to a chosen landing place, thus are worlds apart from a *being suspended* in empty space, with the ground *fleeing* from one, or from a state of helpless falling. Existence is itself *action*, concerted and self-determining, in the former, passivity in the latter case—either, as in the first instance, in the forms of worldless isolation, or, as in the second, of an object-like exposure to the objective world forces. In a manner that cuts across their own order, falling and rising as normative possibilities of all existing thus are differentiated again by the polarity of true mundanization versus *Wahn*,[8] self-transcendence versus self-isolation, the self as direction and form versus the self in dissolution, the world as challenge and response versus "world" as a pressing-in or fleeing apart, weighing-down or leaving-one-suspended heterogeneity of the *factual*. Likewise, the specific temporalization modus of existence tends to crystallize itself in dreams—from those phenomena of a *standing* and a *growing-from-within* of the present that correspond to an intensification of experienced spatial *presence* itself (as a pervading being-at-hand of one's world) to the pressure and rush of time as a presentless precipitation of its passing, as in those states of existential dread which radical self-objectification may induce. Where, as in some forms of acute schizophrenia finally ensuing on such states, the self, no longer able to catch up with *public time*,[9] has quite literally "broken" with, and away from, it, a "death" or standstill of time may be experienced. Having stopped to play along with the intolerable racing of the world of things that pass, the schizophrenic existence, in such cases, finds itself confronted with a vacuum the former occupant of which— *original time*[10]—has been so lost in that rush of things interminably and senselessly fleeing by that the "negative now" of "no time at all any more" (of there being *nothing present*) becomes its lot.

The temporal and spatial conditions of the self and the world thus cross-differentiate those modi of temporalization that inhere axiomatically in an individual life course, and the self and the world, for their part—the *who* and the *what* of an existence—are differentiated by the ontological spread of the *factual* modi-of-being that occur to the person in the form of the symbolic. Somewhat simplifying, Renato de Rosa, in the passage on Binswanger of his survey of existentialist psychopathology,[11] puts the entire order of norms of existence and their concrete modifications under the focus of Binswanger's theorizing in these words: "Knowledge of the fundamental structure of the psyche is, to him, the normative instrument of the analytical judgment. The analysis itself is conducted according to a paradigm the principal concepts of which are the being-in-the-world, transcendence,[12] the self, and temporalization. Genetically, the different psychotic manifestations always are traced to a primary modification of the fundamental structure of the psyche. This modification determines the form of existence, as for example the being-*hole* of many a schizophrenic. All world-regions of psychotic experience and thought are being influenced by this in a characteristic manner. The self of the being-*hole,* or of existence *as a hole* becomes, for example, a dried up plant in the world of vegetation, a thrown-away peel or shell in the world of things, a worm in the animal world, a mere tube or gut, stuffed and emptied again, in the body sphere, and so forth".[13] The existing-as-a-hole, of which de Rosa speaks, refers to the published *Daseinsanalyse* of Ellen West, one of Binswanger's three most famous case studies of schizophrenics, which are singularly representative of his diagnostic thought and method and of which *The Case of Jürg Zünd* has been referred to before.[14]

In all three cases Binswanger finds an identical over-all characteristic of schizophrenic worlds, a peculiar narrowing and impoverishment, as though a cancerous growth was draining away the potential abundance of *Dasein.* But the supervalent ideas, the blocking-off *Wahn* fixations in which in these and all such cases the existents' world accesses are stuck,[15] are fundamentally different in each; even though the patient's existence is pervaded and involved always and inevitably in the entirety of its fabric, the priming points of the abnormal world-modifications met with lie in different spheres of the basic *being-in* of the person—Jürg Zünd's in the allopsychic, Ellen West's in the somatopsychic, Lola Voss' in the autopsychic spheres previously pointed out.[16] What makes all three cases so instructive is the appearance in them of a universal lawfulness: the symptom-picture of each becomes compelling in its specificity, in the subtlest details of its behavioral and characterological physiognomy, once the perception of its *center,* of a just as specific primary failure in successful self-transcendence that inheres in each of these existences has clarified itself. Clinical understanding here is clearly no longer a deliberate enactment of any vague empathizing; as spontaneous empathies—emotional participations that are too unconditional to *know themselves*—are always and necessarily, it is perception and thought, and the more it is only these two, the less can the clinician help engaging his entire being.

The world of Jürg Zünd[17]—prototype of the socially self-conscious —an awkward and frustrated intellectual withdrawing suspiciously from personal contact, shows all the features of homelessness, of a severance from the eternal as the true presence of *being*, which we discerned as the inevitable implication of a radical objectification of self. The patient's anxieties, his experience of an unfathomable senselessness of existence, are traced to a primary splitting-apart of a purely "judgmental" ego (taking its stand *outside* of itself *as body* and *in front* of a world consisting of the side-by-side of things[18]) from an incalculable, irrational self vainly now seeking realization in world contacts: the patient's attention, upon encountering any opportunity for contact, is drawn the more inexorably to the "outer" image of his body and body behavior (as though, in that very situation, seen by others), the more important that situation is to him, the more, in other words, it had initially stimulated him toward engagement. Since the self as original transcendence, as authentic beholder of "world", is a captive of Jürg-Zünd's ego image geared to the all-powerful phantom, the pseudo-world, of the *being-with as a being-one-among-many*, Binswanger finds the dual modus of existence here totally overthrown by the plural. A purely "worldly" (in the sense of *profane*) communication-modus with the others, the things, and oneself, a calculativeness that sees everything in the image of physical forces and their manipulation, remains as the only conceivable world-contact according to the innermost conviction in the idea of which the pattern of existence here is set. Phenomenal space, deprived as it is of the genuine *here* and *there*, the self-thou relation of spontaneous spatialization,[19] *is* stereometric ("objective") space in the case of Jürg Zünd. This means that things in it collide with one another, tend to displace one another, that they are mutually uninterpenetrable, and, incapable of reconciliation and unity, turn space itself into a dimension of danger. Jürg Zünd's Rorschach, accordingly, is full of such apperceptions as "furniture where one is liable to bump one's knee", and "centrifugal spheres[20] shooting off from a fly-wheel, that fly into my face, in mine, of all people's, though they had been fixed to the machine for decades; only when I approach something happens." "Everything about the patient", Binswanger writes, "is angular and occurs abruptly. But between the single jerks and thrusts, emptiness reigns".[21] Zünd's existence is dominated by anxiety in its modus as flight.[22] In this modus, anxiety, as Binswanger puts it, and as we have had occasion to recognize likewise,[23] is "compulsory perpetuation of the past"; Zünd's

existence, therefore, is not "ahead of itself" but is caught and constrained by a "being already in the has-been". The temporalization
modus of Jürg Zünd's existence, in consequence, is a self-alienation
from *time per se*: the subject, while continuing to find himself "in
the world", finds the world devaluated, in a state of disintegration
and decay, with his observations of such disintegration and decay
serving as building stones in the construction of his *Wahn*. The *Wahn*
is thus a dialogue of existence with itself that takes place "in the
emptiness of time", outside of time as the *coming-toward*. Time as such
is understood as empty[24] here, which means that it only *passes* but
does not *come*, that one "watches" it but does not partake in it with
what one *is*, a situation that turns the temporality of the watched,
disintegrating world, since it clashes with the inhibition of inner time
as stated, into one of pressure or *urgency*, just as the spatiality modus
of the world is turned into one of oppressing narrowness and nearness.
The patient's self-objectifying ego preoccupation, which *succeeds* in
rendering him conspicuous in fact, brings forth that effect by means
of his trying to be *inconspicuous*; in the authentic spirit of his self-
encounter as *pure object*, Zünd attempts to be one among many. In
alternation with a just as spastic masculinity pose that he assumes at
certain times, he cultivates the idea of detached poise, of being just
flaneur, of suggesting to the outside that he feels himself to be like
any other person, a particle of a crowd, but precisely this idea, since
it pervades his motor behavior with the incoordinations of the deliberate rather than inhering in it physiognomically as a truth of his
being, makes it "stilted", "awkward", in brief, "gives it the lie". The
lie calls for detection, and detections, just as collisions, are sudden;
Zünd therefore is the physiognomic incarnation of the idea of suddenness, which as fate—from the side of his world—of guilt and
concealment on his own part, partakes in the central theme of his
anxiety and his whole *Dasein*. This theme Binswanger discerns as posed
by the patient's fundamental homelessness, his severance from the
eternal: since time as *inner* time depends on participation, the *sudden*
—with Kierkegaard's words, to which Binswanger refers in his study—
"cannot be worked into a continuity, nor be transferred into one";
(the sudden) "is there one moment, the next one it is gone, and as
it is gone, it is again and completely there." The standing "outside"
of time is thus equi-originally a passive state of exposure *to* time as the

locus of the "accidental"; *accidents,* therefore, ever breaking into the
false security of Zünd's existence, must trespass and disturb also his
isolation from the element of inner time.

Since he senses such invasions as *uncanny,* as a total threat to his
self, which could not be understood unless that isolation, that refusal
of world-participation, were aiming to hold the self in a state of concealment, the primary self-interpretation of existence in this its improper modus "has" the self as the *secretive per se.* As though that-
which-conceals would not ultimately be identical with the self
concealed, as though it were disposing of those limitless powers of self-
manipulation ever only *claimed* by the ego, the *intended* self-conceal-
ment and the *resulting* physiognomic conspicuousness of Zünd's
"nonchalant" behavior with its expressive conjuring-away of the
sudden ever lurking in the dark, are understood by Binswanger as
the two sides of one existential error or riddle, the key to which is
provided by the very "wanting" of the secret ever to come to light.
"The concealed is the involuntary disclosure", Kierkegaard writes,
and Binswanger quotes him, and "For the weaker an individuality
originally is, or the more elasticity is being consumed in the service
of concealment, the more easily will the secret break out of the person
in the end".[25] Accordingly, shame and guilt, while emphatic in the
case of Jürg Zünd, are just as emphatically non-genuine, that is,
passive: the first being a fear of involuntariness, of losing deliberate
control, of finding himself "embarrassed" (Zünd's most violent and
most perpetual acute dread), the second a fear of being "mistaken for
this or that" by the "others". The latter line of self-objectification can
be traced to Zünd's tacit determination of his ego as a pure standpoint for judging; in always "taking" others *by* certain of their social
behavioral traits, he displays a horizonlike conviction that implies his
own vulnerability to such judgments. His guilt is caught in self-misunderstanding[26]: instead of being what authentically it *is,* a challenge to existence to take hold of its own ground, it becomes an instrumentality of self-alienation through which a wall of resentment—of
distrust, suspicion, envy, and hate—is maintained between the subject
and what otherwise *could* be his world.

As we might expect, a nostalgia for an open encounter of the world
and the self pervades the inner life history of Jürg Zünd: he would
like to get out of his autism, to be united with the others, the non-self,

in the dual modus of love; senses, what Binswanger terms at one point "the most terrible *Gestalt* loss that can hit existence", as slowly depleting, destroying him; but already in his visualization of his problem as a whole he again seems caught in its misunderstanding as a primordially calculative-manipulatory, "behavioral", one conceived in the projected image of *past-ness*.[27] As we recall, a problem of this kind only begins with the projection of that image into an empty, nothing-but-dimensional "future"; the fixation of Zünd's inner set therefore cannot be loosened by any "insight" that continues in the line of his inveterate self-objectification. His case is that of a typically depressed schizophrenic: the ego here is too hypertrophied to allow unsatisfactory *ersatz* worlds in the crude sense to arise, sever his conceptual and interlocutory contacts with the "others", and thus cloud the existential moorings of his symptom-picture (Zünd's *Wahn*, significantly, does not behold any delusional "new reality" but only insists on the inner impossibility of the original one). This makes him a paradoxical challenge of the first order to the psychotherapist; existence seemingly having become mechanized throughout in his case, nothing visible is left in it that could affirm itself in front of the mechanisms of the psyche, and psychotherapy would therefore seem to remain without a foothold here that could permit it even to begin. Self-objectification, in Zünd's case, carries to the point (unlike the case of Ellen West, it only does not start out from there) where his body itself has become the enemy; it is the alien *per se,* the locus of an incalculable immanence calling for calculation, indeed the original and constant source of the threat of sudden embarrassment. Intimately interlinked with his love frustration, his body experience, accordingly, alternates between the theme of the "secret wanting out" (fear of *erection in public*) and an inability to "believe" that his body can hold together: the patient, without any medical indication, wears a suspensorium at all times. Existence, as Binswanger concludes, is here never *itself,* has never been *chosen,* let alone "laid hands on"; the patient "has survived himself", and now, in the *dead* of time, runs around "as a corpse".[28]

Though the therapeutic problem proper must be deferred, we already recognize a weak point of the mechanisms inasmuch as they involve the patient's self-knowledge in its double status as knowledge of them and as *itself part* of them: in full accordance with our own analysis of the axiomatic structure of morbid self-consciousness,[29] Jürg Zünd "knows" that he "will act awkwardly somehow",[30] but this knowledge is strikingly unlike a genuine one, a knowledge of anything as being what and how it is independently of one's own act of knowledge.[31] For Zünd also knows (or could be made aware) that without his "anticipatory" knowledge of his embarrassments to come, which *as knowledge* is subject to noetic criteria of proof and thus open to argument, this same knowledge *as an existential state* could never maintain itself; his problem therefore hinges on the said criteria of proof. Already he knows that without his self-"knowledge" (as a state) the awkwardness anticipated never would materialize to start with, and this, then, is the weak point, the foothold, from which, as will be shown in a subsequent chapter, the entire self-obstruction of unauthentic existences, as always revolving around a fundamental conviction that invalidates itself if *the person only dares* to think it through, can be fought.

Zünd's objectified self is the "accidental" one-among-many, his ego that objectifies the self the pure *Standpunkthaftigkeit* ("standpoint-likeness") of the nothing-but-judgmental taking-someone-by-something. A corresponding line of ego-self segregation can be found in Ellen West,[32] but here it divides the ego as an idealized self-image conceived in the spirit of complete liberty from and against the self as formlessly vegetating and weighing-down *soma* good for nothing but to be destroyed. Accordingly, the ego aspires for the "masculine" status of victorious self-determining action—*aut Cesar aut nihil*, is the patient's motto of her adolescent years—while the self is experienced as a pure immanence. As such, it begins in the veil of a receptivity for the active forces of the universe, a longing for liberation, for *being kissed dead*, to quote a lyricism from her early and ethereal, poetically productive time, when her existence, still holding on to its own unity, still responds to the claim for meaning, liberation, world status, on the part of her femininity, her self-as-body. But inasmuch as a phenomenal polarization of this kind must increasingly identify the soma at its most vegetative, most undifferentiated and thing-like, most "massive", the phenomenal self here finally becomes nothing more than the digestive tract, the body not as a whole but a *hole*[33]; the "massive", correspondingly, is quite literally the threat of gaining weight by acceding to the demand of this hole to be stuffed. Binswanger resketches the biography of a brilliant and attractive girl gradually succumbing to what the idea of limitless liberty *qua action freedom*[34] must turn out as hiding wherever the existence is feminine; preconstituted as an immanence in *want* of being-opened, being acted-toward, it *a priori* contradicts that idea in its literalness. The idea of limitless action freedom therefore hides *its own opposite* but does not hide it for long; the terrors of a just as untrue, only existentially now far more "real", apperception of the world as mere matter and weight, a "merely worldly" world in the sense of what we might term a self-interpretative secularism of existence, breaks through, first gradually, then ever faster. To quote Binswanger: "We could describe this secularization, this 'profanation' of *world* thus: in the place of the freedom of a *letting things happen* there appears the *bondage* of a being overwhelmed by a specific world conception; in the place of the freedom of the formation of the ethereal 'world' there ever more appeared in Ellen West the bondage of an *inevitable* drowning in the narrow world of the grave and the swamp. Since 'world', however, means not only world-formation, world-design, but, on the ground of such an image and design, means also the *how* of being *in* the world and of one's attitude *toward* it, we were able to register this metamorphosis of the ethereal into the grave-world also in the form of the conversion *of existence as a bird rising jubilantly into the air into one appearing as a blind and slowly creeping worm.*"[35] Binswanger's last-quoted references are taken from ideations of Ellen West during the opening and closing phases of her illness. What happens in her case is that the "phobia" of gaining weight, the "obsession" that stirs her to do anything, from semi-starvation to a sleepless self-sacrificing in excessive work, to prevent it, gradually, and with the patient herself watching this process in full consciousness, becomes the central and supervalent idea by which the entirety of the original richness of her existence is consumed, while the idea kept in repression, the idea of eating-until-full, at times succeeds in conquering her identity.[36] Rather than the *massive* as feared (obesity), the *massive* of her compulsion to fixate her attention on obesity accomplishes the cited conversion, *bird* to *worm;* in the end, in one of her many fits of depression, it was this central, supervalent idea, horizonlike, at this stage, to any thought and action impulse that occurred to her, but discerned at last in its imprisoning power by the patient herself, that drove her to suicide. In sketching that conversion, furthermore, an entire physiognomic and *Gestalt* modus of what clinically tends to be lumped together as flight of ideas undergoes a phenomenological clarification: the "flight" as what, according to Binswanger, it is in Ellen's case, a thought procedure of *orderly jumping,* is distinguished from the disorganized flight of ideas as an existential *whirl* or *vertigo* that may happen to a person. Like the final "jump" (the suicide), the "orderly jumping" of Ellen West's ideas, which Binswanger describes, can fully be understood as a necessity of her existence as, noetically and therefore factually, her existence has determined itself: in order for her being—as idea, form, spirit, action-freedom—to escape at any point a being-glued-down by the ever waiting swamp of materiality,[37] indeed only *jumping* remains as the guarantee of a free exit.

The case of Lola Voss,[38] finally, allows Binswanger to extend his analysis of existence to the auto-psychically centered version of *autism*: a severe hallucinatory persecution psychosis, complicated by "a highly intricate suspicious oracle of words and syllables, according to which the patient acted or refrained from acting" and, at first glance, suggesting the field of interpersonal relations as the home province of its conflict, is traced, beyond its social vestiges, to its true origins in the immediate confrontation with one another of two "absolutes", the *self* as *soul* with the *world* as *cosmos*: what unfolds in the psychosis of Lola Voss is not a world conception reduced to push and pressure, as in the case of Jürg Zünd, or dynamically laden with incompatible forces, as in that of Ellen West, but, in implementation of Heidegger's word about the "uncanniness", the exposure to nothingness, of the being-in-the-world *per se,* about existence itself as the source of anxiety.[39] Accordingly, Binswanger finds the world apperception of Lola Voss reduced to the categories of familiarity and unfamiliarity (uncanniness). He goes on to say: "Existence here was perpetually threatened and ambushed by an impersonal but deeply hostile *power.* The incredibly thin and threadbare net of artificial combinations of syllables served to protect the existence from being overwhelmed by this power and from the intolerable exposure to it. It then became very instructive to observe how simultaneously with the vanishing of these protections a new and wholly heterogeneous (since not at all *intentional* any more) protection appeared against the invasion of this undefinable *dreadful*— the persecution *Wahn* proper. The impersonal might of the unfathomably *uncanny* was replaced by the *canny* (in the sense of snug, intimate, *secretive*) machinations of the personalized enemy. Against these, now, the patient again was able to defend herself consciously—with accusations, counter-aggression, attempted flights—all of which appeared like child's play compared with the constant helpless state of being menaced by the dreadful power of the elusively *eerie* which before that time had been dominating her inner experience. With this new gain of *existential* security[40] there coincided, however, the complete loss of existential freedom, the total subjection (*Verfallensein*) to the image of the *others* as enemies, psychopathologically: delusions of persecution. I mention this case, first of all to show that we will not understand the persecutory *Wahn* if we start our inquiry with the latter, but rather must direct our whole attention to what precedes it, be it for months, weeks, days, or perhaps only hours. I am convinced that in other cases, too, we will see that the persecutory *Wahn*, similar to the phobias, connotes a protection of existence against its invasion by something inconceivably dreadful; it is only in comparison with this unspeakably weird, non-objective power that the definite cunning of the machinations of the enemies are still far more easily tolerated, since the enemies, in contrast to a wholly formless dread, can yet be *taken* (perceived, figured out, warded off, resisted) 'by' *something*. The other reason that I mention the case of Lola Voss, is to show you that no longer are we bound today to the dilemma raised by the double status of the 'life of the psyche' as open to our empathy and yet hiding *from* it, but dispose of a method, a scientific instrument through which we can bring closer to scientific comprehension that so-called unintuitable life of the psyche also. It naturally still remains up to the powers of imagery of the individual explorer and physician to what extent his own capacity of experiencing enables him to relive and resuffer what the daseinsanalytic research with the planfulness of method opens as experiential opportunities to his scientific grasp."[41]

The clinician's personal powers of spontaneous identification, then, of "intuitive" perceptiveness and understanding, *are* required, self-evidently, for every single step of his task, yet have no bearing at all on the inner order of that task; just as the independence of the inner order of a musical score from the intuition, the powers of re-experiencing, on the part of a conductor, and the requirement for the same conductor to command an utmost of these same "subjective" powers, do not in the least contradict one another according to the structure of

music and of musicality, so the functionalist's reproach of alleged subjectivism in all clinical qualitativistic theorizing completely by-passes,
with the pregiven structure of existing, also that of the relationships
between the existences of the clinician and his patient. Reference to
Binswanger's definition of the psychological quest—in distinction from
the historian's how-has-it-really-been, the natural scientist's how-has-it-
come-to-be-this-way—as solely wanting to know, *how is it really*, has
been made before, and the full meaning and logic of that maxim are
now fast becoming more tangible: as nothing can be translated from
one language into another without first being fully understood in the
original, so also no "translation" of occurrences of and to the psyche
into the language of *any* theory is admissible as scientific unless the
"original", the authentic inner state of the subject, is *understood* (re-
experienced) *first*; the first task of psychology, then, is a re-actualization of inner states according to the specific clues lent in each individual
case by what of them is communicable—understandable—at all.
Wherever, now, there is communication, wherever there is understanding, there is *world*; what constitutes *world* is precisely the transgression
of the absolutely immanent, the in-itself of Sartre, which the cited
concepts connote. The re-actualization of experience-worlds, as the first
principle of *Daseinsanalyse,* is therefore not just a postulate for the end
of obtaining greater immediacy of cognition; no other way of gaining
psychological cognition is genuinely open to start with. A verification
of this statement does not require any closer acquaintance with
existentialist literature; nothing may corroborate it quite so well as *any*
analysis just of what in the objectivistic theories themselves and in
their nomenclature makes them communicable, that is, open to comprehension.[42]

But this concentration of existential analysis on the actuality of inner
states in their *presence*—always the presence of a world—is anything
but a neglecting of the genetic aspects of existence; Binswanger's own
concept, one of the categorial center-pieces of his whole theorizing,
of the inner life history of an existent, in counter-distinction only from
the same "history" as an ever-hypothetical functional process, connotes the exact opposite of such a view. The childhood trauma of
Freudian fame is not even denied its direction-setting import; what is
realized is rather something far simpler and more fundamental, namely
that just the direction-setting capacity of experiential events belies their

causal-mechanistic interpretation as in Freud's doctrine. A true cause-effect connection, in order even to be made out as one, requires the isolation of a process supposed to have its form from its topographical embankments set for it by the conditions of the field wherein it takes place; the latter, regardless of whatever happens "between" them, have set the direction of that process from the start, so that the cause-effect connection as such is a purely one-dimensional affair by an *a priori* of its own definitive constitution. A direction, contrariwise, presupposes a multi-dimensional domain *wherein* it is one, and accordingly it can never be constructed without its *whereto,* the locus of all of its possible goal-points; that which in the future "will result" from the childhood trauma, must be given *already* in order to be "explained", and this requirement is visibly at odds with the natural-scientific meaning of causality. This difficulty, now, is precisely the one met with in the case of the psychoanalytic usurpation of the principle of strict causalism[43]: in order to claim to know that B is the effect of A, one must be able to deduce from an objectively given A that its effect *will be* (rather than *has been*) B, a requirement psychoanalysis never meets since its whole interpretation, even its "knowledge", of A is, vice versa, determined by its knowledge of B *as a datum.* As partaking in the patient's present state (B), his own mnemonic knowledge of A *objectively belongs* to that datum; but this means that just objectively the knower and the known can never be disentangled. What causally is thus never reducible to any of its states of the past, the referent of his own inner life history, the *who* of an existence, registers, pre-reflectively, what amounts to a reversal of "causality"—a reversal of the objective functional order of genetic evolutions *qua processes*: in phenomenal time, not a childhood trauma A is the cause of an adult symptom picture B, a connection which only mnemonic reflection can establish here as *phenomenal* causality[44] with all its misleading implications that we reviewed before. On the contrary, what A *is* is wholly determined by the present state of the existence (B); for *being* presupposes *presence,* and what *is* present here of A but a memory that, as such, belongs totally to B?

An at least equally important observation of the psychology of immediate experience discerns the dimension of *focalized* vs. *horizonlike,* which has been introduced before and which renders in phenomenological terms the actuality of the conscious-unconscious polarity;

since the latter, despite Freud's misunderstanding to the contrary, does not cover such mechanisms of the psyche as underlie hysteric fugues and amnesias, neither does its phenomenological correlate just referred to. Coordinating our earlier observation[45] of a "horizontal" rather than "vertical" splitting of the psyche in hysterical and other paroxysmal states characterized by temporally alternating rather than (as in dementia praecox[46]) simultaneously clashing whole "ego" sets with the results of our inquiry into the problems of inner identity and of its changes,[47] we recognize that what in fugues and amnesias is banished from the center of the field of awareness is not primarily certain memories or other experiential *contents,* but rather their beholder, namely that particular *who* of the paroxysmal existence to whom as focal relevancies they themselves refer. In most instances, this does not mean two sharply segregated but only two overlapping fields of awareness; or we may speak of one field with two or multiple sometimes rigidly fixed "selves" as *focalizing* centers (*"here* positions"; cf. p. 205). The incisive difference between this and the normal structure of attention does not lie in the variability of the phenomenal *heres* as such, which is constitutive to any psyche, but rather in the person's inability to shift fluidly between them and thereby retain a continuity of orientation: as throughout his staccato-form existence on both its inner experiential and physiognomic-behavioral sides, the paroxysmal—hysterics, epileptics and so forth—must alternately perseverate and, tearing himself violently away from what binds him in his perseveration, must *jump* also from one specific temporary identity of his self to another. This presupposes the availability to him of these different specific identities, as distinguished from the successivity of their actualizations; what determines the central tendency of an existence is never the past of process time nor, as a misinterpretation of modern biological finalism has it,[48] its "future", but what in an existence, in ever-recurring biographically, is *timeless.*

What *is* timeless here? An orientative norm, a paradigm of believing, the essence of an apperception of *world* as the implicit and inherent idea of one's whole being. If Heidegger's dictum concerning existence as a "throw"—of being into its Truth, of being as immanence into being as knowledge—were really a speculation and nothing besides, the entire morphological aspect, not only of humanity and the human individual, but of the animal kingdom as well would remain incomprehensible; but instead, biology now finds that the stepladder of phylogenesis culminating in man implies that very tenet. The evolution of its forms can be explained by the well-known mechanistic theories only in its *mechanics*; the forms as such and their unfolding (concretion), which is not identical with the objective procedure of their actualization in time, refer to a dimension of "inwardness", of self-representation, self-interpretation, of the making apparent of a specific *conception* of being, that rises in importance from the lower animals toward the higher.[49] Far from discarding genetics, then, phenomenology only for the first time allows the facts of a genesis to speak for themselves; and what it finds that they utter where the genesis is a course of human life is a pervading unity of existential themes. These themes, in turn, occur as dimension-setting alternatives at once of the existent's biography and of his innermost and most enduring preoccupations, a truth which Binswanger exemplifies by many of his cases but most poignantly perhaps by that of a young girl, "to whom, in her fifth year, when taking off her ice skate, it happened that the heel of her shoe remained stuck in the skate, which caused an inexplicable anxiety and a fainting spell".[50] Let us quote from Binswanger's comments once more *in extenso*.

Since then the now twenty-one year old girl is seized by indomitable anxiety whenever she notices that a heel is not firmly attached to the shoe, that someone is touching his heel or even only speaks of one (the heels of her own shoes had to be nailed on). If she cannot run away in such instances, she faints. Psychoanalysis showed with all desirable clarity that behind the anxiety—revolving around the loose or severed heel—were birth-fantasies, both in the sense of being born—severed from the mother—and of the birth of a child of her own. Among the many severances of continuity which the analysis produced as frightening, the one between mother and child turned out to be the one most properly meant and dreaded. . . . Before Freud one would have declared that the event on the ice in the fifth year of life, though in itself it is entirely harmless, had caused a 'heel phobia'. Freud, as we know, showed that it is the *fantasies* attaching themselves to such an event or preceding it that are 'pathogenically' effective. But both before and since Freud still another explanatory reason was kept in readiness to make understandable why the event—or those fantasies—just affected *this particular* person, namely his or her constitution or predisposition; for everyone experiences the 'trauma of birth', and many a person loses a heel without getting a hysteric phobia. Even though we do not propose by any means to unfold the problem of *predisposition* in its entirety at this point, let alone to solve it, I confidently claim that what we call predisposition can to some extent be illuminated further from the side of our anthropology. What happened is that

in later studies we could show that one still can go farther, penetrate 'behind'
the fantasies, precisely by searching for and examining the world design that
constitutes the primary possibility of such fantasies and phobias. That particular category now which serves the world design of our little patient as a
guide line is the category of *continuity,* of contingence, context, and cohesion.
This means an immense narrowing, simplification, and voiding of the world
content, of the otherwise so exceedingly complex totality of its references and
relations. Everything that makes the world significant submits to the rule of
this one category. It alone is what makes the world and the being in it *stable.*
Therefore the dread of any *severance* of continuity, any *rent,* any *tearing* and
disjoining, separating and *being ripped apart.* Only this 'world image' makes it
understandable why that common human experience, the severance from the
mother, as the arch-separation of human existence, could become so 'supervalent'
that any severing event was fit to *represent symbolically* the dreaded separation
from the mother, drawing on to itself, and activating, the fantasies and day
dreams. We only must not believe that this situation is really mastered by our
understanding if we define the excessive ('pre-oedipal') mother-attachment as
the explanatory reason for the appearance of the phobia; rather we are forced
to the insight that such an excessive mother attachment is possible only on
the basis of a world design founded on the exclusive category of contingency,
continuity, and cohesion. Such a world apperception, always implying such a
mood (or timbre) also, must of course not be 'conscious'; neither, however,
must we call it unconscious in the psychoanalytic sense, for its place is beyond
that polarity. In itself, it is nothing psychological; its reference is to a *world,*
to what only makes possible the psychological facts as one finds them. It is
here that we encounter the actually and properly 'abnormal' of this existence;
yet, and with this we return to our 'psychological' point of start, all the less
must we forget that wherever the world design has become so narrowed, the self
must also be hemmed in and be prevented from maturing. Everything here shall
remain as of old. If the *new,* the severance of continuity, yet forces its approach,
it becomes evident that this can only mean catastrophe, panic, the acute anxiety
fit; for now the world in plain fact collapses, and nothing stable is left in it at
all. In the place of inner or existential maturing, of authentic temporalization
opening itself to the future, there appears here the over-weight and dead weight
of the past, of the *being-there-already.* This world must stand as it is, nothing
may happen, nothing change; its contingency must be guarded as it ever has
been before. From this temporalization-modus alone it is that we can hope
to comprehend that the world-temporal phenomenon of *suddenness* gains the
enormous significance always attained by it in such cases; for suddenness is
the time-character of what rends, fragments, cuts into pieces the thread of
continuity, thrusting existence as it *has been* out of its tracks and putting it
in front of the awful, naked horror, an event that psychopathology most sum-
marily simplifies by referring to it as *anxiety attack.* The severance of the heel
from the shoe on the ice does *not* constitute an 'explanatory reason' for the
appearance, which we are forced to infer, of this pre-occupation prior to *any*

severance of continuity; nor do the fantasies concerning birth and the maternal body. Only because (as self-evidently holds true for the infant) the attachment to the mother meant world stability *per se*, could those fantasies gain such import, and for the same reason it was that the event on the ice attained its own traumatic portent; for precisely here it was that the world took on a wholly different physiognomy, that it showed itself from the side of *suddenness*, of the totally *different*, the *new*, the *unexpected*. None of these phenomena has any 'place', any steady home in the world of this person, nor can it fit itself in with her *design* of one; they therefore must remain on its outside, so to speak, without being integrated, mastered, and absorbed. Instead of being, in the word's full sense, *wieder-holt* [51] (Kierkegaard), that is, fetched back into the inner hold of existence, so that its meaning and content may be lifted and spelled out, what here becomes of it is the existential senselessness of a merely 'worldly' repetition of the *same*, the ever-repeated inroad of the *sudden* into the standstill of the world clock. This world-design, it is true, does not *appear* prior to the traumatic occurrence—it manifests itself, to use the Kantian expression, only on the occasion lent to it by that event; yet, as the transcendental forms *a priori* of the human mind only make experience possible as what it *is* at all, so also the form of that world-design alone is what creates the axiom, the constituent *condition*, for the event on the ice to be *possibly* experienced as traumatic.[52]

The implications are clear; never contenting himself with the *operational* order of categoriality, the psychodiagnostician, as explorer of existences, must look through and beyond the surface of his patient's words[53] in the manner more of a poet than of either a lexicographer or psychoanalyst. The phenomenal content of what in an existence is categorical must be clarified in his inner experience in accordance with the patient's own, an effort which the tendency of words severed from their phenomenality first to freeze in their objective connotations, then to lose their meaning altogether, hampers, but which is aided and supported by another trait of the psychodiagnostician's and psychotherapist's first-hand material. Wherever there is a true existential idea, an entire dimensional alternative, and with it a scenery, a world, is opened; a mere term devoid of any points of ecological reference that define its meaning in the concrete can occupy wholly different positions of phenomenal significance in the patient's and the therapist's world apperception. A preoccupation with the *ground* on the part of a subject, unchecked as to its elaborations within each of the three spheres of existing and their counter-parts in imagery previously pointed out,[54] can mislead the clinician into orienting himself to a vertical polarity,

pneuma versus *chthonic depth, rising* versus *going down* or *falling,*
as a spatial scheme of reference for his understanding of that subject;
in the case here referred to, the case of a patient whose clinical history
the present author had occasion to study, "ground" had the entirely
different connotation of horizontal expanse. It encompassed the simple
dimensional alternative of an existence-axiomatic *here* and *there;* gods
and demons stayed in their places in his world, they never ventured
forth. Favored by a monosyllabic attitude of the patient, the psychiatrist's thought fixation endured dangerously long; what allowed to
correct it in the end were three—only "spherically" different—manifestations of the patient's unitary mode of being.

The patient, first *dreamt*—and recalled his dream—of a cavalcade
of the many countries he had lived in, lands which, instead of his
passing from one into the other, now were passing in front of him,
with his own position at rest. It was at the same time that his migra-
tions, stopping in space, were internalized, "temporalized" into an
entirely new passion: historic studies and collections were taken up
by the subject, a line of interest that contributed a great deal in the
end to his conquest of the depression for which the therapist's
assistance had been sought. The traces of his motor behavior, second,
which by-passed—in his *handwriting*—every opportunity for either
pressure or etherealness, reaching up or digging down, towering or
tumbling, showed a totally "flat" type of enlivened variation; what
appeared in the skeletal directions of its letter-figures was a timeless
characteristic of the world of the wanderer, an existence image such
as actualized in old-Egyptian murals and reliefs. Finally, there was
the *Rorschach*—interpreted by a Rorschach worker who through a
year's course in scoring and rating had somehow managed to maintain
his vision and his grasp of those relevancies of experience that only
its *contents* lay bare. The theme that determined the patient's apperci-
tions in the specificity of what he actually saw in the cards was that
same dynamic horizontality: roads, riverbeds, and railroad tracks
appeared throughout the performance. Had that idea failed to express
itself clearly in his original utterances with their repetitions of the
word *ground?* It had not, as it appeared—his verbal economy notwithstanding. It only had failed to register on a mind preoccupied, for its
part, with the *ground* as the one of interment—of decay and germina-
tion, ghouls, and, aye, *all ids.*

NOTES

1. Throughout the virtually countless number of documented intuitive beholdings of this symbol in the myths and the literatures, it is the psyche *in its objectivity only* which is seen as water; the identities of other phenomenal elements (fire for states of compassion or divine inspiration, air, of free action or thought, altogether of world-facing courage, with the forces of fate seen as winds, earth, of submersion in the sensuous and the demonic) are assumed by the soul whenever, in transcending itself toward *world*, it is its own authentic self. As water, on the contrary, it either remembers (reflectivity) or *waits* (for the winds of fate to stir and ripple it) or does both of these at once. Heraclitus' astonishingly modern insight into the perils of "narcissism", of the *psyche in its objectivity*, becomes most telling in his warning that for souls to become *wet* is their "delight, or rather death" (*Ancilla to the Pre-Socratic Philosophers*, p. 30).

Cf. also the previous discussion on inner identity, pp. 206–08, and on the essence of *symbols*, p. 171. A soul symbol of such richly documented universality as water very evidently is not a "symbol" in the Freudian sense—not an allegorical substitute *for* the soul—for no concrete eidetic appearance of the soul *as a reality* that would either be more immediately intelligible or closer precisely to the *objective* phenomenality of that entity is even conceivable, hence none is there to be replaced allegorically to start with; it is indeed more than anything the *simplicity* of this pre-given fact of existence that shows up in the axiomatic status of the water symbol throughout the range of its historic documentation.

2. Cf. p. 61.

3. Since the psyche just in its *objectivity*, its "stillness", is primarily *memory*, reflection of images that like slowly wandering clouds shape up against the empty "sky" (emptiness-unreality; concerning the *no longer* as a "dimension", cf. p. 114) of an hour of windless quiet, what the psyche reflectingly beholds "prior to" and "around" the emergence of the narcissistic ego image is, quite literally again, the cavalcade of its own "evaporations"—its *past*. Supplementing at this point the phenomenal evidence of the water symbol, its genetic explanation—epistemologically quite in order here precisely on account of the *factual* "objectivity" of this particular state of the psyche—likewise becomes available, as objective evolution simply verifies this qualification of the phenomenally beheld past (the "objective" soul, or *life*) as *in fact arising from the water*.

4. Cf. p. 286. The first "glance" of Heidegger's fundamental ontology, which resolutely centers on the *ground* of existence, yet disposes of all the freedom of orientation and minuteness of perception of the "position above surface" here pointed out, equals the narcissistic focus only in its *direction* but decisively differs from it in terms of its attention-set, as it "blinds itself systematically" precisely for the ego image as a reflective surface effect of the focalized *true self*. Except as a perceptual "obstacle", a "misunderstanding" (if an ordinarily necessary one), the ego is first of all ignored here in order to penetrate the actual "three-dimensionality" of the true self, discern its own *being* and its transparence *for* being—which, in turn, are recognized as the constitutional premises even of

what *hides* them, the "reflectiveness" of the self as condition of the ego as an *image*.

5. Cf. p. 134.

6. Simone de Beauvoir, *Le Deuxième Sexe*, 1949, vol. 1, pp. 256–64.

7. Accordingly, the *actual* female equivalent of male narcissism does not center phenomenally on what here would rather preclude it, the self as *external* body image, but neither on what spontaneous female love, as active receptivity, discerns as the dimension of existential transcendence set in its case—in an "inverse" direction, the world here "being toward" the self—by the "polar" image of the male. The comparable phenomenal focus of female inhibitive self-consciousness, the basis of ego hypertrophy here, is the self not as *immanence* in Beauvoir's sense (as body image) but as a "dynamic", "aggressive" counter force to *receptive transcendence* striving to undo the stated reversal of the latter's direction. Dependent on the degree of its power over the subject's apperception of her being-in-the-world is the degree of masculinity appearing; correspondingly, in male narcissism, the degree of appearing femininity depends on the power of the ego as external body image over the self as self-identity. The male self as a mode-of-being thus strives to tear-into whatever immanence blocks it from the *open*; the female, to open itself *as*, be the opening *of*, immanence. These axioms of existence have nothing to do with functional determinants in any causal sense; they are ontic possibilities or *norms*, determining—"equi-originally"—the spirit and the eros of the person.

8. Cf. p. 161.

9. Cf. p. 113.

10. Cf. p. 114.

11. R. de Rosa, "Existenzphilosophische Richtungen in der modernen Psychopathologie", in *Offener Horizont, Festschrift für Karl Jaspers*, Munich, Piper, 1953.

12. *Transcendence* here translates the *Über die Welt sein*, being-over-or-beyond-the-world, a concept which Binswanger takes over from Jaspers; in distinction from Heidegger's world concept which implies transcendence already in its very constitution as the "open" *into which* existence "ek-sists", Jaspers, as similarly Sartre, conceptualizes "world" *per se* as contingency or immanence. While the distinction may seem definitive and therefore "academic", it assumes the most burning existential actuality in the "dialectics" of the world of the manic-depressive where it unfolds in the form of a periodical alternation of the horizon of existence between a *being-in* demanding an *exit* and a *stepping-out* demanding an "obstacle", a "receptacle", and thus once more the fullfillments of a *being-in*. For some facets of the problem, cf. L. Binswanger, *Über die manische Lebensform*, Zurich, 1944. It is on the same ground that de Rosa's reproach of eclecticism in Binswanger's doctrine, which he raises at this point, may miss its aim.

13. Op. cit., p. 190.

14. Cf. p. *143*.

15. Cf. p. 294.

16. Cf. p. 156.

17. Cf. p. *143*.

18. Cf. p. 324.

19. Cf. p. 201.

20. Literal translation of *Zentrifugalkugeln,* a schizophrenic neologism of the patient.

21. L. Binswanger, "Über die daseinsanalytische Forschungsrichtung in der Psychiatrie", in *Ausgewählte Vorträge und Aufsätze,* p. 209.

22. Cf. p. 121.

23. Cf. p. 116.

24. It is of the most critical importance to arrive at a clear distinction between the schizophrenic experience of *dead time* and the normal experience of *boredom*; catatonics, significantly, are not bored even by those of their most drawn-out petrifications of posture which "suggest" the idea of inevitable boredom to their first-hand observers. In boredom, which especially in retrospect can appear as creative period inasmuch as it necessarily *challenges* creativity, existence finds itself exposed, not to the emptiness but on the contrary to the abundance of time, to time as *coming-toward* the existent, without his having only an appropriate "receptacle" at hand to "dispose" of this wealth.

25. Quoted from Binswanger, "Der Fall Jürg Zünd".

26. Cf. p. 107.

27. Cf. p. 116.

28. *Ibid.*

29. Cf. pp. 134–36.

30. Namely in front of *groups*; he does not seem to see the single person as such, or when he does, that single person has significance only as a group representative; true inter-subjectivity in Marcel's, the dual modus of existence in Binswanger's term, has no chance here to open up anything like a true world.

31. Cf. p. 7.

32. L. Binswanger, "Der Fall Ellen West", *Schweizer Archiv für Neurologie und Psychiatrie,*   .

33. Cf. p. 223.

34. Cf. p. 240.

35. L. Binswanger, op. cit., p. 195. Italics supplied.

36. Cf. p. 206.

37. We recognize here the threat to the *soul*, pointed out earlier in the dream-theoretical section of this chapter, of one of the "four phenomenal elements"— *earth* or *mud*—to assume its identity. In the psychoanalytic literature, this entire theme of the specific dynamisms of the four elements as inherent in the phenomenal constitution of each of them is penetrated most profoundly by the studies of Bachelard (*La Psychanalyse du Feu,* Paris, 1942, *Lautréamont,* Paris, 1939, *L'eau et les Rêves,* Paris, 1942), but without the results yet being anchored in the only possible scientific ground they themselves refer to, that of an anthropology, phenomenology, ultimately an ontology, of existence as *being-in-the-world*; instead of it, and despite his own actually phenomenological achievements in the mentioned studies, Bachelard still refers the whole matter to the immanence of a *somehow given* sphere of the "forces imaginaires de l'esprit", a reified subjectivity or "psyche-object".

38. L. Binswanger, "Der Fall Lola Voss", *Schweizer Archiv für Neurologie und Psychiatrie*, 1949, vol. 63.

39. M. Heidegger, *Sein und Zeit*, p. 184.

40. Binswanger's own footnote at this point: "I deliberately avoid the expression *attempt at self-cure* since neither an intentional attempt at all nor actual progress was involved; the patient at present is more uncured, even more incurable than ever. All we can say is that the existence now has *entangled* itself in a specified world design, that no longer it stands as an authentic self in front of the intolerably, intangibly horrible, but is delivered up to the world of the enemies as an *improper, self-alienated self.*" (Italics supplied.)

41. L. Binswanger, "Ueber die daseinsanalytische Forschungsrichtung in der Psychiatrie", in *Ausgewählte Vorträge und Aufsätze*, pp. 210–12.

42. Cf. pp. 3, 247.

43. Cf. p. 180.

44. Cf. pp. 36, 180.

45. Cf. p. 172.

46. Cf. p. 228.

47. Cf. p. 206.

48. Cf. p. 82.

49. The extent to which this is verified by the most recent advances of modern holistic biology is illuminated with much cogency by Adolf Portmann in his studies; esp. *Die Tiergestalt*, Basel, 1948; "Etudes sur la Cérébralisation chez les Oiseaux", *Alauda*, Bd. 14 (1946), 15 (1947); "Um ein neues Bild vom Organismus", in *Offener Horizont. Festschrift für Karl Jaspers.*

50. L. Binswanger, *Ausgewählte Vorträge und Aufsätze*, p. 204.

51. Literally: repeated (wiederholt). Binswanger, alluding here to Kierkegaard's interpretation of the origin of the word, which its composite structure lays open, hyphenates it deliberately to make visible, in the tenor of Kierkegaard's analysis, at once its own phenomenality (the image of a *fetching-back* or *-again*) and the latter's implications for the authentic phenomenality of existential time. Concerning what constitutes the *background* of Kierkegaard's and Binswanger's hermeneutic of the concept (expressed in Danish and German by words of the same origin and composite structure), cf. our discussion of the phenomenological approach to language, pp. 9, 124–25.

52. L. Binswanger, op. cit., pp. 204–7.

53. Cf. pp. 23–24.

54. Cf. p. 156.

CHAPTER 10

The Psychotherapeutic Situation and the Theory-Practice Relation—Intuition and the Objectivist—Some Sidelights on Psychosomatics—The Neurotic in Our Time—Resistance and Transference—Blind Alleys in Psychotherapy—Psychotherapy and Education—The Case of L. G.—An Excursion into the Problems of Amnestic Aphasia—The Case of L. G. (Concluded).

EXISTENTIAL PSYCHOLOGY DEMANDS THAT ANY account of man and of his world, to be authentic, must start out from a person's situation as unalterably—and therefore unobjectifiably—his. But this *his* implies a unity of the self of the person; unless we have reason to assume that such a unity—a core of self-undoubting being-what-one-is—lies hidden beneath the hesitancies and stallings even of the most directionless neurotic, it is not to be seen how the typical starting situation of treatment ever could meet the existentialist demand. We have, however, found reason to believe that such a core, such essential unity, maintains itself behind the neurotic's self-dissension that arises from his inveterate reflection of himself *qua* his own ego; psychotherapy, then, must first of all be a challenging of this true self of the neurotic patient to come out of its concealment: to assert itself and, through its assertion, to give the lie to the deep-rooted reflective conviction out of which the person has habitually been "by-passing" himself.

The concealment, for its part, betrays itself in contradictions that inhere in the neurotic's first report in entering treatment. These contradictions follow a well-known pattern of guilt attribution: the direction of the attribution is invariably away from the true self. The gap between the true and the objectified self becomes startlingly wide here: as far as the latter is concerned, it may take the patient's blame as readily as anyone or anything in the world. But the self *qua* the who of the neurotic complaint, the self not *reported* but *reporting*, never is blamed; the more fundamental the self-doubt, the less funda- mental—however facile and seemingly extensive it may be—the readi- ness for self-criticism with its free assumption of responsibility, its responsible holding-on to freedom. This factual dichotomization be- tween the true and the objectified self is assisted by other theoretical facilities that the Cartesian world split lends it: *what*ever the neurotic experiences that is inimical to him is seen as object, and inasmuch as reflection may acknowledge it to be induced by one's own mecha- nisms-of-the-psyche, the self-as-object will be blamed for it: but *who*ever, in that inimical experience, is the one that experiences (and now does the complaining) evades the blame.

The express or implicit inclination of many neurotic patients *a priori* to restrict the therapist's task to certain "parts" of their personalities which they desire to have "changed" may be cited as an example for the resolute strategy with which self-objectification undertakes to disarm its challenger even prior to any coming to grips with him; yet for the therapist to set his counter-strategy is incomparably more difficult than any clear discernment of this situation. Reproving the patient on theoretical grounds will not suspend self-objectification as a fact of his inner state; it will, on the contrary, consolidate its hold on the patient by inducing him to become even more alienated from the sources of his being in viewing himself objectively. Evidently, the therapist must neither accede to the patient's restriction nor oppose it didactically; his rejection of it, instead, must take the form of a re- fusal to deal with any one but the indivisible self beyond those artifacts of a self-conscious account. This indivisible self, in turn, is not reached by conjuring it up *nominally*, which would make it just another *factor*, but by being in communication with it already; but how should such communication prior to any objectified theoretical knowledge of the patient's psyche be possible, unless there is reason to revise the customary account of the relation between psycho- diagnostic theory and psychotherapeutic practice also in terms of their temporal succession? Since what the objectivist must sense as para- doxical in the stated requirement undeniably calls for what he now terms—half-awed, half-condescending—intuitive faculties in the thera- pist, it becomes imperative to analyze what he means by "intuitive" more closely.

The axiom of *theory preceding practice* is valid under the presupposition that the subject matter of either answers certain criteria of its primary relation to the theoretician and practitioner. In brief, it is valid wherever theorizing means an inventory of all factual data that occur in a field of pure objects, and where practice, accordingly, *can* mean their manipulation by the inventory-taking observer. The fact, which has been shown, that this is completely untrue of any situation in differential psychology, has explosive implications for the cited axiom: it does not call for its mechanical reversal, for any blind activism, but, far more radically, questions the very notion of successivity that is its horizon-like premise. What, first of all, makes the axiom axiomatic, is, of course, not the conventional acceptance of what it literally stipulates, but the pre-given truth that any meaningful act presupposes orientation. Evidently, therefore, the axiom does not preclude a theory that *as* a theory is its own ultimate purpose, one that does not care for any practical consequences it may have, but only for the truth; no genuine theory, as only technicians may find amazing, indeed has ever cared for anything *but* the truth, and as the example set by physics shows, it is this kind of theories alone that in any ultimate sense has been of any *practical* consequence whatever. Correspondingly, the maxim does not preclude that there may be practical situations, situations illuminated only by a prior understanding of their norms, not yet their specific contents, which would *lead* to a pure theoretical penetration of these contents and thereby establish the orientative premise for the next (and accordingly already far more specific) practical step, for what *is* pure theorizing here, in distinction from what it is supposed to be according to objectivism? *Theorein* means to look, to discern with detachment; the "detachment" is from oneself, from one's own momentary preoccupations or private interests, not from whatever is engaging one's *attention;* consequently, one has nothing to do with one's own fleeting motivations as one *discerns,* no attention, unabsorbed by this engagement, is left for what one wishes, all is claimed by a beyond-oneself—but does that preclude any active quality of the engagement? The complete absence of attention for any purposive motives of one's own, the nothing-but-the-truth as the existential content of one *purely orientative* moment rather seems to be the required condition for a next, "practical" moment capable of maximally effective *action.* Not only the history of all successful science confirms this law; in a way rather close to the situation of the therapist, its validity is shown also by the rapid and constant changes between these two radically opposite sets, complete attention and complete activity, in the artisan and the marksman: visual-motor coordination, which is the form this rapidity and constancy assumes, is the objectively indisputable *coincidence* of the two phases named without any compromise between their polar inner sets, the directions of which here turn out to be one rather than being coordinated by any kind of data-calculative deliberation. The phenomenon of effective visual-motor coordination indeed gives the lie to any Cartesian style dualism that *a priori* sees an ego cognizing confronted with an object cognized: on both its orientative (purely theoretical) and motor (purely practical) sides it is not taking place outside the situation under the artisan's or marksman's focus but, on the contrary, so completely engages them *in* their situations that the "theory" that partakes in the engagement (their visual orientation) can for that very reason never be an "objective" view *of* these situations—never one of such a phantom as a pure field of facts-for-inventory unrelated to the person *as a person.*

It is—as in school psychology it never has been—from this angle alone that the entire problem of anticipatory knowledge, in the form of dreams, "intuitions" or whatever, can be tackled sensibly: in the situation of the marksman, the experienced sureness of aiming is an anticipatory *knowledge* of the hit, and, as any observing marksman will readily confirm, the surer the former, the "surer" the latter as well. Correspondingly, experiments with so-called extra-sensory perception have shown that an unquestioning belief in the objective *possibility* of ESP tends to increase the successfulness of the experimental subjects in the ESP tasks given them, a result explosive to the objectivist's entire picture of the world, the self, and their interrelationships, since no *objective* way at all leads from a difference in the intensity of *believing* to one in the supply of sensory data at the subject's disposal, which a functionalistic theory of experience must conceptualize as factual or fact-relational items somehow being computed by the mechanisms of a brain. The impossibility of correct non-calculative anticipation remains, of course, completely true for any objective cognitive task, any that leaves man on the "outside" of the thing cognized, but in order to find cognitions not subject to this criterion of an objectifying externality of data computation or assessment it now appears that we do not have to go to the lengths to which Dr. Rhine of Duke University has gone; we do—for this purpose— not have to consider *either* ESP phenomena obedient (and trivial) enough to submit to experimentation in the first place, *or* the historic fact of the success precisely in reality orientation and world activity that authentic religious experience ever has been able to impart. All we have to do is look at the simple everyday phenomenon of successful visual-motor coordination accomplishing its anticipatory tasks without analyzing its data.

Contemplating these issues a little longer, we find that *intuition*, in the objectivist's vocabulary, is a name which according to his own understanding and negative evaluations of what he is naming there he at least should give to all non-quantified, non-measurement-derived perceptions and insights of his own and thus to the entire scope of his own spontaneous world orientation, including his fundamental approach to science—yet this he never does; inconsistently, he restricts the term to such perceptions and insights as he personally, and those like him, do not have. In the process of changes in applied connotations of words, *metaphysical*, in psychology, has by now come to mean any concepts for such human experiences as do not fit into the objectivist's picture of what man *should* be like; *mystical*, whichever of such experiences threaten to be echoed by what he unreasonably has pigeonholed as the irrational in his own bosom; and *intuitive*, whatever others see and understand that he does not. Intuitions, provided they are true ones, are perceptions and insights that exceed the sensory and noetic grasp of him who cares to call them intuitions; yet, rather than realizing this, the objectivist is quick to conclude not only that what escapes him must be a disorderly sort of knowledge, if any, but also that those who have it have everything to fear from the Argus eyes of statistical verification. Since it is here that the greatest surprise from the side of phenomenological psychology—to be revealed a little later —lies in store for him, we may confine ourselves at this point to analyzing the logical absurdity inhering in the very constitution of a concept such as *extrasensory* perception as presently used in certain experimental sections of objective psychology. The implication of a beyond-the-senses here presupposes that sensory perception, the contours of which are supposed to be exceeded by the phenomena meant,

has been calibrated in its precise expanse and beyond a reasonable
doubt, a feat not accomplished by any experiments thus far reported
and indeed inconceivable in any such manner as would set sensory
perception apart from "extra-sensory". For, in the absence of any
such knowledge of the "objective" nature of phenomenal perception
as experimental psychology has only been able to refer to non-objective
principles[1] but has not been able to *supply*, what remains as the sole
criterion for such calibration if not the optimal perceptual success of
which human beings are capable? That this optimal capacity is currently classed as extrasensory not only shows the conventional arbitrariness of the conceptual tools with which objectivism operates; it
also, since a function demands to be studied where it shows itself at its
best, suggests a complete reversal of psychologists' approach to the
study of "sensory" perception. In the past, perception—as pointed out
before—has been studied from the side of sensory "elements" that
the psychologist presupposed to be its building stones, only to find
out that they were not; the conclusion, a systematic testing of the
phenomenological hypothesis that knowledge precedes perception—
that elementary to perception are not sensations but essences—seemed
too bold to be drawn, but can it be put off much longer?

What stands in its way are not only such likely misunderstandings
as an attribution, by the objectivist, of the hypothecated precession—
knowledge before perception—to the successivity of process time, as
if the temporal precedence of an *actualization* of knowledge was contended[2]; what stands in its way is at least as much the natural scientist's
unsuspecting tendency to accept as paradigmatically human what holds
true only for the phenomenally impoverished—"unintuitive"—human
being of today. If the scientist were more aware of the horizons which
historicity sets for his own thinking, his chance of discovery of what
lies beyond them would be substantial; instead, having decided (in
fact, if not in principle) that his rationality allows him an observation
post over and beyond all historic horizons, his chance is nil. Together
with his human subjects, he is caught in the fallacy of his age, which
is that of quantitative progress: in the idea, which he no longer even
comes close to examining *as* an idea, that nothing he encounters
within or without should not be subject to his manipulatory deliberations, not be improvable, whatever it be in and of itself, through the
ever-expanding facilities of organization and apparatus. The sway

which the image of organization and apparatus holds over the objectivist in the psychology of today shows all characteristics of a totemistic
obsession; it has become the one absolute to which his thinking unconditionally submits, but since he no longer discerns any alternative
contender to the throne of *principium primum,* his perceptions lack the
background even to make out what is holding him in bondage.

To give an inkling of this powerful preoccupation, we may cite two
examples from the Wechsler-Bellevue Scales by the standard of which
the intelligence of hundreds of thousands of Americans has been
"measured". Both are from the comprehension sub-tests. The first question inquires into what the subject would do if, sitting in a theatre,
he were the first person to discover a fire. Since this supposition—
the supposition of anyone being *first* in that discovery—is senseless
unless the fire is still small at the moment of discovery, the situation
which the question conjures up is one in which an intelligent human
being jumps from his seat to put out what he discovered; yet however much ruin his deed might avert in actuality *if* that question is
to make sense, answering accordingly in the test would ruin his credit.
Instead of putting the fire out—a possibility which apparently had not
occurred to the test-designer and which the test manual therefore
nowhere even considers—the concept of intelligence operated by the
rules of the test requires the subject to report the fire to an usher or
the fire police; organization, and the more so the more anonymous
it is, being considered as that omnipotence which it is not nice, perhaps, but safe for human beings to trust in, intelligent behavior, in
the *instrument for educatc s* from which we are exemplifying, is implicitly defined as the giving up and passing on of responsibilities that
befall and test a person. The second question we have in mind wishes
to know—and measures the test subject's intelligence accordingly—
why it is generally better to give to a charitable organization than
to a street beggar; it wishes to know, not whether, but why such is
the case, and it is deaf to the laughter that answers its hypocrisy, its
virtuous and heartless civic-mindedness from the direction of the
fifteenth century as loudly as, presumably, from that of the twenty-
fifth. A comprehension sub-test for test-designers that would involve the
problem of value-free science might conceivably have helped in this
matter; but who, in its absence, could help admiring the strength of
the convictions of the designer of the Bellevue scales?

In returning to the problems of psychotherapy, the question arises what we are to conclude from observations of this kind. As Robert Lindner's most recent book has pointed out in detail,[3] psychology, since, instead of holding on to the sovereignty of its office as a science, it submitted to beliefs of the age that conflict with the very gist of the being-human, could not possibly be expected to detect their ruinous effect on the human subjects it explored; yet for the psychologist and psychiatrist to regain their freedom as theoreticians and therapists requires them to be free, in the last analysis, as persons. The readiness for unconditional personal engagement which we saw discouraged by the Wechsler-Bellevue, is a "private" prerequisite of the therapist's profession without which no intelligent handling of his tasks is possible; and to illustrate the interdependence of intelligence and courage in this orbit we may briefly re-sketch Binswanger's report and theoretical account of one of his own most dramatic and adventurous experiences. He is being called to a girl whose treatment he has only started, so that his genetic knowledge of her case is still limited, and who has just incurred a condition against the frequent precedents of which all attempts of clinicians have been fruitless: unfailingly, during her menstrual period, she gets into a state where she utters at brief and regular intervals a rattling sound, while simultaneously undergoing "rhythmical" spasms that extend to the entirety of her respiratory muscles. Though the sensorium is free, there significantly is no "feeling" for her body in her in that condition—a feature always pointing, according to Binswanger, to severe disturbances of the *awareness* of being one's own body and thereby of this most fundamental identity relation in its actuality. "What must decide in such cases," Binswanger writes, "is your daring and your trust in victory, not 'theory'. I remember how suddenly there came to me the inspiration, if you prefer, the *revelation,* quietly to walk towards the patient lying in bed, to put the fingers of my right hand around her neck and so strongly to compress the trachea that, short of breath, she tried to ward off the grip, to swallow hard when the pressure let off for a moment. This abruptly broke off the whole movement of *singultus* which totally ceased after the same strategem had been repeated two or three times."[4]

Not "theory", then; no theory, that is, in the usual sense of an inventory of facts, a data-analytic account that would have preceded

Binswanger's action in his mind, but quite a theory if the latter concept is "thought back" to its original and true connotation as an act of pure—ego-detached—orientation that here unfolds not prior to, but in coordinated simultaneity with a just as ego-detached action impulse; an action impulse that it not only steers and illuminates as it gains clarity and sureness, but from the determination and success of which, as the act itself proceeds, it derives its own certitude, its growing sense of direction. But just because a theory of this kind is so "pure" *as* a theory, it is also far more valuable for practice than any standard prescriptions which "theories" as a rule are now expected to yield but which could never be abstracted from this act and its success; as Binswanger points out, its premise, as holds true for artistic inspirations as well, is on the contrary its complete spontaneity. Spontaneity, in turn, is not the impulsive arbitrariness of dilettantes (as again in art; and psychotherapy is an art at least as much as a science) but the opposite of anything unlawful: the immediate presence, pervading the therapist's *decision* both as "knowledge" and as "performance", of a preconstituted order, exactly as in the inception of a great violin concerto that first imposes itself on its composer, later on his audiences. This does not mean that every therapist can do what *he* wants but on the contrary that he completely ceases to be *willful*— becoming *willing* instead, namely open to a given structure, with its own conveyances, its specific necessities, its wants, its imperatives. Every lawful act of therapy thus demands its own "stylistically" compatible "composer": the specifically *lawful* in each case must inhere in the personality of the therapist as much as in the essence of the act which he performs. What, in the case we referred to, is that law? What is the theoretical truth that so much inheres in Binswanger's action that any explicitness of it *prior* to the performance would have conflicted with its coordinative sureness? Against the psychosomatic disturbance, the hysterical splitting apart,[5] of a *Gestaltkreis*,[6] against the inversion of body experience and body behavior which it connotes as an axiomatic possibility of the existence, a different power, able to be its match, is called up from the even more axiomatic recesses of a self still unified in its depth—the power of respiratory distress, of a peril to the very life of the person, of an immediate, nearly inescapable emergency, of the threat of *suffocation*.

The implications are manifold. For one, we have before us a form

of shock therapy, something that may contribute to our understanding
of why shock therapy, always a challenge to the patient's existence,
works at all; but at the same time we may understand why the usual
routines of shock treatment can at best result in fleeting improvements
of the symptom picture, never an actual liberation of the self of any
subject. As the quintessence of spontaneity—the categorical counter-
force to anything *automatic*—the hidden true self cannot respond to a
purely mechanistic way of "calling" it; the action-scope of that procedure, then, as far as the phenomenal side of mere "shock" is concerned, is restricted *a priori* to the mechanisms of the psyche. Among
these, it restores a sounder temporary order by the mere fact of its
power to "polarize" experience focally; but it does not extend to the
existence-constitutional premise of *their* power, to the fundamental
self-misinterpretativeness of any disordered *Dasein*, its state of untruth.

Implementing this criticism with the gist of countless concrete
observations, we notice the thoughtlessness with which the routine
brands of shock therapy, while not pampering the brain of the patient,
pamper that of the clinician as though there was any conceivable worth-
whileness in such a service: instead of first discerning what particular
functional area, rather what area of *interest*, in either the phenomenal
"body" or the phenomenal "soul" sphere of a patient's existence his
case at hand may itself articulate as *strategic*, it is decided *a priori*
that the shock called for ought to disrupt the continuity of the inner
life history of that person, temporarily reducing his existence to a state
of alternately fearful and unconscious vegetating at the mercy of an
impersonal apparatus and its anonymous technicians. Contrariwise,
and just as surely, Binswanger's "challenge" is "shockingly" applied
to the existential disturbance itself: *if* the conviction which that disturbance expresses is true, *if* the respiratory muscular system, rather
than sharing in the body-*identity* of the patient, is indeed another
"who" that, alien to "her" self-identity, may follow its own law of
"peristalsis" and "utterance"; *if* legitimately it may lend itself as its
storm center to the rebellion against the unity of the self of an entire
identity-*version*, a partial (and frustrated[7]) *who*, then it must also be
inaccessible to existential danger, unmovable by any threat imperiling
the body substrate of that abrogated unity of the self. The conviction
failing the test, more than "temporary order", more than sensory-
motor coordination of the respiratory system as an objective sphere

of body functions, is restored: what sustained the recurrences of the symptom—the dualization of the phenomenal soma—is itself compelled to cease here, for what alternative would still be open to it? The *idea* that gave rise to the conflict, and of which the somatization is itself the enactment, is led *ad absurdum;* so irrefutably, indeed, is it disproved *that it must be given up.*

The axiom that existence exists as *noesis* is thus followed into, and found true in, the remotest corners of the orbit of psychosomatics. As in the phenomenal body sphere the experienced heart-beat, the experienced respiration, altogether the integrity of the soma, its capacity of resistive endurance if only "awed" into self-unity, constitutes the powers to which to appeal an "unjust" sentence that the "ego" imposes on the self-as-body, so in the phenomenal soul-sphere of existence it again is the *heart,* in its connotation as the innermost zone of conviction and compassion, the very locus of the true self, that must be appealed to wherever, as in the typical psychoneuroses, existence is peripheralized—fleeing, as by a centrifugal force, from its own center. Only by challenging whatever still has ultimate reference to that center can the therapist, as a co-existent of the patient not *seeking* to "shock" him but communicating with him, intersubjectively, in the open space of Truth, accomplish in many instances what *post hoc,* by objective analyses, may be theorized as a recentering of the patient's existence through the instrumentality of psychological shock. Wherever self-objectification holds sway, the *here* of experience and impulsivity is displaced towards the periphery, with the consequence not only that the self factually *becomes object* (subject to the "mechanisms"), but that the existent, in centering his attention on the self-as-object, is turning his back to the world; the world, de-phenomenalized, thus is severed from him, turned into mere factualness, and accordingly the power of the factual becomes tyrannical.

Since the factual is of itself not the real but rather what reality always and already *has been,*[8] this tyranny cannot but paralyze the natural human powers of spontaneous understanding, of "spatial" sharing and "temporal" intuiting, which derive, along with the eidetic creativity that avails itself of them, from an unbroken access to being, "within" as "without"; but moreover, the factual becomes all-powerful also as that "situation" or "condition" which a technicalized world is offering the person like a pre-fabricated vacancy or reservation. The

making room for one's existence, that room, however small or spacious
it may be, which befits only oneself and nobody else, is replaced by
the looking-for-a-job, a job that anonymous collectives have prepared
for "one"; unlike the artisan, the peasant, or the better professional or
artist even of a modern technicalized society, the functionalized individual no longer can identify with the tenor of his work but rather
sells his working time as an employee and loses himself in the process.
This effect is evidenced by nothing quite so pathetically perhaps as his
helplessness in front of his own "leisure" time, his need to "organize"
or let organize this, too—his complete obliviousness, in brief, precisely
for the essence of *leisure*. It is only a commonplace determinism, a
truism of the *has been* as evidently irreversible and therefore "necessary", to say that the Industrial Revolution and its division of labor
are *forces majeures* of our age; they obviously are that, but just as
obviously are going to hurry to change their form from top to bottom
once the contemporary, no longer contenting himself with rights
society can grant him, begins to live up again to his sacred duty to *be*.

Before exemplifying by a specific case the existential-analytic attack
on the typical neurosis of our time, some further principles of existential
psychotherapy, of *communication as action*, ought to be introduced.
From our previous analysis of what in the Freudian doctrinal structure
the daseinsanalytic school appreciates and what it must reject, it will
cause no difficulty of comprehension that with everything else that
is *perceptive* in that doctrine, the two concepts of transference and of
resistance are taken over also; yet it goes without saying that what
it *is* that is taken over here are these conceptions inasmuch as they
behold authentic phenomena of the therapeutic *situation*. Concerning
their theoretical interpretation, Freud, as in many similar instances,
appears to have been peculiarly blind for the possibilities of a more
even distribution of human shortcomings between the analyst and his
patients, altogether for the incisive significance which the personal
element in their relationship attain at the *therapist*-pole; taking over
the nineteenth century identification of scientific accuracy with
calculative exactitude without first examining its applicability to the
subject matter at hand, the founder of psychoanalysis treats of resistance and transference as though of positive and negative electric
charges, yet fails even to allow for the possibility that a wholly new
kind of "charge" ever may enter the closed field of those currents and

exchanges. His stipulations that are known foreclose the question of *who* transfers *what* to *whom*, of *who* resists *whom why;* yet, since with every new patient-therapist relation it poses itself afresh, this question can in principle not be pre-decided at all. As is readily visible, transference must characterize the therapeutic situation because it characterizes every truly personal rapport—this phenomenon, which Freud registered with a somewhat disturbed surprise when finding himself first confronted with it, because in an impersonally conceived treatment situation it indeed seems out of place, is not an adjunct but an axiom of therapy that neither submits to speculative justifications nor calls for any; defining it (as well as resistance) in any terms of standard images, such as "father", and re-applying it, thus defined, to an individual clinical case in which a father-image is qualified in an endless number of possible different ways by the inner life history of the patient, without first examining specifically *what* "father" means in the world of this person in an axiomatic sense, may prejudice the entire problem his existence poses from the beginning. Likewise, we may in many instances be justified in saying that resistance is resistance to the proposition *per se* of treatment, but we cannot take it for granted before examining simpler possibilities; at any rate, it never is a "complex", "mechanism", or traumatic experience *content,* what in any fundamental sense may resist so stubbornly, but always a conviction, an *inter-est,* a *who* of existence, which allows these instrumentalities to play their role. "If such a (psychoanalytic) treatment fails", Binswanger writes in his paper on psychotherapy, "the analyst inclines to assume that the patient is not capable of overcoming his resistance to the physician, for example, as a 'father image'. Whether an analysis can have success or not is often, however, not decided by whether a patient is capable *at all* of overcoming such a transferred father image but by the opportunity *this particular* physician accords him to do so; it may, in other words, be the rejection of the therapist as a person, the impossibility of entering into a genuine communicative rapport with him, that may form the obstacle against breaking through the 'eternal' repetition of the father resistance. Caught in the 'mechanism', and thus in what inheres in it, *mechanical repetition,* the psychoanalytic doctrine, as we know, is altogether strangely blind toward the entire category of the *new,* the properly *creative* in the life of the psyche everywhere. Certainly it not always is true to the facts if one attributes the failure of treatment only to the patient; the question always to be asked first by the physician is whether the fault may not be his. What is meant here is not any technical fault but the far more fundamental failure that consists of an impotence to wake or rekindle that divine 'spark' in the patient which only true communication from existence to existence can bring forth and which alone possesses, with its light and warmth, also the fundamental power that makes any therapy work—the power to liberate a person from the blind isolation, the *idios kosmos* of Heracleitus, from a mere vegetating in his body, his dreams, his private wishes, his conceit and his presumptions, and to ready him for a life of *koinonia*, of genuine community."[9]

This passage, in disclosing the essentials of the existentialist interpretation of transference and resistance, also introduces us to the dynamics of any psychotherapy inasmuch as it *succeeds*. For it is not, as Freud understood it, with one "part" of the psyche against another that the therapist is called upon to side. It is evident that where one sides one no longer can be impartial about the issue that divides the two "parties"; instead of striving for genuine reconciliation between them, for an organic re-establishment of the lost organic unity of world, the analyst uses his influence to decide their conflict by the sheer overweight—which his siding must induce—of the one of them that he supposes to represent health. While it is not to be seen how such forcible decisions can establish lasting peace any more in the world of the soul than in the world without, it is the supposition just named which contains the whole error. Where existence is so split with and against itself that one "part" of it *can* side with another existent while the other must defend itself against him, in essence what is sick is this state of splitness; consequently, neither of the two parties, themselves only products of the split and hence of sickness, represents the whole which is lost, any more than does the other. It goes without saying that the conflict in the patient as concerns the therapist's role will always be found as only one among the countless possible self-elaborations of the world-conflict; yet would not just the therapist have to insist on aiming, with every single one of his communicative acts, at the only conceivable *thou* of a true act of communication, at that ultimate self of his patient in which the two conflicting world designs, like a several-stemmed growth in its root, are still one? The immense prominence which the entire idea of defense, of the *mechanisms of defense,* enjoys in the preoccupations of psychoanalysis, also enjoys the protections of the taboo with which, of all motivational undergrounds of human beliefs and conceptions, psychoanalysis as an ideology has covered only its own; yet we do not ourselves have to speculate psychoanalytically, nor concern ourselves with the analyst's motives, in order to discern the implications of this state of affairs. Nothing "conative", indeed, must even be touched upon, only the logical and phenomenal structure of the concept of defense be examined to comprehend that wherever there is defense it is an attack that the defense attempts to ward off—that wherever defensiveness of an existent in his communicating is charged by his communicant, it is in the form of attack that the latter has set his approach.

But why does *defensiveness* sound so "shaky", so "guilty", whereas *protection,* a term of which, strategically, psychoanalysis hardly ever avails itself where according to the testimony of the phenomena at hand it actually could, retains the halo of legitimacy? It becomes clear—and here phenomenological analysis penetrates to the human core of the psychoanalytic situation—that the image of defense which the Freudian concept of it conjures up in us is not the image of a legitimate defense of one combatant party against another. Instead, the original *existential* situation from which the Freudian concept of defense so imperceptibly is borrowed that the fact has escaped even the attention of phenomenologists, is the situation of a defendant in court, but of a defendant only holding back on his confession while already deserving of being convicted according to the judge's still silent opinion as he views the evidence that gradually is shaping up. Or is there no need for any *evidence* on the part of that judge? Is there, perhaps, no actual *judge* in the first place? Are the roles of prosecutor and judge, of which the latter is supposed to be radically independent of the former according to a pre-constituted knowledge of perennial man, instead only played by two functionaries of one party, a party that "assigns all roles"—by an omnipotent *state*? On still another ground, if another ground it is than grounds we named before, it become significant that psychoanalysis and the idea of the party state arose during one and the same historic period; the technique of siding with one *who* of an existence against the other can lead to catharsis (as psychoanalysis understands it) but it can lead also to the well-known confessions, which are more drastic only in their circumstances and consequences, of the victims of certain purges of recent historical fame.

Binswanger's reference to Kierkegaard's characterization of the free (and freeing) "openness"—the noblesse—with which Lessing at the same time probed and challenged and yet elevated and distinguished his communicants, may be remembered here and be seen in its contrast with the whole gamut of applied deterministic ideas. Also, one characteristic conception that inheres in all existential-analytic therapy can now be stated without calling for added explanation: in the same way in which productive existential communications work by uncounted more means than just the communicants' views of whatever is topically under their focus, in the same way in which the physiognomic-expressive presence of certain attitudinal qualities of the character and spirit of a person—his speaking, glancing, smiling, being silent—partakes in what makes such ordinary communications productive, so, in order to be true to its model, must existential psychotherapy. The role of the physiognomic-expressive acknowledged here must not, however, be mistaken for anything deliberation can bring forth; any deliberation that applies itself to this entire area of the unconscious *how* of behavior, which legitimately is forever of one's *being*, only results in that mechanization of conduct as which Bergson first discerned the essential nature of all mannerisms.[10] While this precludes self-consciousness in the therapist, it does not preclude that immediate self-awareness which characterizes all existences that know themselves as action-modi. as *directions*; self-knowledge in this sense is not focal but horizon-like, and like all horizon-like knowledge genuinely serves the person's orientation in his action-field. Wherever the power of the physiognomic-expressive is in fact engaging, its psychological genesis traces, not to self-manipulation at all, but on the contrary to those frontal and thereby behavior-unifying engagements in the non-self which existential analysts demand of themselves as they emphasize the importance of such engagements for their patients. If this attitude is pointed out as one, the reason, then, is not to make the practicing psychotherapist more self-conscious but to define as sharply as possible the theoretical difference between the psychoanalytic and existential-analytic methods as actual modes of operation: whereas psychoanalysis works primarily by interrogations and judgments ("interpretations") of which the premise is a conception of the thera-

peutic rapport as a subject-object relation, *Daseinsanalyse,* to sum-
marize this introduction of one of its essential elements, works by
setting attitudinal examples.

In any of the countless factual situations (such as the one in which
Binswanger cured a case of psychosomatic rattling) to which the thera-
pist-patient relation as a personal one can lead, the attitudes thus set
as examples may not be noetic but pragmatic ones; what matters is
that in any case they are not, as a deliberate permissiveness, an artificial fatherliness or motherliness cannot help but be, conventional
formulas, abstractions pre-distilled from the observed factualness of
certain personal powers, tendencies, or virtues, but are the appearance
of an inner orientation of the therapist to the open horizon of Truth
on which all world designs depend for their becoming realities. All
horizonless indoctrination—all propaganda—forfeits what it proclaims,
the possible truth of its own doctrine, by setting the example of a
visible distrust in that same truth as far as its potency is concerned to
speak for itself, without being isolated in the tube of a didactic mono-
logue; vice versa, all setting of examples for a wake readiness of world-
sharing cannot but work towards the recovery of Truth. This "working"
is silent in the sense of being catalytic; it is the effect of the sheer
presence, the visibility to the patient, of personal openness as a *possible*
attitude of humans. In the same way in which a new principle of
patterning introduced, with proper impact, into one sector of a fluid
field of forces must communicate itself to the entire field, without need
for the first carrier to displace itself or spread in the process, so it
is by the presence of one existence in the "spaces" of another that a
communicative spirit may transfigure the design of a *world.*

Such presence, in turn, becomes impossible if the striving of the
therapist, instead of being guided by what implements a catalytic role
in its application to human relations, will be guided by so abstract and
self-conscious a physicalism of role definition as just catalysis; since
the therapeutic situation demands *frontal* engagement, the therapist's
focus of attention in that situation must not continue to center on its
objective aspect *as* a situation. If the named misunderstanding assumes
the form of a theory—a theory of non-directiveness—the therapist's
resulting attitude easily becomes one of listening to words of mouth
as though they were revelations from another planet; but the adoption
of so deliberate a role, which *can* only be a pose, cannot change the

fact that this is a revelation in reverse, a revelation out of immanence.
This inevitability, in reflecting itself somehow in the non-directive
reformer of the Freudian treatment catechism as he "listens", does,
in turn, not *have* to do so in his thoughts, since in greater loyalty to
the very principle of immanence, that governs therapeutical approaches
of this kind, it rather may do so in the form of a complete void of
thought. A mirror then faces a mirror, a resonance resounds empty
time; but the cheat and self-cheat of the magic binds time only as long
as time's allotted portion is not up, and unfailingly, then, the truth
must break through in the end that nothing is deader and more isolating
than a mechanical syntony in the mask of an attentive listener or
recorder. Likewise, therapeutic influence can in the long run only be
corruptive if sought by means of imposing (rather of maintaining, as
such impositions may be necessary at the start) any authority upon
the patient; a prolonged colonization of one self by another ends at
worst in hatred and bilateral demoralization, at best in that form of
Boston tea party at which Eliotian cocktails may or may not be served.[11]
This cancels out in principle the traditional approaches of psychotherapy from "below" or "above" the position of a free existential communication in the Binswanger sense: the dead formulas of non-
directiveness, of any auditing, of the therapist as resonant or registrar,
are as little compatible with communicative frontality, person to person,
as is a suggestive method, with or without hypnosis, a treatment "from
above"—which Binswanger indeed expressly rejects. Yet, as in any such
productive interpersonal relation as *Daseinsanalyse* recognizes as its
model from "ordinary" life, the unfolding of full intersubjective
rapport may need support from such adjuncts as the exercise of a
loosening-up influence on a too heterogeneous and immobile social or
private environment of the patient; the therapist, then, must not any
less refrain from exercising such influence—through directive coun-
selling or even more immediate steps—than would a friend. Or the
whole gamut of bodily existence and experience (accessible most
directly to methods of motor or respiratory rhythmization) may be
so deficient in the pattern of the patient's daily routines that again no
proper foothold for a full flow of intercommunicativeness may be given
at the first contact; rhythmization practices then become directly required in the interests of establishing the communicative rapport. On
the same ground, wherever a condition of the latter kind should call

for it, even such measures will be legitimate as may deviate from the daseinsanalytic norm of verbal communication, such as transitory uses of suggestion; what decides such questions is no strictly speaking doctrinal criterion at all but may rather be the availability of any practical way of inducing an attitude of openness in the subject and thus readying him for the central—communicative—tasks of the treatment.

In defending this freedom of their method, existential psychotherapists observe that each and any of the *technical* formulas referred to before is contingent on the unproven premise of an intrinsic psychological relevance of certain dimension-setting abstractions—such as directiveness, non-directiveness—that pre-occupy the theorists. Existential analysis does not submit to such artificial criteria; instead, it insists on the therapist's unceasing orientation to the concrete experience-contents, the just as concrete action requirements which the endless spread and shift of inter-existential situations apt to serve as models for the therapeutic one mark out. Of all paradigmatic forms of productive rapport between two humans, the one most allowing psychotherapy to "recognize" and "understand" itself in its image is doubtless education; yet the reason that this is so is that education, in the thought-world of the thinkers of existence, means again at long last what it *does* mean. It neither means the indoctrination of youth in any ideology the tenets of which are never questioned or allowed to be questioned, nor a mechanical memorization of carelessly selected and even more carelessly carved up fact materials *a priori* deprived of their meaning; not preparation for conventionally defined societal roles, roles as everybody somehow conceives of them, nor for specialistic jobs and careers of which an anonymous technological collective is setting and changing the pattern.

Nor is education compatible with any *libertinage*: with the arbitrary stirring of allegedly individual impulses never challenged, probed, rallied into action, and affirmed in the end by that sole criterion of reality, the presence of such obstacles in the way of a personal growth as, in any educational context, only the inherent order, that discipline which no instructor can impose, of a context of tasks of inspiring sensibleness can put up. The present dearth of personalities intimately relates with our standard ways of "cultivating" personality where there is no such thing yet and where only an ego, that most secret and solid pillar of conformism, in missing out on the essence of freedom, which it believes to consist in a disregard for given structure, must insist on protecting the right of what in actuality it hampers, the right of "free self-expression" of a person as the guarantee that the person will express himself—that he will express anything—*freely*. Individuality, where it happens to occur, neither needs nor wants individualism as an ideology; and the be-who-you-are of ultimate knowledge is worlds apart from the systematized lovelessness of our present-day indifferent grow-as-you-want. Under a doctrine of education as entertainment, which only does not propose entertainment but proposes to meet "needs" as they arise, it is the *wants* of a novice what is never now permitted to grow in him; even though they *need* such growth, to stir him toward *his*, neither denials nor, for that matter, satisfactions, only the fastest, shabbiest hand-outs of a pre-digested standard culture are his lot. Most of the current pedagogic surrogates, which have long cheated the neophyte out of any world as they rush him toward what he supposes to be its final entrance, are not even aware of the meaning of the idea of *education* any more, which in its timelessness connotes the leading-out-of-and-forth of an existence: its gradual piloting into that openness of world horizons in which human beings as *human* ones, as beings first and last concerned with Truth, can share.

The attention paid by all existential thinkers, philosophers and anthropologists alike, to the central task of education of man in our time thus is anything but incidental; in correction of errors of education it is that psychotherapy can take lasting effect at all. Though not freed from its eggshells of deterministic misconceptions, this truth, like so many others, is meant already by Freud's insistence on the unique import of environmental influences in the formative years; the task of both education and psychotherapy is to lead the existent out of the *idios kosmos*, with Heracleitus' word for it, out of the pseudo-world of the dream and of all "dreaming". But this leading-out—from the standpoint of the dream itself—must be a realization of the anticipatory substance of its content; for the untruth of the dream, as we recall, never lies in its status as a world-immanent species of knowledge, in which on the contrary it allows the dreamer the greatest factual immediacy of experiencing his own Truth, but inheres in its tying-down existential status, its status as a situation. As a situation of "participating noetically" without yet being "in the open", it potentially perverts the very end of knowledge, and from it the novice must be guided into that community of existences in their genuineness, their power to transcend the confines of a mere pragmatic living. Since this is impossible without training at once the patient's reflective powers and his intuitive grasp of the *true*, the task of the therapist in the existential-analytic view can be defined as a bringing into focus of theretofore horizonlike convictions. This is not identical with their relativization or devaluation; far from it, it serves the end of enabling the patient to face them squarely, namely to see them for the first time against anything like a background. This background—the new horizon which the therapist must help open—is set by the conceivable and never before conceived alternative to the conviction, a shift in the patient's orientation that means anything but an abandonment of his world design in its original truth; it rather means an opportunity for him to expose it to the fresh wind of challenge, to examine it and recognize its fundamental idea, and thus to purify it from destructive misunderstandings that may have distorted its imperatives and clouded its authentic content.

The psychotherapy of L. G. was in this original sense an education: its centering on the spirit, which is the common end of the "intellect" and the "instincts" (as, ever opposed to the ego's objectification of them that stunts and corrupts them into personality "functions", they strive to interpenetrate and unite in one status of transcendent *being*), at once warded off two perils that had inhered in his life pattern. For not only was a self-consciousness overcome that had continued to frustrate the strivings of his "intellect" and his "instincts", but in overcoming it the treatment could avoid the pitfalls of either intellectualization or a burrowing in the "conative" for its own sake. The "conative", in this instance, was what the patient would term his *weak cravings*—it was with the announcement indeed that he was suffering from weak cravings, as well as the other, that his *intellectual functioning* was not doing so well any more, that L. G. made his entry. He was a painter in his early thirties, unmarried, who had served with the army in the Pacific in the Second World War and later had studied art under the G. I. Bill. His parents, both European immigrants in New York City—his father had come from a German family in Prague, his mother from Switzerland—were divorced since he was twelve; his only sibling, a sister five years his junior, who like himself had remained with the mother at the time of the parents' separation, had been hospitalized as a "mixed" schizophrenic for nearly three years. Otherwise, only one aunt on his father's side, now living in Munich, was known to him as having suffered from depressions; he knew little about his grandparents, none of whom, even though one of them was still alive, he had ever seen. Religion had played little if any role in his upbringing; his parents, being of different denominations, had solved the difficulties posed by this constellation by ignoring the religious dimension of education altogether, an attitude which at least on his mother's part had continued after the divorce. Both parents were well-to-do, but had become so only of late; his father, whom he had seen little since the division in the family, had been a salesman at the time but was now an executive of the same firm; his mother, whom he described as having developed into a typical business-woman (and a miser), was co-owner and manager of a thriving fashion store. According to L. G., she had developed this business out of virtually nothing after having divorced L. G.'s father. The patient rarely set his foot into the store; he hated the place. The mother had remarried since; her new husband, one of her former employees and now her associate, was loathed by the patient who identified him with the fate of the family and with what in his mother he rebelled against. According to L. G., both her personality in general, which he characterized as tyrannical and worried at once, and the second marriage in particular had much to do with the psychosis of his sister; but he would not volunteer to elaborate on this, and the point was never pressed.

Except for summers at camp, he had spent his entire childhood in New York City. The parents' separation had caused much upheaval in his life at the time, but otherwise it seemed that his younger years had rather been devoid of drama. He had always "had friends", a few of them, as he had shunned the crowd, but he would hesitate to assert that there had ever been a single real friend. How could there have been? Even the conception caused him difficulty. He had learned at an early time to live with inner (or the "inner" sides of outer) experiences which, in consideration of all "standards", seemed unthinkable to communicate; the experiences were not of a nature to submit to any *words*. —What kind of experiences, for instance?—But if he attempted to name them, what good would it do? He had been unafraid of death in the Pacific and had felt some reasonable measure of pride in being able to stand his frequent exposure to it, but now he was *dying*, if in a different sense, and ashamed of it. Had one ever heard of anyone ashamed of dying (and actually not even doing so)? and could one risk saying it without being labelled schizophrenic?—On the other hand, he always had appreciated the importance of being what he termed *accepted*; indeed, it was evident to him—so evident that it took him quite some time to know it—that one could never want or think anything of importance except after a consideration of its chances of *reception by the others*.

By this he meant that what one *wanted*, where the want was ill-received, one could not have; that one would not utter a thought that others might fail to understand the way one thought it? That, as he later recognized, would have been, as he called it, more logical; as it was, however, he would in plain fact never have thought—never before he had come here—that it was shameful to feel crushed inside, or *wanted* to be sick and taken care of by a team of—in his words—consulting women friends; by which he meant that not even to himself he would ever have "named" such thoughts or wants, which yet obtruded on him all the time. Since language was thus his problem, since there was a preoccupation, and more of one than he knew, with the *word*, all these specifications, which he would formulate in a peculiarly indirect and often round-about way, were elicited only gradually and painfully. Being "one" for himself and "another one" outwardly (outwardly he existed as the "verbal" representative of his own self in the world)—that fundamental status of duality was conveyed by numerous signs from the hour of his first visit. The perhaps most drastic symbolization of that back-to-back "posture" of the selves in him was an appearance of the same constellation in his handwriting, the little *n*'s of which curved leftward in their first, rightward in their second downstrokes. But hardly less was it demonstrated by the enormous difficulties it caused him even to penetrate to a statement of his actual complaints—of his *suffering* as, authentically, it kept impinging on him all the time; it was neither the weak cravings nor the malfunctioning of his intellect but so simple and understandable a condition as that he was *desperate*.

Since he was desperate about *nothing*, nothing had ever suggested, legitimatized the use of that word, which at last occurred to him without being offered. That it should describe his state so perfectly, was itself a revelation that stunned but also served to free him, and in more than one sense was the word *desperate* true to his condition, as he not only could state but also improve it through its use, as he soon noticed. How was this possible? What took place in L. G.'s experience with the word *desperate* was not a cure of his despair; but it was its objectification, and such objectification, in taking him "out" of his self that was desperate, temporarily also removed him from the actuality of the being-desperate as a *condition*. While this is plausible, it cannot help being unsatisfactory: why had L. G., a highly intelligent man, not made use of such a verbal facility of self-help before coming to us? Because he had not *dared* to think of himself as desperate—the shame of feeling crushed inside which he only subsequently came to describe was a very real experience of his indeed. But what was it in any mere feeling (such as feeling crushed inside) that could thus be shameful? What L. G. had discovered, only without knowing how to say it, was the unspeakable *my death*[12]—the common ground of the self-loss of the person self-unrealized and of the biological self-loss that is physical dying. For precisely what is the status of despair but a staring into a purely private, incommunicable, abyss, and what else constitutes that dizzying fathomlessness that makes it into an abyss than its incommunicableness? Incommunicableness, now, characterizes all self-knowledge of which the *communication* would bring about a loss of dignity, of status: the incommunicable *per se*, therefore, can according to its own phenomenal constitution occur in identity with the shameful, as it had to L. G. At the same time however, the incommunicable, excluding any communicant as it does, also excludes the self of self-communication, the person's *understanding*. What does this signify? The ununderstood is inevitably the dreaded, the territory without way or compass, that wherein no form or order is known that would allow one to orient oneself in it, in brief, the land *beyond words* (the unstructured); communicating the incommunicable, as through the word despair L. G. finally did communicate it to himself and the therapist, therefore means two contradictory things. *Conceiving* of such communication actualizes the essence of the dread that the incommunicable imparts, whereas doing it—communicating—actualizes the power of communication *per se* to free one from the terrors of this dread since they no longer now are "private": the word, true to its primal task and status in the existence of man, makes order, sets a horizon, restores *orientation*.

This, at first glance, would argue for the value of self-objectification; but it only argues for the imperative of reflective awareness, with which human existences must be led in order not to lead nowhere. In L. G.'s case, the horizon of reflective awareness had been blocked from any conceiving of himself as desperate, while the impulse to engage in reflective awareness was of rare strength; as a result, he objectified himself constantly if inarticulately, and seldom did this activity of his mind happen to coincide, as it had this time, with a liberating push toward the horizon; despair he had not dared admit to himself, but wherever there was (or rather was "trying"to be) a moment of joy, "this is a joyful moment", he would find himself compelled to think, and immediately the joy, thus registered in advance *as though seen in* biographic retrospect,[13] would fail to arrive. How, on a summer excursion, could one stretch out on the grass in perfect relaxation? There was nothing relaxing in knowing that one was supposed to relax, nothing happy in saying to oneself, that these indeed were happy circumstances. This peculiar petrification power of the *categorial*[14] is of the essence of self-consciousness for self-consciousness interrupts the flow of phenomenal time by fixating tombstone-like images of that which-is, rather of what always and already *has been.*[15] Such a petrified image was what interfered immediately with any open encounter between L. G. and his world, and the magnitude of its power, the sway of which was such that he could never grant himself the right to any hour of unmarred serenity, also showed in his response to his conceptual discovery of his despair.

But with all the liberating power of the word, the mere statement of his inner condition hardly could make lasting the liberation that its occurrence to him momentarily had been able to impart. True, he was too substantial a character to feel bothered by the fact that finding oneself thus "classified" with the *hommes foutus* was not nice; at least in theory he was aware of the truthlessness of most of the smoother existences around him, and desired no part whatever of their nicety. But was what he had "won" not just an illusion of this "nice" kind? Did the fault with it not lie precisely in the opposite direction? His apprehension was that what he termed a superficial intellectual self-understanding (which he mistakenly believed that spontaneous discovery of his represented) was most misleading and even harmful, as he had been told by his analyst (an orthodox Freudian treatment had, when his *Daseinsanalyse* started, already run its course for well over a year). It was then that he was made to see that the apprehension itself, not what it was about, was of a nature to justify apprehensions of its own kind: self-suspiciously, as it were, it was calling into question what had freely revealed itself to him as an open truth of his condition. The true, now, never could be either harmful or superficial; the difficulty was only to find out what it really was that was true. But did this difficulty not hide something fundamentally simple? *True*, for example, was joy, as he himself knew; but just to be true it had first to be allowed to *be*, to present itself to him in actuality, and this presence was what he replaced by the untrue representations-in-advance of it that he mistook—and always had mistaken—for an imperative of truthfulness.

This tendency his Freudian analysis had fostered; nothing would come up during the entire first part of his new treatment that he did not already present in terms of a self-objectifying theory almost at once, indeed in many instances *before* it could be ascertained from his statements what specific experiences or features of his life history he was putting in these invariably psychoanalytic formulas. He had come to the point where the know-yourself has replaced the be-yourself so completely that no being which such knowledge even could subject to itself remains in the first place; the self-perceptions, then, being inevitably unoriginal—since they are empty—have nothing at all that would substantiate their claim to knowledge, for knowledge stands or falls with the phenomenality of *discovery*, of the *new*, the breaking-through to an unblocked or widened horizon, and thus precisely in instances of a radically self-objectifying attitude of one's awareness, existence as *human* existence least of all fulfills its pre-constituted imperative to *exist as knowledge*.[16] L. G.'s amazement (when he knew he was desperate) that he could still make discoveries about himself, and that what they disclosed was so much simpler and more sensible than the borrowed abstractions in which he had fixed his self-image, repeated itself frequently during the five months of his therapy. But it took him some time to abandon the attitude of a psychological theorist of his own self, for the conviction that sustained it lay deeper than any acquired beliefs on which his mind quite readily could focus. The substitute horizon around the field of his awareness, that hidden design of his being-in-the-world that constantly led him to take stock of himself (like a fugitive traveling by night who must shun the eyes of the police is taking stock of some illegal possessions) seemed to feed on a central proposition that he had no rightful place in this world, that his very existing was lawless, and therefore could be terminated, so to speak, at any time.

It is evident that a horizon-like notion of this kind must escape the categories of psychoanalysis; only the *rightful*, a spontaneous idea even of young children, is what makes the *allowed* and the *forbidden* sensible to them (or, if it fails to *be* sensible, senseless), and thus it can never be derived from the incidental *what* of the factual permissions and prohibitions around them. The rightful cannot be reduced to any drive quanta or to parental authority as represented by the *superego*, or to "reality" as the *ego* deals with it, for all these entities are, as such, purely factual and hence temporal; the rightful, contrariwise, implies the awareness of an order that transcends temporality because it is true. The unconquerable resistance-to-analysis which Freud so regretfully had noted in his compulsive patients, and which amazed him because it was obscured for so long by a deceitful cooperativeness in which the patient followed the analyst's interpretations with all signs of interest—this resistance[17] did not develop in L. G., even though his self-interpretativeness was characteristically awake. It did not develop because no requests inappropriate to his character (such as "freely" to "associate") were made, and because nothing that he uttered was ever questioned on grounds other than the truth or untruth of its *content*—never, that is, on grounds of ulterior or "unconscious" motives. Yet, it was evident that his self-objectifying in these first sessions satisfied some more than "intellectual" interest in him; it was gaining him security—but what *is* it that an interpretative cooperativeness of this kind can possibly secure?

Since the patient's attitude in such a case is one of opening himself to the analysis, laying bare willingly whatever in him can be objectified (the "mechanisms"), it is misleading to speak of any such thing as a withdrawal of the patient behind a "facade" of cooperation. The cooperation, on the contrary, demonstrates the true self as untouchable by any (even the farthest extended) inventory-taking of psychoanalysis; the inventory-taking is thus convicted of its essential non-intrinsicness, its fatedness under all circumstances to by-pass what the patient knows to be his self. The analysis must by-pass the true self because the latter escapes temporality-bound categories; the fundamental convictions which govern existences are transcendental, world-constitutive. If, as in the case of L. G., the content of such a conviction is *that living itself is guilt,* the frequent observation that such ready cooperativeness in self-inventory, in providing the psychological theory of one's failures past as well as present, is an attempt to acquit oneself of one's responsibilities for them, so that practically everything in one's life pattern may stay put, only scratches the surface of what motivates such conduct in a neurotic. What lies beneath this surface, however, is not any animal within (which on the contrary is here exhibited most freely) but precisely the most human in the patient, his self-as-knowledge:[18] knowing he is guilty and persisting in this most horizon-like idea through no matter which situations, he must assert that conviction and keep it intact against all conceivable aquittals through self-objectification that may challenge and intrude upon its claim to truth. Now, to make such a "test" real, all conceivable aquittals through self-objectification must first of all be put into practice, and exactly this is what a cooperative readiness to psychologize about oneself achieves.

Of what was L. G. so guilty? Of *existing,* as we said—but why, by what conceivable standard, was that guilt? His art work was of some help in searching for the answer. It was of little compellingness on the whole, being one of many restatements of the abstractionist tradition of the past two decades which have turned this tradition into an unmistakable monotony: the pattern of distribution of whatever talent and originality L. G. did show in his paintings, his woodcuts, and his drawings, was strictly complementary, reciprocal, to the one that his self-conscious programmatizing marked out. Only what he himself seemed to disregard as unrepresentative of himself, as incidental to the real tenor of his work, had any power (if only the power of a promise) ; those productions which attempted to focalize his own independence and uniqueness, were lacking in these attributes almost completely. Instead of daring (anything), they followed a safe and well-known formula of daringness; and as though in these constructions he seemed intent on conjuring up expressive power, the demonstrativeness of the *individualistic* that resulted not only was short of that power—which consents but to *unconscious* service—but by the same token was strikingly unindividual *in fact.* L. G.'s therapy-as-education began— in a more proper sense—at this point, and, as always, took the form of an exploding of fixed and sterile basic notions and of their false alternatives that had blocked his existence as an artist from the horizon of Truth: he was led to see that self-expression never *had* been the focal point but the self-evident power of artists whose accomplishments displayed this power most compellingly. Fra Angelico, Giotto, Bosch, Grünewald, Munch or Cézanne, all of whom he cherished, had never been concerned with their own egos when painting, nor had they antici-pated their own positions in art history on the basis of any program-matism of aesthetic theory that legitimately remained to be abstracted *post hoc* from their works by the historians and aestheticians; these masters were able to gain freedom of expression because they had been ready to humble themselves before their tasks, submit to the discipline that inheres in these tasks as their own order, and realize themselves, as man possesses no other way of doing, through a frontal engagement in their *world* as both *resistance* and *requirement*. That *obstacle* experience was the condition of one's own *reality,* that facing it and taking-up its challenges was the condition of *realizing* oneself and thus the essence of freedom, was a discovery of L. G. that struck out against the fundament of a "progressivism" which had taught him to pursue self-expression as an *intellectual goal* in a vacuum of deliberately sought impulsivity. His persuasion—in theory—was almost immediate; what subsequently helped to consolidate this overcoming of individualism as a stereotype was the abundance of historic evidence that precisely where the rule of individualism as a mode of conscious orientation was most absolutely uncontested, a growing dearth of actual *individualities* could hamstring whole civilizations.

Once he had had a taste of spiritual sovereignty, discerned the entire depth dimension of reality which is its paradoxicalness and irony, its eluding of categories, his passion for dialectic reflection was aroused in its whole depth and breadth. He understood that the alter-natives in which his thinking had moved up to that time were traps. He realized that it was only because the actual tenor of his work (which his horizon-like "individualism" had prevented from *being* indi-vidual) had focussed on his ego as on the most deceitful token of his being "different", that his conscious focalization had centered on an abstract *collectivity* of the functional. Thematically, his attention had been drawn toward the impersonal and hence, though he knew this only now, on the *inhuman:* the more lost he had felt in the anonymous world of technicized man, the more had he felt obliged to indulge in the

essential emptiness of its forms. Giving up "individualism" meant also
giving up its dimensional opposite, collectivism; on the other hand,
giving up the vague programs that had guided him in his *constructing*,
meant anything but a return to the copying of nature. Underlying the
antagonism between nineteenth century naturalism and the abstractionist
tendencies of the first half of the twentieth in its art, is the mistaken
notion of modern man that the *factual* world (the *data* of which the 19th
aspired to imitate) is the concrete world; experiencing the essential
shallowness of the *merely factual* was therefore bound to mislead the
early twentieth century artist into seeking the essential in the opposite
of a concreteness thus defined—in the *abstract*. But an abstraction from
sensory data remains an abstraction from sensory data in art as much
as in psychological theory;[19] it does not open the road towards the
reality on which all sensory data hinge, the reality of authentic ideas,
of ideas as *images*. Once L. G. had been helped to explore this dimension of early twentieth century error, thus shedding untrue convictions
that had blocked him from a frontal rapport with his world, he was
free to participate, free to emerge from the ego-stuck privacy behind
him, free for an eidetic encounter with the *sensible* everywhere. Yet,
inescapably, this freedom was at first only a *tabula rasa* of his intellect;
what was forthcoming at first were not images but the *tabula rasa*
itself, the "blank" as a status through which his existence was passing,
in one word, the *naught*.

The sharp increase in anxiety, or rather in the nakedness of its
encounter, with which the collapse of his world left him after the first
storm of intellectual awakening had passed over without replacing what
it had torn down, manifested itself in his *Rorschach* as in all other
media of self-articulation: where before alternations between stereotyped
wholes and unusual detail responses of deliberate eccentricity had
reigned, now an anxious holding on to smaller detail *concreta* (apperceived in a child-like manner but without the child's unawareness of
the possibility of conceptual organizations beyond them) turned up.
Instead of sticking evasively to peripheries as in his first record, L. G.
now, at other points of the new one, went into intershaded areas in a
manner that seemed near to being hallucinatory. What was happening
to him? The recent expansion of his horizon had been accompanied
by much new and unusual reading, altogether by a relative withdrawal
from his own being as the being of his body; it now became evident

that nothing that could implement the new position of his self-as-knowledge from the side of his situation as one actually *lived* had yet appeared.

It is in these moments of therapy that the danger of psychosis looms large: the effect of exposing even a disenchanting conviction as an untrue ideology is further disenchantment before it can become anything better. Moreover, in the rhythm of existence any advance of theoretical knowledge demands vertification and affirmation by a corresponding advance of knowledge in its *immediacy*, a widening of the existence-basis, an increase in self-transcendentness through an actual engagement of one's *being*. L. G.'s love life had continued to be shrouded behind generalities that pretended to be specifics: there were two girl friends, Isabelle and Lenora, between whom he seemed to waver eternally. Isabelle, the first woman in his life, was an agile intellectual, a sprightly and dapper little person, who had "discovered" and "seduced" him; he however never felt quite comfortable in her presence, experiencing a restraint that carried over to his physical contacts with her (his enjoyment of which he described as "limited"). He felt that she had a legitimate claim on him, that he had to justify his existence in her eyes; that it was important for him to be accepted and affirmed by her (which, rather taking him in her stride, she never quite seemed to do). Leonora, on the other hand, a woman of intelligence though with little personality, whom he described as both sensuous and lazy, as "midsummer-like", bored him as a person, but all the more was a living opportunity for "full" physical relaxation. Though in the intervals between their contacts he tended to despise himself for this relationship, it was in the states of tormenting loneliness that regularly visited him that he just as regularly, all previous propositions to the contrary notwithstanding, fell back on the availability which in every sense she represented.

Not only had he never loved; the very proposition that he might do so seemed to frighten him, as his avoidance of the very word *love* and the irritation showed which he displayed whenever the therapist would use it. Yet in quite extrinsic contexts he would make up for this by using the word freely, saying, for instance, that he loved a certain feeling or idea, a certain color contrast, a certain line or shape where a term of lesser weight would have done these things full justice. What this ambivalence hid in his case, may best be comprehended by searching for a psychological law that could allow of comparing it with phenomena materially different yet akin to it in their structure and even in their functional dependence on the same action medium—that of *language:* the phenomena which such a search most plausibly suggests are those of the typical pattern of *amnestic aphasia.* In amnestic aphasia,[20] the person has difficulty in remembering a certain word only when focalizing its conceptual place; he may be found using it quite self-evidently the minute before or after this failure, when what requires its unconscious use is a sentence of different conceptual centeredness, an effort to focalize a different conceptual "place". What is going on in instances like this? According to Gestalt psychology, the requiredness of the forgotten word in and by the meaning context of an action configuration (the whole sentence wherein the word *is* remembered since it is used) guarantees its availability; though this theorem is as plausible as are all or most specific problem solutions of Gestalt psychology, it does not inform us about the primary reason for the unavailability of the word *when focalized.* The reason that the Gestaltist explanation is insufficient is not a dearth of conceptions; the figure-ground principle to which we have to resort to overcome it, is itself a mainstay of Gestalt theory in its numerous applications. The reason for that insufficiency is rather that Gestalt theorems, as objectifying abstractions, call for their phenomenal implementation in order to permit of re-experiencing;[21] in order to know *which* Gestalt principles apply to a certain personality condition *how,* we must first *dare* to re-experience that condition in its authenticity. The experience of terminological focalization is one of a concept *taking form;* the taking-form of something—of anything—occurs out of a formless background; this background, therefore, has to be seen first to understand any such emergence. Without that ground—which in the case of conceptual terms is the locus of all *essences*—being accessible in its ever-presence, the word, whose "place" must be "seen against" that ground whenever focalized, cannot be found, whereas it self-evidently will be at hand where a different ground for its emergence is still available; the latter possibility comes into play when another problem of word-focalization— one involving a different "conceptual place" as the goal of attention— serves in that role as a sentence-building background of essence, and amnestic aphasia thus is amnestic for whatever happens to occupy the *ultimate point* of momentary conceptual aiming.[22] The phenomenological theory of amnestic aphasia presented here is confirmed by the occurrence of such phenomena as the fleeting—split-second-long—occurrence (on the "tip of his tongue") to the speaker of an imperfect word "shadow" (*Vorgestalt*, with Conrad's term)[23] that a deficient figure-background polarization tends to bring forth. It becomes evident that only when a "where" is provided beyond the point of focal aiming, in other words, where the horizon of ideation, which we know to be the horizon of Truth,[24] is free,[25] can it also be free to serve, in this sense, as ground; to the extent to which it is blocked at all, aphasic tendencies unfailingly will appear. Many instances of normal word forgetting become understandable from this insight; what distinguishes psychogenic cases altogether from *organic* ones, is the selective specificity in them in the placement of the block. Nothing less, now, than the horizon of existential truth against the background of which the conception of love must "figure" in order to derive the light of its own evidence from that "ground", had been blocked by the experiences of L. G.'s early years: throughout his life, the notion of love had, to him, quite strictly speaking been truthless. Yet it can never be cast out from its place among one's *possible* ideas—never where a strong notion of the importance of that place inheres in one's fundamental awareness as it had in L. G.'s; and so he used any opportunity that a *substituted* essence-ground—accidentally provided by something he found to his liking—would grant him, to declare his *love*.

That this was effeminate, was his first preoccupation when his attention had at last been drawn to it; the danger of a homosexual panic altogether loomed large at this point, as the collapse of his world also threw him back upon a collectivized self-image.[26] His adolescence, which had focussed determinedly on the masculine status ahead, had by-passed that image without "looking back" at it; it had not made it what for a brief time it now became, an object of *re-flection* and hence of awareness. The maxim of *Daseinsanalyse*, that the cure of a negative reflectivity lies in a deepening of the reflection profound enough to anchor its images in the timelessness of *true future*[27] instead of in the finiteness of the phenomenal past,[28] proved itself at this point: once L. G. understood that a homosexual impulse lies on the way toward heterosexuality rather than standing in any kind of polar apposition to it, the danger point was past, the future kept open. Indeed, it stayed open to him only from here on; but in the paradoxical manner that marks all relations between being and knowing, the idea of openness of future as he held it had itself to be revised: this idea was untrue if, in contradiction to itself, it should turn out to mean an adolescent *keeping open* of all existential "possibilities" as a self-perpetuating attitude of precluding the realization of any single one of them. This very definitely proved to be the case in L. G.'s existence. The difficulty revolved around his negative attitude toward his guilt. A fresh start in the patient's time apperception and practice had to be induced to enable him to face his guilt, enable him at last to make it out as what it *is*. What *is* guilt? A knowledge of one's debt, one's not yet being truly, one's not yet having vindicated oneself, one's *obligation*.

The ground of L. G.'s guilt, we had said, was existence *per se:* its content was his failure to do the present full justice. Self-programmatizing by no means had characterized him only in his art work; wherever he went, a conception of real life as of a *not yet,* a future that a plan or project would one day materialize, had gone with him. He had not lived toward but "in" the future; in the true fashion of modern western man he had deferred his own being. He had not allowed any presence to present itself to him in full and in turn to find *him* present in the sense of a fundamental readiness for whatever it might have offered him if he had been; and uncounted opportunities for the gist of happiness—adventure—uncounted occasions for his *schedules* to be tossed to the winds at a moment's notice, had thus been allowed to pass him by. What was the essence of this self-cheating? In the uncertain, that marks the phenomenality of true future, there inheres as a positive constituent the quality of unprotectedness as a *conditio sine qua non* of freedom; freedom, indeed, is a *willing* exposure of the self to whatever is ordained to turn into its presence. The more the future as a general direction-locus of abstract time is pre-occupied already, the more, in other world, it is prejudiced factually by its subjection to an all-out scheduling inevitably[29] conceived in the image of the past, the less can remain what constitutes *true future*. Planning and scheduling, where they remain ready for revision as well as possible abandonment unforeseeable in their *why, what,* and *how,* are legitimate means of the *present* to gain durability, to "maintain itself through time"; but unfailingly will they turn into destructive forces where the present never is made man's own in the first place, the unforeseeable of future never granted its right of turning up new presences that may radically call into question the plans, schemes, and programs. L. G., for all his focussing-away from the present, had essentially lived as a man without a future, and nowhere had his living in a perpetual *subjunctive* been more obvious that in his tendency not to contact women whom he "would have liked" to contact as they came into his sight at "unfortunate" moments.—Why unfortunate, had it not been fortune that they promised?—Still, and even more so for that, they had been unfortunate moments that his scheduling, his inner set, in its striving-away from the *now*, had supposed to be mere stepping stones on time's way to some never-never future. Isabelle and Lenora were left as institutions, so to speak, that had somehow gotten into his life: handed over by a past that, as it never had been a full present, seemed impersonal to the point of being accidental.

Ever stronger in L. G., as he was making these discoveries, grew the who-am-I, the question of his ultimate identity. It was fortunate that in this accentuated form his true problem occurred to him only after the first critical moment had already passed, at a time when the "homosexuality" was virtually forgotten and when he dared to have dates outside the false alternative between Isabelle and Lenora and the equally false one between no future and a planned one. It was about that same time that he understood that impulses of wanting to hurt physically, which he had newly experienced in his relation with a love partner, and which worried him for a time because he felt no *anger* toward her, were signalling his way toward a fuller union—fuller in tenderness as well as joy—with this partner, signalling his way out of the lovelessness of his inveterate existence-form.[30] For only as the *wherefrom* of his existence—as his position of start on that new way —did this lovelessness, in "coloring" its very own conquest, lend these wishes and their fulfillment a unique yet passing significance that withdrew as rapidly as it had appeared; what helped in this was that the relation admitted of these wishes without even questioning their home-right in the universe of love. Yet it was this encounter with his own "sadism" that first put in sharper relief for him the general problem which was posed by his ever-recurrent experience of finding himself alternately within, and outside of, a certain set of his momentarily most impelling interests, his existential and noetic focussing—when what had been good and right on the inside of it could look "horrible" from without, or when, vice versa, what had been painful in finding oneself engaged in it, yet "revealed itself" as a truth of life once its spell was gone in its acuteness and one would find oneself cut loose from the powerful status of being what one was, which it had granted. The idea, first articulated by Heidegger, of existence as a *being-to-the-ground*, the idea that, to consolidate his new gains, a deeper and truer self-identity, in which those outsides and insides had their common root and point of reference, was to be made accessible more dependably and lastingly, now occurred to the patient almost without assistance. A second phase of passionate ideation was starting, and as—anxiety itself continually receding at this stage—his steps in it were surer than the first time, his *ideas* no longer remained severed from his living.

As it occurred to him that the essence of being *who one is* was daring, he began looking for whatever daring in thoughts or deeds he had failed to muster in his past. It had been clear to him since the time of his psychoanalysis, and to some extent he had known it always, that his parents, and his mother specifically, were responsible for much of his trouble, that she was responsible for what in the beginning of his treatment he at times would call his mother-dependency; but making her thus responsible, what did it mean? A confirmation of this same dependency, he now understood; was not the gist of maturation precisely that one stopped holding one's parents responsible for one? His mother, who had been overprotective and cold at once, had made it hard for him to love, but where in the world was the power which, as long as it let one live, could forbid one the main business of living? He had been told that Isabelle was in his life because she represented a mother figure; Lenora, in turn, had been accepted into it because she nurtured in him the *illusion* that he could be and do to her as his father had been and done to his mother. But his father, who had never occupied his thoughts much, did not occupy them any more when he had been with Lenora; and it was not as a mother but as a woman that Isabelle had stepped into his life. As a woman, however, she most closely corresponded to the first image of woman that had axiomatically engraved itself in him: as the first woman in his life, his mother, indeed, had been the model for that image.

Only now, as Isabelle and Lenora no longer were around, did he comprehend the roles the two had played. He remembered the contemptuous and forbidding attitude with which his mother had treated not only the first assertions of his love interests when he was fifteen, but in substance every more personal interest that he had shown at any age and that did not agree with her conceptions of enterprises in life that promised *advantage*. This philosophy of hers, which had destroyed his sister's happiness and health, he had not long allowed to determine his orientation and movements in the world. He had not allowed it to determine them as far as he knew them focally, but a wound, a void, had remained; he had refused to acknowledge the *justice* of his mother's judgment, but her right to the *position* of judge that should have belonged to his father as he now recognized, he never had questioned. This had left the entire life interest of *loving*, of a search for the true, the truth of his own being, with a mark of illegitimacy, of the forbidden, the hopeless; though this alienation of love as the gist of all *seeking* left its yearning, its power to stir, which he had always known was of the earth, undiminished, it could detract from the *freedom* of the search as from that in it which comes "from above" (from the *father*). What of "satisfactions" were left for this *interest* could therefore be substitutes only, as Lenora had in plain fact been a substitute; his mother's power had thus asserted itself and defeated him even in a domain explicitly refused her domination. Against her will, he had become an artist; yet just as an artist the paralyzing power of lovelessness had frustrated him throughout. Even now this power was frustrating him, for some peculiar reason; for at least in his art work, in his recent, not very numerous accomplishments, the new freedom and strength that he sensed had hardly appeared yet. Isabelle's position, contrariwise, had mirrored that usurpation of the role of *judge* his mother's title to which he had so completely failed to challenge; what he had sought from Isabelle had been a *revision* of the mother's judgment. Yet this replacement of the original judge by another would not have been convincing to him had Isabelle been the person to actually grant such a revision; she had, as it were, become more accepting only of late, when he had been about to stop accepting her.

In all daring, the sight of the absolute peril that this self-probing, self-realizing, of existence implies, is withstood and mastered because the existent is braced against its terrors by his just as absolute identity with his action, which in any ultimate sense he *is* rather than *does* in such a situation. If in turn this bracing could undo, in an insurance-like manner, the danger of daring as such, one could not speak of it as *daring:* any *facing* of terrors will indeed master them in the end, but in itself, and as the price of such a victory, must first of all mean that the terrors are experienced *as terrors.* Daring is in substance a readiness for authentic experience for the sake of its authenticity, and there is no exposure to the authenticity, to *anything* authentic, that is not—in some sense—dangerous *objectively.* L. G. had dared to face his past rebelliousness against his mother in the impotence that had inhered in it: as a plain *fact* of his biography, the rebelliousness had been part and parcel of the same dependency, against which its unfree stirrings had been directed. On good noetic grounds—grounds of immediate theorizing—a discovery of this kind tends to be of paralyzing impact: for if it is only afterwards, after what one thought was the freeing oneself from a chain, that one finds this same chain has secretely determined every movement of the "freeing", who can say that a similarly disillusioning aftermath is not going to follow any new act of self-liberation? It is in this manner that the sheer weight of the past, by forcing the future to be conceived in its image, may threaten to suffocate whatever in the existent *is free;* Hamlet's despair, which L. G. at this point came close to sharing, is the beholding of this possibility as an *absolute inner contradiction* of existence. What is beheld in that despair, is an impossibility to keep the future open as one's own without cutting oneself off from any actual chance of *having* one; the impossibility, unless one ballots for such violence, to escape what ever threatens to take one back, to swallow one up—*the past as mother.* Is one not coming from death as much as going toward it? If, in turn, by going toward death determinedly it is death that one escapes from—that death which is *behind* one—what remains of the terrors of a death that, unlike the one that *is* the past, only the others will (once it has become a fact) be left to know of? It is evident that mastering the terrors of death can mean widely different attitudes concretely; the suicidal ideas of L. G. which arose in him once he *saw* himself in his past, had at least on the face of them nothing panicky but the air of a free resolution.

It was the last crisis in his therapy; but for a couple of precariously tense days his past in this new disguise of it, as *resolution-stretching-towards-the-future,* once more seemed to imperil the entire accomplishment of recent months. What saved it and him was that by this time, after the fourteenth week, his situation had opened up unprecedented

opportunities for re-experience and re-vision of the axiomatic image
of the woman-mother that had endured through his life; the place of
love in his world no longer was vacant. Without its new occupancy,
which the therapy had encouraged him to dare make real, the therapist's
argument that exploded the new disguise of his *past* might have
reached L. G.'s "intellectual" comprehension, but it is uncertain whether
its resonance in him would have been nearly as powerful as it turned
out: his earlier proposition to "quite become himself", to refer self-
disidentifying contradictions of experience to the very ground of his
being, at last was implemented by a metamorphosis of his world. The
woman-mother image, before, had traditionally occurred to him in two
polar versions, as the incarnations of which—in strict accordance with
the truthlessness of such duality—those incidental girl friends, Isabelle
and Lenora, had served; the image had been split, but since—as that
of a primordial power of being—its claim to oneness, to self-unity, is
a constituent of that absolute which in all existences it *is*, it could not
split without splitting the beholder also. L. G. had in fact been two,
as only now he knew; he had been one *who* vis-a-vis of Lenora, a
different one in his relation with Isabelle, and both of these two
"selves" had been but indirect and inarticulate versions of his ever-
veiled identity. This identity, now, was what found itself in Dora's
presence—the presence of an unassuming girl whose readiness for
complete engagement was her one outstanding characteristic. She still
did not occur to him as the love of his life; but she was the first
whole woman in it, a new and unsubduable reality that at last spelled
out for him what love *was*.

Accordingly, the new unity he found occurred to him not first of all
as his own; what implied it was the encountered unity of the woman-
mother as an all-pervasive principle of being. This was not the abstraction which we have to put in its place to connote it: to his experience,
it was the quintessence of the *other*, the *thou*, and since this *eternal
feminine* was now seen beyond any of her individual manifestations
that represented her in the foreground of temporality, any imperfect
ones among them could at once be referred to her perfection. It was in
this manner that L. G. freed himself from the negative woman image
that had bound him: the freeing, as he now experienced it in actuality,
took the form of a reconciliation between his mother and him not in a
literal sense—for there was no overt conflict—but in his inner order

of experiences: once his personal mother no longer was the ultimate she had been standing for, once one was free from the shadows of her own unfreedom, one could afford feeling indulgence and even sympathy in her regard. Learning that the one and only way of liberating oneself is to be free already (in one's actions), he at once now discerned where it was that, with all his rebelliousness, he had in fact remained unfree all his life, had allowed himself to be hemmed in by conceptions and their alternatives that belonged to his mother's world, not truly to his own. He had become an artist out of protest—essentially —against her utilitarian standards; but had not precisely this kind of motivation, which as such was purely negative, granted her existence the right to keep on determining his? Did one become free of someone by doing or saying the mechanical opposite of what he did or said? Projected against the superscreen of contemporary history, the belief could readily be read off in its unmendable mistakenness; it shone through uncounted features of the world scene of which the newspapers were full. L. G., in those days, came to doubt that he was meant to be an artist, an artist at least in the sense in which he had thus far specified the scope of that vocation in his case. He did not question his talent (but what is talent!) but his calling, and he might not have questioned it even then, had not a positive alternative occurred to him already. Although the latter had not actually yet taken a too definite shape at this point even as a conception, it soon developed that a decision had become impending that did not allow of being deferred even for a week: what speeded it was the threat of success as an artist that arose at that moment. An influential critic had liked some past productions of his at an exhibition; L. G. did not like these any more and liked that expert's write-up even less. An offer to become art instructor at some fashionable college in Westchester was one of the effects of the review; it was his first chance of financial independence in any more substantial sense, but it meant nothing in terms of his new direction as he already sensed it, and he *dared* turn it down.

His mother had always been contemptuous of his profession; but the sight of success having almost absolute power over her, the new prospect, of which she had heard, had half reconciled her to it when the news of the rejection reached her. Her anger and desolation seemed boundless, but there was nothing she could do, for even cutting his means of support no longer promised any possible effectiveness; the second *factual* freedom which he took simultaneously with the first was already establishing his independence of income. The income, which was limited but comparatively not bad, would be from a part-time job he had accepted—teaching school children how to draw, but not in school; he was to instruct them as part of the publicity of a department store at its toy department. While this lay along the lines of his past training, it involved far less of his time than the instructor-ship would have, and its matter-of-fact demands were only for crafts-manship, not for a certain attitude and ideology, as implicitly had been expected of him in Westchester. The job left him the opportunity to concentrate on his new plan for work and study; the sureness with which he decided and contracted for it and which was unprecedented in his life, equalled the sureness of other steps that he took about this time. He had not seen his father in years; now, against a silent taboo of his mother's which he had just as silently continued to respect throughout his rebellions, he paid him a visit.

He had always taken his mother's judgment of her former husband at face value. This judgment had stressed the father's carefreeness and lack of ambition and drive. L. G. had failed to question not so much her standards in judging as the truth of the factual accounts on which the judgment was based; even when he had otherwise been inclined to question her standards, this had hardly ever extended itself to these matters, that were so horizon-like, so near the dawn of his own memory. The circumstances under which, as he recalled it, the separa-tion had become event, had favored this inner restriction of his, and so had his impressions of his father at their later and infrequent meet-ings; an atmosphere of embarrassment, dulling and mildly toxic, had enveloped every one of them in the manner of a gas. This element failed for the first time to interfere with their poise as they were meeting; though the father's person could not give or reveal to him anything new, any more than he had expected, the encounter was pleasant and L .G. well received. His new freedom was consolidated by the complete openness in which for the first time they talked, and so, even more drastically, was his experience of a restored identity of his world, an identity even more durable than he had previously surmised. The breach in this identity, as he had long comprehended but only now was realizing with all fibres of his being, had used the breach between

the parents as its evidence, the first proof of its conception. What was
it, then, that so almost secretly had restored unity to his existence?
L. G. would not have conceived of visiting his father, if his "aphasia"
had ceased only for the place of love, the female and maternal principle
of being; once the horizon of an existence is unblocked at all, the
androgynous polarity inherent in the *truth* which such unblocking lays
bare cannot but prove compelling. The power of the male principle, the
reality of the spirit, was what took hold of him at this stage. A third
wave of passionate thought was sweeping up, and for the first time—
in his treatment as perhaps in his life—he was concerned, as it were, with
anything except himself.

Instead of the self, a thousand observations and reflections, sights
and thoughts, seemed to compete for his attention as he went along.
His world for the first time opened itself to him in all its wonders,
and with the capacity of astonishment of an open-eyed child he took it
in. This awakening of true "object" interest, always the one reliable
sign of psychic healing and signal for the conclusion of treatment
could, in his case, avail itself of powers of spontaneous understanding
that had long lain dormant. As though the *communication* that he had
received obliged him first of all to pass it on, his perceptiveness spilled
over in an abundance of insight into personal situations with which
he could, and often did, do good. He freed a friend from an obdurate
affliction with headaches, which had resisted all treatments, by prevailing on him to cut his budget of expenses; and a girl of his acquaintance, whose luck had receded with her body weight in recent years,
was told that the world would, once more, treat her in softer forms if
it was in them that it should find her. Could it be that, with such
awakening of his physiognomic intuition, his *eidetics,* the images still
were not coming on which he knew the future of his art depended?
Since he no longer defined himself as an "artist", since he had understood that art itself had to be freed again from its isolation and segregation, its abstract and museal position as a reservation of the sensible
in a disenchanted world governing itself by functional determinations
—that once more it had to grow, self-evidently, from a broad basis of
everyone's doings and makings of everything every day—the images
came. His *playfulness* in this work orbit, that which against his
programmatism had shown his powers at an early time of the treatment,

was clearly on the rise, and conceivably, at some time in the future, when instead of either copying nature (as the nineteenth century had done) or its reflective shadows (as the early twentieth had) he would paint the *beings* of things as Bosch and Breughel had succeeded in doing, he again would "exhibit"; but the center of his attention, as in already discernible outlines it beheld his future course, was clearly occupied by a different interest at this time, a concern no longer with the visual, but the verbal.

It was stated in the beginning that the *word* was L. G.'s problem—the identity between the unfree and the inarticulate, which is a lawful characteristic of existence as human existence, could not show greater evidence than it did in his case, and neither could, now that his spirit had awakened, the unalterable dwelling of this power in the element of language. He had begun to write—stories, poems, essays, a diary—and was trying, not without some success, to place the few first productions of his pen that passed his own criticism as he went through them; moreover, an intense interest in the comparative history of languages had irresistibly arisen from his recent experiences—in his therapy as in the beginnings of his literary work—of how language unfolded its sensibleness and power from an at last unveiled homeground of Truth as the self-evidence of being. This interest was not altogether new in his life, but he never before had heeded its call; now, fostered by the contact with language as the new medium of his creativity, it became the basis for a whole plan of studies. L. G., though, did not wish to confine himself in libraries; his idea was to travel, to come to know tongues and dialects as people spoke them in their distant lands. His father, in all probability grasping little of the new project, but understanding, it appeared, that it was one change in L. G.'s life that had brought forth his conception of it and for the first time allowed them to talk freely, did not hesitate long with an offer to assist his son financially in this; he evidently had the means for it at this time, and his attitude in proposing it to the patient was leisurely enough not to cause his son compunctions.

This new (and even more literally *daring*) world-hunger of L. G., this appetite for *adventure in space* rounded out the picture of the restoration of his identity: among the more inconspicuous (if not less incisive) forms which the *block* in his world rapport before had taken, a certain shunning of topographic orientation, of full bodily encounter with the layout of spaces, had persisted over the years and shown up in a number of peculiar restrictions of his action freedom. The actual —if to him never satisfactory—form which his learning had taken had leaned toward a classification of objects severed from their contexts of growth; he had had difficulty with maps, as with anything not reducible to abstract rules, and often had failed to trace back his steps in unfamiliar geographic surroundings. He had kept close to the buildings in the street when walking, for fear of open spaces; when in an unknown city, he had ascertained his directions beforehand most of the time. He had ascertained them by a detailed noting down of every turn of the way he was to follow; he had never really conceived of his freedom of understanding what was to be his course from an insight into the city's layout *as it was*. His intelligence had, in application, been rat-like: the more than quantitative difference between the narrowly maze-orientative uses to which (disregarding like the rat the *in itself* of the world, the world in its being) he had put that intelligence, and such uses of it as could rightly be called *human*, had not then dawned on him any more than it has on an entire generation of experimental psychologists.[31] Only now it was that understanding, the inner communication with the meaningful that dwelled everywhere he went, had become his uncontested privilege and most evident and silent power; from the freed horizon of being that at long last had found him, an ever more sensible world was continually coming his way. On the day —the day before he sailed for Greece—when, after an intensive treatment of five months, his *Daseinsanalyse* was completed, his guilt had not vanished; it had turned into a debt he owed his world, which only unreserved engagement could pay off. His symptoms were gone; his anxieties full of courage; any *dread* was itself but a challenge, a single exhortation *to be*. He had learned to love and anticipated future loves with confidence; his hopes were free from scheduling; his Rorschach, full of hope. He had left his clique with its spiritless intellectualism; but for the first time a few true and well-chosen friends had been drawn into his life. In his therapy as we look back on it, the intricacies of the relation between being and knowing stand out revealingly; the problem they pose transcends the confines of a single case by far, and once more, in bidding L. G. farewell, we sense its challenge.

NOTES

1. Cf. pp. 3, 34, 39, 57.

2. Cf. p. 18.

3. Robert Lindner, *Prescription for Rebellion*, 1953.

4. L. Binswanger, *Ausgewählte Vorträge und Aufsätze*, p. 137.

5. Cf. p. 234.

6. Cf. p. 159.

7. Cf. Binswanger's biographic comments, which clarify the requiredness of the specific line of "somatization" in this case, op. cit., pp. 140–41.

8. In any authentic account, the world not only *is* never "facts" but never *was* either: the imperfect rather refers to the image of a present that is past as such, in other words, to the authentic historicity of *lived situations.* The perfect, as in the perfection of the *fait accompli,* gives the closedness of the event from without, in abstract time: its phenomenal *wherefrom* (its essence) is obscured by retrospection since retrospection, as a shortening of perspective, must turn events into mere time-points or sequences of such. Cf. also pp.   .

9. L. Binswanger, "Über Psychotherapie", in *Ausgewählte Vorträge und Aufsätze,* pp. 142–43.

10. H. Bergson, *Le Rire,* Paris.

11. T. S. Elliot, *The Cocktail Party,* 1950.

12. Cf. p. 121.

13. Cf. pp. 115–16.

14. Cf. p. 124.

15. Cf. p. 253: also, as their findings ostensibly apply here, our discussions of anticipations retrospective in their eidetic structures—apperceiving the future in the image of the past; pp. 115 and 225–27.

16. Cf. p. 91.

17. Freud's observation of this particular type of resistance, though uncomprehendedly and unadmittedly, struck at the root of his whole theorizing.

18. Cf. p. 107.

19. Cf. p. 25.

20. Modern revisions of Wernicke's early classification and theory of the aphasias have recognized this syndrome as a broad continuum stretching all the way from its share in the symptom pictures of the true organic aphasias via those of hysterical amnesia to the normal everyday experience of having a word "on one's tongue" without being able to "grab" it.

21. Cf. p. 35.

22. Cf. pp. 72, 129, and the conspicuous tendency of language to identify the absolute of a complete transcendence as the *unspeakable,* which in turn is reflected by the resistence in some religions against a citing of the name of God.

23. K. Conrad, Über den Begriff der Vorgestalt und seine Bedeutung für die Hirnpathologie, *Nervenarzt.* 18, 1947, 289.

24. Cf. the traditional proverbial dictum of folklore that a "word" someone had "wanted" to say but has forgotten "must have been a lie".

25. This freedom is lacked both by hysterics *incapable* of self-transcendence and by brain-organics *incapacitated* in it.

26. Cf. pp. 157, 160.

27. Cf. p. 114.

28. Cf. p. 115.

29. For a previously given reason, and because only past experience is available also *materially* for such constructions.

30. Cf. p. 307.

31. Cf. Erwin Straus, "Der Mensch als ein fragendes Wesen", *Jahrbuch für Psychologie und Psychotherapie*, Würzburg.

CHAPTER 11

Being and Knowing (II)—Genetic and Inner Biographic Time—Reality and Its Losses—The Problem of Wahn— *The "Subjective" Turn of Psychopathology and Psychotherapy—The Problem of the Sexual Perversions—The Investigations of Boss—The Universality of the* Love **Norm.**

THE TRADITIONAL CONCEPTION OF KNOWLEDGE HAS knowledge follow temporally the co-presence of two *things.* The conception is axiomatic to objectivistic psychology which can seemingly demonstrate it by confronting, in the usual O-S manner, a subject (the organism) with an object (the stimulus) ; knowledge of the object by the subject then ensues in the specific forms of perception, thinking, and judgment. There is no fallacy in the demonstration *as such,* but what is it that is being demonstrated in it? Fallacious is the account of it which objectivism has provided. The essence of that account, which we have cited, never is demonstrated; one tacitly presupposes— and self-evidently (as though not just an *experimental* attitude would require one to take nothing for granted) slants one's interpretation of experimental findings accordingly—what everybody already believes to be "evident" about the nature of knowledge.

This silent premise, which the present text has examined from multiple viewpoints, is itself not several but only *one;* but an inspection of it may be made at many different depths or levels of inquiry, which on their part constitute a succession of implementations of a first and still rather formal discovery, which is that of a sleight-of-hand identification by the objectivist between the event-nature of knowledge and the nature of a field event effected by the coming-into-contact of two objects: an effect of the latter kind always is given in the form of measurable sensory data, a status which emphatically is not the one of the phenomena of knowledge. The radical behaviorist, who is exempt from the present criticism because he is concerned, in the situation here spoken of, only with the measurable sensory data that *represent* knowledge objectively, by-passes the phenomenon of knowledge *topically*; the less self-consistent type of objectivist, contrariwise, *misses*—epistemologically—the phenomenon of knowledge because in disregarding its constitutional *givenness* beyond the entire sphere of object-fields he assumes—against all evidence—that any event, and therefore knowledge, too, must admit of being constructed theoretically as an event within physical time-space.

So far, however, our criticism has not only been formal; it has also been negative in the sense of centering on a mere logical (or epistemological) want of theoretical prudence. Yet one can go farther than this and make out a peculiarity of knowledge itself—overlooked in the objectivistic account of it—that hints at the very core of the problem: what is *known* in any given form of knowledge is known always as *being what it is; is* connotes essential identity maintaining itself through time; by no means a momentary constellation, then, such as sensory data in a certain stereometric distribution, is what ever is known as a *thing*. Therefore, it is not what replaces the *thing* in the experimental O-S paradigm of objectivism—a stimulus aggregate— that is encountered by the organism's knowing to start with; what becomes manifest as its orientative behavior is on the contrary an *essential* or *identity* knowledge, the presence of which in turn explodes the presuppositional notion of objectivism that knowledge would submit to any account in terms of any "present moment" of mathematical (process) time and of its ever-fleeting fact pattern as the gamut of objects. The substance of knowledge being the identity of the *known* which is nothing that *happens-in* but on the contrary is that which *resists* time, knowledge itself cannot be constructed as those temporal events by which it only actualizes itself or occurs, but only as the— itself sense-transcendent—presence-*to*-the-mind of what the occurrences both *pro-duce* and depend on—*identity*. Identity, in turn, presupposes being.

Confronted with this argument[1] which—there being nothing acci- dental about the grown structure of language—plays with perfectly good conscience on the opportunity language itself grants to distinguish between *something* and its *occurrence,* the objectivist charges that one is manipulating words; one should rather, he insists, say that knowledge comes about than that it thus comes. But how does it come about—objectively? To this day, the objectivist, having worried about the question for a century and concentrated on it with ever-intensified labors lately,[2] still owes us any answer that would even be a single step forward on the road to solution. Knowledge does not come about, it occurs, appears, irreducible forever either to sense data or memory traces, and it could not do so unless it were already, *prior* to any occurrence.

The genesis of the occurring of any phenomenon of knowledge, any *idea*, in consequence, does not necessarily coincide with that temporal order of its *remembered evolution* as a biographic succession of experiences that a retrospective analysis of the biography itself may map out. This discovery is nothing less than academic: in phenomenological psychology, it becomes important in view of the impossibility (constituted by the status of thought as a temporal succession of insights) to analyze something like an existence-inherent idea otherwise than as though the phases of insight into what makes the idea *compelling* were themselves temporal phases of its evolution in the life course. To give an example, the idea thus conveyed by the typically neurotic can be epitomized as that of a world that cannot be trusted. The distrust in it is founded upon the person's experience of the blind and accidental character of the purely mechanical laws that govern it. The rule of these laws extends itself to the person's self inasmuch as the self objectively partakes in the world-context; the self, then, as that part of the world-context with which one deals all the time and most closely, can be trusted least, since it is never distant enough from one even to allow of a sufficiently objective survey. This means that one must watch it not only all the time but with particular anxiousness and alertness; such watching, in turn, blinds one's attention for that of which it forms a part, the world in its openness, its claim upon the person to engage in *action*; the blindness initially attributed to the world law, its accidental and accident-threatening character, with which the "watch" over the self originally is justified, is thus further enhanced by the effects of the watch itself on the acute appearance of the world image as it impinges on the watch from behind.

What results is a strengthened conviction on the person's part that the world is unworthy of trust. But is this resulting to be understood *causally?* It is evident that precisely what is axiomatic in the expe-

riential cycle of neurosis according to the analysis of it just presented
must be missed completely if the phases of that cycle are taken literally,
in other words, are misunderstood as necessarily bio-genetic ones that
must be distinguishable in the individual case in order to justify this
interpretation; their successivity as a genetic one may be reflected
by the biographic facts in one case or another but does not have to be
since no factualness of such a genesis is claimed by the interpretation
in the first place. What more truly here is *genesis* is not an actual
process externally observable (or internally, for that matter, in view
of the structure of *self*-observation) but the stages of a phenomenological inspection that unfolds analytically what is given all at once
in the world idea of the typically neurotic. From the standpoint of a
critical theory of knowledge, such a situation is of course not new:
an insight into a *mathematical* problem, as into a quasi-spatial logical
order, may occur to the mind all at once yet require its temporal
unfolding in terms of a phaseology, a succession of steps, to be
accounted for analytically; the inspection, here, too, does not claim
to reflect the pattern of any factual process time of the insight analyzed.
Its "time" is a different one—it is that of *analyzing* as the temporal
unfolding of a unitary whole, by which act the space of eidetic
experience in which the phenomenal order of an idea distributes itself
in accordance with its essence, is converted, not into genetic time, but
into the *time of thinking*.

This realization is important to preclude the objection to phenomenological inspection of existences that the order of experiential
successivity in terms of which they epitomize their findings are arbitrary from the standpoint of factual verification; if the successivity
of its biographic facts would already, as it never does,[3] give the order
of an existence in its inner temporality, objectivism would not have
failed so badly in tracing genetically the contents of psychotic worlds.
How can we even hope to understand their genesis, however, if we
do not understand these worlds themselves in their presence? It no
longer is necessary to point out that any understanding of alien
worlds hinges on that of one's own—on the theorist's *power* of understanding, but such insistence on the pre-categorial as well as pre-
quantitative nature of original cognition does not conflict any more
with the postulate of systematic communicableness as the basis of all
science than would hold true for such a similar order as musicology.

The postulate, on the contrary, can be realized to the full extent of its strictness *only* by phenomenology; thus, in turning to what may tentatively be comprised in the standard term *psychogenic psychoses*— grossly organic ones not lying within the province of psychotherapy— we are in need of a principle that would reliably differentiate the world contents of the *alienated* from both the neurotic and the normal.

School psychiatry, inclusive of psychoanalysis, has never actually tackled, let alone solved, this question; as is not difficult to see, any answer to it depends on a phenomenological clarification of the spontaneous concept of insanity (*démence, Verrücktheit*). What is meant by these terms, some kind of understanding of which can be seen to precede any theorizing on psychosis? The usual formulas circle around the notion of a loss of reality. The notion does not throw any light on what is lost in these losses.[4] It throws back a turbid image of the factualness of the loss. The loss itself is obvious in certain schizophrenias; the obviousness, even though in biological principle all neuroses are reality losses, dims out toward the fringes of the orbit of dementia praecox. The manic is losing reality not in the sense of an advancing alienation from it; he loses reality as a form of world conduct because he grabs far more of it than with the greatest effort he can hold. The reality, which the depressed loses, is contrariwise not grabbed at all; he has difficulty to lose that portion of it that weighs on him like indigestion. But why does he hold on to it, if not for fear of losing it? Why, in turn, does he fear to lose it if not losing it turns out to be his loss? Is the compulsive post-encephalitic, in the torment of his over-scrutinizing reality perceptions, at the health pole of the dimension of which loss of reality constitutes the other? Has not the epileptic, with his inability to get on from one sensory experience to another, his inability to experience anything except in the concrete, a hold on reality that should make him a model of sanity, *if* reality were indeed that concrete to which his emotions must "stick"? But have not his most prototypical verbal indulgences in the "descriptive" characterization of experiences so exceedingly concrete, rather an indirectness, an abstractness, that forever leaves vague precisely the contents of these experiences in terms of any communicable—concreteness? The peculiar oscillation of the meaning of *concrete* and *abstract* that overtakes these concepts once their application is out of focus[5]—which it is whenever they are applied "backwards" to the structure of experi-

encing itself—is, of course, anything but accidental, since not even
categories can be expected to illuminate what they themselves receive
their light from.

Since reality—as has been shown before[6]—eludes with the same
categoricalness the same kind of misuse of the categorial, there is
nothing surprising about the oscillations of its meaning which appear,
as we just noticed, in the field of psychopathology as we view it under
the category of loss of reality. Reality not submitting to any standard
account of "reality", the essence precisely of those reality losses which
most drastically occur as just that, either to the loser or to his human
surroundings, is not grasped by any conception that presupposes such
a standard account, that hinges on the notion of insanity as a deviation
from standard. It is for this reason that the concept of delusion, which
is commonly defined as "distortion", "misjudgment", "misinterpretation" of reality (of a *public standard* of it by which the ideas of
the insane are cognized) fails to grasp the subjective plausibleness of
the contents of psychotic ideas. This fact not only shows up in the
unconquerable vagueness of the definitive boundary between "delusion"
and "illusion"; it also accounts for the impotence of the concept to
distinguish in principle delusions that are "clinical, of course" (that
are insane) from delusions with which one ideologist may charge
another—or at times an entire society or group—in his propaganda.[7]
Since it is evident both that the latter are substantially different from the
clinical phenomena and that yet the concept of delusion, which ignores
the pre-given multi-interpretability of world, contains nothing that
would allow of any definite differential determination of either, the
concept of delusion yields neither intrinsic enough nor consistent
enough criteria for developing any true theoretical account of the
phenomena of insanity as they occur to the insane.[8] The ontological
contingency of reality on *Truth* has been pointed out before, as has
the logical and phenomenological constitution, altogether different from
that of delusion, of the concept of *Wahn*.[9] *Wahn* refers not to reality—
which, in accordance with the predicative order of the truth-reality
relation, it may distort, but of which it can never be defined as *the
distortion*—but to Truth; it is a blocking off of Truth, an untruth
in which existence is caught in its entirety, so that its erring tends to
be incorrigible.

Wahn, then—as does its opposite, truth itself—has reference to the primacy of understanding in man; it is understandable—solely but also completely—from the vantage point of the existence of the person caught in its fangs, rather than being seen already, as *delusions* always are, as the ununderstandable that stands against understanding. Just like the concept of delusion in its wider and ever more vague usages, that of *Wahn* surpasses the boundaries of a psychosis-concept based on the extrinsic—since purely managerial—criterion of a mere factualness of lack of social rapport; yet, unlike the fuzzy end of the range of significations of delusion to which we alluded, *Wahn* in its technically speaking non-psychotic forms, of which Binswanger's *Case of Ellen West* gave an example, is just as much *Wahn*, if not necessarily quite as socially alienating a form of it, as it is in the ideations of a verbigerating hebephrenic. In distinction, moreover, from the isolated clinical data which the category of delusion, operating, like any other superimposed conceptual scheme, in a direction transverse to that of the manifestations of these symptoms, fixes into a record of peculiarities of thought that catch the eye, the understood phenomena of *Wahn* cast light on the essential unity of the psychogenic psychoses, which cuts across the characterological and symptomatological boundaries between them.

The manic-depressive conditions for example (the noetic aspects of which one seldom used to illuminate in full) no longer must continue to dangle beyond the reaches of the thought disorders proper, without —except in the speculations of psychogenetic theorizing—seeming to relate to them organically enough to make visible a common ground; that common ground is nothing that escapes understanding. It is itself a possible fundamental condition of human existence *qua* knowledge— and has spontaneous language, which always knows better than the abstractions we may borrow from it, not known this common ground since time eternal? Not by chance, it possesses one original concept of erring for the erroneous and the erratic: the being-in-error and—in a now archaic connotation—the directionless erring in the sense of an aimless wandering around. This duality of secondary meanings which historically unfolded—in English as in countless other tongues— from a single original one, reflects precisely the difference between the schizophrenic being-stuck in a specific position of existential untruth and the ultimately aimless restlessness of the manic-depressive unable to steady his eyes on any possible truth of existence and consistently realize it in his life course. The appearance of *Wahn*-like ideas, not justifying—since no incorrigibility is observed—the frequent switch from his proper diagnosis to a paranoid or schizophrenic one, occurs in the manic not in representation of a different disease process, altogether not as any equivalent of *Wahn in its purity*, but in consequence of a valuative bewilderment in which a loss of enduring existential orientation is met by desperate and necessarily arbitrary attempts at forcing the fixation of some kind or other of horizon.

Since the existentialist psychopathologists, helped by their interest in the immediate phenomenal conveyances of language, have been pioneers in pointing out and exploring the often stunning literalness with which abnormal phenomenal experiences in both the sphere of sensory world contacts (Jaspers) and of psychosomatic conditions (Binswanger) tend to state but the actual existence-status of the person, the contents of *Wahn* ideas, as shown before, did not remain long beyond their comprehension once they realized that nothing human is inaccessible to human understanding—nothing indeed, unless the clinician, whether "knowing" it or not, already is determined to admit of the ununderstandable as an acceptable quality of any phenomenon in his field; the opportunity which objectivistic theorizing granted to replace the *who* behind the phenomena by an anonymous process that at least one could claim to understand whereas the phenomena themselves escaped one, has, of course, supported that negative attitude as perhaps nothing else. Accordingly, the problem of *Wahn* occupies a central position in existential-analytic theorizing. Jaspers[10] and Wyrsch[11] accentuate the presence of creative urge in the structure of more developed (systematized) *Wahn* ideas, a feature we may understand from the opportunity the collapse of reality itself, the encounter with nothingness, establishes in some instances; like any creativity, that of the *Wahn* operates against the background of a neutral blank inviting differentiation as the blank sheet of paper invites the writer, the uninitiated hill slope after a fresh snow fall the skier, or virginity the first night. The preferability of fighting the whole world, suffering from the whole world, over being lonely, as one aspect of the inner situation from which paranoid ideas may spring has been pointed out by E. Kahn[12] ("exoprojected antinomy"). Müller-Suhr, in tracing the genesis of *Wahn* from its inception in a form of self-objectification, that in distinction from the neurotic one would seem incomparably more radical, with the self-as-object image externalized more absolutely and distantly and with a correspondingly greater depth of the self-noetic split of the psyche, pointed out that *Wahn*-like experiences in the widest connotation of the word "make their appearance when a person becomes emotionally aware of his *being-different,* of his individuality as a human being in the proper sense of the word: *Wahn* itself appears when he cannot stand that. The particularity of the *world* of the *Wahn* patient also makes the incorrigibility of the *Wahn* itself compelling."[13] A liberation from self-objectification the genuine *Wahn* may bring wherever its incorrigibility as a self-protection of existence in its new "world" (Binswanger) is complete (where its mundanization attempts have been crowned by an at least "formal" success), a possibility which Binswanger has been emphatic in demonstrating; among the three case studies of his we reported, only the *Case of Lola Voss* with its full-blown and wholly victorious *Wahn* shows its actualization. Wyrsch[14] refers to the same possibility as he expounds the genuine *Wahn* patient's greater freedom from experienced self-objectification as a challenge to the clinician which the clinician must be able to meet with a corresponding, only truer, freedom from self-objectification of his own: an exceptional capacity of immediate experience is required of him, if he is to hope to understand the patient. Kunz, finally, gives an illuminating formulation of the different geneses of *Wahn* in its wider connotation as a supervalent idea gradually draining the person's being-in-the-(true)-world and of *Wahn* in its narrower sense as a successful world substitute conceived in existential untruth: "The psychopathic-paranoic *Wahn* constitutes the explication of a private modification still occurring within the dominant *common* being-in-the-world of the everyday, whereas the primary *Wahn event* forms the break-through and actual beginning of a radically heterogeneous mode of existence that differs sharply from the ordinary."[15]

It is only a matter of course that the existential psychotherapy of *Wahn* (in its widest sense), as the central phenomenon of all true psychogenic psychoses, is limping behind its existential psychopathology: the difficulties both of establishing rapport and of mastering the phenomena of transference and counter-transference where rapport is established often are insuperable. Progress, nevertheless, is constantly being made in those lighter cases of psychosis where the truth-untruth polarity of the world of an existence is still, however precariously, in balance, and at any rate there still continues to grow, unabatedly, the emphaticness with which the imperative to "get oneself into" (or as near as possible to) the world-contents constituted by a clinical case, to "live with the patient", follow his actions from *within* (actively re-experience their motor impulses) to understand their meaning, is being pointed out by Binswanger, Kuhn, Minkowski, Minkowska, Szilasi, and by many of the followers of the Jaspers school as well, and which has had its parallel in the United States most of all in the tenor of the work of Frieda Fromm-Reichmann.[16] With or without the philosophical articulation and theoretical penetration which qualify this tendency of the most recent psychiatry and psychotherapy in its strict daseinsanalytic form, it thus first of all appears as a spontaneous assertion from many sides at once of the timelessly and irreducibly human and of the universality of this status as in principle unlimited even by the most far-gone and perplexing alienations. What, then, is this tendency? Nothing more or less than a common and simultaneous anticipation, not only of the psychiatry and psychotherapy of tomorrow but of what alone can lend any theory or practice dealing with existences anything like a solid orientative direction; the very wanting-to-be-born of a—yet future-shrouded—science of man.

Underlying both the theoretical and therapeutic work of *Daseinsanalyse* proper, the conception of existence as the unfolding of a world-idea, a fundamental and design-like conviction that by no means is unconscious but horizonlike and therefore, as such, no matter of ordinary focal awareness on the part of the existent who "is" rather than "has" it, finally allows of a clarification of symptom patterns more or less incomprehensible before its time, such as the so-called ego-alien impulse experiences of compulsives, obsessives, and phobics,[17] the addictive personality,[18] and the sexual aberrations or perversions, on the latter of which the work of Médard Boss, probably the most independent one[19] among the post-Binswanger representatives of the existential school of psychotherapy, has centered.[20] The position of Boss is important on two accounts, as the by far most advanced and exposed one at this time on the road of theoretical conquest into the thicket-like frontier of problems traditionally surrounding the "perversions" of the love impulse in man and deriving, just as traditionally, this jungle-character at least as much from the humanity or inhumanity of the theorists themselves as from that of the phenomena and whole

existences under their focus; and as a testimony to the enduring fruitfulness of the achievements of Heidegger's fundamental ontology,
scarcely even tapped as yet in the vastness of its scientific implications, for any future ways of psychic healing, as the bold attempt is
made by Boss to derive the principles of his theorizing as well as his
psychotherapy from the existential-analytics of *Time and Being* directly.
This means that instead of Binswanger's "anthropological" additions
of more and more *empirically* possible conditions or situations of
existence believed to be sharing in the fundamental status of dread
and care, only these two, which Heidegger himself had pointed out
as the most immediate alleys of a radical self-encounter, are admitted
as legitimate starting data for existential-analytic inquiries of no matter
what specific aim or province (in the sense of field of study or academic
endeavor); for as dread and care it is that existence finds itself when
radically alone, and only when existence is alone with itself, with the
person's attention unclaimed by the misleading notions of the world
and of its being-with, can existence fully know itself as ground, in the
intolerableness of its limitations, its isolating factualness, its immanence,
which must fully be faced noetically precisely in order to derive,
from such encounter, any true conception of the existential imperative
of self-transcendence or love that alone can break that isolation; love,
then, is not another modus-of-being as according to Binswanger, one
which in the manner of Binswanger's standard work[21] can meaningfully
be arrayed with its opposite, loneness, on one plane of encyclopedic
classification of existence-forms objectively *occurring.* The factualness
of their occurrences as equi-ordinated objects of observation notwithstanding, the relationship between these two, love and loneness, is no
more one between equi-ordinated "species", each final as a quasi-
phylogenetic form, than can be said of the relationship of a cater-
pillar to itself as butterfly; Heidegger's onesidedness, which Binswanger often and explicitly deplored, in "insisting" on dread and
care as the only *Grundbefindlichkeiten* of existence, therefore does not
ignore love but on the contrary only allows for the first time of its
full penetration by the light of understanding.

   A host of new problems unfolds from this epistemological position
of Boss, which we have tried to convey more *in extenso* than his own
rather lapidaric and, relative to their briefness, uncompelling statements
in *Meaning and Content of the Sexual Perversions* and in "Beitrag zur

daseinsanalytischen Fundierung des psychiatrischen Denkens"[22] can be said to do, both as regards his deviations from Binswanger and the criterion of logicity to which his proposition directly to derive from fundamental ontology a method of applied existential analysis must ultimately submit like any other proposition in science; what, especially, his recourse to the unmitigated immediacy of insights and discoveries of Heidegger means in the concrete, can far better be inferred from his cogent and often truly brilliant case studies than from his philosophical and methodological explications. Most of the—more implied than explicit—criticism of Binswanger in these explications is not of a kind that *phenomenological anthropology* could not answer, and the difference between these two directions of *Daseinsanalyse* seems altogether far less one in substance than in theoretical emphasis; however, it is obvious that precisely a difference in theoretical emphasis can easily become a very substantial one in applied diagnostic theorizing and even more in therapeutic practice. The danger of a renewed objectification as inherent in the "anthropological" turn which Heidegger's existential analytic undergoes in the encyclopedic thinking of Binswanger consists of an almost unnoticeable prejudicing of the existent's authentic situation as one already here supposed—not in theoretical principle but all the more easily in actuality—to answer a certain *norm* of the being-in-the-world, a norm which the classification system of the modi-of-existence provides the more readily as it approaches the inevitably misleading perfection that inheres in all category-bound systems as such; it is not enough—this appears to be the gist of the dissidence of Médard Boss, who in his critique of the anthropological theory of perversions[23] nowhere opposes Binswanger himself but all the more deteminedly the hypotheses of von Gebsattel and E. Strauss—it is not enough that a teacher of exceptional circumspection is able to stay aware of the contant necessity to re-experience categories from the side of their phenomenality, to re-think norms of existence from the side of the being itself that, in the unrepeatable and unabstractible time-space of its *here,* its historicity, implements these norms in the concrete, but care must be taken in the formulations of the system to avert any actual restoration of the Cartesian subject-object split, any prejudicing-from-"without" of psychiatric cases *as existences* by the less circumspect disciples and practitioners to follow the teacher. This formulation of what in Boss' criticism appears paradigmatic does, of course, not mean to reflect the relative historic positions of Binswanger and of the other mentioned "anthropologists" who can hardly be called his disciples; from certain of their teachings, to which frequent references are contained in his own writings, he never incisively distanced himself, and only this seems to have challenged Boss to attack "anthropology" as a pitfall.

Boss' critique of the anthropological theory of perversions is joined by one of the psychoanalytic theory covering the same subject, and both prepare the way for his central contention that all sexuality, regardless of the specificity of its aims, strives to return to a primordial totality of being, to being in its absoluteness, and hence must transcend itself into that affirmation of the absolute value of the other which is the world-transparency of love.[24] Breaking out of what ever hems love in, the clod-like mode-of-being of an "isolated, autocratic, petty, and fear-laden individual"[25] and bridging the deadening gulf that separates its own factualness (temporality, immanence) from that of the fact-world by the "swinging" love-unity of the being-in-the-world of the lover, it is by the conquest of space-time, by the conquest of both the world and the self, that the totality of being meant by the sexual interest *extends* itself to the experienced universe as it *centers* on aims of a peculiarly unique import. That this "unique import", which under the "universal love norm" is always one and the same, is found attached to multiple specific aims, must not detract from its essential oneness any more than the mere fact of the attachment of this unique import mostly to normal aims makes the latter any less peculiar precisely from a standpoint of radical detachment than can be said of the perverse ones. Indeed, the first and perhaps most important teaching about these abnormalities which Boss finds confirmed by every single one of his case studies, is that they are confirmations precisely of the truth— which in principle already Scheler had stated[26]—that love, as the essence of the sexual interest in man, is *one* throughout its manifold elaborations of aims and even in the remotest and most "shocking" urges they engender; it is more than anything this imaginative freedom of goal formation as a possible freedom from "functional" purposivity that, as the representative of a spiritual (world-interpretative) principle interpenetrating with a biological one, distinguishes human love from the sexuality of animals which nowhere escapes the exclusive rule of the biological principle of species propagation.

What allows Boss to claim the identity of the "love norm" throughout the expanse of the ordinary and the deviant forms of sexual
striving, is quite evidently not the criterion of pleasure which is central
to the psychosexual theory of Freudian immanentism and naturalism,
for no bridge leads from pleasure to the *motif* of self-sacrifice in love,
and altogether to the loftiness, the spirituality that incisively characterizes the phenomenal situation of loving; even whether the phenomenality of the orgasm is truly understood if—with a want of observingness that may seem no less typical of retrospective falsifications of
its experiential structure than certain retrospective theorizations of
dreaming are of the dream situation—it is understood as an extreme
quantity of pleasure is a problem we may only pose in passing. Most
of all, the hard time psychoanalytic theorizing has had in incorporating
the phenomena of maschoism in its account, the ever greater remoteness from phenomenal observation of masochistic *experience* which
has appeared with every revision and modification of the Freudian
hypothesis on this perplexing propensity of the soul, raises the question
whether psychoanalysis did not perhaps miss the essence of the love
instinct altogether and already at the point of Freud's first perceptions of its psychological nature; as has been pointed out before,[27]
this possibility would by no means preclude the attainment of a roughly
correct theoretical picture of the *genesis* and *mechanisms* of the psyche.
Boss himself states[28] that the Freudian calculations of the psychosexual
genetic process in terms of quantities of drive energy and of the varying
constellations and combinations which they enter do account—much
better than any previous theory—for the finite[29] biographic data from
which they are abstracted; they only fail, like any other such abstractions, and for the same intrinsic reasons, to allow of any valid theoretical understanding of the phenomenal *presence* of a psychosexual
situation from the vantage point of the existent. How—the formal *why*
which applies here having been answered before—does psychoanalytic
theory fail in such understanding? Should it be that pleasure, which
everybody is so sure is the most concrete (therefore most quantifiable)
thing in the world, is, actually, like all mere quantities, a rather *abstract*
category that no longer allows those who think in its terms any true
phenomenal re-encounter with the manifold qualities and structures of
immediate experience from which one derives its typically immanentistic concept? Should it be that radical phenomenology, which

has been seen as reversing so many "evident" predicative relations,[30] has to revise the one between pleasure and love striving, too, and that, rather than sex being understandable in terms of the "pleasure principle", it is pleasure that turns out to be a *concept of limit* denoting an imperfect (insufficiently transcendent, or, in Boss' term, world-transparent) state of loving? Phenomenological evidence would argue for this, as we experience no inner coercion in applying the concept of pleasure to gastronomic satisfactions, satisfactions outside the orbit of inter-subjectivity (of radical and polar self-transcendence) but immediately are aware of a slight if perhaps deliberate preposterousness in hearing someone say that he *loves* a certain dish. Contrariwise, the delights of sexual love in any of its forms, which phenomenally are characterized by a *liberating* engagement of existence in its time-pervasive wholeness, seem coerced categorially by applying to them the concept of something so shallow as pleasure, but this situation must and will be obscured by the actual shallowness of such satisfactions of the sexual interest in which the existent, already following a con-viction of the Freudian type—a conviction that sex is just a pleasure—is realizing this conviction by prejudicing *in actu* the possible scope of love experience through a narrowly *ego-bound* manner of experiencing. Finally, why would Freudianism have found itself in need of the obscurantist speculations surrounding *Eros* and *Thanatos*, the pleasure principle as bounded by a hypothetical death drive, if the truth of that speculation were not inherent *in* rather than focally beheld *by* it, namely if that death which is the fate of the pleasure principle according to the hypothesis itself would not inhere, as an unmitigable phenomenal deadness, in its own constitution as a concept?

The fundamental inaccessibility, to the psychoanalytic grasp, of any of the inspirational states, the enthusiasms, of existence, as in principle irreducible in their transcendency, defying an immanentistic account, has been clarified before. Many observations testify to the truth of that criticism but nowhere, perhaps, does it apply more crucially than to the phenomena of sexual love: as Boss points out, the experiential quality common to all of its strivings as they approach and even more as they attain their aims is a "widening" of existence, in brief, *joy*, not pleasure—which, of course, centrally partakes in this joy but which is here transfigured, so that nothing remains of its self-boundness, of the ordinary consummative quality of all mere pleasure. Joy, now, is the one ubiquitously human experience which psychoanalysis not only most completely but also most drastically fails to account for, since, with all its intrinsic, indeed, constitutional, spirituality, joy is far too elemental and immediate a state of the self to even allow of any theoretical account in terms of such roundabout and derivative abstractions as "sublimation". If pleasure is not the comprising norm of love, if that norm is joy, why prejudice from the start what a widening of existence such as joy connotes may do to pain as well as pleasure? The Freudian error here can most simply be stated in this form, that the concepts of pleasure and pain, in being applied psychoanalytically to the phenomena of sexual love, are brought to these phenomena from without, with an understanding of them that itself is one of existence in its ordinary isolation—of existence precisely in that modus of it which emphatically is not the one of love, indeed is its opposite. In its isolation, its immanence, existence submits to the narrow interests of the organism as the organism's subjective correlate, the equally narrow ego, understands them, and it is these interests that articulate themselves according to the polarity of pleasure and pain as an orientative dimension of self-protectiveness.[31] From this it does not follow that existence in its *dual modus* must have the same interests and indeed the same notions *a priori*; it does not follow that love may not have the power of *transfiguring* what pleasure and pain, and the latter just as much as the former, mean in the most real situation of being-beyond-oneself that is known. The power of love to transfigure pain, too, to fill pain, as a potentially spiritualizing, life-intensifying challenge to life,[32] with existential meaning, is documented by human testimony far beyond the narrow and arbitrarily assembled panopticum of the *psychopathia sexualis*; what blocks contemporary accesses of understanding to this primal relation between love and pain is the hostility to human experience in its authenticity of everybody's everyday notions rather than experience itself, the collective ideology of an unhappy age pursuing happiness through anaesthesias rather than thought. Precisely the fascinated interest in the atrocious, in every form of inhumanity testifying to the dictum *homo homini lupus*, which characterizes so much of the sensationalism and brutality of the mass civilizations of our age that it appears but as the unofficial underside of their official humanitarianisms, stands in an inevitable, indeed most lawful relation—a relation of mechanical and depressing compensa-

toriness—to the sentimental philosophy of maximal comfort, a
philosophy to which suffering just in its meaningfulness has become the
quintessence of evil. The sado-masochistic complex of impulses as one
of Boss' case studies enucleates its motivational core, does not side
with but on the contrary rebels against that state of affairs: in its
own quite literal manner, it only puts into action a truth, which is
one of existence *per se* inasmuch as existence is human, the truth that
any suffering, whether in the forms of pain or of dread, inclines to
be meaningful, and that, wherever meaningful, it is qualified by two
conditions, of which voluntariness or affirmation by the existent (the
amor fati of Nietzsche) is one, the capacity of existential challenge
on the part of the suffering—the capacity of intensifying the sense of
being alive and widening its "spaces"—the other. Contrariwise, meaningless (merely passive) suffering, which today appears as the un-
avoidable historic consequence of the trivial mass ideology of painless
pleasure hunting, is characterized by nothing so much as this, that
it always and only happens-to the sufferer (who here hides his face
from it), appearing so-to-speak as the revenge of a life-power expressly
rejected as such. Accordingly, it is in the negative, not in an enlivening
but a deadening form that experience encounters it; be it in the form
of the slowly dulling pain of the noise and atmosphere of modern
traffic, politics, and office routines, or of the equally unfaced and, in
consequence, slowly paralyzing anxiety which the insecurity of existence
in these dismal and unprecedented conditions of factual comfort brings
forth, or of the constant panicky flights from it, which so totally contrast with an attitude of *standing the gaze of the naught*—of a productive dread—that even their panicky character, which the available
distractions of social living ever stand ready to conceal, remains unad-
mitted. Yet, in any ultimate sense even this senseless suffering may be
far from meaningless: historically, it could be through its very instrumentality that the spiritual destination of human existence, which will
eventually reclaim its rights, elects to remind the existents that these
rights are inalienable.

While Boss' criticism of the anthropological theory of perversions
reveals less of a cleavage between his position and that of von Gebsattel
and E. Strauss than between his conception and that of psychoanalysis,
it is no less incisive in objecting to the constitutionalism (structuralism)
that inheres in their version of phenomenological anthropology, comple-

menting at all points the error of environmentalism in Freudian doctrine. As the child's and the growing person's openness to all kind's of "seductions", of which psychoanalytic doctrine makes so much, cannot be understood theoretically without the assumption of a prior conceivability to the individual (which psychoanalysis fails to account for) of the attractiveness of the seduction in its specificity as *unique import* and of a corresponding selectivity of the psyche (which objectivism must overlook because this selectivity becomes manifest only in the factualness of the selection as a biographic datum), so the structuralistic conception of perversions as *a priori* "deformations" of the love instinct confounds the essence of the love striving of the sexually deviant with the particularity of those existential conditions of their being-in-the-world in and against which the norm of love (which in itself is always *one*) rather must assert and vindicate itself in their cases. Correspondingly, just as the one most decisive characteristic of sexual love, its self-transcendentness, is missed altogether by psychoanalysis, so the aforementioned version of anthropological theory, by misidentifying self-transcendentness with the interest of the race and its functional economy from an objective biological viewpoint of species propagation, misses it precisely where its powers to "convert" and "transfigure" the immanent—the conventionally meaningless and even repulsive—are in fact most stunning. In his case studies which comprise what approximates the whole range of the sexual deviations, Boss, therefore, develops the essential elements of what could be organized into a kind of sliding scale of different norms of the being-in-the-world in their relation to a universal love impulse that most consistently strives ever to widen the very form of man's existence: not the love impulse, although in the perversions as much as in normal forms of sexuality it may be weak, is itself ever deformed, but the whole existence of the person may in at least one of its dimensions be narrowed in such a way that its opening focus falls restrictedly on a specific sexual aim. In otherwise "ordinary" existences this aim may be the ordinary genital one; for less ordinary ones a general tendency of the love impulse to center on what ordinarily is a preparatory matter or phase can be observed, and this preparatoriness may apply in either a psychogenetic sense (Freud's oral and anal fixations) or in the more literal one of the preparatory acts of love play and of the many whims and notions that—normally in a fleeting way and therefore only un-

noticedly—accompany love play precisely where its powers of engagement are greatest. Since a successful breaking-through that available
opening of the existence-form means in any case its widening—means
a lessening of the existence-conditioned restrictiveness of the focal
interest of the love striving—any actualization of the striving in its
given aim[33] brings its aiming nearer to the opportunity of a spontaneous re-direction, of *normalcy*: the deviating impulses therefore
become stronger—not only in their impulsive power *per se,* which is
not a function of their deviating but the force of the love striving, but
also in their very deviating— to the extent to which they are kept in
a state of frustration that inevitably must disidentify the existent from
and against his own self. By the same token, they become weaker—
precisely in their deviating—as they are being actualized; but actualization here does not just mean that, in a perhaps rather half-hearted
and mechanical, all too often hounded manner, they are "practiced",
but that first of all they are understood and affirmed, as genuine representatives of the universal norm of love as it applies to the given situation of his existence, by the existent in his striving for self-realization,
for world.[34]

As a workable theory of psychodiagnosis and psychotherapy in this
realm, Boss' propositions, like their epistemological underpinnings
already spoken of, have something tentative, at least insufficiently
rounded out, which does not detract from their power of vision and
illuminating qualities in dissipating typical commonplace notions of
objectivism, but does arouse the desire for a greater elaboration and
unification of principles that would allow of an integration of his
insights with a comprehensive existential-analytic theory of personality;
as far as the sexual deviations as such are concerned, we may, however, already attempt to formulate Boss' findings in terms of what these
findings accentuate, their meaning for the patient's existence, and of
those most fruitful implications of their existential messages of which
psychotherapy would have to be the actualization and activation: the
deviations, from this standpoint, are not to be seen in any dynamic
sense of ultimate existential direction, but are stations on the road to
erotic integralness, which the subject's existence-norm has put between
him and normalcy; he must therefore be encouraged to conquer and
occupy these "stations" precisely in order to gain any chance of passing
them. It is evident that the principle, formulated in this form, would

apply only where fixation is already definite, the field of psychosexual experience, owing to the social probability of a frustration of the love striving in that preliminary form of it which the fixation connotes, no longer fluid; moreover, other principles connected with the concrete particularity of each deviation and in fact of each individual case will evidently have to be co-applied with it in order to determine its more specific modes of application. One aspect—articulated by all homosexuality—of the universal love norm that according to Boss directs all sexual strivings is the totality and bipolarity of that male-female *anthropos* image to the "archetypical" reality of which, in Plato's *Symposium*, Aristophanes refers in expounding the essence of love as an eternal striving to *restore* that totality; according to the universal love norm, the homosexual is seen as striving for his "opposite number" not any less than the normal. What makes the difference is that his starting position—his *existence*—is not unambiguously male (or female); it conflicts with itself in such a manner that sexual bi-polarity already characterizes the self in its immanence, so that it is not in terms of a simple bi-polarity of strivings but of the extra-polarization of a complementary bi-polar partner image that the self of the homosexual transcends itself in his love in some instances; depending, however, on the given degree of possible existential identification (self-identification in the proper sense) with the psychosexual counter-pole within (with a *who* of the sex opposite to that of the—extra-polarized— biological self), a partner image that represents exclusively the sex of that biological self may quite radically and unambiguously come to occupy the focal center of the love interest in other instances. It is obvious from their existential premise as just stated that it is more in the latter than in the former cases that a conflicted self- and world-norm narrowing the person's existence and thus jeopardizing the starting position of his love striving will be at the root of the homosexual deviation. In any case, then, it is not from the love impulse as such, let alone from sexuality as a functional entity, but from the existence-norm, the character of a person, that, with all sexual deviations, the homoerotic ones also demand to be understood. All questionableness of Karen Horney's therapeutic conclusions notwithstanding, as the first psychoanalyst—pointing out the unconditional primacy of character— she reversed the predicative order between sexuality and personality contended by Freudian doctrine—an exceedingly timely clarification or rather re-clarification to the merits of which Boss' work explicitly refers.[35]

Since the book by Boss is one of the few pieces of the literature of existential psychopathology thus far available in an American edition, we have given the task of enucleating its theoretical essence and its comprehensive implications-in-principle for psychotherapy preference over any closer description of its ramifications into a differential theory of the various perversions. As he himself has freely recognized, Boss owes many important elements of his view to theoreticians he opposes —the "anthropologists", Freud, several dissidents from orthodox psychoanalysis; among the latter, Jung is the one to whom this debt is most emphatically acknowledged, as he "was the first among modern psychologists to recognize the precise correlation between the inner structure of the soul and the outer worldly possibilities of love for humans. He has demonstrated the strict relationship between 'animus' and 'anima' (which are his names for these intra-psychic images of male and female essence) and the chosen empiric concrete love partners of the outer world. This represents a correction of Klages' one-sided misleading definition of love as a lonely idiopathic erotic intoxication. At the same time, C. G. Jung developed a clear and decisive insight into the general correlative unity of man's Self and the picture of his world which will become so decisive for our own investigations."[36] We may add that existential analysis would not have had to transfigure so incisively this theoretical heritage if the transfiguration would not also call for a quite different, less manipulatory,[37] more sharing form of psychotherapy than just the Jungian.

NOTES

1. We are purposely not considering the problem of meaning here, of which both the Gestalt and the radical-objectivistic conceptions have been dealt with before; cf. p. 117.

2. Cf. p. 28.

3. Cf. p. 204.

4. Cf. p. 25.

5. The focus of application of the polarity of *concrete* and *abstract* is a classification of isolated concepts—concepts already severed from their order of phenomenal emergence—that is undertaken according to the sole criterion of nearness to, or remoteness from, *sensory* reference; the focus of application is toward the categorial context of language as an *operational* one, which means that it

turns its back on (or "presupposes") phenomenal experience, hence cannot shed light on it.

6. Cf. pp. 80–81.

7. Mention may be made here only of Else Frenkel-Brunswik's study in racial prejudice (in collaboration with R. N. Sanford, "Some Personality Factors in Anti-Semitism") with its naive exclusion-from-consideration of the phenomenal experience-contents of racial bias *as they occur to the biased;* already the *a priori* use of the concept of *prejudice prejudges* what such a study should *investigate,* the temporal order of experience and judgment in the biased. In consequence, E.-B. fails to attain any vantage point beyond racial conflicts, namely beyond the group notions and beliefs, the purely reactive concepts (such as prejudice) with which, as a *participant* in historic processes structured by the presence of racial bias, she self-evidently identifies. The more, then, as its implicit claim is scientific detachment, her study, rather than contributing to the theoretical understanding of racial bias, may contribute to the bias.

8. The inconsistency in interpreting *guilt* experiences of pathological intensity but devoid of specific self-indictments without factual basis as *delusional* (as which in clinical practice they are habitually diagnosed) appears immediately from the absence of any conceivable "reality" standards for "normal" degrees of intensity of guilt experiences according to the phenomenal constitution of guilt.

9. Cf. p. 161.

10. K. Jaspers, op. cit.

11. J. Wyrsch, *Die Person des Schizophrenen,* Bern, 1950.

12. E. Kahn, *Arch. f. Psych.,* 88, p. 435, 1929; *M'schr. f. Psychiatrie,* 119, p. 65, 1950.

13. A. Müller-Suhr, *Z. Neur.,* 177, 1944; *Fortschritte,* 18, 1950.

14. J. Wyrsch, *Z. Neur.,* 121, p. 186, 1929.

15. H. Kunz, *Z. Neur.,* 193, p. 671, 1931.

16. F. Fromm-Reichmann, *Principles of Intensive Psychotherapy,* Chicago, 1950.

17. Cf. pp. 331–35.

18. Cf. p. 330.

19. Cf. p. 158.

20. M. Boss, *Meaning and Content of the Sexual Perversions,* New York, 1949.

21. L. Binswanger, *Grundformen und Erkenntnis menschlichen Daseins,* Zurich, 1942.

22. *Schweizer Archiv für Neurologie und Psychiatrie,* 47, 1951, 15–19.

23. M. Boss, *op. cit.,* pp. 16–26.

24. Cf. pp. 202–03.

25. M. Boss, *Meaning and Content of the Sexual Perversions,* p. 37.

26. M. Scheler, *Wesen und Formen der Sympathie,* Bonn, 1923, p. 233.

27. Cf. p. 163.

28. M. Boss, *op. cit.,* p. 8.

29. Cf. p. 255.

30. Cf. pp. 73, 76.

31. Significantly, the phenomenon of anxiety, which is the experiential repre-

sentation (or "presence") of existence-in-its-isolation and therefore (as Boss rightly identifies it) the absolute counter-pole to love, refuses to submit to that kind of "orientation": it is, in any phenomenologically strict (literal) sense, strikingly *painless*. Accordingly, the less bound to anything that *pains* from within or without, anxiety occurs to the existent, the more purely *is* it anxiety, and the more deadening (unless they are *faced*; cf. p. 123) are its terrors.

32. Simone de Beauvoir, op. cit., vol. II, pp. 163–167. Beauvoir, in a shift of terminology which seems to restrict "masochism" to a character type, separates the (potential) significance of pain as an element of love play (and of submission in an analogous status) from the personality problem of the female masochistic character who submits out of dependency and irresponsibility and thus does not possess the imaginative freedom on which, with all true existential presence, also any form of love play depends. The possibility of a conceptual differentiation of this kind would, of course, at least not guarantee its empirical applicability, as there are instances of masochism which follow at once both lines of motivation yet behaviorally testify to the unitariness of the motivation behind them, so that to speak of any admixture of motives in them would be arbitrary; the question which they raise seems exactly whether Beauvoir's conceptual differentiation may not already prejudice a unity of motivational experience that defies any categories of social evaluation that in the manner of all *ideological* value schemes are superimposed on it from *without* the authentic situation of the existent.

33. Only in rather specific cases of homosexuals with psychic hermaphroditism, of which Boss reports one in his book, such an actualization hardly seems possible; while existences of this type do not in principle exceed the limits of the homosexual type-category formulated on p. 308, the definiteness of their self-identification with the biologically opposite sex would for all practical purposes seem to shift their problem from the area of psychotherapy to the areas of social philosophy, philosophy of law, and legislation.

34. Cf. pp. 8, 116, 156.

35. Cf. M. Boss, *op. cit.*, p. 17.

36. *Ibid.*, p. 31.

37. The "world" manipulated by Jungian therapy is, of course, not the factual structure of the patient's environment, which the therapist as an existential-communicative partner of the patient, a person in his world, may in certain instances not only have the right but the duty to try to improve (cf. p. 260) but is the patient's world-*design*, and this world-design *not*—as would again be legitimate— as a noetic proposition open, as such, to radical argument and debate, but as a "psychological" fact-datum, an *object*. Cf. also p. 181.

CHAPTER 12

A Glance at Jungian Thinking—The Problem of Typologies—The Objectivity Problem Re-posed—Conrad, and Growth Tendencies—*The Infinity of Possible Type Concepts—The Double Status of "Ideas"—A Cinderella of Psychology—Expressive Phenomena and* Validation—*The Ubiquity of the Expressive in the Media of Psychology, and First Proposals for a Basic Professional Qualification Requirement—The* Worlds *of Human Beings and the Analyst—The Concept of Compulsivity and Its Fate—The Magic, Mythical, and Mystic—The Sacramental and the* Wholesome—Symbols *and the Rationalist—The Case of K.—The Problems Surrounding* Attention—*Radical and Descriptive Phenomenology—Categoriality as a Trap—The Science of Man of Tomorrow: Feats and Foretokens.*

For all its desultoriness, our encounter with the acknowledgment of a certain heritage of existential psychology at the conclusion of the preceding chapter was not incidental, for Jungian theory contains the seeds of *Daseinsanalyse* like an egg the fledgling that wants out: at a certain point, the egg's containment, having meant absolutely positive protection before, comes to mean just as absolutely negative a constraint. The solidity with which the doctrine of a fundamental ambivalence inherent in all world horizons inasmuch as they are identified (as in any ultimate sense they never can be truthfully) with certain factual constellations is reflected in biogenetic phenomena, is a perception which, in contemplating the image just used, we may register in passing; what matters more at this point is that the applicability of the image—as we did apply it—is confirmed by every essential trait of Jungianism as from our newly gained position it shapes up in retrospect.

Thus, a strict co-relativity of self and world is already seen by Jung, but not yet the truth (or trans-factualness) of being that only unfolds

312

the polarity of the two. The destiny of the psyche to *actualize what it is* is understood already; not yet, what it *is* that it "is". Objectification, of course, is as incomplete here as it cannot help but be: a self-conscious ego that aspires unconsciously to actualize its unconscious counter-pole by conscious strivings is mistaken for the agent of self-realization. Static intra-psychic compensatoriness, never accounting for *what* is being compensated-for by *what*, is mistaken for the principle of the self-world rapport, *knowing* becomes *wishing*, the spiritual a kind of invisible matter indispensible for the consumption of certain, if central, "func-tional" needs of the psyche, while Truth is misidentified with what in the *light* of it may or may not appear true.[1] The causally inexplicable simultaneity of events that relate in their meanings does not as yet lead to the meaningful quest after the—definitively "simultaneous"—wholes (which the researcher only does not happen to have noticed or con-ceived of) in which the media wherein such events occur may be found to participate, but to the likely bewilderment of physicists leads to the introduction into explanatory science of *synchronicity* as a "principle of nature" competing with *causality* on one and the same plane-of-understanding of the cognitive quest.[2] Psychotherapy is seen as reaching into territories that "were formerly the domain of priests and phil-osophers", but with a peculiar insistence on limping behind the most challenging philosophers of Jung's own time (as well as a few quite challenging ones of its priests), it is supposed to "reach" there by taking up the nineteenth century shibboleth that these competitors have just laughingly and totally thrown away—*Weltanschauung*.[3] Is it surprising that Jungian psychology, with its enjoyable abundance and deplorable unsharpness of perceptions, its fanaticism for, and weakness of, logic, its ability—demonstrated by Jung personally—to explain a case of psychosis equally well in Freudian, Adlerian, and finally its own terms without explaining it in any of these, should also reach into the proximity of a science of man with such accomplishments as its *typology of personalities?* That this typology is not like any of the others now current, that something intrinsically truer-about-man, conceived more from the standpoint of man's existing, is trying to express itself in it, has often been recognized, and there can be no doubt that such Jungian concepts as *introversion* and *extraversion*, which have so much become part and parcel of the accepted psychological vocabulary of our time that the many decided anti-Jungians who use them rarely

seem aware of their origin any more, succeed in conveying something
that at once appears evident. This rather impressionistic kind of evidence,
now, is the one phenomenology explodes as it touches it: what, it would
ask, are the "insides" and "outsides" which here are presupposed to be
so clear? The premise of the introversion-extraversion polarity—as
conceived by Jung—a premise, which has itself never been demonstrated scientifically, but is inherited from Cartesian metaphysics,[4] is
that there is a "fact world" and an "inner-psychic world", that each of
these exists independently of the other at least to an extent that allows of
a separate conceptual determination of either; that, in other words, the
pre-given *spatiality*[5] of existence, from which the apperception of physical space only unfolds, can itself be conceptualized—with any degree
of legitimacy—as it *is* conceptualized in the Jungian categorial polarity
named (in analogy with the space concept of physics).

Reasons which argue against that premise in greater detail have
been presented before.[6] Its fallacy, where it is applied to the construction of a typology such as the Jungian, is concealed behind a prior
implicit selection by the typologist himself among the many possible
perceptions of one and the same existence that may be chosen as guides
in implementing introversion and extraversion concretely. If, for example, "ideas" and "realities" are prejudicially segregated, the former
being identified with *abstractions* of thought, the latter with *sensory
concreta*, it becomes possible to demonstrate, as Jung did, that Schiller
was an introvert, Goethe an extravert. If the counter-observation, diametrically reversing this account, is recorded, that there was a primary
propensity toward histrionic effects in Schiller's work, toward lyrical
meditation and penetration in Goethe's, the analytical psychologist can
answer that we are faced with the compensatory workings of the *anima*.
But this "compensatory" relation, too, can be reversed—without, of
course, its conception gaining in meaning: the cited tendencies in the
two poets were *unconscious* only in the sense that the personalities
concerned, despite much documented self-knowledge, were not preoccupied with any psychological categorizations of them as they were
displaying them in their activities, a point which again, of course,
applies equally well to any psychological categorizations of those of
their propensities on which their placement in the Jungian typology is
based. From whence, then, does any criterion for a conscious-unconscious
dichotomization derive that of itself would apply to the polarities—

which, as such, are unquestionably *given*—within either set of "traits" in each of these two personalities? And, if there is no such criterion, what remains of any possible meaning of *intro* and *extra* here? From the personal "inwardness", the "innermost" of the "heart", from the spontaneous speaking *out* of one's mind (or a violent *being out of it*) do these two concepts not differ precisely in this, that the symbolic "spatialisms" which the others express are themselves spontaneous experiences through which the pre-given "space" of existence reveals its structure without deliberate analogizing? The impossibility of carrying through Jung's naively space-abstracted categories empirically, an impossibility the demonstration of which could be continued on the basis of case materials *ad libitum*, confirms the logical impossibility of it from the analysis of which we started.

The problem of the possibility of a strictly phenomenological typology of personalities is the problem of a typology of existences, of world-*modi;* since a survey—which precisely as a survey is possible only from without—of the existence-norms it differentiates is its indispensable premise, the problem of objectivism must itself be posed afresh. Objectification of the psyche was rejected, at an early point in this study, where in actuality it turns out to be a conceptual reification of subjective experience that, once accomplished, must obscure the authentic phenomenal contents from which it itself is derived through abstraction; what thus is being reified into fictitious "facts" and "factors" is the constitutive "towardness" of experience as a two-way street between a world and a self. But objectivity, in its loose and common usage, means empiricalness; empiricalness not only was not rejected in our study but stressed. While "objectivity", in another loose, if less common, usage, refers to the encounter of phenomena from without (whatever is not part of the self), in any strict sense of original definition the *ob-ject* is not that at all but is a "thing" that is *thrown against* the self and thus is radically severed from the self or from any common ground-of-being which, prior to the objectification, the two may have shared. The radical *ob-ject* then, as already pointed out previously,[7] is the thing that has become completely subject to our measurements and completely closed to our immediate understanding; it is an object such as self-consistent (molecular) behaviorism must wish its objects to be.[8] It becomes evident now that the encounter of things merely from without, as according to that loose definition of objectivity we

last cited, is no guarantee at all of any such radical objectivity: the
world of our existence, and even more emphatically the *human* world
outside of us, is, as shown before,[9] first of all "physiognomic"—accessible
to our understanding immediately. Such understanding, in turn, does
by no means operate solely by way of verbal communications; but
through whatever media it operates, its relation to these media is
characterized precisely by this: it still shares with them that encompassing *sensibleness* both of original knowledge and of what original knowledge knows, which—the ground of being as a common one still
being intact and accessible—forbids such understanding any objectivity
in the aforementioned strict sense of the term. But is this not an asset
rather than a limitation? Has the impossibility for social and anthropological science to do without understanding not been demonstrated
amply? If, in the loose meaning of "objectivity" last referred to, such
cognitive approaches to existences from without and through no matter
which media, which spontaneously avail themselves of the *sensibleness*,
for example, of physiognomic patterns, are defined—which is no more
than a question of usage—as objective ones, phenomenological psychology is by all means objective, for it stresses a studying of the
phenomenal outsides of existences as much as of their insides.

But what media are open precisely to its objective approach?
Language, of course, inasmuch as it is immediately expressive (not
only of its own communicative contents but at least as much of the
being of the communicant); but immediate expressiveness is no
monopoly of language. Moreover, from the *contents it articulates*—and
it is at this level of their greatest articulateness that ideas can be concealed as well as expressed—to the *ways of expressing them* (the less
concealable expressivity of speech and voice) the whole phenomenon
of verbal communication shows itself from a truly enormous number
of what—in terms of the functional distribution of its gamut of
events—may be considered as its different "sides", "levels", "aspects",
or zones of concentration. The continuum the succession of these
maps out only starts off with the *focally articulated content* of verbal
communication, but it is impossible to say where it ends, for this
dimension already leads far beyond even the functional entities themselves of speech and voice, dissipating, as it does, into the more and
more "objective" (unconsciously physiognomic) expressivity of motor
behavior, facial and manual gesturing, body attitude, and of the static

structure of the soma: the intercommunication of meaning between one existent and another turns out to operate at an infinite number of levels of expressive contact at once.

The stunning obliviousness of objectifying psychology for the entire realm of the *expressive movements*—which during the last two decades has only begun to break down—is a significant example of its absurd lack of perceptiveness: its somewhat disconcerted attitude in the face of the static expressivity of the somatotypes (and of the theories which cover them) appears open-minded in comparison with the blind sweepingness which has inhered in that bias. Also, speaking only of the difficulties with which Kretschmerian-Sheldonian anthropography has met, it is rather evident that these lay as much in the insufficient clarification of its earlier conceptions as in any prejudice on the part of its scientific audience: the notion that the whole approach was fatalistic, while peculiar in the mouth of otherwise strictly deterministic critics, not only could feed on their own failure to reflect on the meaning of "fatalism" and "freedom"[10] but at least as much on imperfections of the Kretschmerian personality theory itself. The very concept of type was never thought through too critically. Characterological generalizations from specific, not necessarily type-representative, individual elaborations of some of Kretschmer's types were sweeping. The normal and the pathological versions of certain of the types—even though they had themselves been determined qualitatively (eidetically)—came to look but like different positions along one and the same quantitative continuum: the schizophrenic was but the extreme schizoid, psychotic processes altogether became, as such, phenomena of character, that human beings existed in any such thing as a world seemed forgotten. Fundamental to this structuralism was a misunderstanding of the perceived somatic features and whole body styles; the asthenic and the leptosome especially remained unseparated in principle, and the question whether these types altogether justified their being put on one plane of comparative classification—whether their ontogeneses were homogeneous in terms of a simultaneity of the phases of growth which "produced" them—was never posed.

Since then, the revision of the entire system by Conrad,[11] a monumental undertaking that could draw as much on embryological research as on somatotyping measurements as on a closer phenomenological inspection of the Kretschmerian types and sub-types of personality, has shed much light on the actual order of human ontogenesis from the side of body constitution. According to this revision, what a type concept fixates is neither a multi-individual homogeneity of specific psychophysical qualities nor a certain arbitrarily chosen and limited range of them[12] but a guiding principle of growth, a dominant or co-dominant growth tendency, which is represented in the organism by a consistent structural norm of body style or pattern. Subject to inter-individual variation, intra-individually this norm pervades and objectively determines all spheres of static and dynamic expressivity of the soul-body unity of existence; what implements the type concept, hence, is already an *existential idea,* the phenomenalization of a conception—inhering in the organism itself—of a possible modus of the being-in-the-world. Considering our earlier insight into the ways in which all existential ideas imply their own alternatives, into their representativeness for a dimension-setting topic which they share with these alternatives and which becomes the very *theme* of a biography, it is not surprising that Conrad's growth tendencies, too, are found to occur in (in fact to be determined by) the polarities in which each of them stands to its diametrical opposite; the polarities themselves, in turn (of which there are properly speaking two, while a third, purely pathogenic, one is constituted by the possibly occurring dysplastic inhibitions of growth itself) unfold at different stages of the ontogenetic total process, thus representing wholly heterogeneous single aspects of the organism-personality unity (the typological position of which always lies within all three polarities at once). Only one of the two biopositive ones—the polarity of pycnomorph-cyclothymic versus leptomorph-schizothymic[13]—unfolds *prenatally,* and is subject exclusively to Mendelian laws of heredity. This specification already limits the "fatalism" of the theory even in an objectivistic-deterministic sense, for those traits of personality and biography that correspond to the— most fundamental but also most general—"primary variation of the being-human" (Conrad) of which this polarity represents the range, are just as general and fundamental. This means that they still allow of an infinite number of post-natal differential elaborations of what specifically they *will be* in the later actuality of existence and character; the positions which they specify thus not only exclude an infinite number of developmental possibilities already but also imply one.

The mentioned polarity, furthermore, is an exclusively *inter-*

individual continuum along which the individual always occupies a
definite and unchangeable position exclusive of all others. While none
of these positions is in itself ever pathogenic, let alone pathological,
it is toward the extreme of the range that predispositions (here to be
understood as mere *vulnerabilities*) for personality disorder are at their
highest, and correspondingly they are at their lowest in the
"metromorph-synthymic" center of the dimension; this order of degrees
of predisposition, however, is "cross-differentiated" again by the organism's position along the plastic-dysplastic polarity, the polarity of
freedom versus inhibition of growth *per se*, so that the total constellation of positions in terms of the primary polarities of both growth
tendencies and growth inhibitions that most favors a continuous growth
of personality and existence can be characterized most closely as
plastic-metromorph-synthymic. It is in post-natal interaction with the
environment—which at this stage of ontogenesis no longer is the
environment of a vegetative entity subject to ecological laws that are
purely "functional", but is the world of an existence—that progres-
sively, with each new phase of life finding a more narrowly defined
range of differential determinations still open, the position of the
organism-personality unity within the third dimension of Conrad is
fixed. This third dimension (or the second one, if only those pertaining
to growth tendencies proper are counted) is set by the polarity of
hyperplastic versus hypoplastic—athletic versus asthenic, by an older
terminology. In distinction from Conrad's primary polarity ("round"-
"oblong"), his secondary one ("strong"-"weak"), specifies the typological structure of the organism-personality unity at a less *in*cisive
(fundamental-characterological) but more *de*cisive (differentially determining, biography-directing) level; the "most fundamental and general" positions of the first polarity are actualized by those of the second
in the sense of a specific selection from the range of potentialities of
each.

The polarity of hyperplastic versus hypoplastic represents an intra-
as well as an inter-individual range of variation: it "allows" the
individual to occupy multiple and even contradictory positions (in
terms of possible heterogeneously "strong" or "weak" developments
of motor functional body areas and of their characterological correlates) along this continuum. In distinction from the type of differentiation which inheres in the primary (vegetative) polarity, the actualiza-

tion of existences which the secondary one spells out thus quite evidently depends on patterns of action and action training, on the individual's education and self-education, in brief, on his world relations as an implementation of his freedom; biogenetic "determinism", at this stage of research and thought, indeed reaches the point where at last it seems to call "itself" into question.[14] In distinction from the primary one, the secondary polarity of Conrad is seen as reaching into the realm of the pathological on all sides, and the more extremeness of, or disparateness between, intra-individual positions along its continuum develops, the more difficult the task of personality integration and the more acute the threat of personality disorder. Or should this determination of its scope of pathology be still too wide? "Disintegration" and "disorder", indeed, are no monopoly of the secondary dimension; but it is precisely in distinction from the pathogenic implications of the dimension of "growth-inhibitive" pathology (pathology of a more diffuse and perpetual kind, less inclining toward taking the form of acute processes) which the plastic-dysplastic polarity (epileptic conditions and other forms of paroxysmal defect) represents, that those of the hyperplastic-hypoplastic one can now most readily be recognized: the norms of the self-world rapport to which they point are those inveterately conflicted ones that clinically take the forms of the classic psychogenic psychoses. Only whether—and to what extent— the latter turn out to be of either a manic-depressive or a schizophrenic type or represent any possible combination of their features, is predetermined by the person's position along the primary, of itself never pathogenic, bipolar dimension of Conrad; the actualization of a psychosis, like the actualization of any biographic pattern or event in its concrete existential and historical import, remains bound up in any case with the polarity of action and interaction only.

The unique significance of Conrad's structuralistic theory of human ontogenesis lies in its complete liberation from the onesidedness, the nativistic coercions of psychological phenomena practiced by its predecessors, its capacity of following lines of biographic growth and growth disruption understandingly from within the personalities concerned, and in the circumspection of its theorizing which combines an utmost of logical consistency with an utmost of elasticity in admitting and reconciling any conceivable perceptions and data; biology and phenomenology here constantly affirm and assist each other, and not only the nature-nurture problem but also the problem of a typology of norms of existing which we had posed seems solved at least as regards its most manifest aspects: with the polarities of Conrad not only a highly meaningful three-dimensional distribution of general and clinical personality prototypes becomes possible, but this typology-model—though allowing of a systematic account most of all of the psychodynamics of *phenotypical* clinical patterns[15]—nowhere exhibits that peculiar omniscience which has continued to characterize the ambitions of typologists. It is evident that no differential theory of personality, whether merely classificatory or genetic, can conceivably account for any human characteristics that do not already submit to the differentiating criteria of the theory[16]; since the number of any such characteristics, of the *modi* of phenomenal experience implementing them on the side of the person's subjectivity, and of the polarities these map out is as endless as is the *world* itself into which "existence exists", no such thing as an exhaustive typological theory of man is conceivable any more than it would appear desirable.

What is the secret of this endlessness, which so much falls outside of the finiteness of all objects of nature and even of subjectivity itself, where subjectivity is but the "inside" of an inter-referent constellation of natural objects, a pragmatic context of living[17] allowing to be (or not to be) comprehended as an inconclusive position somewhere on the way from the *in-itself* of Sartre to what he, not quite satisfactorily, terms the *for-itself*, the position of *man?* A tree, such as the one spoken of at the beginning of our chapter I, is a different object in the worlds of the lichen, the tree louse, the ant, the squirrel, the woodpecker, the deer and the dog, but only in the world of man is its meaning not fixed pragmatically, *can* the tree be the many different objects which it is in the worlds of the lumberer, the peasant woman, the forester, the botanist, the vacationer, the painter or poet, and only in the world of man can and does arise the question, what *is* the tree? The power to conceive of *being* and the freedom *to be* are thus one and the same, and as the former can be defined, "from the side of the object", as the conceivability of being, thus the freedom to be, defined from the side of the object, turns out to be that absolute—potential or actual— *openness* of the existential horizon which would not even allow either to recognize "truths" in their "relativity" or thus to misformulate what has become a truism of today's *everybody*, if it were not what is meant by Truth.[18] That man lives in the "open" is the objective-scientific reason that man, to the despair of all those theoreticians of personality who against the testimony of all empiric data believe that he can be figured out, escapes all figures, all quantifications, all statistics, a statement which cannot be taken literally enough: it does not say that an individual or a group cannot be calculated, as both are calculated all the time now by psychologists specializing in advertisement and other instruments of publicity and propaganda; it says only that man escapes the calculation, which means that the individual or the group which in objective terms of *prediction* success *will* act as the calculation expects them to will also—and to precisely the extent of that success—have ceased to be human.

The future of man, then, is at present at least doubtful. The doubtfulness, which after two centuries dominated by the optimism of consistent progress has arisen rather suddenly and to which existential philosophy is only the first attempt to articulate an answer, has no historic precedent that could truly suggest one; it is itself a state of suspension of man between the most enormous threat and an equally enormous hope. A hope implies that freedom of being on which all instituted freedoms are only contingent, and which they can never guarantee, the freedom to live one's own *future*. In order for a future to be lived there must be one. Since a future that can be predicted is no future, it is not the future of his statistics on which man can legitimately stake his own future, except in reverse: the future of man depends objectively on his future ability to invalidate his own statistics.

But why does the openness of man's existence, which we determined as Truth itself, make him so potentially incalculable? Because Cartesianism, which is the forgotten metaphysical premise of the attempts of all constructors of brain models bent on bridging the gap in psychology functionalistically,[19] is wrong: the appearance of any specific elaboration, any idea out of that openness of the existential horizon is not an event that takes place either on a cognitive outside of objective world perceptions or on a conative inside of biological need, nor can it be construed with any justified hope of understanding as a bi-polar field event, except in the sense of a theoretical concept-of-limit, an eternal postulate precluding its own implementation; for the field itself is never objectively given, never knowable to any cognizer (himself forever caught in his own "bi-polar" existence field), nor can it be constructed from any separate renderings of its "poles", since vice versa these poles are already what they are only in their pre-given polarity, their inter-referentness to one another, which in turn has any actuality only as the actuality of the field. An existential idea is thus at once a real state of the self and a just as real one of the world; reducing it to any functional laws, in consequence, would be a proposition functionally to reduce *reality*. To what, except that *nothingness* of understanding in which all functionalistic theories of man indeed and with much consequence of scientific principle have landed, could reality be reduced?

Existential ideas, in turn, are ideas that are *lived*; ideas, implying their alternatives, as we saw, set dimensions—of orientation, hence of existing, hence of personality; the typologies, the possible personality theories altogether which can be built on them, is therefore not smaller than is the number of authentic human ideas themselves, which is endless. Does this not render hopeless any conception of a science of man? It only poses its problem afresh, as problem, first of all, of the fundaments of such a science, which can never be severed from that frontal exposure to the immediate presence of ideas which is philosophizing[20]; secondly, as problem of method. The inadequacy of restricting phenomenology, in either a theoretical or applied determination of its scope, to *verbal* communications, has been pointed out before[21]; in the same context of argument, the province of legitimate psychological objectivism was recognized as constituted by phenomena essentially "physiognomic" or "expressive". Realizing, as we do now, that the number of possible personality dimensions that objectively are given is endless, we can finally understand why these phenomena, and any scientific approach to them, have continued to embarrass the objectivistic psychologist.

The reason for this peculiar hauntedness of his conscience, for the stubborness of his attempts to talk the haunt out of existence, lies in the objective presence, in such a trace of expressive motor behavior as a specimen of handwriting, of that endlessness of personality dimensions which the objectivist—*a priori* if thoughtlessly identifying order with finiteness—cannot reconcile with his ideas of science. That infinity itself which he so shuns is phenomenal in expressive movements and their traces, and the *order* of psychological perceptions of which they allow must therefore be missed, if instead of being permitted to unfold toward the—itself phenomenal—foreground in the authentic direction of all physiognomic perceptions, which runs toward that foreground from an invisible, so to speak trans-spatial point, a point "in eternity", it is prejudiced by the superimposition—following the exactly opposite course—upon the phenomena of behavior of any measuremental scheme that depends on an abstraction. The dimensionality of the physical space into which phenomena are unfolded is, as we have seen before,[22] an abstraction from their own unfolding; things are *distributed* in that space, essences appear. Since space is only inasmuch as anything appears, it is not vice versa in terms of space in its abstractness that appearances can ever be understood or that which appears in them ever be cognized: they can at any time be translated—in their totality, never their wholeness—into bundles of data of a geometric distribution encountered, and this the objectivist would of course be willing to do, but what does it avail him? The translation is a oneway street, the new idiom with which one finds oneself a code without a key, not only in reality can the taking-apart of a living structure not be reversed: expressive movements can be quantified, but there is no way back to any meaning.

This—not the question of sensible validation, which has been solved to a sizeable extent and is solvable to one of ever greater perfection—is the reason that *graphology*, as on many accounts the most representative of all studies of expressive movements, has taken so radically divergent developments in territories where the dominant orientation of psychology was phenomenological from where it was objectivistic. The situation of graphological inspection only confirms the constitution of all physognomic phenomena as stated: it focuses on the "spatiality" of the movements with the trace of which it is faced, but since it does this by following the impulses of movement (visually that *invisible* of which the trace is the appearance and the medium of understanding) into their given space-distributions rather than starting out by measuring the latter, it is able to reconstitute in the inner order of the graphologist's experiences the inner experience of the originator of the sample and of that phenomenal world-reference which it implies. In doing so, graphology discovers that those dimensions of the space of handwriting which can be identified as dimensions of physical space within which the writing either is distributed factually or of which— leaving the foreground of its factual space-distribution already—it is a two-dimensional pictorial projection, form only the nearest aspect of the whole spatiality of the movement trail under its focus, the surface stratum of a depth that points away from space as it appears in it. Yet, precisely in terms of *appearance*, this entire order is encountered *in reverse*: what is seen first, what phenomenally is nearest, is not any such thing—highly meaningful as it may be if understood already—as a ratio between the size of particles of movement lying in different field directions from the central position of the line, but rather such qualities—emphatically underivable from the geometric structure of the space *only into* which they appear—as, for example, the *thorniness* of a pattern. That "thorniness" already is encountered in its specificity, its directedness by the idea behind it, which may appear in the militancy of the form itself, the idea that "world" *per se* is something to be kept at a distance; but this the objectivist, especially if in contact with his human subject he should find himself as part of the world thus to be kept at a distance, would lump together with a thousand other and wholly heterogeneous phenomena from different existences in one concept of hostility, which thus becomes a *trait* and quantifiable—*wrath*, much too phenomenal a quality or state to be of interest to the objectivist as what it is, would be an extreme *quantity* of the same material of which *diffidence* is just a small one.

It is in this manner, that the essence of personality pictures is missed from the start: instead of following topically the existential idea of world-at-a-distance, which in the actuality of personality, the actuality also of expressive motor behavior, may be bi-polarized—as it is bi-polarized in certain schizophrenics—with such an alternative of it as a cosmic immersion of the self, its being "overwhelmed" and "diluted" by the sheer contingency of being; instead of following that idea to its axiomatic theme (of which the said polarity is the unfolding) of the problem of participation, of love in a world of power, the objectivist contents himself with a classificatory characterization that is as pale as it is abstract and that reveals nothing about the subject's identity as a human. It is evident that, to assess the full vastness of the contrast, we do not have to restrict ourselves to the disclosures of the physiognomic where the physiognomic is recognized as just that, in other words, in the area of those psychodiagnostic media that the expressive movements provide; immediate psychological understanding throughout (an in essence all true *world* understanding) is physiognomic perceptiveness and as such operates just as much on the part of any understanding Rorschacher as of a graphologist aware of the expressive nature of all psychic manifestations.[23] How, otherwise, would we be able to explain that early Rorschach studies, undertaken by the founder of the test himself, even though disposing only of a handful of scoring categories, show a discrimination as well as an unconfoundable concreteness of personality perceptions that the typical current Rorschach report seems to be getting ever-farther away from? The impossibility to duplicate physiognomic cognition by measurement, which is itself not more or less than a demonstrated psychological law that axiomatically inheres in the given constitution of perception,[24] the objectivist turns into an invalidation in principle of approaches in psychology that explicitly are physiognomic; but what, in so doing, are his criteria of validity? How objectively valid criteria of verification, rather, can there even be in a science that, as holds true for the psychology of personality, has the unmeasurable itself as subject?

The problem of validation—of any studies or single findings in the field of personality—phenomenological psychology not only does not disregard; phenomenological psychology alone has nothing to fear from its solution. The objectivist is mistaken if he believes that phenomenology is uncontrollable; his greatest surprise is only coming, as we had stated before,[25]—phenomenology not only admits of statistics, it demands, at one decisive point, its services. It admits, as well as demands, statistical validation of personality psychological approaches and of single findings with the self-evident provision that the data on either side of the correlations that measure significance are true *as data,* that they are actually given by the object—personality—a problem to which, unlike to all other problems just in statistics, the objectivist has never yet given the full benefit of his attention. If he had, the contestability of all so-called constant data used as criteria of validity or reliability in the statistical objectification of personality tests or test findings, a contestability which is either one of the data as such or of the inambiguity of the dimensional concepts[26] in terms of which one presents them, would have led him to the one and only result to which all rigorous epistemological examinations of the problem of "validation" in personality psychology yet have led: the only strictly uncontestable criterion here is personal identity, the resulting exclusive standard of objectification, the identifiability of any personality report (or of statements partaking in, or inferred from, one), the only existent as well as conceivable statistical device which tests such identifiability, the *matching experiment*. In the matching experiment, the theoretician either may partake as an experimental subject directly by displaying his understanding of the expressive unity (identity) of personality in the form of a "blind" identification, from a given range either of the behavioral traces of a group of individuals, or of their biographic data, or of any other materials representative of personality in any sense, of the one or ones belonging to the subject(s) under his focus; or his own characterizations of the latter, arrived at on the basis of no matter which medium or media of contact, may be submitted to third judges for such matching; in the latter case, the judges' own pre-tested overall ability blindly to match identities on the basis of samples of behavior from the most heterogeneous specific media is the self-evident prerequisite to qualify them for their office. The cultivation of such experiments, conducted in sufficient numbers, with sufficiently tight experimental controls and sufficient qualitative spread to safeguard statistical significance, would have been the evident duty of the statistical-minded psychologist in the field of personality, and nothing, perhaps, testifies better to the inadequacy of his conceptions, both of man and of himself as a scientist, than his conspicuous shunning of them, which is explicable only from the inevitability of the dilemma with which such undertakings threaten him: quantitative data, which according to his own determination are the only ones that can claim objective validity, here explode of their own the entire remainder of a quantitativism seeking both to quantify—outside of their pre-given dimensional and configurational contexts that alone determine what they *are*—single "traits", and to understand identity recognitions themselves (as a noetic faculty of man) as the function of an additive agglomeration of elements conceptualized (as single sense perceptions and their memory traces) in the same atomistic manner. It is evident that the debunking of "intuition" as "subjective" or "disorderly" which, even though a scientist should adjudge but what he knows from experience, inheres in the objectivist's conception of scientific and unscientific methods in psychology, must end at the point where quantitative data on their part debunk the debunkers, and so an ever growing mass of such data, reported in the literature from all over the field of the expressive movements in recent years is met, no longer even with attempts at disproof, but with silence.

But phenomenological psychology, in dissipating charges that mechanically seem to revolve around a never-thought-through concept of subjectivism,[27] would contradict itself if to beat the objectivist's fictitious trait dimensions ("into" which the latter's data "fall", but out of which no substantial knowledge has emerged) on the objectivist's own home grounds by the instrumentality of matching experiments were an end to be pursued for its own sake; its demand that a Rorschacher, a testing specialist who thinks in categories which themselves are abstractions from the experiential-expressive correlates of a range of possible structures of the being-in-the-world, must be able blindly to determine from his personal contacts with a subject, his reading contacts with that subject's life history, which of a given handful of Rorschach records is that subject's, or that a practicing psychiatrist, confronted with a characteristic off-couch utterance of one of his patients unnamed in his identity must be able to tell that patient's name, quite obviously derives from its tenet—for which we have reasoned before[28]—that the ultimate topic as much as the ultimate problem of psychology is identity; that, before the *who* of an existence is not grasped as nearly as possible, the psyche supposed to be that *who* in its objectivity remains in plain fact unknown, a situation that in principle forbids any kind of subsequent theoretical statements about, or inferred from, that object. This does not mean that in the face of any personality-theoretical tenet as such or of its individual-psychological application in a differential diagnostic study we can be sure of the truth of such theorizing if its claims are supported by the theoretician's or the diagnostician's capacity of successful identity matching; it only means that, with such capacity present, we finally see ourselves in that zone of consequent psychological empiricalness where even to speak of science no longer at least must be preposterous: while matching ability is no proof of theoretical truth, it is its absence which proves that theoretical truth, in a specific case at hand to say the least, cannot possibly have been attained, for what else if not that unity of behavior that was missed in the matching failure is personality—the topic of the theorizing—precisely in its objectivity, its "pre-constituted" and exclusive *givenness* as appearance?[29] What can anyone know about someone else whose identity marks he is not even able to recognize with reasonable sureness? Precisely as an objective science—in the only possible valid sense of that term—the future of psychology hinges as on a minimum requirement on the psychologist's ability at least to match identity successfully, and that this ability happens to be subject to statistical controls by no means only disarms the objectivist as he finds himself confronted with this proposal of phenomenology; it also—a point of greatest importance for the didactic and training status of psychological science—is the only guarantee for a future unity of that science, since it is the only conceivable weapon against the current arbitrariness (both in theory and in practice) of *either* the uncontrollable speculative *or* the "controlled" but otherwise spurious quantitativist varieties which—today as in the future—psychology can command.

While the last named type of arbitrariness still reigns over much of professional psychology, the former has continued to determine the situation in psychiatry. The increasing looseness in the use of diagnostic concepts that developed under psychoanalytic influence testifies against the claim which has protected it in practice, the claim to a better grasp just of personality *dynamics*: no gain in knowledge is achieved by merely extending the scope of application of a term beyond its own phenomenal territory and to the possible point of an inclusion of the precisely opposite phenomena.[30] While the logical and methodological errors that inhere in this practice have been analyzed, its core can only now be determined: to the variability of existence between such dimension-setting alternates that represent *one* theme of existing as a person's preoccupations with his self-experienced clumsiness and with its valued opposite there corresponds one of just as multiple possible perceptions *of* that existence on the part of the observer and inquirer. Dependent on the constellation surrounding the establishment of contact between the two, either the "clumsy" or its extra-polarized opporite, the "refined", will gain the inquirer's attention, to serve as the nucleous for an identification of the person's *being* —which, of course, escapes this kind of categorial nailing-down. The inadequacy of such a categorization may then be perceived, but to the extent that it is, the one of the two polar alternatives of which the inquirer has already decided that it is *untrue* must be debunked with all the more militant partiality. An unconsciously motivated conscious fixation of the subject's psyche may easily be charged in this case, and this line of thinking will the more be convincing to the inquirer the less he has stayed aware of the experiential moorings of his "categories"—of their innate reference to specific and sharply circumscribed characteristics of the phenomenal experiences, the *world*, of his human subject as to the one and only inalienable criterion for employing the categories.[31]

The "dynamic" fate of the concept of *compulsivity* may serve as an example at this point. In the theorizing of Freud who before had accorded the compulsive patient the power of greatest possible resistance to analysis—without ever realizing that this meant also an acknowledgement of his resistance (as an "object" of cognition) to psychoanalytic theoretical understanding—an analogy was found between this syndrome and all rigid adherence to beliefs that psychoanalysis deems *irrational*. As all analogistic thinking of which the analogistic character is not constantly remembered leads to a sweeping identification-in-substance of the *analogates*, Freud's theorizing about the compulsive, as the present scope of application of the clinical concept of compulsivity shows clearly, virtually blotted out the primary differential criterion for a conceptual determination of the whole authentic phenomenon of compulsivity which earlier psychiatry had evolved *phenomenologically*: the criterion of an ego-alien character of the impulses of "compulsive" acts (as, to a somewhat lesser degree of such ego-alienness, of *obsessive* thoughts that are anticipations of catastrophic future events, or to an even lesser one of the static spatio-somatic fears that constitute *phobias*; it is farther on along this continuum that phenomenology encounters the *addictive* impulse patterns, now rarely classified with the ego-alien symptom pictures). What is missed in the psychoanalytic accounts of this syndrome? Evidently, as so regularly in psychoanalytic accounts, the "analogization" by-passes the authentic *situation* of the compulsive: the situation of finding-oneself-compelled as by an "outside" force, a force which yet, significantly, is not allocated delusively in any body-external sphere or altogether in physical space. On the proper grasp of this situation the very notion of compulsivity stands or falls, yet the psychoanalytic account leaves it virtually indistinguishable from the situation of a vaguely defined *compulsive personality*. In distinction from the true compulsive, the latter finds himself *identified* with the

tenor of his "rigid" acts and habits; therefore, and with a well-known
arbitrariness,[32] he must first be "debunked" as *rationalizing* for what
psychoanalysis claims are the "ulterior motives" of his acts and habits
in order to make his "compulsivity" visible, his *experienced self-identity*
invisible, the analogization itself compelling.

In all true (experenced) self-conflicts, as of the Faustian *Zweiseelen-
kampf*, the phenomenal self is "claimed" by different specific identities[33]
as by *possible* elaborations of the *being* (the "who") of the person;
where self-conflict no longer is true as such, as in the multiple existences
of hysterics and epileptics (or, at that level of more definite and stable
and therefore more drastically disparate forms of self-identity, of "ego",
which distinguishes their position from the paroxysmal ones, in the
multiple personifications of schizophrenics), the plurality of the self
as such no longer is experienced by the existent, whom all the more it
comes to characterize from the vantage point of an environment observing him. In the ego-alien phenomenon, now, a third possibility of
pluralization of identity appears, and this is what early psychiatry—
more phenomenological than the later "dynamic" psychiatry but not
phenomenological enough (so that existential psychopathology now
everywhere has to take up where it left off)—discerned as the characteristic experience-modus of the obsessive-compulsive: the self as the
other, excluded from the self's apperception of its own identity as of
its *action tenor*, occurs to itself (to itself-as-ego) in accordance with the
significance of the exclusion as already an encountered fact; it occurs
to the ego from *without* what the ego is to start with—the *who* of all
rational purposive operation, "knowing" itself as a *sovereign intellect*
and knowing the *world* as nothing but raw material for its calculative
analyses, dispositions, and manipulations. While the corresponding lines
of self- (and world-) division which apply to obsessive, phobics, and
prototypical addicts[34] can just as clearly be traced to their fundamental
conceptions of their being-in-the-world, the frame of the present study
commands our concentration on the phenomenology of those ego-
external impulses that most drastically interfere with the ego. The most
real of all media of experienced self-identity quite evidently is the
sphere of *action* and thus of the *motor impulses;* since it is with the
latter that the compulsive impulses proper, the experienced and obeyed
compulsions to do or not to do certain things, interfere, the compulsive

in the strict sense is indeed the one of the four sub-types we have named whose experiences represent the extreme of phenomenal ego-alienness.

While the magic character of the compulsive "rituals" was recognized by psychoanalysis, the essence of the element called magic was not. Phenomenological analysis of the experiences of compulsive patients reveals a necessity to reverse, as usual, the customary account: evident to the compulsive is not that he *has* to obey his compulsion—precisely this *must* is what forever remains alien to him, and the "evidence" to him which the customary notion of compulsivity has in mind, far from being that of any obligation, is one of his obedience to the impulse as of an always already evident *fact* of his own acting. Incomprehensible to him, in turn, is not what in standard psychiatric texts is supposed to be senseless to him, the *content* of the act; a compulsion to form four tiny balls of mud between one's fingers, group them "in a lively asymmetry" on one of them, blow them against a piece of paper all at once and repeat this performance until the resulting sound pattern is *satisfactory* (until the patient distinctly has heard four sharply separated clicks not dull in the tonality of any one of them) has, to him, a quality of *noetic evidence* that is accentuated rather than lessened by his difficulty—which merely reflects the experiential *nearness of this knowledge*[35]—to put it in *words*, for his speech itself is totally in the service of what this knowledge (which is *near* only the ultimate self in him but all the more is an outcast of the narrowed orientation system of his "ego") inevitably must defy. It is evident that this defied authority that dominates his ego is no other than *rationality* itself—rationality as the principle of *causally comprehensible* means-ends connections, as *purposivity:* however evident the content of the compulsive impulse may be as it *occurs* to him, a purpose—this is what makes the fact of his obedience to it so alien to himself—it has not.

The obvious hint which this situation offers us is to search for other human action types that happen to defy the *rationally purposive.* Just the *magic* ones, which are rather demonstratively purposive, would seem out of question here at first; they would seem so if we already understand them "operationally", as means to ends, as in the habitualized magic of rites that survive by mere force of tradition. The cultic purpose of the magic with which according to some petrified formula of it the magic act may be identified, indeed tends to obscure the origin of its meaning at a later stage. But what kind of meaning is this? What is the theory originally behind the use of words and things for *purposes* such as invocation and conjuration? Evidently one which knows significances of *actions* other than those which can be defined in terms of a causal-temporal successivity of events, for while we can account for a magic rite as a means-to-an-end operation in terms, say, of a primitive theology, the evidence, in turn, of the *content* of the primitive faith, of the specific conviction underlying an attribution to the magic of its power to work can never be comprehended as the outflow of any observation of *causality*. What evidence, then, is this if not that immediate and pre-categorial[36] one which inheres in all true symbols? The magic, in order to be understood, must be thought back to what it partakes in. Magic *experience*, in turn, is not the only form of immediate participation in the evidence of the *symbolic*. It may, in fact, be the most precarious one among the three prototypical forms of such participation, of which the other two, the mythical and the mystic,[37] are far less endangered by that—historically ever recurrent—self-and world-alienation, self-and world-pertification, which appears to be the fate precisely of magic thinking in all existence-contexts wherein time and again it has emerged. How can its phenomenal content help us to explain such sterile ending as its rigid and formula-like practices inevitably disclose? The peculiarity of ego-alien experience is but a specified version of a more ubiquitous one with which we meet at this point: the *absolute*, to which all symbols have reference, occurs in magic experience, as emphatically it does not do in the two other forms of symbol-participation, in the image of the uncanny, unknown, the not-to-be-trusted—of *existential dread*.

This holds true for the phenomenal origin of magic cults as much as of compulsion neurosis; in both, what is incorrectly called the *mystic* preoccupation precisely with numbers quite frequently and literally testifies to the abstractive and calculative setting of the self-world relationship which, as in modern Western civilization, is bound to ensue upon that primary alienation of the phenomenal world—originally meaningful throughout—which is the premise of any awareness of a fundamental homelessness of the existent—of that situation or condition in which the dreadful *per se*, the dreadful in its absoluteness or formlessness, (in which it *is* the *naught* and hence uncanny) makes its appearance. The truth that thus holds for the rigidity of either type of rites, the code-bound and the ego-alien, is implemented in turn by what we know to be the basis of *anxiety*, an isolation of the existent in a world *disenchanted* either by hostile surroundings (the emergence of magic forms of faith in tribes not sharing in a common culture with their neighbors) or by even more fundamentally heterogeneous ones (modern technicized man) ; only in the latter case, however, does "reality" itself come to consist of just as isolated fact-things, of "items" of which no immediate understanding remains except for the under-standing that they can be counted. Whatever symbol still has power at this—nihilistic—stage of self- and world-rationalization to point to the *whole*someness (sacredness) of being and thus to serve as a token of continuity in a *futureless and therefore truthless*[38] cavalcade of fleeting events[39] and of their behavioral counterparts (streamlined actions and beliefs) inevitably must be identified with the literalness of a fact-thing, for nothing else remains *real* in the actuality of world experience here; but not from the vantage point of *immediate,* only of *self-alienated* experience, the superficially reflective experiencing of the ego, can the magic act attain to the point of concealing even that symbolism itself wherein it roots. The peculiarly "fetishistic" tendency inherent in all cultic ritualizations that are known, and likewise in the contents of all true compulsive impulses which a too narrowed ego finds alien, derives precisely, then, from their primary roles as last remnants and tokens of the truth of being—of what forever *defies* the abstractive-manipula-tory order in the cloak of which they are themselves forced to appear here: the *sacred*. At this point we encounter the common phenomenal basis[40] for the entire expanse, first of all of the sacred in its closer sense as the holy and the sacramental, of whatever mainstays of human faith anchor themselves beyond the calculative schemes of a purely operationally defined intellect and of its spiritless accounts of *self* and *world;* for the experienced "erogenicity" of body parts that, most stunningly in its encounter by adolescents, are suddenly understood as transcending their own *functional* purposes; for their possible roles (and those of certain just as symbolic *practices* of sexual love) as tokens of the absoluteness of love, as in Boss' theorization of the sexual perversions; and for the other ununderstood, since externally met-with *uncompromisingness,* as well as the power, of the contents of neurotic compulsions in the outspokenness of the convictions they convey. Precisely the "irrational" in all of these phenomena does not, as Freud believed, defy reason but attempts to restore reason by defying that dead abstractness of a purely utilitarian self- and world account which forever evades the question of what can possibly be the cause behind all "causes", what the purpose of its entire web of "purposive" (functional) determinations—that rationalization of "reality" of which Freud became the pontifex and the prophet. What conclusion remains to be drawn at this point? Not only are the sexual perversions, as we have seen, a single testimony to the unity of the human; such "obviously senseless" phenomena as the compulsions of motor behavior, too, are far from violating it, for what else are they if not utterances of a *protest* characteristic of the entire situation of modern western man?[41] What protests here is by no means only the ultimate and forgotten *who* of the compulsive's individual existence as an outcast from his own "ego"; it is on the contrary just in the compulsive that this *who* still seems vigorous enough to raise its voice at all. But what is the protest *against* if not that *unreasonableness* of the rational ego with its pervasive technicalism of purposes and the primary purposelessness of its being, that insists on first alienating, subsequently debunking, an entire dimension of the very being-man?

It has become a commonplace that conceptions such as the sacred have no place in science; but while the belief that they do not can be traced, as we have traced it before,[42] to a rather clumsy error in scientific logic (confounding of phenomena with conceptual tools for their grasp), the axiom that if there is any one place that is never a place in science it is a commonplace, is conveniently overlooked by the objectors. The sacred itself, of course, must remain ununderstood if it is "understood", as it is by all debunkers and disenchanters of the universe of man, as a kind of last reservation of traditional ritualistic conventions in a world of causal and purposive rationality in which one might as well do without it; any rite or cult that—in the true experience of its followers—submits to such a formula, already has ceased to be sacred because it has ceased to stand in living communication with its own phenomenal sources in *experience*. Precisely this severance of communication with the immediate *sensibleness* of the symbolic, which first takes the *form* (and subsequently, at its more advanced stage, becomes the *fate*) of magic thinking, is but the outcome of that alienation of the "place of God" itself of which Heidegger speaks in his essay on Nietzsche[43] and into which causal-purposive rationality inescapably must force the sacred, as it is doing in our time. The sacred, then, like any phenomena immediately understood by the psyche, can never even conceivably be understood by using that same dubious rationality for an analysis of the last fuzzy shadows which that—now nothing but "peculiar"—entity still manages to throw into our midst, but only by re-experiencing it in its authentic revelations, which a magic-rationalistic[44] ideology ever serves to obscure. What are the experience-forms such revelations appear in? Even where the enduringly *fundamental* situation of an existence itself compels, as in the *sacred of love*, to be first encountered in the "magic" form of the fetish,[45] in all authentic experience of the *absolute* (or sacred) this element does not occur in any *isolation* from the "profane" but rather shows an effusion-like and all-engulfing quality: it issues from (and has its strongest concentration in) the focal phenomena of true mythical experience but on its way into more and more peripheral (profane) experience-zones it passes over without sharp boundaries into those concentrations of lesser "density", lesser immediacy and timelessness, lesser sacredness of the sacred, which the concepts of the *sound* or *wholesome* and finally of the *whole* itself connote;[46] not without compelling reason, the *whole, holistic, health, healing,* all linguistically relate to *holy.* The sacred, then, does not begin in the sphere of religious cults, let alone of their ritual surfaces no longer apprehended, but begins with any spontaneous human experience of everyday living the immediate significance of which, no matter whether sanctioned by official religion or convention, transcends a causal-purposive account of *existence* by the operational *ratio*—a qualification which, as we may recognize at this point,[47] implies an essential identity of all immediate experience with the encountered presence of the meaning of true *symbols.* Precisely this is what utilitarian man, with the position itself of his understanding *outside* of the immediacy of his own being that calls for it from *within,* has difficulty to grasp; his relation even to the things nearest to him, the things he owns, has become so empty that, to paraphrase a word by Rilke, he is used to mass-produce or purchase his book, his apple, his house, his vehicle, today and consume or sell it tomorrow, and he cannot understand that none of these entities has any but the most extrinsic similarity with those objects (*categorially identical* with those we named) into which, to quote Rilke directly, "the effort and love of our ancestors had entered".

He stands on the outside of the myth of being, which only for this standing outside of it *is* to him[48] a *myth;* he stands on its outside in the same sense and manner as L. G., who, as we remember, was sometimes "on the outside" of his own interests, his realities, his engagements. That the myth only therefore is one to the utilitarianist critic, does not question the veracity of the latter's debunking impulse; it only questions the truth of the world-rapport which he attains through it, which is the same as saying that what it questions is the truth of his existential position that gives rise to the impulse. The utilitarianist critic is right about the myth as he understands it; what is not right, what in fact simply tends to be missing, is solely his understanding, which by definition is knowledge of something from *within;* the actuality of the myth, since it is a mode of world apperception and thus horizon-like to the myth-bound psyche, since, in other words, it already in its own constitution presupposes that inside knowledge in order to *be* at all, is therefore the diametrical opposite of the "appearance" of the myth to the one or ones who perceive it from its outside. Since perception of appearances, however, can be a penetration towards their essences,[49] the enlightened critic, if he follows the legitimate Socratic rather than the less expensive utilitarianist tradition (and besides happens to be a reasonably good observer), must not, when finding himself faced with the facts of human symbolic experience, get stuck in pragmatist platitudes about it; he may come to the realization that the magic, for example, is at its root no "primitive" misunderstanding of *causality* after all—primitivity rather being a mark of this theory *about* it— but a function of immediate expressiveness that has nothing to do with deliberate reasoning to start with. Owing to the *a priori* externality of his own position vis-a-vis the phenomena of symbolic experience, however, he cannot go farther; since he must misidentify *thought* with an abstractive organization of data,[50] the immediate noetic content of symbolic experience escape him as much as the concreteness in which authentically they occur: in the previously considered Gestaltist manner,[51] the symbolic, then, becomes itself a function of abstraction.

Both phases of the error can be discerned with exemplary clarity in Susanne K. Langer's *Philosophy in a New Key.*[52] The misunderstanding of symbolic experience as *abstract* may occupy us first: treating of magic, which Langer fails consistently to distinguish from the two other forms, she says (of a "savage") : "It is not ignorance of causal relations, but the supervention of an interest stronger than his practical interests that holds him to magical rites. This stronger interest concerns the *expressive* value of such mystic acts".[53] Yet it is evident[54] that precisely the *expressive* value of an expression does not concern the one who expresses but the analyst of the expressive product, the physiognomist; whoever spontaneously does "express" (and the more so the more expressive, or immediately convincing, his expression turns out to be) is not concerned with a *post hoc* external abstraction from his act of expressing as a psychological object, not with his own expressivity (which precisely in this case never would be what it is), but with *what he has to express*. But what, then, does the "savage" express in the magical rite? Langer, a few lines later, arguing that it is natural for primitive man to perform it, leaves no doubt about what she means by *natural* by comparing this type of act with the "spontaneous" acts of bees and birds. It is significant for this naturalism that her power of observation breaks down only under the weight of such speculation: the acts of bees to which she links the magic rite can be accounted for throughout in terms of recognizable practical purposes they serve; to the extent to which the acts of birds seem to transcend these, on the other hand, the information that they are natural is no more informative than it is in the case of the magic rite itself.

This abstractionist by-passing of the immediate noetic contents of any authentic ritual—of the primary truth-reality unity embodied in the holy, the wholesome, and the whole—inevitably leads to other breakdowns of observation; the attitude of knowing-everything-already which, regardless of whether they know themselves as rationalists or not, is characteristic of all objectifiers of subjectivity,[55] inheres not necessarily in the individual theoretician, who may honestly strive for the detachment of true empiricalness, but in the position itself which his theorizing *a priori* is occupying. The consequence, however—which challenged phenomenology into existence—must be an increasingly hasty and superficial way of looking at phenomena, at any of them at least which at the same time seem remote and yet half-way understandable. Being half-way understandable means that the noetic contents of authentic phenomenal experience underlying their "appearances" can be re-experienced *vaguely*; in the now already known manner of confounding one's own understanding of a symbol from without its original eidetic sphere with the understanding of the original beholders from *within* it, the vagueness will itself then be attributed to the latters' way of thinking, with an *impressionism of the symbolic* as the quite certain theoretical result. Langer, functionalizing *images* into *instruments* "for abstracting concepts from the tumbling stream of actual impressions",[56] argues for this position by referring to what she seems to sense as the inexactitude of the fact that "fire is a natural symbol of life and passion, *though* it is the one element *in* which nothing can actually live".[57] The error is, of course, not in the symbol but in the *though* of the sentence we quoted. The symbol itself connotes an *identity* (in essence, not in fact) between *life* and *fire*. The *in* connotes nothing of the sort but the environment that surrounds the life-fire: it connotes a *duality* relation. It only yields the logical surface of the error to say that the constitutions of an environment and of what it surrounds are two different matters; it does not yield as yet the truth of the symbol—its strength on precisely the ground on which Langer contends its ("sense-experiential") weakness.[58] In order to recognize the latter, we have first to re-experience in the concrete (as the ancients themselves experienced it) the timeless truth of the theory of the *phenomenal elements* as inclusive of all being[59] (position A); furthermore, we have to think through— position B—the implications of the rapport (self-world) between a *being* and whatever it is *not* (its "environment"), a rapport of which the O-S formula of behaviorism gives but a pale and uncompelling shadow. The O-S connotes a side by side of object-*items*, one of them defined as organism, the other as stimulus, which the formula arbitrarily confronts with one another in abstract space; the *existential rapport*, contrariwise, on the irreducible notion of which this formula depends without admitting it, is in essence a polarity. Polar to one another is what substantially *excludes* one another: if only what is not fire is left to be life's *world*, life itself (*vide* position A) *is fire* already by the logic of elimination. Langer's facts thus confirm fire as a life symbol; the impressionism, which her chapter on "Life-Symbols; the Roots of Sacrament", charges, is not on the part of the image which her discussion takes up but on that of the discussion.

With the regaining of immediate accesses to immediate knowledge the problem of therapeutic rapport, of therapeutic rapport especially with the psychotic, stands or falls: "symbolic experience", which is our abstract and roundabout term for immediate knowledge,[60] inheres in the psychotic's every word or act that strikes the diagnostician as

unintelligibly odd or bizarre. We remember the schizophrenic highly
skilled in arithmetic who yet failed every *additive* problem, if only by
one position which he added to or subtracted from his solutions: five
plus five invariably was eleven, forty-eight plus seventy-three invariably
one hundred twenty-two. What *was* it that he added? He did not
know it, if knowledge means the payment of focal attention to the
known, which he was afraid to pay, as his reaction to questions
showed why it was that he did it; yet all the more he *knew* it, as a
man knows that he can speak when what he is speaking shows his
attention centered not on his faculty of speech but on Peruvian
excavations. Does this move his knowledge that he can speak into a
nebulous subterrane of his psyche which we could sensibly call unconscious? It only removes it, and on one plane of consciousness, from
the phenomenal midst of his attention field where matters are *present*
to him conceptually, toward the periphery, the horizon—into the self-
evident and thus *ever*-present perceptual ground with which the "figure",
that his attention focalizes as he speaks, contrasts. It was not different
with out schizophrenic. Horizon-like, or rather that which blocked the
horizon in his case, had become the knowledge that *he had always been
left out,* and this knowledge was but in strict accordance with the
facts of his biography.

Once this was understood, nothing was more natural than that he
should always add *himself* where the opportunity of *adding* arose in
the first place; but he not only added, he also subtracted himself, when
subtraction was the task of the hour, for it was not self-assertion that
motivated him, but world-sharing: he had been left out from the world
as the locus of *participation,* so he participated as the *one* he knew he
was, in whatever engagement or action (and however self-sacrificial
was its demand) the world called for; multiplication and division, as
soon came out, included, though not visibly so, as the role of the *one*
in these operations made its induction inconspicuous.

It was said after this had transpired, that K.'s was a case of con-
cretistic thinking; yet, in his arithmetic and elsewhere, he gave every
sign of unimpaired capacities of abstracting. What was meant by that
concretism (the true instances of which, in other cases than his, only
result from such fixations, as they increasingly may immobilize thought)
was something generically wholly different, which escapes the polarity
of abstract versus concrete:[61] the literalness with which he experienced

his *situations*. This immediate occurrence of existential significances, which, as we saw, is of the essence of the ritual, demanded priority over the purposive scheme of rational operation as it always and legitimately demands it—in love, in religion, in art, in play; but in distinction from the free assertion of this title in the mentioned spheres of symbolic experience and activity, in distinction also from that unfree rebelliousness with which, in the ego-alien phenomena of compulsive neurosis, it breaks into the nothing-but-operational action system of the ego, to challenge the ego's claim to *be the self*,[62] it was behind the rationality of the interfered-with operation itself that this *interest* of the patient's existence here hid: K. never, as later in his remission he remembered, was unaware that his act would have been arbitrary, a violation of logic and thus of the very world order which he cherished, *if* he had induced into his problems a "factor" they them-selves did not contain. ·

The gist of his position was precisely that they *did* contain that factor to start with; only those who handed the problems to him were, in their blindness, oblivious to the evidence of it. They merely passed the problems on to him like messenger boys who mutilate a text they fail to grasp in relaying it to its addressee; the receiver of the message then has to reconstruct its true wording according to what seems sensible in terms of its topic as he knows it. That, being left out of the world everywhere, it was *everywhere* (consequently in any arith-metic operation too) that he was called upon first to correct that original error of his very universe, an error which inhered in the world's standard account of *it all* and which therefore its account of any single task was bound to contain on its part, *seemed sensible.*

Once this was understood by the therapist, the patient's isolation was broken: no longer was he left out, his fundamental experience was shared, the stationary pressure which the effect of knowing oneself as isolated—further isolation—had exercised on him, removed; his arith-metic was not the only line of behavior which at once registered the change. To find himself understood did not in itself yet constitute existential liberation; but the road toward such liberation, which as always led via a discovery of the *active* character of "participation", of participation as *engagement,* of an opportunity which the patient had forgotten and which yet was ostensibly his, to *live his own truth,* was unblocked for him by this first experience of finding himself understood. Therapy, in consequence, not only was possible with this psychotic but was successful; it was successful because the therapist *a priori* did not subscribe to the psychoanalytic tenet according to which a liberating insight—which itself of course meant something very different here from what it means in psychoanalysis[63]—must be an event on the patient's part; the liberating insight that unhinges a schizophrenic fixation is without exception an inner task of the therapist which the therapist does or does not accomplish. This task is in most cases incomparably more difficult than it was in K.'s; the treatment situation in this instance, with its relatively ready transparence, is not typical, certainly, of the degree of the ordinary complexity of treatment situations encountered in the face of schizophrenia. Yet it was typical of the *kind* of complexity inherent in this illness, paradigmatic of the essence of what in schizophrenic experience *is* schizophrenic, and so precisely what was exceptional here, the relative ease of the understanding and cure of which it allowed, may contribute to furthering the cause of understanding and cure of the schizophrenic in general.

What it points up as the condition *sine qua non* of any future progress in this area is a better understanding of the structure of knowledge itself and hence of *attention;*[64] if qualitative clinical observation had not fallen to a low in our time compared with which the descriptions and studies of early psychiatry often astound by their brilliant perceptiveness, already such a simple phenomenon as the craving of some psychotics for opportunities of centering their attention on *something*—on anything—in order to escape the mortifying submersion in hallucinatory experience-floods[65] they know so well should have drawn the attention of psychiatrists and psychologists to the problems-in-principle of attention and of its engagements. On these phenomena, their sound forms and their sick ones, all theorizing about consciousness and the unconscious indeed hinges with the greatest emphaticness conceivable, and this dictum, which is only one of strict empiricalness, is not restricted to a demand for clinical (*external*) perceptiveness of the diagnostician and the therapist, since the other necessity on which the phenomenological revisions of psychology were seen as hinging at least as much —a critical attention for the phenomenal background of one's own most "ready" *conceptual notions*—requires the same detached openness of experiencing and attention in the theorist. Unless the latter requirement, which in the concrete means a living distrust in the *categorial per se* is met as much as the former, existential participation such as all true psychotherapy requires remains obstructed by fixations within the therapist such as were shown at the end of our chapter IX; an observation that sheds light on the difference between the two main streams of psychopathological theorizing that the philosophy of existence inspired and that we may roughly designate as the Heidegger and Jaspers schools of thought.

Somewhat simplifying, we may say that a division of roles has developed: the Jaspers school poses problems, the Heidegger school (Binswanger, Boss, R. Kuhn, *et al.*) re-thinks (and often explodes) them from the standpoint of the existences by whose cases and case histories they are posed. The passion for systematicness that inheres in Jaspers' psychopathology as it does in his philosophical work also predisposes it toward the task of a mere recording and formulating of such discrepancies between normal and abnormal modes of world apperception as themselves tend to escape a normal mode of understanding unless and until the latter is allowed to avail itself of the instrumentalities of phenomenological reduction; it is not, on the other hand, any lack of understanding for the necessity of full existential participation on the clinician's part, which he perhaps was the first both to practice and to demand of others, that restricted Jaspers *therapeutically*. *Allgemeine Psychopathologie*, with its magnificent exemplifications and discoveries, as besides it Jaspers' revolutionizing pathographic studies on Strindberg, Van Gogh,[66] Hölderlin,[67] Swedenborg,[68] and Nietzsche,[69] testified to the unreserved intensity of this participation, and so does a personal statement of Jaspers which Kolle[70] reports: "What we are missing!" Jaspers said: "What opportunities of understanding we let pass by because at a single decisive moment we were, with all our knowledge, lacking in the simple virtue of a *full human presence.*"

Jaspers' concluding distinction, in this statement, between human *presence* and human *knowledge*, a distinction *Daseinsanalyse* does not recognize as valid in any ultimate sense,[71] hints at the reason for the restriction we spoke of: phenomenology, in Jaspers' conception of it (which, except for a rather limited range of classes of eidetic objects,[72] does not acknowledge phenomenology in its status as a reduction of experiential contents to a sphere of axiomatic essences accessible in principle to human intellection[73]), is itself restricted to what might better be called phenomenography, a descriptive recording of immediate subjective experience as reported, for example, by a person under psychiatric examination, without questioning the share in such a communication of the ego; with a determination of the ego Jaspers himself would not concur in, this share is, in substance, that of the conventional semi-reflectiveness of *language* and of the perennial self-misunderstanding of existence of which, in its operational usages and the small talk of everyday, language inclines to make itself the instrument. Thus, a psychopathology of the Jaspers type may record the catatonic's *body* sensitivity, visual and haptic hallucinations, phenomenal separations between experienced movement initiatives and objective motor impulses which he witnesses, and his typical *cosmic Wahn* ideas; the paranoid's *ego* sensitivity, auditory hallucinations, separations between objective and *assumed* ego identities, and *social-speculative Wahn* ideas, but either of these patterns it would record only as clinically occurring symptom constellations; what unifies each of them and marks out the evident contrast between them as an essential polarity (if a polarity on one plane of schizophrenic disruption of the being-in-the-world), the implicit reference in each of the catatonic symptoms named to a primary self-understanding of existence as *spatial,* in each of the paranoid ones of existence as *temporal,* escapes such recording. It escapes it, certainly not because the observations just referred to lie beyond the reach of the theorists' power of conception here but because as observations—otherwise they would indeed be purely speculative—they presuppose that readiness for the perception of essences as realities, of which only an acknowledgment of the possibility of inter-existential communication, of world-sharing, as a systematic scientific one—not merely a matter of the presence or absence of full human alertness as a momentary fact of the clinician's attitude—admits in principle.

The same holds also for the problem of amnestic aphasia, which in a different context we had occasion to look into,[74] and for such a problem as Gruhle poses in his paper on "Psychopathology and Academic Training".[75] He first recapitulates the Jaspers tenet[76]—perhaps the most epochal empiric discovery of this thinker—that schizophrenic experience (and schizophrenic *thought* at least as much as reality experience) lacks characteristics which are self-evident (*focally* unknown, as we would say) to the normal, so that it is of these characteristics that the clinician has first to gain conceptual awareness if he wishes even to have the fundament of a chance to understand the experiences of schizophrenics. The two characteristics of this kind that make all the difference in the case of such experiences as concern the phenomenal *identity* of a person with *manifestations of his own psyche* are experienced *Ichqualität* (ego-quality, here meant to connote the quality of a partaking in the self) and experienced *Impulsqualität* (impulse quality). Gruhle denies these characteristics not only for the schizophrenic but for the mediumistic person and the inspired, a determination which—especially as concerns the latter—radical phenomenology not only would question as a probable distortion by means of insufficiently descriptive (and insufficiently many) concepts but which Gruhle himself half takes back a few lines later by granting *Ichqualität* to the experience of the occurrence-to-one of an *idea*. His real question arises from a comparison between the *role* of the medium, who is but an executive organ of some alien subjectivity, and the *situation* of a schizophrenic who experiences his thoughts as authoritatively made and imposed on him by someone else. The two categories, *Ichqualität* and *Impulsqualität*, which are true only in their phenomenal origin as conceptualizations of the basic difference between normal and psychotic thought experience in its comprehensive polarity but become untrue, as happens to categories so often, once they are turned into instruments of sub-differential analysis,[77] fail here, as Gruhle admits, for do we not know that mediumistic and schizophrenic thought experience are substantially different matters? The same terms "stand for entirely heterogeneous matters", Gruhle writes. "All one can do, without such make-shift really being satisfactory, is to assume that the medium's disturbance or paralysis of ego-initiative is itself subject to some kind of intellectual steering that conceivably distinguishes it from the meaningless one of schizophrenics".[78] This almost automatic attribution of meaninglessness to something ununderstandable which one experiences as such is, of course, nothing new; the assumption of intellectual steering in the medium would, on the other hand, seem too sensational to be convincing. The limits of the Jaspers conception of clinical phenomenology show up at this point: *passivity* and *receptivity* are not reflected in their *a priori* and pervasive heterogeneity,[79] and neither is the obvious relation between the experience-modi Gruhle deals with and the—themselves forever irreducible—arche-phenomena of *masculinity* and *femininity* seen at all. It is in this manner that the essence of personality divergences is missed: the fundamental differences between the "feminine" receptivity of the medium, the "masculine" receptivity of the inspired, and the object-like *passivity* of the schizophrenic self according to the convictions of his own ego and therefore[80] according to the facts of his existence receive no chance to clarify themselves.

The limitations of the Jaspers conception of phenomenology and the unlimited and gratefully acknowledged richness of Jaspers' clinical observations and enucleations of problems, this contrast about circumscribes the position of the Jaspers school as it shapes up in the vista of *Daseinsanalyse*. While such investigations as Minkovski's into time experience[81] or into the genesis of contact anxiety,[82] Kuhn's into the therapy of simple existences,[83] Conrad's into *Vorgestalten*,[84] or Minkovska's into the experiential structures of "combined" psychoses,[85] are possible only from a standpoint of radical phenomenology, existential analysis, at this time of writing, appears but as the central current within a much vaster movement of re-thinking the status and scientific nature of man. This movement, which in its entirety feeds on the psychopathological studies and literary work of Sartre as much as on Kierkegaard, on inspirations by such theologians as Barth, Brunner, Tillich, or Buber as much as on Jaspers' insistence on the impossibility of a pre-reflective transcendence, on Heidegger's most recent inquiries into the *quadruple insufficiency* of all past determinations of being[86] as much as on Marcel's less daring, if not less amiable, phenomenological analyses, is in any actual sense no longer even limited to Europe. Books only recently published in this country, such as Fromm's *Forgotten Language*,[87] Tillich's *The Courage to Be*,[88] and Rollo May's *Man in Search of Himself*[89] have taken up topics and exhibited conceptions of unmistakable affinity to the observations and themes of the thinkers of existence, and Schachtel's studies in Rorschach "factors" and exceedingly perceptive paper on memory[90] may be cited as tokens of a first audacious pioneering into the vast and virgin territory still awaiting cultivation by an American phenomenological psychology to come.

As we view the comparative history of the sciences, a striking difference between the developments of psychology and of physics appears. Before physics was drawn into the limelight of public attention by the enormity of its practical consequences for man and his society, it enjoyed that serene independence from pragmatic needs and pressures, that undisturbed privilege of dealing with its problems for the sake of Truth only, without which it would not have grown as a science in the first place. It is evident that psychology, to gain that maximum of freedom from inner restrictions of its theorists on which it depends so badly, was even more in need of such splendid solitude for its tasks, yet it has grown faster as a profession than as a science, stimulated more by needs of a pragmatic kind than by its own problems in their pureness. In principle, nothing can be more unhealthy for any science, including, ultimately, any applications of science; yet, since this development cannot be reversed, should psychology not be able to turn its plight into an asset by being true to Truth at last—by using its newly won societal influence against the very interests that fostered it? Is it not time for the psychologist to refuse and reject the abominable assignment to any such tasks or role definitions as *human engineering?* In the past, psychology had allowed itself to be used as one of many levers in the rapid mechanization of man that our century has seen; but if its growth as a profession was thus founded on a fundamental untruth, one of the fruits which that same growth has left it is an unequalled opportunity for making good where it has failed. The new tyrant holding man and his future in bondage is the robot within and without. The struggle to cast off his yoke is only now opening. Anyone, and any whole branch of knowledge and of practice as well, that should still prove responsive to the situation and essence of man, can lead in that fight. Psychologists have not missed, nor irreparably forfeited, their chance. Their task—the hour of their trial—is only coming.

NOTES

1. Cf. p. 55.
2. Cf. C. G. Jung, and W. Pauli, "Synchronizität als ein Prinzip akausaler Zusammenhänge", *Naturerklärung und Psyche*, Zurich, 1952, 1–107.
3. Cf. C. G. Jung, "Grundfragen der Psychotherapie", *Dialecticon*, 1951, 5, 8–24.
4. Cf. p. 62.
5. Cf. p. 10.
6. Cf. p. 20.
7. Cf. pp. 61–62.
8. Cf. p. 3.
9. Cf. p. 32.
10. Cf. p. 132.
11. K. Conrad, *Der Konstitutionstypus als genetisches Problem*, Berlin, 1941.
12. Cf. pp. 21, 43.

13. For the body-constitutional and charactological definitions of these and of the other differential concepts used by Conrad, we refer to Kretschmer's own original work.

14. Cf. pp. 133–34.

15. Cf. p. 344.

16. Cf., K. Conrad, *op cit.*: "According to again different principles-of-growing, a different set of *types* could be established." This, of course, implies no arbitrariness or fictitiousness of such *types*, nor does it detract from the lawfulness inherent in each of their *possible* sets: the "principles of growing" themselves which Conrad's typology follows up are no speculative but phenomenological ones; they are not established through abstraction from "traits" of dubious psychological relevance and even more dubious identity of substance, but, like the classic *temperaments* and like Kretschmer's original types, are *perceived*. Such perceptions, while actualized by the empiric encounter with individual phenomena of immediate typological representativeness, are according to their own phenomenal constitution no cognitions of anything fleetingly factual but of essential possible qualities (and sets of such qualities) at once of the being human and of the whole gamut of spatio-temporal *Gestalten* (physiognomic-eidetic *ideas* in their objectivity) of which the potential or the norms inhere axiomatically in the *animate per se*. In accordance with this idea-bound constitution of typological *perceptions*, however, not a single required position within one set of types can any more coincide intrinsically—in the sense of any true identity—with any one within another set of types than is the case in respect to certain "ambiguous" arrangements, allowing of multiple and mutually exclusive *phenomenal identities*, in the experimental psychology of perception. Typologies, therefore, are by necessity mutually exclusive; they can never be interrelated directly but only by referring any two or more of them to their common "ground": the *type*, in both its essential *Prägnanz* (eidetic definiteness) and its *temporal* variability, is at once an "idea" of the typologist and an *idea* unfolded in its "objectivity" by the *being* itself which he cognizes. Cf. also p. 235.

17. Cf. p. 213.

18. Cf. p. 9.

19. Cf. pp. 28–58.

20. Cf. pp. 138, 211.

21. Cf. p. 316.

22. Cf. pp. 124–25.

23. A more detailed discussion of this subject would exceed the limits of this study. Concerning the problem it poses, cf., besides the foregoing passage and p. 238, K. Jasper's *op. cit.*, pp. 214–32.

24. For at least one aspect of the entire *paradoxicalness*—from the empiricist's viewpoint—of the constitution of perception, cf. K. Jaspers, *op. cit.*, p. 221: "In the case of rough proportions, the measuring instruments are safer than our estimates, in those of the subtle morphological proportions, which *physiognomically* matter most, the *eye* is far more sensitive and exact."

25. Cf. p. 247.

26. Cf. pp. 237–38.

27. Cf. pp. 14–15.

28. Cf. pp. 11, 91–92, 200, 205.

29. *Appearance*, of course, in the fundamental *physiognomic* sense that applies here, is not what underlies the de-phenomenalized perceptions of the typical contemporary and his world approach; it is not appearance in terms of the traditional theological and metaphysical antinomy of *being* and *appearing*, but in the much older sense which this antinomy itself came to obscure and has continued to obscure since. Cf. M. Heidegger, *Einführung in die Metaphysik*, Tübingen, 1953, esp. pp. 75–88; also, p. 27 of the present text.

30. Cf. p. 316.

31. Cf. our analysis of Freud's confounding of "horizontal" with "vertical" intra-psychic polarities, p. 172, and of the characteristic partiality of the psycho-analytic attack, p. 257.

32. Cf. pp. 169–73.

33. Cf. p. 206.

34. Within the multi-dimensional domain of a typology developed according to such criteria as Conrad's (cf. pp. 317–20) the entire group of personality types inclining toward ego-alien experiences can be shown to occupy positions in the *center* (at once of Conrad's first and of his third polarities), with phobics and addicts closer to the "dysplastic", obsessives and compulsives to the "plastic" pole of the dimension of growth impediment (third polarity); the actual development of pathology itself would depend, as elsewhere, on the individual constellations of growth tendencies in terms of the second polarity, hyperplastic-hypoplastic. Correspondingly, the specific sub-type of ego-alien pathology that results is independent of its own actualization by the post-natal personal history of a subject: this actualization as such is comprehensible in terms of positions within the second polarity, but *what* it actualizes remains determined by what in Jungian concepts has been called the ambiversion of the obsessive-compulsives (the nearly equal participation in their make-up of pycnic and leptomorph tendencies of growth). In terms of Conrad, accordingly, this ambiversion can be defined as a central range of positions within the first polarity, the dimension of primary organic *forms*. The correspondingly indecisive balance of the obsessive-compulsive's world apperception, which motivationally-noetically implies its very opposite (the imbalance of all *uncertainty of direction*) raises problems of homeostasis in the face of which the formation of ego-alien patterns of experience is the typical attempt at solution in all those cases where conflicting growth tendencies of the second polarity *actualize* the problem of balance itself as a conflict unsolvable within the boundaries of the self-as-ego, forbidding any such answers to the problem as do not in themselves involve an experiential alienation of one whole pole of the self. While we must abstain from a closer tracing of these dynamics and of their sub-varieties in the different syndromes named, it may be emphasized on this occasion that the decisively actualizing role of the person's world rapport for his health or pathology, which Conrad's theory of psychobiological genetics so accentuates, implies *in principle* an accessibility to psychotherapy of all (non-organic) abnormal personality patterns; the person's "somatotype" in

its position along the second bi-polar dimension of Conrad is no more than a physiognomic statement of his post-natal *past*.

35. Cf. pp. 172, 211.

36. Cf. pp. 171, 175.

37. The mythical, the magic, and the mystic not only are ever recurrent historic forms of human experience as a *participation in being* (occurring as an immediate sensibleness of the *symbolic*) but can be understood in terms of one set of phenomenological laws that renders visible their necessity, their combined *inclusiveness* for human symbolic experience, and their tendency to *exclude* one another in their concrete occurring. Their realm comprises all spheres of existential interest, but their role is less obvious in such a sphere as the economic interests of man as compared with the evidence of its position in love, religion, political ideation, and so on. The three forms of symbolic experience, futhermore, govern different forms of experienced *time*, from the standing ever-presence of the mystic via the *finite time* ("beginning" and "end of time") of the myth to "time" as a *threat to continuity* (compulsive and magic form of time experience; cf. p. 218).

38. Cf. the derivation of the German *währen*, to last, to endure, from *wahr*, true.

39. Cf. p. 212.

40. The following are named together only as diverse types of human experiential reference to the *sacred*; just their forms of encountering the sacred can, however, show mythical or mystic as well as magic forms. In the magic form, which always appears to serve a role complementary and compensatory to a state of radical dualism between *self* and *world*, to *rationalism* as the prevalent orientation modus of a person or whole society, the sacred only becomes most fetish-like (becomes so isolated and factualized that its *immediate truth* becomes obscured by the codified role which it is forced to assume in such an instance). Contrariwise, in the mythical and mystic experience-forms the sacred pervades and unifies the self and the world; what distinguishes them, is its fluid-like encounter as a force tearing down all isolating boundaries of individuation in the mystic, its childlike definiteness and *at hand* character (taking the form of an evident sensibleness of all *things as such*) in the mythical experience-forms; accordingly, in the extent to which any succession of them within *one* biographic or historic existence can be made out at all, the mythical form tends to precede, the mystic to follow historically, the magic. Since the magic-mystic-mythical differentiation of experience applies to the sexual interest as to all others, Boss' theory which we outlined might be clarified further by examining the given forms of the love interest in man in the light of the order of experience-forms here referred to; the ritualizing character of *fetishism* has often been noted, but precisely the *obviousness*, here and elsewhere, of a subtype of magic experience, as compared with the mythical and the mystic, seems to inhere in its "specialistic" qualities, its tendency toward an isolation of certain objects in their facticity (their *abstractness*; cf. pp. 62, 78). Methodologically, this observation forbids to infer from the *evidently* magic character of fetishism any exclusiveness of its participation in the three modi of symbolic experience named; empirically, the phenomenal structures typical of the two others can be shown not any less plausi-

bly to coincide with those of many different (normal as well as abnormal) elaborations of the *norm of love* (cf. p. 301).

41. Only in passing we may note that, in distinction from such simpler and understandably *perennial* forms of pathology as the manic-depressive, schizophrenic, epileptic, and hysteric, for which documentation exists from almost all periods, the historic past of the compulsion neurotic is at least uncertain; his exclusive appearance in societal circumstances dominated, as our civilization has been since the eighteenth century, by rationalism as an *existence-modus,* would not seem inconceivable. Cf. pp. 96–97.

42. Cf. pp. 15–16.

43. Cf. p. 129.

44. The historical affinity between the magic and rationalism shows up in the magic nature of modern technical civilization, which is gradually being perceived by a greater number of thinkers, especially by thinkers reflecting on its concrete impacts on the situation of man. As a glance into *space fiction* or the average comic book, the preoccupation with push-button miracles and uncounted similar observations make clear, modern technology—at its *present* stage—is primitive wish fulfillment almost throughout. The airplane, for example, in which man steps into a cabin isolating him from the lofty element through which he rides, has nothing in the least to do with the Icarus *myth* and the timeless *orientative* theme of human existence it embodies: what stirs Icarus is the eternal challenge man faces to overcome his earthly bondage, to act against his given condition, to *fly regardless.* The airplane, contrariwise, reveals itself as a realization of the oriental (and Mephistophelian) *wish* theme of the flying cloak or carpet, a topic of wishing traditionally linked with the might of *magicians.*

45. Cf. M. Boss, *op. cit.,* pp. 39–55.

46. M. Heidegger, Über den Humanismus, pp. 36–37.

47. Cf. pp. 124, 127.

48. Cf. p. 16.

49. Cf. pp. 140–41.

50. Cf. pp. 23, 74, 125.

51. Cf. p. 73.

52. S. K. Langer, *Philosophy in a New Key,* New York, 1949.

53. *Ibid.,* p. 39.

54. Cf. p. 271.

55. Cf. pp. 16, 60, 164.

56. *Ibid.,* p. 117.

57. *Ibid.;* italics supplied.

58. *Ibid.*

59. Cf. p. 239.

60. Cf. pp. 120, 123–25, 357–58.

61. Cf. pp. 71–73, 293–94.

62. Cf. p. 205.

63. Cf. pp. 174–75.

64. Cf. p. 27.

65. Cf. Bonhöiffer, *Die akuten Geisteskrankheiten der Gewohnheitstrinker*, Jena, 1901; Schreber, *Denkwürdigkeiten eines Nervenkranken*, Leipzig, 1903; Jaspers, *op. cit.*, pp. 117–18.

66. Jaspers, "Strindberg und van Gogh." *Versuch einer pathologischen Analyse unter vergleichender Heranziehung von Swedenborg und Hölderlin;* Sammlung "Arbeiten zur angewandten Psychiatrie", Bern 1922.

67. *Ibid.*

68. *Ibid.*

69. Jaspers, "Die Denkweise Nietzsche's im Ganzen seiner Existenz", in *Nietzsche, Einführung in das Verständnis seines Philosophierens*, Berlin 1936.

70. K. Kolle, "Pathologie des sozialen Kontaktes", in *Offener Horizont, p.* 179; italics supplied.

71. Cf. pp. 125, 130.

72. Cf. pp. 149–51.

73. While this is in agreement with Husserl's dictum that no ultimate *whats* or "quiddities" are ever given in and through sensory experience, it fails to appreciate Husserl's insight into the essence-approximational structure of "purified" appearances-to-the-mind with which reductive phenomenology deals.

74. Cf. pp. 274–75.

75. H. W. Gruhle, "Psychopathologie und akademischer Unterricht" in *Offener Horizont.*

76. Cf. pp. 24–25.

77. Cf. pp. 80–81.

78. W. H. Gruhle, *op. cit.*, p. 159.

79. Cf. p. 110.

80. Cf. pp. 135, 153.

81. E. Minkovski, "Que veut dire 'Ancestral'?", *Archives Suisses de Neurologie et de Psychiatrie*, 1951, 47, 66–74.

82. E. Minkovski, "Le Contact humain", *Revue de Métaphysique et de Morale*, 1950, 2.

83. R. Kuhn, "Daseinsanalyse im psychotherapeutischen Gespräch", *Schweizer Archiv für Neurologie und Psychiatrie*, 1951, 47, 52–60. This study is important especially in view of the sometimes heard yet quite baseless conjecture that the existential analytic method of therapy could "reach" only the intellectual and the educated, an idea which the disturbing sight, for example, of Binswanger's humanistic erudition may explain; the erudition of Rousseau, Pestalozzi, or Herbart, as we may observe here, not only never prevented them from "reaching" children but seems positively to have had something to do with their powerful practical effects most of all on elementary education.

84. K. Conrad, Über den Begriff der Vorgestalt und seine Bedeutung für die Hirnpathologie, *Nervenarzt*, 18, 1947, 289.

85. (In connection with their constitutional and hereditary aspects;) F. Minkovska, *Epilepsie und Schizophrenie im Erbgang*, Zurich, 1937.

86. M. Heidegger, *Einführang in die Metaphysik*, 1953. *Being* as "reality" (that-which-is) is traditionally delineated against *becoming, appearance, thinking,* and

the *ought*, which however *are*, so that the stated delineations are interpreted by Heidegger as attributes of the inherent self-confoundingness of existence in that now climaxing (and perhaps *closing*) historic phase of a *severance from being* of which man's insufficiently *radical* reflectiveness (cf. p. 133) became the tool.

87. E. Fromm, *The Forgotten Language*, New York, 1951.

88. P. Tillich, *The Courage to Be*, New Haven, 1953.

89. R. May, *Man in Search of Himself*, New York, 1952.

90. E. G. Schachtel, "On Memory and Childhood Amnesia", in P. Mullahy, *A Study of Interpersonal Relations*, New York, 1949.

EPILOGUE

"For any theoretical determination of our being we have to pay; any such determination is a grip that clutches the *practice* of our future existence in advance; on it depends what shall become of us. *As man sees himself, thus he becomes*; in this there consists his freedom, to which he has to hold firm to be *human*. If we should fail to know how to limit our objectification of ourselves by a respect for the unrecognizable of our being, we shall resign our liberty, and the power of disposition over ourselves will be our death". These sentences of Plessner[1] sum up the position of existential thought in psychology as pithily as it can be summed up; they contain all or most of the keys to the discussions of the pages behind us; at the same time, they bring into focus an over-all determination of the relations between being and knowing that is the exact reverse of what the nineteenth and early twentieth centuries had thought of these relations.

The nineteenth and early twentieth centuries had thought of knowing as a registering of facts, which in turn they had stopped distinguishing from the truth about them; they had not been perceptive enough to note, either that knowing understands rather than registers or that understanding stands or falls with the notion of being as that which resists time (identity), whereas all facts are fleeting. The notion of *being* which, even though they never do without it in practice (for example, in their *is*-statements) must appear so strange and "metaphysical-sounding" to positivistic scientists as they behold its prominence in our study, is therefore no speculation of metaphysics in the least—which, inclusive of the metaphysics of positivists, it on the contrary has the power of exploding—but the first empiric datum of existence as *human* existence; just as compellingly, since the notion of being was seen to be absolutely underivable from "facts", its first implication is the *factualness* of transcendence as the central constituent of every single specific datum of our daily existences *as such*. This secures the legitimate place in psychology of the concepts of being and of transcendence;

354

since any even approximative solution of the problems which surround them—and among which that of the relationship between being and knowing is the one most fundamental—continues nevertheless to depend on immediate perceptiveness as much as radical reflection, what is exploded by this recognition is not more or less than the arbitrary and artificial boundary between philosophy and psychology as fields.

What is the *empiric* reason for its breakdown? Since such a statement as Plessner's which we quoted is backed up by observations *ad libitum,* the inference which he draws cannot but be drawn as one in a context of *psychological* theorizing; at the same time, the inference questions psychological theorizing as one has grown used, under positivism, to conceive of this endeavor. Psychological theorizing in that form is supposed to nail down facts; now the discovery is made that instead it tends to *produce* them. This is itself a psychological fact of the first order; can the philosophers, then, be blamed for it that its implications happen to transcend psychology? What are these implications? The form in which we stated that existentialist discovery is likely to create some misunderstanding: we spoke of the power of knowing to create its own realities. Is knowing arbitrary, then? Can one become what one "wants" by choosing to know oneself as this or that? We have a model case here for the complete confusion that must arise in the mind of the average scientist in the social and anthropological fields if he attempts to apprehend one tenet of existential reflection that revises a customary notion of psychology without at the same time following, and succeeding to understand, the revision of all others. Knowing does not preceed being; their predicative order is the other way around. But *being,* which is not *facticity,* as all facticity is contingent on being, takes the *form* of knowing in man, takes this form "constitutionally" and at all strata of his "psyche"; knowing, therefore, as it represents an absolute presence, as it represents what timelessly maintains itself through time, is that very stretching-towards-the-future, as which Heidegger determined its essence: *understanding.* Yet, in order to see this, one has first to free oneself from what knowing "pretends to be" according to the *post hoc* abstractions *from* it by which one has grown accustomed to account for its accomplishments. The nature of these abstractions consists in this that they make order among the residues ("facts") of the past according to the operational (categorial) system of logic. Existential reflection does not question what logic derives its compellingness from; it questions an obliviousness for that origin that inheres, for example, in the doctrine of "symbolic logic". Logic as a *positive* (operational) system remains dependent on precisely that notion of identity *the entire problem of which it by-passes*; but this makes it clash with itself implicitly, for the "facts" to which it is being applied do not stay identical with themselves even from one split second to the next. The problem of time and being thus is the absolutely first one precisely in those sciences in which the relationship between being and knowing becomes relevant, the sciences of man; the answer to it which we attempted to sketch in approximate contours in this book may not be shared, but neither can the problem itself any longer be escaped by scientists. This compellingness of the *problems* of existential reflection and of the dimensions of thought they open up is satisfaction enough; as only in an age of operationalism, in a world "adjusting" itself to the technician's unprecedentedly narrowed horizon, could be forgotten at all, even a problem unsolved is better than one capable of "solution" at the price of essential untruthfulness in the very act of posing it.

The technician's "separation" of science and philosophy has never been honest, if honesty shall be more than a matter of intentions; if it had, we would not constantly discover him *in flagranti* of tacit premises in his theories neither deriving from experience nor seemingly "known" to him in their strictly presuppositional status. The nature of ideology is that it enunciates the opposite of what its protagonists practice, and it is in this sense, the same in which we had found the empiricist a dogmatician, that we find a "freethinker" like Reichenbach restricting and censoring man's birthright to be a being that—from the child's spontaneous *why* on, that hence is as elementary to his nature as anything "animalic"—*asks questions*.[2] What form does this censorship take? The form of dividing questions into admissible and inadmissible ones; the latter are those which the "free inquirer" cannot answer and which he therefore deems unanswerable, or, with his synonym for what escapes him, *meaningless*. "The elimination of meaningless questions from philosophy", Reichenbach writes,[3] "is difficult because there exists a certain type of mentality that aspires to find unanswerable questions". But has not all knowledge, all insight man has ever found at all, been in answer to questions that *somebody* had deemed unanswerable? Who can read the quoted passage from *The*

Rise of Scientific Philosophy and not think of an embarrassed father who, after having encouraged his child to ask questions finds, not without some resentment, the questions beyond him? Reichenbach's attitude in the face of such questions as he finds comfortable to discard as meaningless is in strict accordance with the sensational redefinition of philosophy which is implicit in the world picture of the scientific specialist and which the author has had previous occasion to formulate in substance: philosophy is the locus of all points which the technician leaves unanswered.[4]

According to the nature of psychological and psychiatric work (as a type of work dealing with universes), specialization works against its own purpose when applied in these existent branches of the yet non-existent science of man; no mind whose very scope of experiences reaches beyond the investigator's can possibly be understood by that investigator. That this failure of understanding is due to occur where the investigator is a specialist—where his scope of experiences, his phenomenal *world*, is limited by his specialization as a categorial and operational scheme arbitrarily imposed upon a subject matter (man) that of itself extends *beyond* any such schemes[5]—is the perhaps most incisive one (in a sense of training significance) among the many revolutionary insights existentialist criticism of contemporary culture carries with it. The crisis of man, in one of its major aspects, is a crisis of his specialism, of the division of labor and of "professional viewpoints", and existentialism as the most articulate answer to this crisis so far would be untrue to its mission in *both* philosophy and "anthropological" psychology if it were to fail to demand an abrogation in principle of specialism as we know it. But in posing this demand, the last claim existentialist thinkers conceive of as a means to implement it is that complete falsification of an already questionable truth which sails under the flag of a popularization of science; if man in his present calamity shall make his way back to the truth of *being* he has lost, neither fiction nor "facts", only a courageous attack upon the fundamentals of his situation, can cut his path.

What *is* the truth that existential reflection "remembers"? Like anything that is *true*, something fundamentally simple; but is the simple necessarily the "popular"? In a technicized age that has come to hold this mistaken belief along with many others of its kind, an age mistaking its everyday abstractions for realities, its manipulations of the laws of nature for creations, the way back to the simplicity of essential truths, the way of communicating them to an audience educated only to pass them by, is paved with terminological complexities precisely on account of the position of the starting point that audience dwells at. Hegel's ironical words, according to which "when the people are supposed to think, they believe it has to be something particular", apply to this situation in an exemplary manner: the greatest difficulty the present study will have to overcome in its readers is the mistaken belief nurtured by two millenia of speculative ontologies of first the "metaphysical", later the "scientific" varieties, that thought can master anything specific, anything-that-is if it has not first *become* thought by probing itself on the fathomless "datum" of being and of its just as general but also—as the supreme fact of contemporary man's anxiety is demonstrating empirically—just as *real* opposite, the *naught*. It may appear "hard to follow" or even "speculative" to propose, as we have, that, for example, the customary dichotomy in psychology between the cognitive and the conative "functions" of the human psyche is in any ultimate sense fictitious rather than empirical; but is not precisely that "complexity" a consequence of the psychologist's by-passing, under a empiricistic *ideology*, of a tangible simplicity that only observation can convey? Is the "complexity" of that conception any longer a complexity if we only *dare* think it in the immediacy of its content? If we do—and it is not to be seen how thought that is not daring, that refuses to be a constant adventure in that *unknown* that is Reichenbach's "unanswerable", can be *thought*—we find the "complexity" turning into the simplicity of, for example, so pretty and inconspicuous a little fact as that, in English, one word, to *ask*, connotes at once the demand for *getting* something and for an *answer* that can "feed" one's knowledge. "Historic developments"? But what *axiomatic possibilities*, inherent in man's status, of verbal apperception as an articulation of the *sensible* allowed such "developments" specifically to take *that* course?

As we look back, the treatment of many matters still seems insufficiently elaborate; especially of those which, while of central relevance for psychopathology and psychotherapy, refer of their own nature to inquiries we were only permitted to trace, inquiries which to present exhaustively would far have exceeded the planned boundaries of this

study; likewise, only the most passing attention could be given matters
of such specificity as naturally refuse to be treated in a first introduction to the principles of a doctrine so radically deviating from all
the now current ones as *Daseinsanalyse*. The decline, during the first
half of this century, in the practice of thought truly *free*—free from
operational coercions, self-disciplined and self-steering—which the dis-
couragement of philosophy under the pretense of discouraging the
metaphysical idleness of the philosophies of yesterday brought about
under the very auspices of one of them—positivism—is nowhere more
painfully felt than in contemporary man's action problems of everyday
living; and psychotherapy is in a very substantial sense a study and a
practice dealing with action tenors. Heidegger's uncovering of the common roots of ontology and ethics, which to no one may be of greater
concern than just the psychotherapist, could be re-sketched only in a
nearly dehydrated condensation, and so could uncounted other subjects
of central significance for the present and the perennial situation of
man—subjects which an entire and still virtually untranslated literature
unfolds *in extenso*. Since psychoanalytic doctrine only now dominates
the scene of psychiatric thinking in our society, much space, finally,
had to be devoted to clarify the radicality of the departure of existential
analysis from Freud's fold; the criticism needed for such clarification
could not help being just as radical, but at least to those many of our
readers not bound to the alternative of black or white according to
which *simplified* man of our time, man not able any longer to hold
more than one "conception" at a time, is having his opinions, the
heavy implications in this criticism of an unreserved acknowledgment
of the merits both of Freud himself and of the whole movement he
started will not have escaped. A similar hope may be expressed for
the reception of our treatment of Gestalt psychology in its essential
difference from the phenomenological movement; if Gestalt Psychology's own *phenomenology* in those sectors of its science which it
took up would have been adhered to into the very core of its theoretical
conclusions, if instead of the stimulus error of physicalistic speculation
the principle of nothing-but-experience, so fruitful in the Gestaltist
clarification of the phenomenal *constancies* of perception, thinking, and
learning, would have been followed to the end in the theory of
experience and subsequently been applied in personality psychology,

the split that has taken shape would never have occurred. To appreciate the truths and merits of both movements, psychoanalysis and Gestalt psychology, we have to rethink them from the side of the impulses of theorizing from which they sprang and of the situations of their take-off; their accomplished historical forms already tend to obscure these origins to our vista, and thus their cases themselves bear witness to the difference between being and facticity, authentic and abstract *historic time,* with which we found ourselves in need of dealing.

The situation of man—of modern man in his ever-growing isolation from being, inclusive of his own being—which in essence both doctrines have passed by is, at this time of writing, approaching a climax of criticalness that permits of no theorizing about him unless such theory is true to the experiences of whoseever lot it is to *live* that situation. Of the new horizons radical which reflection opens up to man, *Daseinsanalyse,* and "existentialist" thought altogether, constitutes the promise rather than its fulfillment; but no restraint that is our duty must be misunderstood as requiring us to overlook the obvious and simple truth that among movements of the intellect at least of the nearer part of modern history none has been more filled with that passion of seeing and of thought which at long last is proving again its power of inspiration. As shown by the proceedings of the 1951 International Convention of Psychotherapists[6] at Lindau on Lake Constance, with the abundant strength of the new conceptions it put in relief, no other movement, moreover, has made deeper inroads into science in recent times than the themes and contemplations of the thinkers of existence have already, and yet, that tide of man's self-rallying in our day, which the existentialist movement spells out, hardly has started to expose its fast-swelling momentum. What land of human error are we leaving? To what distant and long unseen coast, waiting for us though it hides beyond our horizon, will that current, this night wind we sense, restore us, one far morning, as masters?

When shall Truth lie with us at last, and safely below us what Jaspers has diagnosed as the nadir thus far in the history of man as man knows him? Which course will prove to have been ours? What hour see us land? The author does not know the answers. He should be untrue to his entire proposition for man of a destiny uncoerced, a tomorrow uncrippled by schedules, could he even wish, in any seriousness, that he did.

NOTES

1. Helmuth Plessner, "Über die Menschenverachtung", *Offener Horizont*, p. 327. Italics supplied.

2. Cf. p. 75.

3. H. Reichenbach, *Op. cit.*, p. 214.

4. U. Sonnemann, "The Specialist as a Psychological Problem", *Social Research*, 1951, 18, No. 1.

5. *Ibid.*

6. E. Speer, Ed., *Die Vorträge der 2. Lindauer Psychotherapiewoche* (The lectures of the second Lindau Psychotherapy Week), Stuttgart, Georg Thieme, 1952.

BIBLIOGRAPHY

Adler, A.: *The Neurotic Constitution*. Moffat, Yard, New York, 1917.

------: *Problems of Neurosis*. Cosmopolitan Book, New York, 1930.

Ancilla to the Pre-Socratic Philosophers. Cf. Freeman, K., Ed.

Angyal, A.: *Foundations for a Science of Personality*. Commonwealth Fund, New York, 1941.

Arnheim, R.: "The gestalt theory of expression". *Psychological Review*, 1949, 51, 358–74.

Bachelard, G.: *La Psychanalyse du Feu*. Gallimard, Paris, 1939.

------: *Lautréamont*. Gallimard, Paris, 1939.

------: *L'Eau et les Rêves*. Corti, Paris, 1942.

------: *L'Air et les Songes*. Corti, Paris, 1950.

------: *La Terre et les Rêveries du Repos*. Corti, Paris, 1948.

------: *La Terre et les Rêveries de la Volonté*. Corti, Paris, 1948.

de Beauvoir, S. *Le Deuxième Sexe*. Gallimard, Paris, 1949.

Bergson, H.: *Le Rire*. Alcan, Paris, 1900.

------: *Essai sur les Données immediates de la Conscience*. Alcan, Paris, 1908.

Binswanger, L.: *Ausgewählte Vorträge und Aufsätze*. Francke, Bern, 1947.

------: "Der Fall Ellen West". *Schweizer Archiv für Neurologie und Psychiatrie*, 1945, vols. 53, 54, 55.

------: "Der Fall Jürg Zünd". *Schweizer Archiv für Neurologie und Psychiatrie*, 1946–47, vols. 56, 57, 58.

------: "Der Fall Lola Voss". *Schweizer Archiv für Neurologie und Psychiatrie*, 1949, vol. 63.

------: "Die Bedeutung M. Heideggers für das Selbstverständnis der Psychiatrie". In *M. Heideggers Einfluss auf die Wissenschaften*. Francke, Bern, 1949.

------: *Grundformen und Erkenntnis menschlichen Daseins*. Niehans, Zurich, 1942.

------: *Über die manische Lebensform*. Niehans, Zurich, 1944.

------: *Einführung in die Probleme der allgemeinen Psychologie*. Springer, Berlin, 1942.

------: *Wandlung in der Auffassung und Deutung des Traumes von den Griechen bis zur Gegenwart*. Springer, Berlin, 1928.

------: "Geschehnis und Erlebnis". *Monatsschrift für Psychiatrie*, 1931, 80, 266.

Bonhöffer, K.: *Die akuten Geisteskrankheiten der Gewohnheitstrinker*. G. Fischer, Jena, 1901.

Boss, M.: "Beitrag zur daseinsanalytischen Fundierung des psychiatrischen Denkens". *Schweizer Archiv für Neurologie und Psychiatrie*, 1951, 47, 15–17.

------: *Meaning and Content of Sexual Perversions*. Grune & Stratton, New York, 1949.

Brunswik, E.: "Remarks on Functionalism in Perception". *Journal of Personality*, 1949, 18, 56–65.

Collins, J.: *The Existentialists*. Regnery, Chicago, 1952.

Conrad, K.: *Der Konstitutionstypus als genetisches Problem*. Springer, Berlin, 1941.

——: "Über den Begriff der Vorgestalt und seine Bedeutung für die Hirnpathologie". *Nervenarzt*, 1947, 18, 289.

Dessauer, F.: *Die Teleologie in der Natur*. Reinhardt, Basel, 1949.

Descartes, R.: *Discours de la Méthode*. Maire, Leyden, 1637.

Dilthey, W.: *Aufbau der geschichtlichen Welt in den Geisteswissenschaften*. Teubner, Leipzig, 1921.

——: *Briefwechsel zwischen Wilhelm Dilthey und dem Grafen Paul Yorck von Wartenburg, 1877–1897*. Niemeyer, Halle, 1923.

Eliot, T. S.: *The Cocktail Party*. Harcourt, Brace, New York, 1950.

Freeman, K., Ed.: *Ancilla to the Pre-Socratic Philosophers*. Harvard University Press, Cambridge, 1948.

Frenkel-Brunswick, E. & Sanford, R. N.: "Some personality factors in Anti-Semitism". *Journal of Psychology*, 1945, 20, 271–91.

Freud, S.: *Collected Papers*. Hogarth Press, London, 1927.

——: *Totem and Taboo*. In *The Basic Writings of Sigmund Freud*. Random House, New York, 1938.

——: *Vorlesungen zur Einführung in die Psychoanalyse*. Internationaler Psychoanalytischer Verlag, Leipzig, 1922.

Fromm, E.: *Escape from Freedom*. Farrar, Rinehart, New York, 1941.

——: *Man for Himself*. Rinehart, New York, 1947.

——: *Psychoanalysis and Religion*. Yale University Press, New Haven, 1950.

——: *The Forgotten Language*. Rinehart, New York, 1951.

Fromm-Reichmann, F.: *Principles of Intensive Psychotherapy*. University of Chicago Press, Chicago, 1950.

Goldstein, K.: *The Organism*. American Book, New York, 1939.

——: *After-effects of Brain Injuries in War*. Grune and Stratton, New York, 1942.

——: "The effect of brain damage on the personality". *Psychiatry*, 1952, 15, 234–60.

Gruhle, H. W.: "Psychopathologie und akademischer Unterricht". In *Offener Horizont, Festschrift für Karl Jaspers*. Piper, Munich, 1953.

Hegel, G. W. F.: *Die Phaenomenologie des Geistes*. Duncker, Humblot, 1837.

Heidegger, M.: *Einführung in die Metaphysik*. Niemeyer, Tübingen, 1953.

——: *Holzwege*. Klostermann, Frankfurt, 1950.

——: *Sein und Zeit, Erste Hälfte*. Sixth Edition, Neomarius, Tübingen, 1949.

——: *Vom Wesen der Wahrheit*. Second Edition. Klostermann, Frankfurt, 1949.

——: *Vom Wesen des Grundes*. Third Edition. Klostermann, Frankfurt, 1949.

——: *Über den Humanismus*. Klostermann, Frankfurt, 1949.

——: *Was ist Metaphysik?* Fifth Edition, Klostermann, Frankfurt, 1949.

——: *Existence and Being*. With an Introduction by W. Brock, Regnery, Chicago, 1949.

Horney, K.: *The Neurotic Personality of our Time.* Norton, New York, 1937.

——: "Culture and neurosis". *American Sociological Review*, 1936, 1, 221–230.

——: *New Ways in Psychoanalysis.* Norton, New York, 1939.

v. Humboldt, W.: "Über die Verwandtschaft der Ortsadverbien mit dem Pronomen in einigen Sprachen". *Gesammelte Schriften*, vol. VI, Section 1, 304–330, ed. by the Prussian Academy of Sciences, Berlin, 1829.

Husserl, E.: *Ideen zu einer reinen Phänomenologie.* Niemeyer, Halle, 1922.

——: *Logische Untersuchungen.* Niemeyer, Halle, 1921.

Jaspers, K.: *Allgemeine Psychopathologie.* Fifth edition, Springer, Berlin, 1946.

——: *Psychologie der Weltanschauungen.* Springer, Berlin, 1919.

——: *Strindberg und Van Gogh.* Second edition, Springer, Berlin, 1926.

——: *Die geistige Situation der Zeit.* Fifth edition, de Gruyter, Berlin, 1932.

——: *Philosophie.* (Three volumes). Springer, Berlin, 1932.

——: *Nietzsche: Einführung in das Verständnis seines Philosophierens.* De Gruyter, Berlin, 1936.

——: *Existenzphilosophie.* De Gruyter, Berlin, 1948.

——: *Der philosophische Glaube.* Piper, Munich, 1948.

Jung, C. G.: *The Psychology of Dementia Praecox.* Nervous and Mental Disease Publications, Washington, 1914.

——: *Psychology of the Unconscious.* Moffat, Yard, New York, 1916.

——: *Psychological Types.* Harcourt, Brace, New York, 1923.

——: "Grundfragen der Psychotherapie" *Dialecticon*, 1951, 5, 8–24.

——: and W. Pauli. "Synchronizität als ein Prinzip akausaler Zusammenhänge". *Naturerklärung und Psyche*, 1952, 5, 1–107.

Katz, D.: *Gestaltpsychologie.* Schwabe, Basel, 1948.

Kierkegaard, S.: *Gesammelte Werke*, 12 volumes. Diederichs, Jena, 1909–22.

Koehler, W.: *Die physischen Gestalten in Ruhe und im stationären Zustand.* Verlag der Philosophischen Akademie, Erlangen, 1924.

——: *Gestalt Psychology.* Liveright, New York, 1929.

——: *The Place of Value in a World of Facts.* Liveright, New York, 1935.

Koffka, K.: *Principles of Gestalt Psychology.* Harcourt, Brace, New York, 1935.

Kolle, K.: "Pathologie des sozialen Kontaktes". In *Offener Horizont. Festschrift für Karl Jaspers.* Piper, Munich, 1953.

Koppel, S. E.: *An Inquiry into the Validity of the Concept of Projection.* Unpublished Dissertation.

Koppers, W.: *Der Urmensch und sein Weltbild.* Herold, Vienna, 1949.

Krech, D.: "Notes toward a psychological theory." *Journal of Personality,* 1949, 18, 66–87.

Kuhn, H.: *Encounter with Nothingness.* Regnery, Chicago, 1949.

Kuhn, R.: "Daseinsanalyse im psychotherapeutischen Gespräch". *Schweizer Archiv fuer Neurologie und Psychiatrie*, 1951, 47, 52–60.

——: "Daseinsanalyse eines Falles von Schizophrenie". *Monatsschrift für Psychiatrie und Neurologie*, 1946, 112, Nos. 5 & 6.

Kunz, H.: *Die anthropologische Deutung der Phantasie.* Verlag für Recht und Gesellschaft, Basel, 1946.

Langer, S. K.: *Philosophy in a New Key.* Mentor Books, New York, 1948.

Lindner, R.: *Prescription for Rebellion*. Rinehart, New York, 1952.

Löwith, K.: *Das Individuum in der Rolle des Mitmenschen*. Drei Masken, Munich, 1928.

——: "Die Auslegung des Ungesagten in Nietzsches Wort 'Gott ist tot' ". *Die Neue Rundschau*, 1953, 64, 105–37.

Marcel, G.: *Journal Métaphysique, 1913–1923*. Gallimard, Paris, 1927.

——: *Etre et Avoir*. Aubier, Paris, 1935.

——: *Homo Viator, Prolégomènes à une Métaphysique de l'Espérance*. Aubier, Paris, 1944.

——: *Le Mystère de L'Etre. Tome I: Réflexion et Mystère, Tome II: Foi et Réalité*. Aubier, Paris, 1951.

——: *Les Hommes contre L'Humain*. Aubier, Paris, 1951.

May, R.: *Man's Search for Himself*. Norton, New York, 1952.

Minkovska, F.: *Epilepsie und Schizophrenie im Erbgang*. Zurich, 1947.

Minkovski, E.: "Le contact humain". *Revue de Métaphysique et de Morales*, 1952, 2.

——: "Que veut dire 'ancestral'?" *Archives Suisses de Neurologie et de Psychiatrie*, 1951, 47, 66–74.

Nietzsche, F.: *Werke*. 11 Bände. Kröner, Stuttgart, 1921.

Pfänder, A.: *Phänomenologie des Wollens*. Barth, Leipzig, 1900.

——: "Motive und Motivation". In *Münchner Philosophische Abhandlungen, T. Lipps gewidmet*. Barth, Leipzig, 1911.

——: *Zur Psychologie der Gesinnungen*, 2 vols. Barth, Leipzig, 1913.

——: "Grundprobleme der Charakterologie". *Jahrbuch der Charakterologie*, 1924, 1.

Picard, M.: *Hitler in uns selbst*. Rentsch, Erlenbach-Zurich, 1945.

Planck, M.: *Scientific Autobiography and other Papers*, Philosophical Library, New York, 1949.

Plessner, H.: "Über die Menschenverachtung". In *Offener Horizont*, Piper, Munich, 1953.

Portmann, A.: *Die Tiergestalt*. Reinhardt, Basel, 1948.

——: "Etudes sur la Cérébralisation chez les Oiseaux". *Alauda*, 1946, 14; 1947, 15.

——: "Um ein neues Bild vom Organismus". In *Offener Horizont*, Piper, Munich, 1953.

Rank, O.: *Technik der Psychoanalyse*. Deuticke, Leipzig, 1926.

——: *The Trauma of Birth*. Harcourt, Brace, New York, 1928.

Reichenbach, H.: *The Rise of Scientific Philosophy*. University of California Press, Berkeley, 1953.

de Rosa, R.: "Existenzphilosophische Richtungen in der modernen Psychopathologie". In *Offener Horizont*, Piper, Munich, 1953.

Sartre, J.-P.: *L'Imaginaire: Psychologie phénoménologique de l'Imagination*. Gallimard, Paris, 1940.

——: *L'Etre et le Néant: Essai d'Ontologie phénoménologique*. Gallimard, Paris, 1943.

——: *L'Existentialisme est un Humanisme*. Nagel, Paris, 1946.

——: *Situations, I, II, et III*. Gallimard, Paris, 1947, 1948, 1949.

Schachtel, E.: "On Memory and Childhood Amnesia". In Mullahy, P., ed. *A Study of Interpersonal Relations.* Hermatige Press, New York, 1949.

Scheler, M.: *Wesen und Foremen der Sympathie.* Cohen, Bonn, 1926.

——: *Vom Ewigen im Menschen.* Neuer Geist, Leipzig, 1921.

——: *Die Wissensformen und die Gesellschaft.* Neuer Geist, Leipzig, 1926.

——: *Die Stellung des Menschen im Kosmos.* Reichl, Darmstadt, 1928.

Schilder, P.: *The Image and Appearance of the Human Body.* International Universities Press, New York, 1950.

Schopenhauer, A.: *Über die vierfache Wurzel des Satzes vom zureichenden Grunde.* Brockhaus, Leipzig, 1891.

Sonnemann, U.: *Handwriting Analysis as a Psychodiagnostic Tool.* Grune & Stratton, New York, 1950.

——: "The Specialist as a Psychological Problem". *Social Research,* 1951, 18, No. 1, 9–31.

Speer, E., Ed.: *Die Vorträge der zweiten Lindauer Psychotherapiewoche.* (The Lectures of the Second Lindau Psychotherapy Week). Thieme, Stuttgart, 1952.

Stekel, W.: *The Interpretation of Dreams.* Liveright, New York, 1943.

Straus, E.: "Der Mensch als ein fragendes Wesen". *Jahrbuch für Psychologie und Psychotherapie,* Würzburg. Undated reprint.

Tillich, P.: *The Courage to Be.* Yale University Press, New Haven, 1953.

Tolman, E. C.: *Purposive Behavior in Animals and Men.* Century, New York, 1932.

Thorndike, E. L.: *Human Learning.* Century, New York, 1931.

v. Üxküll, J.: *Theoretische Biologie.* Springer, Berlin, 1928.

v. Weizsäcker, V.: *Studien zur Pathogenese.* Thieme, Leipzig, 1935.

——: *Der Gestaltkreis. Theorie der Einheit von Wahrnehmen und Bewegen.* Thieme, Stuttgart, 1950.

Welsh, E.: *The Philosophy of Edmund Husserl: The Origin and Development of his Phenomenology.* Columbia University Press, New York, 1941.

Wyrsch, J.: *Die Person des Schizophrenen.* Haupt, Bern, 1949.

Zsilasi, W.: *Wissenschaft als Philosophie.* Europa Verlag, Zurich, 1945.

——: "Die Erfahrungsgrundlage der Daseinsanalyse Binswangers". *Schweizer Archiv für Neurologie und Psychiatrie,* 1951, 67, 74–82.

INDEX

Abstract behavior, so-called, losses of, 23, 25, 71, 72
Addictive Personality, 330
Adler, A., 181, 182, 184, 185, 187, 313
Aestheticism, 47, 48, 99, 271
Air, as soul symbol, *239*
Allopsychic origin of psychoses, 156, 223, 228
Ambiversion, *349*
Amnesia, hysterical, *287*
Angyal, A., *11*, 70, *93*, *143*, 171, 173, 193
Anima, 88
Anschauungen, fundamental eidetic, 23
Anschauungsformen, Kantian, 19
"Anthropolological" theory of perversions, 300, 301, 305
Anxiety, 71, 103, 104, 119, 121, 122, *142*, 235, 236, 272, *310*, *311*
Aphasia, amnestic, 243, 274, 245, *287*, 344
Archetypes, 150
Aristophanes, 308
Aristotle, Aristotelian, 19, *50*, *141*
Arnheim, R., *51*
Associationism in psychology, 7
Attention, 23, 27, 172, 191–197, 205, 245, 342
Autopsychic origin of psychoses, 156, 223, 230–231
Awareness, structure of, 191–197, 234
Awe as phenomenon, 122, *142*
Axioms of directional meaning, 10, 207, 221, 222

Bachelard, G., *241*, *362*
Barth, K., 346
Beaufret, J., 109, 110
de Beauvoir, S., 220, *240*, *311*, *362*
Behaviorism, 3, 14, 21
  molar, 3, *11*, *51*, 136, 339
  molecular, 3, 289, 315
Being vs. *Having*, 95, 135, *144*
Bergson, H., 20, *27*, 64, 98, 101, *287*, *362*
Binswanger, L., viii, x, 26, 38, 44, 134, *143*, 145–*161*, 162, 163, 188, 191, 200–203, 215–219, 221, 232, 235, *240*, *241*, *242*, 250, 251, 252, 255, 258, 259, 260, *287*, 295, 301, *310*, 343, *352*

Birth trauma, 235–237.
Bleuler, E., 36, 200
Bohr, N., 65
Bonhöffer, K., *351*, *362*
Boredom as phenomenon, 108, 241
Bosch, H., 271, 285
Boss, M., viii, *161*, 200, *216*, 289, 298, 299, 309, *310*, *311*, 334, 343, *350*, *351*, *362*
Brain disease, organic, 23, 25, 53, 76, *287*, *288*
Brentano, F., 7, 17
Breughel, P., 285.
Browning, E. B., *217*
Brunner, E., 346.
Bruno, G., 67
Brunswik, E., *52*, *93*
Buber, M., 346

Cardiac neurosis, 199, 202
Care, 95, 104, 107, 149, 299
Cartesianism, Cartesian, 11, 15, 19, 30, 31, 53, 60–62, 90, 91, 97, 104, 120, 201, 202, *216*, 244, 245, 300, 314, 322
Catatonia, *241*, 344
Causalism, radical physicalistic, 63, 65, 68, 233
Causality, phenomenal, 63, 179, 233
de Cervantes, M., 150
Cézanne, P., 271
Charcot, F. M., 36
Clod-worlds, 145, 157
Cogitatio vs. *extensio*, 60–62
Cognition, esp., 17, 28–52, 84–89
Collective unconcious, *190*
Collins, J., 19, *27*, 31, *140*, *363*
Compulsive, post-encephalitic, 293
Compulsivity, compulsion neurosis, *248*, 293, 312, 330–335, 341, *349*
Conation, esp., 7, 17, 84–89, 263
Conrad, K., 275, *287*, 312, 317–321, 346, *347*, *348*, *349*, *350*, *352*, *363*
Conscience as phenomenon, 107, 147, *160*
Consciousness, 5, 6, 18, 22, 23, 25, 171–173, 175, 233
  and the unconscious, 191–197